Comparative Performance of U.S. Econometric Models

Edited by
LAWRENCE R. KLEIN

D0068728

New York   Oxford
OXFORD UNIVERSITY PRESS
1991

Oxford University Press

Oxford   New York   Toronto
Delhi   Bombay   Calcutta   Madras   Karachi
Petaling Jaya   Singapore   Hong Kong   Tokyo
Nairobi   Dar es Salaam   Cape Town
Melbourne   Auckland

and associated companies in
Berlin   Ibadan

Library of Congress Cataloging-in-Publication Data
Comparative performance of U.S. econometric models / edited by
Lawrence R. Klein.
p. cm.   Includes bibliographical references.
ISBN 0-19-505772-4
1. United States—Economic conditions—Econometric models.
I. Klein, Lawrence Robert.   II. Title: Comparative performance of
United States econometric models.   III. Title: Comparative
performance of US econometric models.
HC103.C7344   1991
330.973'001'5195—dc20   90-6730

1 2 3 4 5 6 7 8 9

Printed in the United States of America
on acid-free paper

Preface

The United States has been the main world center for empirical work in macroeconometric model building, and there are many different models of our economy in active use at the present time. This situation of supremacy in the volume of effort may change, but it probably will not do so in the near future. Given the plethora of U.S. models, it is only natural to try to draw some conclusions from a comparative study of the various systems. This comparison effort is aimed not only at serving the external users but also at helping the model builders themselves in improving their systems.

During the second half of the 1970s leading model builders in the United States came together for repeated seminars that culminated in a series of research papers that were first published in *International Economic Review,* 1974–75, and then put together in a single book volume published in 1976.[1]

Following the U.S. experience, there were model comparisons for Japan, Canada, and United Kingdom, and possibly other countries or areas. Recently there have been comparisons of international models.[2]

There was a hiatus in U.S. model comparisons after the original effort. The work had been supported by a grant from the National Science Foundation and channeled through the National Bureau of Economic Research. The program was known as Conference on Econometrics and Mathematical Economics (CEME). One branch dealt with comparisons of national macroeconometric models. This branch ceased activity temporarily, after the publication of the first book of the research results, but other CEME subject area groups continued to function. In 1985, it was decided to resume seminar activity on the subject of model comparisons. The work of British modelers through the center at Warwick organized by Kenneth Wallis was certainly a stimulant.

There was such enthusiastic response among leading US model builders when asked if they would participate in a new round of comparisons that it was easy to decide to resume operations. The results of the second phase are reported in this volume. At the present time, while the manuscripts are being prepared for publication, there is no sentiment for discontinuing seminar operations as we did in 1976. The seminar functions are presently on-going and new issues are being examined.

Most of the material in this volume is concerned with comparisons among *mainstream* models, which are largely or basically natural evolutions of the original group from the late 1970s. Two participants who propose significantly different kinds of models—John Taylor with a rational expectations alternative and Christopher Sims, with a vector autoregressive alternative—were not ready with completed chapters at this time, but it is to be hoped that their models will be included in a subsequent collection of reports. There are, however, important new features in this second round of comparisons, namely, condensed IS–LM versions of large models, error decompositions, combined models of high and low frequency data, and model forecasts under consistent assumptions.

In the first volume, an outsider was invited to comment on the comparisons, and all participants found Carl Christ's remarks to be constructive, stimulating, and suggestive. Again, in this second round, we have benefited from external comments by Ignazio Visco and Robert Shiller.

There have been enormous improvements in computer hardware and software. These changes have contributed to the success of the seminar deliberations and in the provision of instructive graphics. It was possible to present computer-based graphics across models in strategic comparisons at seminar meetings, to assemble and store vast files of replicated forecasts under different specified conditions at successive time points and to prepare more tables of relevant calculations. Stochastic simulations open potentials for more meaningful comparisons. These are computer-intensive calculations and will become more easily accessible as time goes by.

The model comparison seminars that generated the several chapters of this book were stimulating research meetings. Best practice techniques have worked their way across models; unusual behavior in some models has been detected; and in thinking up new comparison exercises, fresh model applications have been generated. As editor of these collected works and as organizer of the seminars, I want to record my thanks for excellent cooperation requiring very serious efforts by all and am continually pleased by the enthusiasm of the seminar participants for our line of research.

NOTES

1. *Econometric Model Performance* L.R. Klein and E. Burmeister, eds. Philadelphia: University of Pennsylvania Press, 1976.
2. *Empirical Macroeconomics for Interdependent Economies,* Ralph Bryant et al., eds. Washington D.C.: Brookings, 1988.

Contents

External Reviews

Contributors

F. Gerard Adams
Professor of Economics
University of Pennsylvania
Philadelphia, Pa.

Lewis S. Alexander
Economist, Division of Internal Finance
Board of Governors, Federal Reserve
    System
Washington, D.C.

Albert Ando
Professor of Economics
University of Pennsylvania
Philadelphia, Pa.

Flint Brayton
Chief, Macroeconomics and Quantitive
    Studies
Division of Research and Statistics
Board of Governors, Federal Reserve
    System
Washington, D.C.

Roger E. Brinner
Data Resources Inc.
Lexington, Mass.

Bryan W. Brown
Professor of Economics
Rice University
Houston, Tex.

Michael R. Donihue
Assistant Professor of Economics
Colby College
Waterville, Maine

Ray C. Fair
Professor of Economics
Yale University
New Haven, Conn.

R. Jeffery Green
Professor of Economics
Indiana University
Bloomington, Ind.

Bert G. Hickman
Professor of Economics
Stanford University
Stanford, Calif.

Albert A. Hirsch
Bureau of Economic Analysis
U.S. Department of Commerce
Washington, D.C.

E. Philip Howrey
Professor of Economics and Statistics
University of Michigan
Ann Arbor, Mich.

Saul H. Hymans
Professor of Economics
University of Michigan
Ann Arbor, Mich.

Arthur Kennickell
Division of Research and Statistics
Board of Governors, Federal Reserve
    System
Washington, D.C.

Lawrence R. Klein
Professor of Economics
University of Pennsylvania
Philadelphia, Pa.

Stephen K. McNees
Vice President
Federal Reserve Bank of Boston
Boston, Mass.

Roberto S. Mariano
Professor of Economics
University of Pennsylvania
Philadelphia, Pa.

Robert J. Shiller
Professor of Economics
Yale University
New Haven, Conn.

Joaquin Vial
CIEPLAN
Santiago, Chile

Ignazio Visco
Servizio Studi
Banca d'Italia
Rome, Italy

OVERVIEW

CHAPTER 1

Past, Present, and Possible Future of Macroeconometric Models and Their Uses

LAWRENCE R. KLEIN

HISTORICAL INTERESTS

As the twentieth century enters its last decade, there is unusual interest in documenting the historical roots of econometrics, which is fundamentally a development of this century. At the present time there are still some survivors among the pioneers, and it makes sense to do as much historical research as possible while firsthand accounts are available.

Econometrics, as a total subject, is older than macroeconometric model building and deserves a separate historical inquiry. Early investigations of demand–supply functions, income distributions, family budgets, cost, and production functions have been the subject of historical study.[1]

In a somewhat narrower vein, the joint founding of the Econometric Society and the Cowles Commission for Research in Economics represented the beginnings of major steps forward from the decade of the 1930s. The fruits of these efforts in econometrics are just over the half century mark and have been highlighted by papers delivered at the fiftieth anniversary celebration of the Cowles Foundation at Yale and ongoing historical writing. In addition to some of the papers presented at the Cowles Foundation anniversary party, there have been some separate studies by scholars from the group.[2]

A third line of historical scholarship involves tracing the foundations and development of econometric models of complete nations, starting from the early modeling efforts of Jan Tinbergen for the Netherlands and the United States before the second World War and continuing to the present. Major postwar efforts were mounted in the United States, organized to no little extent by the Cowles Commission's research effort, and continuing in isolated centers during the 1950s and 1960s. From 1970, we find an intense proliferation of macro model building—all over the United States and in country after country round the world. The proliferation encompassed developing countries, centrally planned economies, and complete worldwide trading systems of all countries together.

This proliferation has been good from an intellectual point of view. There has been a great deal of scientific challenge, reconsideration, recapitulation, and the gradual enforcing of tight scholarly standards. Many flowers have bloomed and many excellent ideas, for both economics in general and econometrics in particular, have been developed in this expansionary phase, but the user is confronted with a perplexing problem of choice. Which model is to be used in particular circumstances and which model is to be believed when the results appear to be different?

More than 10 years ago, a seminar was organized to compare models to appreciate their differences and to look for commonalities.[3] In a first phase, the Model Comparison Seminar looked at distributions of multipliers across models, and the outcome of common applications of control theory. Control theory was used mainly to examine the relationships among inflation, unemployment, and growth during the late 1960s and early 1970s, to see whether alternative policies could have achieved a better macroeconomic outcome. The findings of the first phase of work for the Model Comparisons Seminar were published in issues of the *International Economic Review, 1974–1975*, and reprinted in a single volume.[4] The findings of the exercises in optimal control were separately reported.[5]

Outside observers found the variations in different models to be large, probably disturbingly so. For practitioners, however, who are more familiar with model sensitivities, the dispersion of results was no great surprise and some significant common aspects were detected.

Prior to the first round of comparisons, conventional thinking had been that fiscal multipliers built up dynamically to maximum levels and held steady. In the set of models available in the early 1970s, it was found that a form of crowding-out caused fiscal multipliers to rise and turn down, unless accommodated by monetary policy. This phenomenon was observed in several models. In this period, too, there was generally more appreciation of the significance of monetary policy. Most models showed sensitivity in this respect. Also, the optimal control exercises showed in all cases that inflation could not have been totally avoided, but that better employment performance (after Vietnam) could have been achieved without appreciably more inflation.

The Model Comparison Seminar avoided the issue of *forecast* comparison in the first phase. Nearly all the models involved were being used in forecasting the economy. Some retrospective studies were made for ex post extrapolations or in-sample simulations, but comparisons of ex ante forecasts were not under discussion in the Seminar at that time.

We are now ready for a fresh round of Model Comparisons, and the activities of the Seminar were both resumed and revised in 1985. New models entered the group and new thinking about dispersion and comparison techniques entered the scene.

HISTORICAL EMPHASES OF EARLIER MODELS

Before we turn to the work of the Seminar on Model Comparisons, it may be worthwhile to review briefly the focal points of interest during the historical period of macroeconometric model development.

Tinbergen's early studies in model building were greatly concerned with the phenomenon of the business cycle. This concept had been much studied from time series data, without formal model guidance, and also without a strong basis of macroeconomic theory. The impressive contributions to macroeconomics of J. M. Keynes inspired much of the work in model building, Tinbergen's in fact, but the emphasis was not on business cycle dynamics, as such. But other econometricians, notably Frisch, Kalecki, and Slutsky, emphasized the cyclical problem. If we write the general linear model as

$$A(L)y_t + B(L)x_t = \Gamma(L)e_t \tag{1}$$

and its solution as

$$y_t = K\lambda^t - [A(L)]^{-1}B(L)x_t + [A(L)]^{-1}\Gamma(L)e_t \tag{2}$$

it can be said that Tinbergen concentrated on the cyclical properties of λ, the vector of characteristic roots of the system, whereas Frisch and Slutsky concentrated on the contributions of the stochastic component from the error vector e_t. Both Frisch and Kalecki were interested, too, in the propagation aspects of the system, namely the nature of the characteristic roots. Without stating generalized dynamic multipliers in a formal mathematical sense, Keynesian economists were deeply interested in the response of y_t to changes in x_t, exogenous variables. This response is shown by the second term of the right-hand side.

In Eqs. (1) and (2)

$$y_t = \text{column vector of endogenous variable}$$
$$x_t = \text{column vector of exogenous variables}$$
$$e_t = \text{column vector of random errors}$$
$$A,B,\Gamma = \text{matrices of coefficients, where}$$
$$A \text{ is square and nonsingular,}$$
$$B \text{ is rectangular, and}$$
$$\Gamma \text{ is diagonal}$$
$$L = \text{displacement operator}$$
$$K = \text{matrix depending on initial conditions}$$

Most modern models are similar to that in (1), but are nonlinear. Needless to say, a substantial literature on cyclical properties of nonlinear macro models also developed, but Tinbergen's early models were usually approximated by linear expansions.

Some counterfactual scenarios, of what might have been, were made by Tinbergen and his students for the American economy but contemporary applications of forecasting, multiplier calculation, and stochastic simulation were not investigated, understandably, because of the nonexistence of the computer.[6]

The Keynesian theories of macroeconomics that came to the fore in the mid-1930s placed heavy demands on forecasting and policy analysis.[7]

Jan Tinbergen had actually set out to test economic theories of the business cycle when he developed the first U.S. macro model, but that part of the study never came to definitive conclusions. As time passed, different theories or doctrines have been at center stage, and some testing has been undertaken. The Model Comparison Seminar is always interested in comparing the working of models based on different doctrinal hypotheses. The progress has been from Keynesian $\rightarrow$ Growth $\rightarrow$ Monetarist $\rightarrow$ supply side (input–output) $\rightarrow$ neoclassical $\rightarrow$ expectational.

Every doctrinal wave leaves an impression. Models have not become completely growth oriented, but they are now closely examined for accepted long-run or steady-state properties. Similarly, they are not predominantly monetarist, but money and credit market conditions play more significant roles than previously in most models. The input–output system and other conditions of production have been introduced in an inherent way in many models, but they are not purely supply-side systems. The present preoccupation with rational expectations models will not win complete converts to model-generated expectations systems, but it will be evident in that model builders will pay more attention to expectations formation in the models of the future.

A distinguishing feature of contemporary model use, in contrast with the earliest applications, is that intensive and extensive simulation analysis is made for prospective policies. There has always been interest in what might have been, i.e., how different policy actions in the past could have changed economic history, but the use of models to advise policymakers came about gradually and was greatly enhanced by the use of the computer. The fast turnaround on the computer has meant that every large disturbance and every major policy move, in the macro sphere, is examined as closely as possible (often in no more than 24 hours) after the event or in advance of legislative–administrative decisions on new policies. Tailored policy scenarios, together with inventories of standard multipliers, are now commonplace, but were rare in earlier model studies.

Jan Tinbergen, Henri Theil, and others steered model builders into the area of policy optimization. This approach can be formulated as a control theory problem and posed significant computational demands on model operators. At first these demands appeared to be very onerous, but now are fairly routine. Indeed, the first phase of the Model Comparison Seminar demonstrated how the computations could be done with comparative ease and made some contribution to scholarly advances in econometrics at the time the control approach was being considered on a large scale, some 10–15 years ago.

SUMMARY OF A NEW ROUND OF MODEL COMPARISONS

There are now models in existence that were not available for the prior round of comparisons in the 1970s. In addition, there are new kinds of models. The vector autoregressive systems (VAR) built and maintained in Minneapolis (Federal Reserve Bank of Minneapolis and University of Minnesota) are essentially different and are being used regularly in forecast and other applications. The VAR model, in contrast with Eq. (1), is

$$A(L)z_t = e_t \tag{3}$$

where z_t is a vector containing a subset of the variables in y_t and x_t. The main distinguishing feature of the VAR model is that the distinction between endogenous and exogenous variables is absent. When specific policy changes are introduced for comparison with other models, they cannot in general be represented simply as changes in exogenous inputs, but rather require changes in one or more of the equations of the model or the introduction of *innovations,* that is, shocks to particular equations.

All the models in the seminar use expectations variables. These are usually specified as lag distributions in the relevant magnitudes, and these distributions are commonly based on a theory of adaptive or extrapolative expectations. Some models use expectations reported from sample surveys, and these magnitudes are generated by other objective variables in the system.

A model designed by John Taylor of Stanford is based on own-model generated expectations (called rational expectations). There are often problems of uniqueness in the estimation and solution of such systems, but a set of estimates has been obtained, and the model with expectations generated in this way is compared with the others in the seminar.

In general, as will be seen in the next chapter, the time shape of response characteristics to prescribed policy changes is quite different for the VAR and rational expectations models. The VAR models were examined at an early stage and then withdrawn from the seminar. They are presently being reintroduced by Christopher Sims. Also, as before, the special structure of a monetarist model (from the Federal Reserve Bank of St. Louis) causes it to have some distinctive multiplier properties, but it is more often within the range of values of the mainstream models than are the other two. The model of the Federal Reserve Board has very strong cyclical swings along its dynamic multiplier paths and is accordingly distinctive among the whole group. In an addendum to the next chapter, Albert Ando explains this feature of the model that was used. As a result of personnel and related work assignments, the participation of the monetarist group from St. Louis was terminated in 1987.

Apart from making comparisons between unusual and doctrinal models and the mainstream group, the seminar's approach does much to enhance understanding among model builders and operators. The first exercise was to evaluate dynamic multipliers (1975.1–1984.4) for each of the models. These are

Fiscal (spending increases) with
   M_1 (or corresponding monetary instrument) held to a baseline path
   A short-term interest rate held to a baseline path
   A reaction function governing money supply behavior
Monetary expansion through
   Increases in M_1
   Decreases in a short-term interest rate
   Increases in M_1 with a reaction function
Supply shocks through
   Decrease in world oil price[8]
   Decrease in wage rate, with M_1 held to a baseline path
   Decrease in wage rate, with a short-term interest rate held to a baseline path
   Decrease in wage rate with a reaction function governing money supply

In view of the unusual interest in the American J-curve effects that are associated with the recent depreciation of the U.S. dollar, we decided to make some special multiplier calculations (1983.1–1989.4) as follows:

U.S. dollar depreciation below baseline values with
   Full pass-through to domestic prices
   Partial pass-through to domestic prices
Increased economic activity abroad with
   Exogenous exchange rates at baseline values
   Endogenous exchange rates

Decreased U.S. GNP growth with
  An increase in domestic taxes and exogenous exchange rates at baseline values
  An increase in domestic taxes and endogenous exchange rates
  An easier monetary policy (through either M_1 or short-term interest rates) and
    exogenous exchange rates at baseline values
  An easier monetary policy (through either M_1 or short-term interest rates) and
    endogenous exchange rates

All these simulations were designed and executed by some model operators, but only a subset of the specified simulations is reported in the next chapter. It is evident that uniformity and consistency in the specification of the experimental conditions across models are being sought, but some models cannot comply with one prescription or another, and the Seminar's main code is "To let models be models"; in other words, to let model operators interpret a given set of directives as closely as possible, while recognizing that each model has some distinctive characteristics that do not always permit full compliance.

Until one has actually participated in a seminar like this, it is hard to realize how difficult it is to get several independent model operators, all trying to describe the same economy, to use common inputs and techniques for studying multipliers or other model sensitivities. There are problems of units of measurement, nominal vs real input changes, dynamic paths of input changes, management of other related exogenous magnitudes (such as monetary accommodation for fiscal changes), and model adjustment. When model operators come together in face-to-face meetings and look at dynamic multiplier trajectories of all systems charted together they can readily spot unusual (outlying) features and accordingly reconsider what has been done to the outlying system. It required more than a year of repeated meetings to agree on a set of inputs to be used in all models and to be sure that each model operator made the appropriate arithmetic calculations.

Most, but not all, model builders adjust their models, that is, they change the constant terms (or the mean values of additive errors) to produce a "realistic" solution for the simulation period. In ex ante forecasting this is done, in a meaningful way, only for the *current* period's solution viewed as a set of *initial conditions*. This adjustment procedure can be used for ex post simulations, and in the prior phase of this seminar we used *tracking simulations* for some baseline solutions. In a *tracking simulation,* residuals are added to each equation so that the solution reproduces a *specific* data file such as actual historical values.

Constant adjustments are sometimes determined by a mechanical rule and sometimes by subjective decision making. For our Model Comparison Seminar, we agreed that each model could generate its "own" baseline path by using whatever rule was deemed suitable for generating adjustment factors. The rule should be objective, numerical, and used only to obtain adjustment constants for the baseline simulation. No further adjustments were permitted for the multiplier calculations outlined above.

Multipliers are artificial in the sense that the model operator can generate calculations for highly restricted changes, with all other exogenous variables held to baseline values. This may be highly unrealistic, but the exercise provides only sensitivities and not actual or practical policy changes. In a linear system, however, composite multipliers can be obtained by combining different individual multipliers. For example, the combination

$$w_j \frac{dy_{it}}{dx_{jt'}} + w_k \frac{dy_{it}}{dx_{kt'}}, \qquad t' \le t$$

shows the change in y_{it} to be expected when $w_j x_{jt'} + w_k x_{kt'}$, is changed. This composite multiplier can be obtained from separate evaluations of the multiplier effects of x_{jt} and of x_{kt}. In nonlinear systems this property does not hold precisely, but if the degree of nonlinearity is weak, it holds in an approximate sense.

From the tabulations given in the next chapter, it can be seen how the different assumptions about related values change the shape of multiplier paths.

The present rounds of the Model Comparison Seminar are breaking new ground by taking up an entirely fresh problem, the matter of evaluating the effect on ex ante forecasts of differing inputs. These procedures are described at length in the chapter by Stephen McNees, who has compiled a unique set of data. He has had, and continues to have, access to the actual ex ante forecasts, over varying time horizons, of most of the major forecasting groups. His records date back to 1970, and occasionally earlier for models that were used during the 1950s and 1960s (the Michigan and Wharton Models). Side-by-side with the regular ex ante forecasts that each model operator develops, with its *own* input values, McNees also collects from the model builders in the Seminar ex ante forecasts that are generated by *common* assumptions, where applicable, for fiscal, monetary, and rest-of-the-world (ROW) inputs into U.S. models. Everyone lines up on these crucial inputs and then generates forecasts with the fixed rules (of own choice) for residual adjustment factors together with other inputs that are used for the actual ex ante forecasts that are prepared regularly by each group.

For comparison, McNees also collects extrapolations that are based on the fixed adjustment rules and individual input assumptions for exogenous and policy variables. Dr. McNees is trying to separate the contribution of the model from the contribution of the modeler to forecast accuracy. As in the case of the multipliers, there are options. In one case, model operators use a common monetary assumption expressed as an allowable growth for M_1 (given fiscal and ROW inputs). In the other case, the monetary assumption is for a particular path for the federal funds rates (given fiscal and ROW inputs).

He finds that forecast values are less dispersed when some common input assumptions are used, and the reverse in other cases. The details are described at some length in his chapter on forecast performance of models. When a large sample of replicated forecasts has been put together, Dr. McNees will have made a singular contribution to our knowledge about the sources of forecast error.

Stephen McNees has contributed mainly to the analysis of reported forecast error, comparing extrapolated values with actual observations once they are realized, also allowing for data revision. A different approach to forecast error has been elaborated by Ray Fair. He uses the techniques of stochastic simulation with his own model, the Michigan Model, and an autoregressive model to decompose error into the following sources:

1. The additive disturbance associated with each stochastic equation in a model

2. The sampling variability of estimated model coefficients
3. Errors of assigned values for extrapolated exogenous variables.

These are straightforward error sources and have been studied in the past in some models using stochastic simulations.[9] Ray Fair also studies specification error. He fits a model to a subperiod of a time series sample and extrapolates the model into the remaining part of the sample. Relative error within the fitting period compared with that in the part outside this period provides an approximation for specification error tests.

In studying the Wharton Model for the prior phase of this Seminar, Michael D. McCarthy introduced the useful notion that many large-scale mainstream models were actually elaborations and enhancements of an underlying IS–LM system.[10] This raises the possibility of condensing a large model to its underlying IS–LM core. This approach was also used in the Stanford Energy Modeling Forum.[11] In this volume, Bert Hickman extends the energy modeling analysis to the study of core model elasticities on the basis of complete model simulations.

Some condensations of the Wharton Model to its IS–LM core were presented to the Seminar by Lawrence Klein, with the point emphasized that the LM curve, so obtained, was flat, relative to the IS curve. E. Philip Howrey and Michael R. Donihue made very interesting presentations to the Seminar on the IS–LM system within the Michigan Model and R. Jeffrey Green did similar work with the Indiana Model. Their studies provided neat two-dimensional summaries of these two models. They also showed how macro policies induced shifts and slope changes in the two curves (IS, LM). The different approaches of Bert Hickman, the Michigan group (E. P. Howrey, S. H. Hymans, and M. R. Donihue), and R. Jeffrey Green are all reported together in a single chapter.

The multipliers in this new round of comparisons are laid out much better and designed more consistently, across models, but they cover essentially the same range of external changes, namely fiscal and monetary shocks. Some supply side shocks are added, and these contribute a nice feature to the new work. In addition, a set of simulations not previously executed in a broad comparison across models refers to J-curve analysis.

F. Gerard Adams tabulated these J-curve results as well as the fiscal, monetary, and supply side shocks, for several contributing models. They show some gradual improvement in the U.S. current account as a result of exchange rate changes, but not by a wide enough margin to have a significant impact on foreign money markets. Generally speaking, the models suggest that the response should be fairly quick—in the first year—but this cannot be seen in observed data for 1985–1987 except in real terms. On the matter of whether an American recession would quickly improve the nominal trade balance, the models are varied and, as yet, not very informative.

General calculations of standard multipliers or sensitivities are very useful, especially when studied across several models, as in the seminar, but there is no substitute for in-depth examination of multiplier or sensitivity tabulations, particularly for understanding why model results differ. Roger E. Brinner and Albert A. Hirsch do just that in a bilateral comparison of the DRI (Data Resources Inc.) and OBE (Office of Business Economics) models. Their study points to the necessity of going beyond the tabulations of the next chapter, if we are to understand, in a fundamental sense, why models differ.

Ray C. Fair and Lewis S. Alexander also do in-depth comparison of the Michigan and Fair Models, but they focus on relative forecast performance. Ignazio Visco, an invited discussant for the work of the Model Comparison Seminar, looks at comparative performance of subsystems across four models, in a very detailed and interesting way.

When the first round of model comparisons was being prepared more than 10 years ago, computer facilities were good—good enough to do the standard kinds of things that were implemented. But facilities are even better now. Stochastic simulation is much easier now. Many more replications can be obtained. Rational expectations models must be estimated by simultaneously simulating an underlying model repeatedly in iterative steps. Computer demands are much heavier, but there are no approaches, leads, or methods that remain unexplored at the present time because of inadequacy of computer facilities. Large-scale mainframes, supercomputers, and very powerful microcomputers are all drawn on, at one time or another, for the Seminar's work. Our group discussions were significantly enhanced by the real time graphic comparisons made for the assembled group. Many of these graphic computer displays are in the next chapter.

Roberto S. Mariano and Bryan W. Brown do theoretical and simulation analysis of significance tests and forecast error in the presence of nonlinearities. They extend previous work in several directions.

NEW PROSPECTS

It is widely recognized that the world economy is becoming ever more interdependent. With the freeing of exchange rates in 1973, the increasing size and frequency of international capital flows, and the attempts by nations to coordinate international economic policy, it becomes evident that single country studies are increasingly inadequate. It becomes very difficult to analyze economic policy for single countries in isolation, without taking account of international repercussions.

Open economies will not find this situation so unusual. They can note that they have always been very internationally minded and have always taken foreign effects into account when trying to analyze domestic effects of policy induced or other changes in economic conditions. The point is that no economy is any longer closed. All economies are, to one degree or another, open. This is particularly true of the United States. Model building for the United States must bring trade and international payments relations into the system from the very start. In the Model Comparison Seminar this is recognized in the multiplier experiments, the specified consistent international conditions for ex ante forecast evaluation, and the J-curve simulations. Also, John Taylor's model is not only different in the treatment of expectations, but also because it is a multicountry world model, with the United States being just one component.

John Taylor's call to public service as economic councilor to the President unfortunately prevented his contributing a separate chapter on his model, which has been published in an earlier version in a conference on international model comparison.

The implications of internationalization go even further. International modeling of many related economies together is now becoming more and more commonplace. After the venture of project LINK, which is in every sense an international model of truly world scope, there have been many such modeling ventures by the OECD, the Federal Reserve, the Japanese Economic Planning Agency, and several university or research center groups. The community of world modelers is expanding, and this form of model building will eventually be as common as national modeling. A related venture is discernible in sub-LINK systems. Various areas are suitable for regional model building, but the most elaborate are those of the Pacific Far East.[12]

While the Model Comparison Seminar originally focussed on looking at simulations and other properties of several U.S. models jointly, there are new ventures, one of which is reported by F. Gerard Adams and Joaquin Vial in this volume, dealing with model comparisons across different developing countries. It is a challenge, in itself, to undertake model building for individual developing countries. Models for such economies have special characteristics involving the strategic importance of fixed capital in production, the distribution of income in consumption, demographic trends toward urbanization, reliance on primary commodity exports, general importance of the supply side, endemic inflation in a few cases, the bearing of serious debt burdens in other cases, and the primitive state of domestic financial capital markets. But model building in the Third World has progressed to the point at which it becomes meaningful to look at cross-country results to strengthen our understanding of this segment of the world economy.

Increasing attention to developing countries and also to centrally planned economies, a few of which are also developing cases, will be characteristic of new trends in model building and analysis. An initial seminar on the issue of comparison across developing countries was held in Taiwan at the National Central University during May 1987. There have been follow-up seminars on this subject, notably at Project LINK meetings in Seoul, November 1988.

It has been noted that much progress in model building, model analysis, and the very techniques of model comparison is due to advances in computing. A similar advance is taking place in parallel in telecommunications technology. Data files, model estimates, and other pertinent information can be transmitted electronically among research centers to central computer facilities. Also computers engaged in modeling efforts can be linked into a fixed network. Model comparisons can be done from remote locations. Project LINK, moreover, has conducted intercontinental telecommunications experiments using audiovisual hookups together with remote access to computers for instant transmission of model results to widely dispersed participants. This means that researchers in different centers can stay in touch through means of telecommunications. The use of models will be enhanced by these devices, especially for international coordination practices, but also for research contacts.

Another area of model-related research is in the execution of stochastic simulation studies. These have been used for study of models for a few decades already, but increasing sophistication, power, and speed of computers enlarge the horizon of this form of analysis. Many more replications become possible, bigger systems can be handled, and stochastic simulation for the multiple model problem (international model building, e.g.) can now be carried out. Vector and parallel processing enable computers to be much more versatile in handling stochastic simulation. Optimality calculations for a large system, such as LINK, at the international level have been successfully executed by using parallel and vector capabilities.

It has been claimed that economic forecasts have not been improving. This is in contrast to experience in other fields such as meteorological forecasting. The claims may actually be incorrect, as shown by Stephen McNees' studies of error statistics over the years. He finds significant improvement between the 1950s and 1960s, some deterioration during the turbulent 1970s, and recovery again in the 1980s. There may even be a trend toward improvement in the 1980s over the 1960s.

Whether or not an improvement is being realized, users and practitioners will always want *more*. Among the promising approaches toward forecast improvement that have been discussed in the Model Comparison Seminar has been the combination of forecasts, using different models together for the same forecast. One specific line of improvement that is being investigated is the combination of high- and low-frequency data, using different models for the analysis of each.

In a practical sense, high-frequency data refer to monthly statistics (or even weekly or daily), whereas low-frequency data refer to quarterly (or annual) data. Models for the extrapolation of high-frequency data are based on formal time series methods, either in systems of VAR or ARIMA equations. We may try to take advantage of the high serial correlation observed in most economic time series to make very short-run forecasts of high-frequency data—up to horizons of 6 months. Some economic processes, particularly in money and credit markets, are best analyzed in very short periods.

There are many ways of combining time series with structural econometric models, the latter being the mainstream type studied in the succeeding chapters of this volume. One proposal, which is presently being investigated at Pennsylvania, is to accept the time series results, ARIMA based, for very short-run forecasts, and adjust structural models to agree with these estimated values for two quarters. The adjustments are then retained in the structural models for the rest of the forecast period.

ARIMA equations, in a monthly time frame, are written as

$$\sum_{j=0}^{p} \alpha_{ij} y_{i,t-j} + \sum_{j=1}^{m} \sum_{k=0}^{q} \beta_{ijk} x_{j,t-k} = \sum_{j=0}^{r} \gamma_{ij} e_{i,t-j}$$

Estimates of the parameters α, β, γ are obtained by methods of statistical inference from monthly time series samples and kept very current. In the United States a steady stream of monthly values is announced every week, so there are many occasions for updating the results. The monthly values are extrapolated from these equations for 6 months and averaged into quarters. A quarterly structural model, like most of the models in the Seminar, is also extrapolated, using the formula

$$f_i(y_{1t}, \ldots, y_{nt}, y_{1t-1}, \ldots, y_{n,t-p}, x_{1t}, \ldots, x_{mt}, x_{1t-1}, \ldots, x_{m,t-q} \hat{\theta}_1, \ldots, \hat{\theta}_{r_i})$$
$$= a_{it}, \; i = 1, 2, \ldots, n$$

where the $\hat{\theta}_i$ are estimated parameter values and the a_{it} are nonzero values substituted for the mean values of the stochastic error terms of the original specification. The mean values of these errors are zero, but instead of mean values or instead of subjectively imposed nonzero values, a set of a_{it} is selected, over the forecast horizon, so as to bring the solution of the structural model "close" to the ARIMA forecasts in the first two quarters. The adjustments are then retained for the entire horizon of the longer forecast.

A slightly different approach is being investigated at Michigan. A VAR model is used to track a small number of important variables for which monthly observations are available. Forecasts from the monthly model are merged with the quarterly model forecasts in two ways. First, the forecasts of common variables are forced to coincide by adjusting both the monthly and quarterly model forecasts to produce a minimum variance combined forecast. Second, within-quarter monthly observations are used to update the expected values of the disturbance terms in the quarterly model. In principle, these two types of adjustment could be imposed on the quarterly model for the entire forecast horizon.

It is anticipated that forecasts can be improved by the use of these techniques because the increasingly available set of high-frequency series provides added information about the current movement of the economy—information that goes beyond that available in the structural model. But even if the forecasts are not significantly improved, they should not be worsened, and the advantage of this procedure of model adjustment over subjective adjustment is that it is fully replicable by other researchers. It is an *objective* rather than a *subjective* method of model adjustment for the purposes of forecasting.

In Chapter 8 by E. Philip Howrey, the Michigan and Pennsylvania approaches for using monthly data to improve forecasting accuracy are explained in more detail, particularly for the former case. It is worth noting that this line of research actually started in the earlier phase of the model comparison seminar. T. C. Liu and E. C. Hwa of Cornell constructed an interpolated set of monthly GNP accounts and constructed a monthly model that showed significant forecasting promise.[13] In many respects, their work has been continued and extended at the Federal Reserve Board, and E. Philip Howrey refers to the contemporary work on a monthly forecasting model.[14]

Not only are models being compared in some newer ways, particularly in drawing on the increasing power of the computer that is now readily accessible to all, and in an international direction, but models themselves are undergoing change. Indeed, the whole macroeconomic theory basis for the specification of econometric models is being debated by economic theorists at great length and in great detail. The present activities of the Model Comparison Seminar reflect these changes and new directions for our subject.

The introduction of time series methods, in the form of ARIMA and VAR models, not only reflects the fact that such approaches attract a great deal of attention of econometricians now, but it also reflects the dissatisfaction of many economists with theoretical specifications of models. Pure time series models contain little or no theoretical economic specification. They are, in a sense, agnostic or empirical models. These time series approaches, as indicated earlier, are being used and discussed in this book. The VAR models are part of the comparison activity and ARIMA methods are, as mentioned above, being used in conjunction with structural macroeconometric models to automate the system adjustment procedures and to try to improve short-run forecasts. There is no neglect of these new directions; there are serious attempts to integrate them into the main body of work.

A second area of debate within macroeconomics has been in the treatment of expectations. Model builders in the past have treated expectations as adaptive:

$$\Delta y_t^e = \lambda(y_{t-1}^e - y_{t-1})$$

Where y_t^e = expected value of y_t

This makes expected values geometric distributed lag functions of historical ("own") values. There is much empirical support for the adaptive approach, and it is well represented in working models that are presently being used.[15] A more general approach, that includes adaptive expectations as a special case, is one that assumes

$$y_t^e = f(y_{t-1}, y_{t-2}, y_{t-3}, \ldots)$$

Expected values are assumed to be some (distributed) lag function of historical values. This approach is criticized as being "ad hoc," but its origins date back to Tinbergen's original models and was introduced because economic theory simply did not provide any explanation of the expectations mechanism. It merely recognized that expectations are important.

Economic theorists now have a relatively new theory of expectations—rational expectations. These are expectations that are generated by the very ("own") model that the econometrician is attempting to estimate and use. This theory is more in the form of an hypothesis and needs testing as well as exposition. In general, the problem of generating observations for expectations from the very data that are also being used for model estimation poses some questions of identification and uniqueness.[16] The rational expectations model of the United States developed by John Taylor, as mentioned above, is a full participant in the Model Comparison Seminar. This model is identified and its response properties are studied together with all the other participating models. It is the only model in the compilations that relies explicitly and heavily on "own-model" generated expectations, although other models use some form of own-model expectations. The multipliers from John Taylor's model, shown in the next chapter, are, in some cases, different from the general tendency of other models in the comparison, but not in all cases. Fiscal multipliers for his type of model appear to peak quickly and fade back toward zero; also the price multipliers show sustained movement by larger amounts under the impact of shocks. Most models have tended to underestimate the amplitude of induced price changes, while Taylor's model shows more proneness toward inflationary movement in experiments where there is a stimulus to the economy.

Although most working models have not used "own-generated" expectations, some have introduced explicit expectations variables into the system. Many models have equations for investment expectations, taken from well-known sample surveys of businesses. They also have equations for housing starts, which are like business investment expectations in that they serve as anticipatory indicators of realized residential construction. Earlier versions of the Michigan, Fair, and Wharton models used indexes of consumer sentiment as expectations variables (income, price, expenditure, and general economy expectations). Wider possibilities exist in the use of business surveys, and techniques for generating such expectations within the context of complete systems can be used, along the same lines that have already been tested for the Michigan, Fair, and Wharton models. It appears that the next thrust in model building may, in fact, introduce explicit expectations variables through the combination of sample surveys together with macro models that are based on time-series samples.

All the chapters in this volume except those prepared by Ignazio Visco and Robert J. Shiller were directly related to continuing activities of the Model Comparison Seminar. The Visco and Shiller contributions were specifically invited as external presentations and evaluations of the Seminar activities.

Most of the models studied in this volume are large systems, consisting of several hundred equations each, although some are smaller. There is no distinct preference for large or small systems; the only objective of investigation is to determine which can do the job of analyzing the economy best.

As far as understanding, managing, manipulating, and studying systems is concerned, size within the range being considered is no serious obstacle to use. The extensive and intensive uses of the ever improving computer have freed us from most of the size problems. There are still degrees-of-freedom questions and issues concerning statistical method to be dealt with. But there are enough degrees of freedom for system application of the sort being used, and investigators gain familiarity with system properties from highly repetitive applications that are made possible by the power of the computer. Small systems have their advantages and disadvantages too. They all show up in the multitude of comparisons studied in this book.

NOTES

1. See George J. Stigler. (1954). "The Early History of Empirical Studies of Consumer Behavior." *Journal of Political Economy* 62, 95–113, and (1962). "Henry L. Moore and Statistical Economics." *Econometrica* 30, 1–21; Carl F. Christ. (1985). "Early Progress in Estimating Quantitative Economic Relationships in America." *American Economic Review, Supplement* 75, 39–52.
2. See Clifford Hildreth. (1986). *The Cowles Commission in Chicago 1939–1955.* Vienna: Springer-Verlag.
3. This seminar was organized as one branch of a *Conference on Econometrics and Mathematical Economics* (CEME) supported by the National Science Foundation and administered by the National Bureau of Economic Research.
4. L. R. Klein and E. Burmeister. (1974). *Econometric Model Performance.* Philadelphia: Univ. of Pennsylvania Press.
5. A. A. Hirsch, S. H. Hymans, and H. J. Shapiro. (1978). "Econometric Review of Alternative Fiscal and Monetary Policy, 1971–75." *Review of Economics and Statistics* 60, 334–345.
6. A study of wage shocks in the United States through the medium of the Tinbergen Model was made by J. H. Witteveen. (1947). *Loonshoogate in Verkgelegenheid* No. 39, Nederlandsch Economisch Instituut. Haarlem: de Erven F. Gohn, N.V.
7. Many Keynesian economists who were not econometricians did not appreciate or were not aware of the forecasting issue; this aspect became evident in the first efforts at postwar planning in the mid-1940s.
8. Many of the models in the Seminar participated in the Energy Modeling Forum, when oil price shocks were investigated. See Bert G. Hickman. (1987). "Macroeconomic Impacts of Energy Shocks and Policy Responses: A Structural Comparison of Fourteen Models." In *Macroeconomic Impacts of Energy Shocks,* B. G. Hickman, H. G. Huntington, and J. L. Sweeney, eds., pp. 125–198. Amsterdam: North-Holland.

 9. George Schink. (1971). *Small Sample Estimates of the Variance-Covariance Matrix of Forecast Errors for Large Econometric Models: The Stochastic Simulation Technique.* Ph.D. Thesis, Univ. of Pennsylvania. See also C. Bianchi and G. Calzolari. (1980). "The One Period Forecast Errors in Nonlinear Econometric Models." *International Economic Review* 21, 201–208.
10. V. G. Duggal, L. R. Klein, and M. D. McCarthy. (1974). "The Wharton Model Mark III: A Modern IS-LM Construct." Reprinted in *Econometric Model Performance,* L. R. Klein and E. Burmeister, eds., pp. 188–210. Philadelphia: Univ. of Pennsylvania Press.
11. See B. G. Hickman, *op. cit.*
12. Shinichi Ichimura pioneered sub-LINK models of the Pacific Area. See Shinichi Ichimura, ed. (1980). *Econometric Models of the Asian Countries.* Kyoto: Center for Southeast Asian Studies, Kyoto University.
13. T. C. Liu and E. C. Hwa. (1974). "A Monthly Model of the U.S. Economy." Reprinted in *Econometric Model Performance,* L. R. Klein and E. Burmeister, eds., pp. 70–107. Philadelphia: University of Pennsylvania Press.
14. Carol Corrado and Jane Haltmaier. (1988). "The Use of High-Frequency Data in Model-Based Forecasting at the Federal Reserve Board." Finance and Economics Discussion Series, 24. Washington, D.C.: Federal Reserve Board.
15. An excellent example of an empirical test is provided by a careful study of the Central Bank of Norway, Morten Jensen and Morten Jonassen. (1986). "The Formation of Household Expectations—A Test on Norwegian Cross Sectional Survey Data." *Arbeids Notat,* Norges Bank, Oslo.
16. For an econometric analysis of these issues in depth, see M. H. Pesaran. (1987). *The Limits to Rational Expectations.* Oxford: Basil Blackwell.

CHAPTER 2

Performance of Quarterly Econometric Models of the United States: A New Round of Model Comparisons

F. GERARD ADAMS and LAWRENCE R. KLEIN

Many things have changed since the first round of econometric model comparisons, now more than 14 years ago (Klein and Burmeister, 1976). Most econometric models have been updated, not only to reflect the new data and underlying conditions, but also to respond to new ideas about how the economy operates. It is time, consequently, to take another look, to see how the models perform. This chapter focuses on the response of the various models to a number of alternatively specified external shocks.

Altogether 11 model groups supplied simulation results for the model comparisons. These groups represent a cross section of the currently active model operators and forecasters. They ran from the now traditional Keynesian to the monetarist and the rational expectations approaches. The participating model groups and the special characteristics of their models are listed in Table 2.1.[1]

Early in the meetings of the model comparison seminar, the philosophy of model comparisons was the topic of some extensive discussion. It was thought that comparison would require some standardization, but the model operators were reluctant to tamper with the structure of their models or even with the way they were used. Although it rapidly became clear that the alternative simulations would have to be prescribed quite precisely, it was decided to "let the models be models." This phrase was understood to mean that the model operators would use the models in the way they typically did. If, for example, the world economy was handled exogenously, it would continue to be dealt with in that way. If certain exogenous variables called for in the simulations were not in a model, the model operator would be allowed to work with the corresponding variables that were included in the model. Consequently, the standardization prior to making the simulations applies only to the specifications of the simulation runs, not to the models themselves. As much as possible, the simulations are intended to reflect the differing performance characteristics of the models.

The approach of this work was to compare alternative "disturbed" model solutions to a base solution. Each model operator was instructed to prepare a so-called "tracking solution" that would approximately reproduce history over the period 1975.1 to

Table 2.1. Characteristics of Participating Econometric Models

Group	Individuals	Abbreviation	Size of Model: No. of Behavioral Equations	Remarks
Bureau of Economic Analysis Washington, DC 20230	A. Hirsch	BEA	195	Neo-Keynesian contains exceptional fiscal detail for government users
Data Resources, Inc. Lexington, MA 02173	R. Brinner J. Yanchar	DRI	354	Emphasizes cyclical sensitivity, sectoral detail, long-run theoretical consistency
Ray Fair, Yale New Haven, CT 06520	R. Fair	FAIR	30	Emphasizes optimization by agents and disequilibrium
Federal Reserve Board Washington, DC 20551	W. Lee	FRB	128	Emphasis on financial flows and long-run equilibrium
Indiana University Center for Econometric Research Model Bloomington, IN 47401	J. Green	IND	100	Business cycle model with consistent long-run properties
Lawrence Meyer Assoc. St. Louis, MO 63130	J. Prakken	LM&A	90	Neoclassical synthesis
University of Michigan Ann Arbor, MI 48109	M. Donihue S. Hymans P. Howrey	MICH	86	Short-run, partial adjustment, open economy, government budget constraint
Federal Reserve Bank of St. Louis St. Louis, MO 63102	K. Carlson	St.L.	<10	Emphasis on money and its economic impact
Taylor, Stanford University Stanford, CA 94305	J. Taylor	TAYLOR	20 (U.S. only)	Rational expectations model; multicountry system
The WEFA Group Bala Cynwyd, PA 19004	F.G. Adams L.R. Klein J. Hagens	WEFA	281	Ninth version of the Wharton model, I/O linkages at the 1-digit level, use of anticipations variables
The Boston Company Economic Advisors (BCEA) Boston, Ma 02108	A. Sinai	SINAI	210	1987–1988 version, considerable financial system with quick expectations effects in financial markets

1984.4. After some experimentation with different simulation specifications, the following assumptions were agreed on:

SPENDING SHOCKS

1A. Real defense spending is shocked by 1% of historical GNP for each period 1975.1–1984.4 with M_1 (or corresponding monetary instrument) held to its base path.

1B. The same shock as in 1A, but with the short-term interest rate held at its base path.

1C. The same shock as in 1A, but with a reaction function used for money supply behavior.

MONETARY SHOCKS

2A. M_1 increased by the amounts 0.14, 0.73, 1.88, and 2.8% in the first four quarters, respectively. From the fifth quarter forward, M_1 is 3% above the base path.

2B. A short-term interest rate is lowered by 100 basis points, below the baseline path.

SUPPLY SHOCKS

3A. The world oil price is lowered by 20% below the baseline path. There are no other exogenous changes.

3BA. *The growth rate* of an average wage rate is lowered by an *annualized* rate of 2 percentage points *in the first simulation quarter* and then is allowed to grow undisturbed in subsequent quarters. M_1 is kept to the baseline path.

3BB. Wage shock as in 3BA with the short-term interest rate held at its base level.

3BC. Wage shock as in 3BA, but a reaction function is used for money supply behavior.

The adjustments to obtain the "disturbed" solutions were made as closely as possible in accord with the common set of instructions, but as we have noted, the idiosyncrasies of the models forced some substitutions of approximately equivalent magnitude. The results of the simulations were sent on diskettes to the University of Pennsylvania where they were assembled and analyzed.

OVERVIEW OF SIMULATION RESULTS

In this section we summarize the results and attempt to provide some analytical explanation.

The tightest summary of the results is contained in Table 2.2A, which records the average of the results for 10 different models (a smaller number is used in parentheses when some of the models did not provide a complete simulation path that could be averaged in with the other results). For example, the first line of this table compares the average multiplier associated with simulation 1A for the first four quarters (1975.1–1975.4), for the eighth quarter (1976.4), for the twelfth quarter (1977.4), and for the fortieth quarter (1984.4). The "high" is the highest value of the average multiplier observed, the "low" is the lowest average, and the "average" is the average of average values over the entire 40-quarter simulation period. The first panel shows the impact on GNP, and the second panel on the GNP deflator. The third panel shows average impacts on consumption and investment (for the fiscal stimulus simulations only). Table 2.2B shows the standard deviations of the distribution of model multipliers. Figures 2.1–2.3 present average effects across all models. Graphs are shown for GNP, deflator, unemployment, interest rate, government deficit, and balance of trade. Appendix Tables A2.1–A2.12 compare the results of the various models.

FISCAL POLICY (SIMULATIONS 1)

The expenditure simulations involved an increase in public spending without monetary accommodation (Sim 1A), with interest rates kept at baseline values (Sim 1B), and with a monetary policy reaction function (Sim 1C).

- On average, the "high" of the expenditure simulations without monetary accommodation (Sim 1A) is 1.5 after a period of four to five quarters. The lack of monetary adjustment causes the multiplier to drop to an average "low" of −0.4 (after more than 20 quarters) and then to stabilize around 0.1 over the long run (after 40 quarters). In other words, in the long run the average multiplier is close to zero, in the absence of monetary accommodation.
- In contrast, with monetary accommodation to keep interest rates at the baseline level (Sim 1B), the multiplier reaches a "high" of 2.2 (after four to five quarters) and then declines to a "low" of 1.0, which is also close to the long run value after 40 quarters. Over the entire simulation period the average multiplier is 1.4.
- Not surprisingly, the solutions with a monetary policy reaction function (Sim 1C) fall somewhere between Simulations 1A and 1B, though it is interesting to note that the reaction function limits the upward swing of the multiplier to a little below that of the other two simulations.
- The initial effect of fiscal stimulus on investment is strongly positive, but eventually there is crowding out, particularly if money supply is assumed unchanged.
- The impact on the deflator (measured as percentage deviations from the baseline solution) shows entirely different patterns. The impact on prices is zero or even slightly negative during the first two impact quarters. It builds up gradually throughout the simulation period.
- The three simulations differ considerably in their inflationary impact with the price deflator deviations building up to 2% without monetary accommodation (Sim 1A), 6% with monetary accommodation (Sim 1B), and in between with the monetary policy reaction function (Sim 1C).

Table 2.2A. "Average" Dynamic Multipliers[a]
(Selected Periods 1975.1–1984.4)

	1975.1	1975.2	1975.3	1975.4	1976.4	1977.4	1984.4	High	Low	Average
The Effects on GNP										
					Fiscal Simulation (multiplier)					
[1A]	1.06	1.42	1.54	1.55	1.33	0.73	0.15	1.55	−0.42	0.33
[1B]	1.28	1.87	2.13	2.19	2.15	1.70	1.02	2.22	1.00	1.45
[1C]	1.07	1.37	1.46	1.45	1.09	0.50	0.82	1.46	0.16	0.79
					Monetary Simulation (% deviation)					
[2A]	0.06	0.20	0.42	0.70	1.23	1.22	−0.15	1.26	−0.39	0.33
[2B]	0.32	0.75	1.07	1.27	1.78	1.87	1.17	1.87	0.32	1.37
					Supply-Side Simulation (% deviation)					
[3AA]	0.12	0.25	0.34	0.42	0.57	0.61	0.21	0.62	0.12	0.44
[3BA]	−0.04	−0.04	−0.03	−0.01	0.11	0.18	−0.02	0.20	−0.05	0.06
[3BB]	−0.04	−0.06	−0.08	−0.08	−0.07	−0.09	−0.08	−0.04	−0.24	−0.15
[3BC]	−0.03	−0.02	−0.03	−0.01	0.09	0.09	0.06	0.10	−0.13	−0.02
The Effects on GNP Deflator										
					Fiscal Simulation (% deviation)					
[1A]	−0.03	0.00	0.11	0.21	0.82	1.37	2.00	2.16	−0.03	1.58
[1B]	−0.01	0.10	0.29	0.50	1.72	2.77	6.68	6.68	−0.01	3.96
[1C]	−0.05	0.00	0.07	0.15	0.63	1.02	4.10	4.10	−0.05	1.81
					Monetary Simulation (% deviation)					
[2A]	0.01	0.01	0.07	0.07	0.54	1.05	2.27	2.70	0.01	1.75
[2B]	0.04	0.12	0.30	0.51	1.74	2.89	7.28	7.28	0.04	4.30

Supply-Side Simulation (% deviation)

[3AA]	-0.01	-0.12	-0.19	-0.29	-0.44	-0.55	-0.43	-0.01	-0.67	-0.48
[3BA]	-0.13	-0.23	-0.23	-0.36	-0.44	-0.52	-0.21	-0.13	-0.53	-0.34
[3BB]	-0.17	-0.29	-0.30	-0.44	-0.58	-0.73	-1.91	-0.17	-1.91	-1.03
[3BC]	-0.18	-0.31	-0.30	-0.45	-0.54	-0.67	-0.95	-0.18	-0.95	-0.69

The Effects on Consumption

					Fiscal Simulation					
[1A]	0.26	0.44	0.55	0.61	0.60	0.37	0.38	0.64	-0.34	0.13
[1B]	0.36	0.78	1.06	1.25	1.58	1.35	1.58	1.85	0.36	1.41
[1C]	0.33	0.47	0.58	0.65	0.52	0.18	0.80	0.83	-0.03	0.47

The Effects on Investment

					Fiscal Simulation					
[1A]	0.75	2.00	3.02	3.66	3.80	1.34	-2.08	4.22	-3.05	-0.49
[1B]	0.91	2.47	3.89	4.86	5.90	4.11	-0.19	6.00	-0.19	2.40
[1C]	0.85	1.84	2.56	2.97	2.59	0.26	0.10	3.19	-1.48	0.56

ªModels included in computation:

[1A] BEA, DRI, FAIR, FRB, IND, LM&A, MICH, WEFA, St.L, Taylor
[1B] BEA, DRI, FAIR,   IND, LM&A, MICH, WEFA,   Taylor
[1C] BEA, DRI, FAIR, FRB, IND, LM&A, MICH, WEFA, St.L

[2A] BEA, DRI, FAIR, FRB, IND, LM&A, MICH, WEFA, St.L, Taylor
[2B] BEA, DRI, FAIR,   IND, LM&A, MICH, WEFA,   Taylor

[3AA] BEA, DRI, FAIR, FRB, IND, LM&A, MICH, WEFA, St.L
[3BA] BEA, DRI, FAIR, FRB, IND, LM&A, MICH,   Taylor
[3BB] BEA, DRI, FAIR, FRB, IND, LM&A, MICH, WEFA,   Taylor
[3BC] BEA, DRI, FAIR,   IND, LM&A, MICH, WEFA

Table 2.2B. Standard Deviation of Dynamic Multipliers[a]
(Selected Periods 1975.1–1984.4)

	1975.1	1975.2	1975.3	1975.4	1976.4	1977.4	1984.4	High	Low	Average
The Effects on GNP										
					Fiscal Simulation (multiplier)					
[1A]	0.32	0.47	0.55	0.66	0.62	0.36	1.16	1.28	0.32	0.85
[1B]	0.44	0.98	1.08	0.95	0.66	0.32	2.04	2.04	0.30	1.03
[1C]	0.27	0.38	0.50	0.58	0.79	0.68	0.68	1.08	0.27	0.80
					Monetary Simulation (% deviation)					
[2A]	0.13	0.27	0.35	0.44	0.80.	1.16	1.12	1.24	0.13	0.93
[2B]	0.60	1.27	1.59	1.60	1.17	0.77	2.09	2.09	0.60	1.44
					Supply-Side Simulation (% deviation)					
[3AA]	0.12	0.19	0.24	0.28	0.26	0.31	0.55	0.72	0.12	0.44
[3BA]	0.04	0.08	0.12	0.15	0.24	0.31	0.27	0.34	0.04	0.26
[3BB]	0.06	0.10	0.13	0.17	0.29	0.38	0.54	0.61	0.06	0.42
[3BC]	0.06	0.09	0.13	0.18	0.27	0.26	0.31	0.31	0.06	0.24
The Effects on GNP Deflator										
					Fiscal Simulation					
[1A]	0.07	0.10	0.18	0.21	0.54	0.93	1.54	1.65	0.07	1.13
[1B]	0.13	0.31	0.60	0.94	2.51	3.64	3.48	4.04	0.13	3.06
[1C]	0.06	0.09	0.15	0.10	0.32	0.70	4.30	4.30	0.06	1.53

Monetary Simulation (% deviation)

[2A]	0.02	0.06	0.12	0.19	0.46	0.81	1.99	2.15	0.02	1.41
[2B]	0.13	0.41	0.81	1.36	3.82	5.73	5.98	6.56	0.13	5.07

Supply-Side Simulation (% deviation)

[3AA]	0.11	0.12	0.17	0.17	0.29	0.38	0.71	0.71	0.11	0.51
[3BA]	0.08	0.12	0.12	0.12	0.15	0.18	0.22	0.25	0.08	0.19
[3BB]	0.13	0.20	0.22	0.24	0.29	0.42	2.98	2.98	0.13	1.13
[3BC]	0.14	0.22	0.25	0.27	0.31	0.35	0.58	0.59	0.14	0.41

The Effects on Consumption

Fiscal Simulation

[1A]	0.20	0.30	0.34	0.41	0.41	0.34	1.15	1.15	0.20	0.77
[1B]	0.55	0.90	1.04	1.11	1.40	1.05	1.96	2.18	0.55	1.39
[1C]	0.37	0.49	0.59	0.71	0.82	0.72	1.08	1.08	0.37	0.90

The Effects on Investment

Fiscal Simulation

[1A]	0.77	1.26	1.70	2.02	2.05	0.73	3.22	3.89	0.73	2.49
[1B]	0.84	2.13	3.43	4.06	4.16	3.13	3.65	4.24	0.84	2.66
[1C]	0.81	1.45	1.85	2.16	2.47	1.86	3.48	3.48	0.81	2.63

[a]Standard deviation of percentage effects

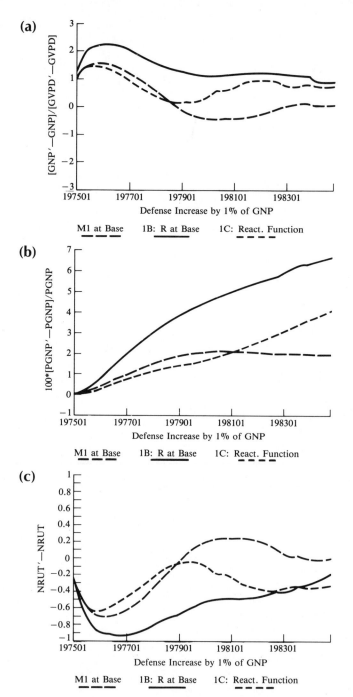

Figure 2.1. Average multiplier paths—fiscal policy. (a) Fiscal simulation: average GNP multiplier. (b) Fiscal simulation: average PGNP percentage deviation. (c) Fiscal simulation: unemployment rate (average deviation).

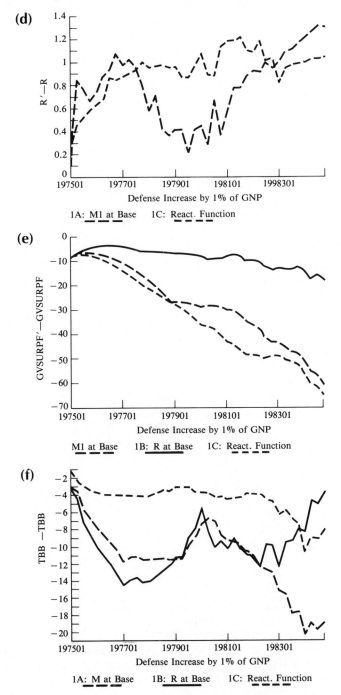

Figure 2.1. *(Continued.)* (d) Fiscal simulation: interest rate (average deviation). (e) Fiscal simulation: federal deficit (average deviation). (f) Fiscal simulation: balance of trade (average deviation).

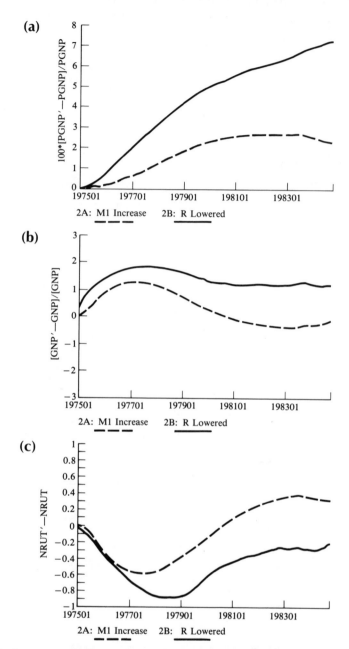

Figure 2.2. Average multiplier paths—monetary policy. (a) Monetary simulation: average PGNP percentage deviation. (b) Monetary simulation: average GNP percentage deviation. (c) Monetary simulation: unemployment rate (average deviation).

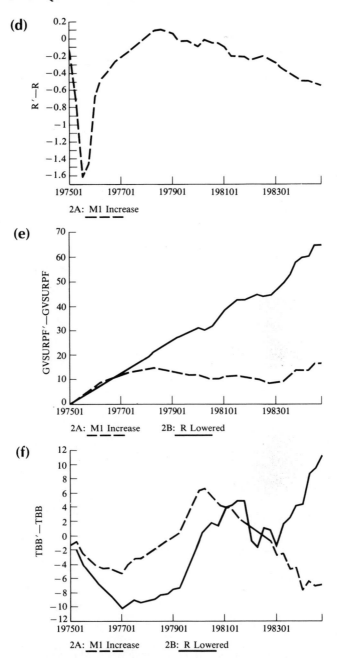

Figure 2.2. (*Continued.*) (d) Monetary simulation: interest rate (average deviation). (e) Monetary simulation: federal deficit (average deviation). (f) Monetary simulation: balance of trade (average deviation).

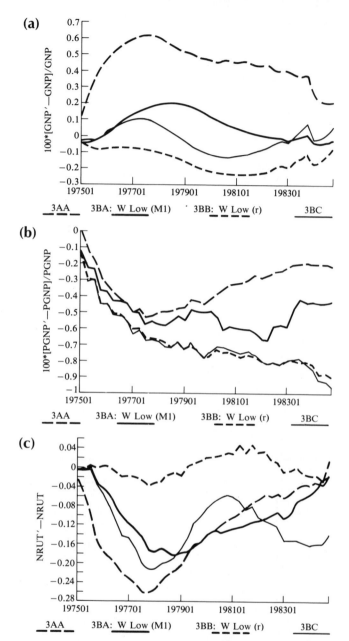

Figure 2.3. Average multiplier paths—supply-side simulation. (a) Supply-side simulation: average GNP percentage deviation. (b) Supply-side simulation: average PGNP percentage deviation. (c) Supply-side simulation: unemployment rate (average deviation).

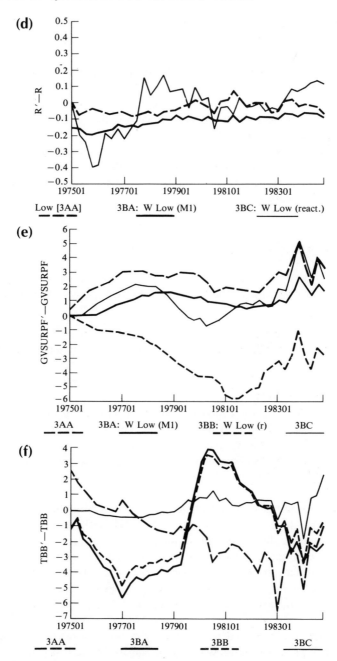

Figure 2.3. (*Continued.*) (d) Supply-side simulation: interest rate (average deviation). (e) Supply-side simulation: federal deficit (average deviation). (f) Supply-side simulation: balance of trade (average deviation)

- The effect on unemployment is greater and more persistent in Sim 1B than in the other fiscal simulations where significant increases in interest rates, up to 1%, occur.
- On the other hand, the fixed interest rate simulation (Sim 1B) shows considerably smaller impact on the deficit than the other fiscal simulations, which indicates continued severe increases in the federal deficit over the entire simulation period.
- Trade balance effects are consistently negative, though much smaller with the monetary reaction function (Sim 1C) than in the other cases.
- The variation between the models is quite large, for example, the standard deviations of 1% of GNP among the results for the fiscal stimulus simulation 1B after three quarters. Long-run differences are even larger, particularly with respect to inflationary impacts.

MONETARY POLICY (SIMULATIONS 2)

The monetary policy simulations involved a 3% increase in money supply (Sim 2A) and alternatively a downward adjustment of 100 basis points in short term interest rates (Sim 2B).

- The impact of monetary ease for the average of the models builds up more slowly than that of fiscal stimulus, reaching a peak 8 to 12 quarters out into the simulation period. A 3% increase in money supply yields a GNP increase "high" of 1.25% (Sim 2A). The long-run effect of an increase in money supply on GNP is close to zero (-0.15).
- In turn, a 100 basis point reduction in the short-term interest rate gradually builds up to an impact on GNP of 1.8% (Sim 2B). The long-run effect is maintained at 1.2% after 40 quarters.
- The effect of monetary expansion on the price level takes a gradual upward path, a 3% increase in money supply yields over 2% higher prices in the long run (Sim 2A).
- The interest rate reduction effects a similar gradual buildup of prices, but at a faster rate reaching a 7.3% impact on the GNP deflator after 40 quarters, but with considerable dispersion among models.
- Both policies produce reductions in unemployment, reaching a maximum of almost 1 percentage point after 12 quarters with the reduced interest rate, but it is notable that the improvement in the unemployment rate fades away later in the simulation period and disappears entirely in the increased money supply case (Sim 2A).
- The effect of the increased money supply on interest rates occurs quickly and sharply. It is at its maximum with a reduction at the interest rate by 1.6 percentage points in the third simulation quarter, but the effect of increased money supply on interest rates also disappears quickly.
- The effect of monetary ease on the budget deficit is substantial, $10 billion in the case of increased money supply, and rising continuously to over $60 billion in the reduced interest rate case (Sim 2B).
- Both monetary simulations show cyclical swings of the balance of payments,

though it should be noted that most of the models take the exchange rate as exogenous and do not include international capital flow effects.

SUPPLY-SIDE (SIMULATIONS 3)

The supply side simulations all involve a downward movement in costs; Sim 3AA assumes a 20% reduction in international petroleum prices and Sims 3BA, 3BB, and 3BC assume a downward adjustment of wages of 2% with money supply unadjusted, interest rates unchanged, and a monetary policy reaction function, respectively. A critical question in these simulations is whether the impact on demand overwhelms the effect on supply.

- The average impact on real GNP is quite small in all the cases considered. Even a reduction of oil prices of 20% yields only a maximum increase in GNP of 0.6%, and that after a gradual buildup over 12 quarters. Over the entire simulation period the effect of the oil price reduction amounts to 0.4% of GNP.
- In contrast, the lower wage simulations (Sims 3BA, 3BB, and 3BC) appear to be dominated by the lower demand, so that the impact on GNP is almost everywhere negative. Not surprisingly, the simulation that maintains the baseline interest rate shows less GNP than the other reduced wage simulations.
- On the price deflator side, the supply side simulations yield lower prices, as anticipated. In the case of petroleum prices the impact is slow in building up. An average impact of −0.5% is obtained but that figure is reached only in 12 quarters after the oil price reduction.
- The lower wage simulations similarly yield reductions in the price level, that is, 2% lower wages results in lower prices by 0.3% with money supply fixed (Sim 3BA), and 0.7% with interest rates fixed (Sim 3BB) and also 0.7% with the monetary policy reaction function (Sim 3BC). In these cases, the effect is more rapid than in the petroleum case, with substantial effect on prices after two to four quarters.
- The impact of supply-side shifts on the unemployment rate is perceptible though not substantial except in the case of fixed interest rates (Sim 3BB) demonstrating the importance of monetary effects in these supply-side simulations.
- Interest rate effects are, however, quite small in all cases except with the monetary reaction function, which introduces some cyclical swings.
- The budget deficit improves somewhat in all cases, except Sim 3BB with the interest rate at base levels.
- The trade balance improvement associated with lower petroleum prices fades away after four quarters. Reductions in wage rates appear to improve the trade balance only after 16 quarters.

CROSS-MODEL COMPARISONS

Comparisons among the performance of different models are considerably more difficult than comparisons among average simulations as the figures in Appendix Tables

A2.1–A2.12 show. There is a considerable, one might even say astonishing, variation in the performance of the models considering that they were estimated over approximately the same time period and are largely, but not wholly, intended for the same purposes. We can no longer say, as did Klein and Burmeister (1976), "Despite such differences, however, with the exception of the FRB St. Louis model, there is a fair amount of agreement among the quarterly models." Some of the differences reflect the different structures of the models noted in Table 2.1. But to a substantial degree differences among the models do not appear to represent so much intended differences in structure specification as differences in sensitivity of interest rates to money supply and nominal GNP, the LM curve; investment and other demands to interest rates, the IS curve; and prices to cost and capacity pressures, the AS curve.

We will make an attempt to look into these issues below. At this point we will review the results obtained in the simulation runs, attempting in each case to identify a group of models that tends toward the average, and noting those that appear to follow distinctly different movements. The discussion of effects on GNP and prices is based on Appendix Tables A2.1–A2.12.

FISCAL POLICY (SIMULATIONS 1)

- The characteristics of dynamic expenditure multipliers without monetary accommodation (Sim 1A), reaching a peak between 1.5 and 2, are shared by many models during the first few quarters of the simulation period. But the equilibrium property of eventually returning to zero is shared only by IND, St.L, and TAYLOR. Some models show great swings, it would appear, in response to movements of interest rates, particularly FRB and, to a lesser extent, DRI. MICH and FAIR show continued positive multiplier impacts throughout the simulation period, whereas WEFA and BEA appear to show negative multiplier impacts in the long run. St.L shows considerable insensitivity, with little movement as a consequence of the spending increase in the absence of monetary accommodation. The pattern of TAYLOR that reaches its peak multiplier in the second simulation quarter is notable.
- Monetary accommodation to maintain baseline interest rates (Sim 1B) alters the picture considerably in that most of the models maintain positive multipliers between 1 and 2.5 (at the peak) over much of the simulation period. The BEA model continues to show a declining multiplier pattern, and DRI shows a mounting multiplier into the 4 to 5 range, presumably as a consequence of its sensitivity to the monetary growth required to stabilize the interest rate.
- The introduction of monetary policy reaction functions (Sim 1C) causes wide swings in the multiplier in a number of the models, for example, LM&A, DRI, and FRB. The nature of the reaction functions and the time phasing of their impact warrant further study.
- There is somewhat more agreement among the models with respect to inflationary impact, most of the models showing a gradual pattern of price increase reaching higher prices by about 1 to 2% at the end of the simulation period, without monetary accommodation (Sim 1A) and 5 to 6% with monetary accommodation

(Sim 1B). There are, however, some striking exceptions, for example, TAYLOR and BEA, who show price increases of 5% (without monetary accommodation), and DRI and IND, who show sharp price buildups with monetary accommodation. St.L shows little price impact, but there has been no adjustment in money supply, and this is after all a monetarist model. FAIR also shows little price impact, approximately 1% after 40 quarters.

MONETARY POLICY (SIMULATIONS 2)

- With some striking exceptions the money supply simulations (Sim 2A) show a common pattern of gradual upward movement, an impact of between 0.5 and 2% of GNP with gradual downward movement to near zero. Exceptions are much wider cyclical swings by DRI and FRB. St.L also shows a cyclical swing, but of a smaller magnitude.
- Monetary simulations reducing the interest rate directly (Sim 2B) show a maintained positive multiplier throughout the simulation period. DRI shows continued very strong upward effects and BEA again shows a cyclical swing.
- For the typical model, the price impact of the 3% money supply increase ultimately works out to about 2%. Again, there are exceptions; DRI shows almost 8% and FRB shows a cyclical peak of almost 6%. On the other hand, MICH and FAIR show little price sensitivity.
- Interest rate reductions (Sim 2B) yield somewhat greater price level increases in some cases, that is, LM&A, DRI, IND, and BEA. On the other hand, there is little impact on prices in WEFA, MICH, and FAIR.

SUPPLY-SIDE (SIMULATIONS 3)

- The typical models show only moderate real GNP impacts from a 20% reduction in petroleum prices (Sim 3AA). The short-term impact is moderate (less than 1% in all cases) but over a longer span some of the models display cyclical characteristics.
- Somewhat surprisingly, the price impacts show substantial divergence. The price path typically moves gradually downward to a decline of some 0.5% below baseline. FAIR, FRB, and MICH show somewhat stronger price declines. BEA eventually shows a positive price impact.
- Lower wages (Sim 3BA) without monetary accommodation have generally positive impacts on real output. This represents a rightward shift of the aggregate supply schedule and rightward shift of the LM curve. The amount of the impact varies greatly among models and tends to fade away over time in most, but not all, cases. The negative path of FAIR is an exception. An interesting result is a gradual decline in unemployment (Figure 2.3), which fades out eventually.
- Lower wages with monetary accommodation (Sim 3BB) show more diverse, and more negative and cyclical effects on GNP. Note that in this case, the baseline interest rate is not permitted to decline as it is in Sim 3BA.

- As we have noted earlier, the monetary policy reaction function (Sim 3BC) tends to introduce cyclical movements in several of the models.
- The price level implications of lower wages are gradually downward between 0.3 and 0.8% over 2–4 years. After that time, prices recover, despite the fact that wages have been continued in the simulation at the reduced level. DRI and WEFA show significant continued declines in prices in simulations with baseline interest rates and with the monetary policy reaction function.

J-CURVE SIMULATIONS

A separate round of simulations was carried out to investigate the so-called J-curve effects.[3] The purpose was to evaluate the response of trade and of other dimensions of the macro economy and the balance of payments to changes in the exchange rate, foreign economic activity, and economic activity in the United States. The simulations carried out were as follows:

J1. *10% Dollar Depreciation* (exogenized exchange rate at baseline levels × 0.9). With pass-through as specified in each model.

J2. *Higher Foreign Economic Activity*—One percent above baseline foreign economic activity. With exogenous exchange rate at baseline level.

J3. *Lower U.S. Growth*—By using fiscal policy (an income tax increase) U.S. growth rate is 1% lower than baseline with exchange rate exogenous at baseline levels.

Average results of the simulations have been summarized in Table 2.3 and detailed results by model are shown in Appendix Tables A2.13 and A2.14. In each case, multipliers are shown after 1 year (1974.1), 2 years, 3 years, and 4 years. In the discussion below, we use the average multipliers to develop some simple rules about model responses.

Simulation J1—Depreciation of the U.S.$ by 10% with Pass-through as Specified in the Individual Models

The objective was to observe impacts on real and nominal trade and trade balances, on import prices, and on economic activity and the price level.

- Import Prices—Average impacts of devaluation on import prices suggest *an elasticity of 0.5 to 0.7 on average*. Although the figure builds up gradually over the first year, these responses seem somewhat higher than recent experience would justify.
- Imports in Volume and Value—The elasticity of imports with respect to dollar depreciation appears to be approximately −0.4 in volume and +0.2 in value terms. *None of the models yields a decrease in the value of imports as a result of dollar depreciation even after 4 years.* On average, the elasticity with respect to import prices is a little less than unity, so that a smaller price feedthrough might marginally change the result.

Table 2.3. Average J-Curve Simulation Results

Effects on	1984.1	1985.1	1986.1	1987.1
10% Depreciation of U.S.$				
		% Deviation from base		
Real imports	− 3.41	− 4.14	− 4.13	− 4.11
Nominal imports	1.74	1.95	2.25	2.51
Real exports	3.39	4.19	4.23	4.06
Nominal exports	4.84	6.48	7.31	8.18
		Deviation from base (bil 1982 $)		
Real trade balance	26.73	33.96	36.12	38.06
Nominal trade balance	10.69	15.90	17.01	18.95
		% Deviation from base		
Real GNP	0.89	1.23	0.96	0.61
GNP deflator	0.12	0.56	1.13	1.97
Import prices	5.59	6.46	6.69	6.92
1% Increase in Foreign Economic Activity				
		% Deviation from base		
Real exports	0.90	0.92	0.96	0.97
Nominal exports	0.91	0.93	1.00	1.18
		Deviation from base (bil 1982 $)		
Real trade balance	2.38	2.38	2.76	3.0
Nominal trade balance	2.53	2.69	3.16	3.49
		% Deviation from base		
GNP	0.17	0.14	0.09	0.07
1% Decrease in U.S. Growth Rate[a]				
		% Deviation from base		
Real imports	− 1.37	− 3.38	− 5.43	− 7.68
Nominal imports	− 1.54	− 3.87	− 6.42	− 9.32
		Deviation from base (bil 1982 $)		
Real trade balance	5.69	14.89	26.51	40.42
Nominal trade balance	5.81	14.12	24.64	38.10

[a]Based on three models only.

- Exports in Volume and Value—Exports in real terms show a response elasticity of 0.3 to 0.4. There appears in addition to be significant price effect, yielding an elasticity in value terms ranging from 0.5 to 0.8.
- Balance of Trade (goods and services) Real and Nominal—In real terms the results are surprisingly similar among the models with a response of $26 billion after 1 year to $38 billion after 4 years (1982$). But in nominal terms the models show smaller and considerably more diverse effects. On average, improvements in the international balance ranges from $10 billion after 1 year to $18 billion after 4 years, a disappointing improvement. But, the difference between the models is from $10 billion for Indiana, DRI, and Wharton to $30 billion for Sinai.
- GNP and GNP Deflator—Impacts on GNP and the deflator are surprisingly diverse and in some cases large. On average, GNP increases 1%. Given the assumption of fixed money supply (in most cases), and the surprisingly large impact on GNP, the GNP deflator impact builds up to an average of 2% after 4 years, and then tends to diminish in the out years.

Simulation J2—Increase in Foreign Economic Activity with Exchange Rates at Baseline Level

The critical issue here is to appraise how much an improvement in economic activity abroad would improve the U.S. trade balance and economic activity in the United States. The models handle the external environment differently and have very different export elasticities for the US.

- Exports (real and nominal)—On average, a 1% higher *level* of economic activity abroad translates into almost 1% higher real U.S. exports, but the figures range from 0.25 (Sinai) to 1.88 (WEFA). Exports in nominal terms are little different from exports in real terms as there appears to be little price impact.
- Balance of Trade (real and nominal)—Balance of trade impacts obviously vary greatly as well. But it is important to note that they are small, averaging about $3 billion. If one were to assume a 1% *rate of increase* in place of *change in the level* of foreign economic activity, one could accumulate the figures shown. Still, the improvement in the U.S. trade balance would be only $12 billion on average after 4 years. The effects on U.S. GNP are small, averaging 0.1%.

Simulation J3—Lower U.S. Economic Growth

Only a few models provided results for this simulation. The issue is simply "Will an economic slowdown (recession), assumed to result from a tax increase, solve the U.S. balance of payments problem?"

- Imports in Real and Nominal Terms—The models show surprising variation in the sensitivity of imports to economic activity. After 4 years of slower growth, reductions in imports average 7.7% ranging from 2.6 to 14.5%. There is little difference between real and nominal impacts.
- Trade Balance—The great variation in imports also shows up in impacts on trade balances. After 4 years, the positive effects range from an impact of only $5 billion to an effect of almost $70 billion. Although the variation between the models is unrealistically large the simulations suggest that with two of the models, slower growth has promise of making a significant difference in the balance of payments.

AN APPROACH TO STRUCTURAL ANALYSIS

Dynamic multipliers illustrate but do not explain the performance characteristics of the models. An approach to structural analysis is to look at the underlying behavioral function structure and coefficients. These can be summarized in the familiar IS and LM and AD and AS curves of intermediate macroeconomics.[4] Hickman (1984, 1986) uses simulations to measure the slopes of these curves. The problem is that the multipliers result from a simultaneous solution of the entire equation system and, in most cases, do not identify the slopes of the desired relationships. An alternative approach (Kuh, Neese, and Hollinger, 1985) is to decompose the block structure of the model and to compute multipliers. This approach would be burdensome and difficult in dealing with numerous structurally diverse models.

Fortunately our simulations make possible a limited measurement of the IS and LM curves. This is shown graphically in Figure 2.4. We illustrate our discussion in reference to the expenditure simulations (Sim 1A and 1B). The broad lines intersecting show the initial IS–LM curve equilibrium at e corresponding to the baseline solution. The increase in public spending shifts the IS curve to line IS2 and equilibrium f. Simulation 1A, assuming no monetary accommodation, leaves the LM curve unchanged (except, of course, for price level change). Simulation 1B calls for a shift of money supply and consequently of the LM curve just sufficient to maintain baseline interest rates. This yields LM2 and equilibrium g. The slope of the LM curve can then be identified as DE/AB from Sim 1A and the slope of the IS curve is approximated by DE/BC, using information from Simulations 1A and 1B. As we have noted, this procedure assumes that there is little or no price increase, that is, the AS curve is flat over the relevant range since an increase in prices, given the money supply, would shift the LM curve to the left. For the same reason the aggregate supply curve cannot be evaluated in a similar fashion in Sim 1A.

Similar computations can be done with the monetary simulations to identify the slope of the IS curve. In that case, our simulations do not enable us to identify the LM curve. The aggregate supply curve can be evaluated in Sim 2B, which sets the interest rate. The supply-side simulations do not permit disentanglement of supply- and demand-side forces. In principle, though perhaps not in many of the models, lower petroleum prices should affect domestic income and demand as well as supply. And wages obviously affect both the demand and the supply side.

In Table 2.4 we present some estimates of the slopes of the IS and LM curves. Columns 2 and 3 show the LM curve slope based on Sim 1A, after a period of four quarters. The figures in parentheses are the corresponding price effects (in %)—note the estimates of the slope parameters are biased to the extent that the price effect deviates from zero. Columns 7 and 8 show for each of the models an estimate, re-

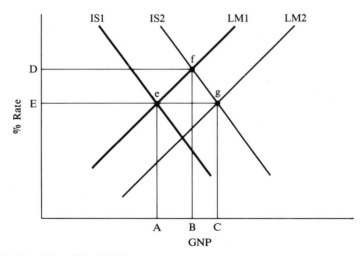

Figure 2.4. Identifying IS and LM curves.

Table 2.4. Estimated IS LM Slope Coefficients

Model	Sim 1A		Sim 1B		Sim 1A % Effect	Sim 1A LM Slope	Sim 1A–1B IS Slope	Sim 2B Based Alt IS Slope
	GNP Effect	PGNP Effect	GNP Effect	PGNP Effect				
BEA	2.5122	0.0000	2.6338	0.0000	0.28	0.11	−2.29	−1.12
DRI	2.0785	0.1887	2.2057	0.1690	0.70	0.34	−5.38	−3.20
FAIR	1.3879	0.1474	1.4496	0.1474	0.22	0.16	−3.67	−2.33
FRB	2.453	0.3443	3.2595	0.4262	2.08	0.85	−2.57	−1.74
IND	1.1964	0.0492	1.575	0.0328	0.50	0.42	−1.31	−0.99
LM&A	1.6192	0.3279	2.3054	0.4918	0.70	0.43	−1.01	−1.08
MICH	1.2853	0.0766	1.3194	0.0703	0.07	0.05	−1.72	−1.52
ST.L	0.1708	0.0818	—	—	0.08	0.48	—	—
WEFA	1.5995	0.1475	1.5995	0.1475	0.00	0.00	—	−2.26

spectively, of the LM and of the IS curve slopes based on the results (at simulation quarter 4) of Sim 1A and Sim 1B. Column 9 shows IS curve slopes based on Sim 2B.

The LM curve slopes are positive, but vary greatly. Note that the slopes are increases in interest rate per $ billion of increase in GNP, so that a slope of 0.85, as in FRB, is quite steep, whereas 0.05, as in MICH, can be seen as fairly flat. The higher slopes (FRB and LM&A) may reflect the bias resulting from inflation which is more pronounced in these models than in the ones with lower calculated LM slopes. In turn the IS curve slopes are all negative, as anticipated. Although again there is much variation, all the IS slopes can be considered steep. The alternative approach to IS produces different slopes, but again steep ones.

More extensive analysis of model structure is needed to confirm the association between the differences in the dynamic multipliers and the structural characteristics of the models.[5]

ACKNOWLEDGMENT

We would like to thank Jirapol Pobukadee for valuable research assistance.

NOTES

1. A number of others participated in the discussions but did not submit results for inclusion in the tabulations. Allen Sinai's model simulations are listed only for the J-curve estimates because he joined the seminar group at a later stage.
2. The St. Louis Fed model went its own way even in earlier simulation comparisons and the Taylor model is based on rational expectations features that appear to accelerate the processes of adjustment.
3. A smaller number of model builders participated in this effort than in our earlier round of simulations. The simulations covered a different period, 1983.1–1987.4.
4. See also the chapters on "IS-LM Curves" in this volume.
5. The chapters comparing the DRI and BEA models and the FAIR and MICHIGAN models make such detailed structural analyses.

REFERENCES

Fromm, Gary, and Lawrence R. Klein. (1976). "The NBER/NSF Model Comparison Seminar: An Analysis of Results." In *Econometric Model Performance*, L. R. Klein and E. Burmeister, eds., pp. 380–407. Philadelphia: Univ. of Pennsylvania Press.

Hickman, Bert G. (1984). "Macroeconomic Effects of Energy Shocks and Policy Responses: A Structural Comparison of 14 Models." Stanford: Energy Modeling Forum, Stanford University.

Hickman, Bert G. (1986). "The US Economy and the International Transmission Mechanism: A Structural Comparison of Twelve Multicountry Models." Stanford University: Center for Economic Policy Research.

Klein, Lawrence R., and Edwin Burmeister, eds. (1976). *Econometric Model Performance*. Philadelphia: University of Pennsylvania Press.

Kuh, Edwin, John W. Neese, and Peter Hollinger, eds. (1985). *Structural Sensitivity in Econometric Models*. New York: Wiley.

Table A2.1.

[1A] The Effects of the Increase in Defense on GNP [M₁ at base]

	1975.1	1975.2	1975.3	1975.4	1976.4	1977.4	1984.4	High	Low	Average
					GNP Multiplier					
BEA	1.39	1.76	2.20	2.51	2.18	1.25	−2.43	2.55	−2.52	0.09
DRI	1.23	1.65	1.89	2.08	1.79	0.72	0.80	2.15	−0.78	0.58
FAIR	0.99	1.27	1.37	1.39	1.25	1.11	1.56	1.56	0.99	1.26
FRB	1.38	1.91	2.23	2.45	2.27	0.87	1.47	2.51	−3.68	−0.21
IND	1.00	1.29	1.24	1.20	0.94	0.59	−0.11	1.29	−0.28	0.29
LM&A	1.16	1.74	1.82	1.62	1.12	0.51	−0.42	1.82	−0.80	−0.02
MICH	0.88	1.08	1.23	1.29	1.32	1.17	1.31	1.36	0.88	1.18
WEFA	1.09	1.26	1.48	1.60	1.51	0.65	−0.73	1.75	−1.36	−0.18
ST.L	0.22	0.29	0.23	0.17	0.11	0.01	−0.03	0.29	−0.21	−0.05
Taylor	1.23	1.90	1.67	1.18	0.76	0.45	0.07	1.90	0.02	0.36
Average	1.06	1.42	1.54	1.55	1.33	0.73	0.15	1.72	−0.77	0.33
Standard deviation	.32	0.47	0.55	0.66	0.62	0.36	1.16	0.63	1.37	0.50

[1A] The Effects of the Increase in Defense on GNP Deflator [M₁ at base]

	1975.1	1975.2	1975.3	1975.4	1976.4	1977.4	1984.4	High	Low	Average
					PGNP: Percentage Deviation					
BEA	−0.17	−0.17	0.00	0.00	0.62	1.45	4.65	5.13	−0.17	2.97
DRI	−0.05	0.02	0.09	0.19	0.61	0.94	0.88	1.20	−0.05	0.80
FAIR	−0.03	0.03	0.08	0.15	0.37	0.51	1.25	1.25	−0.03	0.71
FRB	−0.07	0.03	0.18	0.34	1.46	2.98	1.67	4.10	−0.07	2.33
IND	−0.07	−0.07	−0.02	0.05	0.54	1.19	2.40	2.52	−0.07	1.69
LM&A	0.00	0.00	0.33	0.33	1.09	1.31	1.10	1.51	0.00	1.08
MICH	0.04	0.03	−0.23	0.08	0.34	0.42	1.88	1.88	−0.23	0.91
WEFA	−0.07	−0.09	0.15	0.15	0.99	1.49	0.82	2.00	−0.09	1.33
ST.L	0.00	0.02	0.05	0.08	0.19	0.30	0.30	0.50	0.00	0.34
Taylor	0.09	0.24	0.47	0.74	2.02	3.12	5.09	5.39	0.09	3.70
Average	−0.03	0.00	0.11	0.21	0.82	1.37	2.00	2.55	−0.06	1.58
Standard deviation	0.07	0.10	0.18	0.21	0.54	0.93	1.54	1.63	0.09	1.03

Table A2.2.

	1975.1	1975.2	1975.3	1975.4	1976.4	1977.4	1984.4	High	Low	Average
[1B] The Effects of the Increase in Defense on GNP [r at base]										
					GNP Multiplier					
BEA	1.40	1.79	2.27	2.63	2.53	1.79	−3.24	2.74	−3.24	0.31
DRI	1.23	1.64	1.93	2.21	2.49	2.36	4.37	4.52	1.23	3.20
FAIR	1.00	1.29	1.41	1.45	1.42	1.34	1.88	1.88	1.00	1.48
IND	1.07	1.48	1.53	1.57	1.65	1.56	1.35	1.65	1.07	1.41
LM&A	1.25	2.03	2.32	2.31	2.44	1.74	0.15	2.51	0.15	1.23
MICH	0.88	1.09	1.25	1.32	1.41	1.29	1.63	1.63	0.88	1.40
WEFA	1.09	1.26	1.48	1.60	1.78	1.61	1.94	1.94	1.09	1.42
FRB[a]	1.42	2.08	2.67	3.26	5.55	7.93		10.92	1.42	6.68
Average	1.28	1.87	2.13	2.19	2.15	1.70	1.02	2.71	0.26	1.45
Standard deviation	0.44	0.98	1.08	0.95	0.66	0.32	2.04	1.19	1.40	0.75
[1B] The Effects of the Increase in Defense on GNP Deflator [r at base]										
					PGNP: Percentage Deviation					
BEA	−0.17	−0.17	0.00	0.00	0.62	1.60	6.57	6.94	−0.17	3.85
DRI	−0.05	0.01	0.08	0.17	0.65	1.26	11.79	11.79	−0.05	4.31
FAIR	−0.03	0.03	0.08	0.15	0.42	0.58	1.33	1.33	−0.03	0.80
IND	−0.07	−0.07	−0.03	0.03	0.65	1.64	9.99	9.99	−0.07	4.38
LM&A	0.00	0.17	0.50	0.49	1.86	2.76	5.86	5.86	0.00	3.73
MICH	0.04	0.02	−0.25	0.07	0.33	0.41	2.13	2.13	−0.25	0.97
WEFA	−0.07	−0.09	0.15	0.15	0.99	1.67	6.03	6.03	−0.09	3.05
FRB[a]	−0.07	0.03	0.22	0.43	2.39	7.53		40.57	−0.07	11.57
Average	−0.01	0.10	0.29	0.50	1.72	2.77	6.68	7.29	−0.05	3.96
Standard deviation	0.13	0.31	0.60	0.94	2.51	3.64	3.48	4.21	0.15	2.84

[a] Average and standard deviation include some simulations not shown separately.

Table A2.3.

	1975.1	1975.2	1975.3	1975.4	1976.4	1977.4	1984.4	High	Low	Average

[1C] The Effects of the Increase in Defense on GNP [React. fnc.]

GNP Multiplier

	1975.1	1975.2	1975.3	1975.4	1976.4	1977.4	1984.4	High	Low	Average
BEA	1.37	1.70	2.05	2.20	0.87	−0.56	−0.18	2.20	−0.73	0.20
DRI	1.23	1.66	1.92	2.15	2.20	1.71	1.98	2.90	1.23	2.15
FAIR	0.98	1.22	1.28	1.25	1.03	0.89	1.48	1.48	0.87	1.11
FRB	1.40	1.81	2.04	2.11	2.28	0.39	0.79	2.45	−1.56	1.13
IND	1.02	1.35	1.35	1.36	0.97	0.36	0.44	1.36	0.11	0.53
LM&A	1.25	1.75	1.55	0.96	−0.25	−0.14	−0.10	1.75	−0.58	−0.02
MICH	0.88	1.08	1.22	1.28	1.29	1.12	1.21	1.35	0.88	1.12
WEFA	1.08	1.21	1.37	1.41	1.28	0.89	1.21	1.41	0.51	0.89
St.L	0.46	0.59	0.36	0.34	0.11	−0.17	0.53	0.83	−1.15	−0.01
Average	1.07	1.37	1.46	1.45	1.09	0.50	0.82	1.75	−0.05	0.79
Standard deviation	0.27	0.38	0.50	0.58	0.79	0.68	0.68	0.61	0.94	0.66

[1C] The Effects of the Increase in Defense on GNP Deflator [React. fnc.]

PGNP: Percentage Deviation

	1975.1	1975.2	1975.3	1975.4	1976.4	1977.4	1984.4	High	Low	Average
BEA	−0.17	−0.17	0.00	0.00	0.62	0.87	2.01	2.18	−0.17	1.25
DRI	−0.05	0.01	0.08	0.18	0.63	1.13	7.89	7.89	−0.05	3.16
FAIR	−0.03	0.03	0.07	0.13	0.31	0.42	1.27	1.27	−0.03	0.64
FRB	−0.07	0.05	0.18	0.30	1.38	2.69	14.67	14.67	−0.07	5.30
IND	−0.07	−0.07	−0.03	0.03	0.59	1.29	3.29	3.29	−0.07	1.81
LM&A	0.00	0.17	0.33	0.33	0.47	0.44	0.91	0.91	0.00	0.44
MICH	0.04	0.03	−0.23	0.08	0.35	0.43	1.81	1.81	−0.23	0.89
WEFA	−0.07	−0.09	0.15	0.15	0.90	1.39	4.38	4.38	−0.09	2.30
St.L	0.01	0.05	0.10	0.16	0.39	0.48	0.68	0.88	0.01	0.53
Average	−0.05	0.00	0.07	0.15	0.63	1.02	4.10	4.14	−0.08	1.81
Standard deviation	0.06	0.09	0.15	0.10	0.32	0.70	4.30	4.27	0.07	1.50

Table A2.4.

[2A] The Effects of the Increase in M₁ on GNP

	1975.1	1975.2	1975.3	1975.4	1976.4	1977.4	1984.4	High	Low	Average
					GNP: Percentage Deviation					
BEA	0.01	0.06	0.17	0.31	0.55	0.57	−1.01	0.72	−1.19	0.09
DRI	−0.02	−0.00	0.11	0.47	2.48	3.83	−2.86	3.90	−2.86	0.89
FAIR	0.03	0.19	0.59	1.08	1.43	0.97	0.25	1.50	0.03	0.57
FRB	0.02	0.12	0.38	0.81	2.32	2.99	0.64	3.01	−2.94	−0.20
IND	0.00	0.02	0.06	0.13	0.34	0.40	−0.06	0.40	−0.06	0.20
LM&A	0.02	0.14	0.45	0.87	1.76	1.11	−0.13	1.77	−0.14	0.58
MICH	−0.02	0.01	0.01	0.02	0.25	0.27	1.08	1.08	−0.02	0.48
WEFA	0.07	0.32	0.49	0.75	1.09	1.16	1.22	1.22	0.07	0.88
St.L	0.04	0.25	0.76	1.51	1.78	0.79	−0.63	2.21	−1.61	−0.28
Taylor	0.43	0.96	1.21	1.04	0.31	0.11	−0.00	1.21	−0.01	0.16
Average	0.06	0.20	0.42	0.70	1.23	1.22	−0.15	1.70	−0.87	0.33
Standard deviation	0.13	0.27	0.35	0.44	0.80	1.16	1.12	1.02	1.15	0.39

[2A] The Effects of the Increase in M₁ on GNP Deflator

	1975.1	1975.2	1975.3	1975.4	1976.4	1977.4	1984.4	High	Low	Average
					PGNP: Percentage Deviation					
BEA	−0.00	0.00	0.00	0.00	0.16	0.29	1.55	1.99	−0.00	0.96
DRI	0.00	−0.02	−0.05	−0.09	0.26	1.28	7.37	7.83	−0.09	4.10
FAIR	0.00	0.02	0.03	0.10	0.42	0.52	−0.20	0.54	−0.20	0.23
FRB	0.00	0.00	0.00	0.05	0.67	2.21	1.57	5.78	0.00	3.25
IND	0.00	0.00	0.00	0.00	0.03	0.17	1.61	1.61	0.00	0.74
LM&A	0.00	0.00	0.17	0.00	0.93	1.31	2.38	2.50	0.00	1.78
MICH	−0.03	−0.03	−0.01	−0.09	0.04	−0.05	0.34	0.57	−0.11	0.10
WEFA	0.02	−0.03	0.12	0.02	0.37	0.60	1.71	2.12	−0.03	1.15
St.L	0.00	0.01	0.04	0.12	0.99	1.98	3.44	4.47	0.00	2.88
Taylor	0.07	0.19	0.38	0.62	1.52	2.16	2.96	3.24	0.07	2.31
Average	0.01	0.01	0.07	0.07	0.54	1.05	2.27	3.06	−0.04	1.75
Standard deviation	0.02	0.06	0.12	0.19	0.46	0.81	1.99	2.22	0.07	1.28

Table A2.5.

[2B] The Effects of the Decrease in r on GNP

	1975.1	1975.2	1975.3	1975.4	1976.4	1977.4	1984.4	High	Low	Average
					GNP: Percentage Deviation					
BEA	0.16	0.38	0.62	0.89	1.93	3.06	-2.66	3.34	-2.66	0.15
DRI	-0.02	0.05	0.17	0.31	1.04	1.87	5.04	5.32	-0.02	3.25
FAIR	0.06	0.18	0.31	0.43	0.79	0.90	0.35	0.90	0.06	0.61
IND	0.22	0.55	0.79	1.01	1.95	2.51	1.90	2.54	0.22	1.89
LM&A	0.12	0.38	0.66	0.93	1.91	1.78	2.83	3.50	0.12	2.00
MICH	0.01	0.21	0.44	0.67	1.22	1.28	0.99	1.29	0.01	0.99
WEFA	0.09	0.20	0.36	0.44	0.77	0.88	0.89	0.89	0.09	0.62
FRB[a]	0.07	0.16	0.37	0.57	1.59	2.93		16.36	0.07	5.91
Average	0.32	0.75	1.07	1.27	1.78	1.87	1.17	2.90	-0.29	1.37
Standard deviation	0.60	1.27	1.59	1.60	1.17	0.77	2.09	1.72	0.90	0.94

[2B] The Effects of the Decrease in r on GNP Deflator

	1975.1	1975.2	1975.3	1975.4	1976.4	1977.4	1984.4	High	Low	Average
					PGNP: Percentage Deviation					
BEA	-0.00	0.00	0.00	0.00	0.31	1.02	4.65	5.32	-0.00	3.12
DRI	-0.01	-0.02	-0.03	-0.04	0.12	0.51	13.28	13.28	-0.04	4.16
FAIR	0.00	0.02	0.02	0.05	0.20	0.33	0.00	0.47	0.00	0.28
IND	0.00	-0.03	-0.03	-0.02	0.29	1.19	14.77	14.77	-0.03	5.87
LM&A	0.00	0.00	0.17	0.16	0.93	1.74	8.33	8.33	0.00	3.74
MICH	-0.08	-0.12	-0.25	-0.18	-0.06	-0.07	1.30	1.30	-0.25	0.51
WEFA	0.02	-0.05	0.10	0.00	0.26	0.39	1.03	1.50	-0.05	0.79
FRB[a]	0.00	0.00	0.02	0.05	0.43	1.65		39.54	0.00	8.82
Average	0.04	0.12	0.30	0.51	1.74	2.89	7.28	8.31	0.00	4.30
Standard deviation	0.13	0.41	0.81	1.36	3.82	5.73	5.98	7.13	0.16	4.78

[a]Average and standard deviation include some simulations not shown separately.

Table A2.6.

[3AA] The Effects of the Decrease in World Oil Price on GNP

	1975.1	1975.2	1975.3	1975.4	1976.4	1977.4	1984.4	High	Low	Average
					GNP: Percentage Deviation					
BEA	0.13	0.46	0.71	0.88	0.72	0.69	−0.57	0.92	−0.68	0.37
DRI	0.03	0.16	0.28	0.37	0.90	1.25	−0.47	1.25	−1.14	0.04
FAIR	0.06	0.12	0.20	0.27	0.57	0.76	1.31	1.31	0.06	0.85
FRB	0.13	0.29	0.43	0.60	0.66	0.56	−0.11	1.70	−0.11	0.85
IND	0.10	0.15	0.15	0.15	0.13	0.09	0.44	0.44	0.03	0.17
LM&A	0.20	0.46	0.63	0.72	0.90	0.87	−0.07	0.95	−0.07	0.46
MICH	0.40	0.53	0.58	0.62	0.69	0.42	0.54	1.15	−0.03	0.59
WEFA	0.00	−0.02	0.01	0.01	0.28	0.44	0.42	0.53	−0.09	0.15
St.L	0.02	0.06	0.10	0.15	0.29	0.43	0.42	0.65	0.02	0.47
Average	0.12	0.25	0.34	0.42	0.57	0.61	0.21	0.99	−0.22	0.44
Standard deviation	0.12	0.19	0.24	0.28	0.26	0.31	0.55	0.39	0.39	0.27

[3AA] The Effects of the Decrease in World Oil Price on GNP Deflator

	1975.1	1975.2	1975.3	1975.4	1976.4	1977.4	1984.4	High	Low	Average
					PGNP: Percentage Deviation					
BEA	0.17	−0.17	−0.17	−0.33	−0.16	−0.15	1.09	1.25	−0.33	0.42
DRI	0.10	−0.05	−0.16	−0.23	−0.40	−0.42	−0.94	0.11	−0.94	−0.30
FAIR	−0.17	−0.29	−0.42	−0.52	−0.90	−1.12	−1.49	−0.17	−1.51	−1.20
FRB	0.03	−0.12	−0.33	−0.56	−0.95	−1.10	−0.14	0.03	−1.61	−0.97
IND	−0.03	−0.03	−0.03	−0.07	−0.14	−0.25	−0.26	−0.03	−0.61	−0.36
LM&A	0.00	0.00	0.00	−0.16	−0.16	0.00	0.09	0.27	−0.32	−0.04
MICH	−0.19	−0.35	−0.47	−0.46	−0.56	−0.78	−0.84	−0.19	−1.39	−0.90
WEFA	0.00	−0.03	0.02	−0.16	−0.45	−0.74	−0.97	0.02	−0.97	−0.54
St.L	−0.02	−0.06	−0.10	−0.15	−0.29	−0.43	−0.42	−0.02	−0.65	−0.47
Average	−0.01	−0.12	−0.19	−0.29	−0.44	−0.55	−0.43	0.14	−0.92	−0.48
Standard deviation	0.11	0.12	0.17	0.17	0.29	0.38	0.71	0.41	0.46	0.47

Table A2.7.

[3BA] The Effects of the Decrease in Wage on GNP [M₁ at base]

	1975.1	1975.2	1975.3	1975.4	1976.4	1977.4	1984.4	High	Low	Average
					GNP: Percentage Deviation					
BEA	−0.04	0.04	0.10	0.17	0.28	0.37	0.17	0.40	−0.07	0.21
DRI	−0.05	−0.04	−0.02	0.02	0.29	0.56	0.07	0.58	−0.05	0.26
FAIR	−0.12	−0.19	−0.27	−0.33	−0.47	−0.50	−0.63	−0.12	−0.68	−0.53
FRB	−0.08	−0.15	−0.14	−0.10	0.19	0.39	−0.28	0.69	−0.28	0.12
IND	0.00	0.00	−0.05	−0.06	0.01	0.07	0.13	0.15	−0.06	0.09
LM&A	0.03	0.07	0.11	0.14	0.33	0.36	0.25	0.36	0.03	0.23
MICH	−0.06	−0.04	−0.03	−0.02	0.13	0.11	0.11	0.14	−0.06	0.09
Taylor	−0.03	−0.03	0.02	0.10	0.11	0.07	0.00	0.13	−0.03	0.03
Average	−0.04	−0.04	−0.03	−0.01	0.11	0.18	−0.02	0.29	−0.15	0.06
Standard deviation	0.04	0.08	0.12	0.15	0.24	0.31	0.27	0.25	0.22	0.24

[3BA] The Effects of the Decrease in Wage on GNP Deflator [M₁ at base]

	1975.1	1975.2	1975.3	1975.4	1976.4	1977.4	1984.4	High	Low	Average
					PGNP: Percentage Deviation					
BEA	−0.17	−0.34	−0.17	−0.49	−0.47	−0.73	−0.27	0.00	−0.74	−0.39
DRI	−0.15	−0.27	−0.38	−0.47	−0.67	−0.75	−0.38	−0.15	−0.78	−0.56
FAIR	−0.28	−0.34	−0.40	−0.44	−0.56	−0.55	−0.58	−0.28	−0.58	−0.51
FRB	−0.16	−0.22	−0.32	−0.39	−0.65	−0.70	0.21	0.28	−0.70	−0.21
IND	0.00	0.00	−0.05	−0.10	−0.28	−0.41	−0.19	0.00	−0.46	−0.32
LM&A	−0.17	−0.34	−0.17	−0.33	−0.31	−0.44	−0.18	−0.17	−0.48	−0.30
MICH	−0.05	−0.11	−0.12	−0.29	−0.27	−0.41	−0.31	−0.05	−0.49	−0.34
Taylor	−0.09	−0.19	−0.28	−0.39	−0.36	−0.19	0.00	0.00	−0.42	−0.11
Average	−0.13	−0.23	−0.23	−0.36	−0.44	−0.52	−0.21	−0.05	−0.58	−0.34
Standard deviation	0.08	0.12	0.12	0.12	0.15	0.18	0.22	0.15	0.13	0.14

Table A2.8.

	1975.1	1975.2	1975.3	1975.4	1976.4	1977.4	1984.4	High	Low	Average
[3BB] The Effects of the Decrease in Wage on GNP [r at base]										
					GNP: Percentage Deviation					
BEA	-0.04	0.03	0.08	0.14	0.24	0.34	0.31	0.43	-0.04	0.22
DRI	-0.05	-0.07	-0.08	-0.09	-0.10	-0.09	0.11	0.11	-0.32	-0.13
FAIR	-0.13	-0.23	-0.34	-0.44	-0.68	-0.77	-0.80	-0.13	-0.89	-0.74
FRB	-0.10	-0.20	-0.26	-0.31	-0.47	-0.74	-1.27	-0.10	-1.50	-1.02
IND	0.00	0.00	-0.05	-0.08	-0.07	-0.06	0.06	0.06	-0.08	-0.03
LM&A	0.03	0.05	0.05	0.04	0.16	0.26	0.41	0.43	0.03	0.19
MICH	-0.06	-0.04	-0.03	-0.02	0.12	0.10	0.08	0.13	-0.06	0.07
WEFA	0.07	0.02	-0.01	-0.03	0.00	0.02	0.42	0.42	-0.03	0.06
Average[a]	-0.04	-0.06	-0.08	-0.08	-0.07	-0.09	-0.08	0.17	-0.34	-0.15
Standard deviation	0.06	0.10	0.13	0.17	0.29	0.38	0.54	0.20	0.49	0.41
[3BB] The Effects of the Decrease in Wage on GNP Deflator [r at base]										
					PGNP: Percentage Deviation					
BEA	-0.17	-0.34	-0.17	-0.49	-0.47	-0.73	-0.36	0.00	-0.82	-0.43
DRI	-0.15	-0.26	-0.37	-0.47	-0.71	-0.91	-2.22	-0.15	-2.22	-1.35
FAIR	-0.28	-0.34	-0.40	-0.44	-0.60	-0.64	-0.61	-0.28	-0.67	-0.60
FRB	-0.16	-0.22	-0.32	-0.41	-0.81	-1.31	-10.04	-0.16	-10.04	-3.78
IND	0.00	0.00	-0.05	-0.10	-0.28	-0.44	-0.99	0.00	-0.99	-0.61
LM&A	-0.17	-0.34	-0.17	-0.33	-0.47	-0.44	-0.37	-0.17	-0.58	-0.44
MICH	-0.05	-0.11	-0.12	-0.29	-0.27	-0.41	-0.33	-0.05	-0.49	-0.34
WEFA	-0.45	-0.77	-0.83	-1.05	-1.22	-1.52	-2.26	-0.45	-2.26	-1.58
Average	-0.17	-0.29	-0.30	-0.44	-0.58	-0.73	-1.91	-0.14	-2.06	-1.03
Standard deviation	0.13	0.20	0.22	0.24	0.29	0.42	2.98	0.14	2.90	1.07

[a]Average and standard deviation include some simulations not shown separately.

Table A2.9.

	1975.1	1975.2	1975.3	1975.4	1976.4	1977.4	1984.4	High	Low	Average
[3BC] The Effects of the Decrease in Wage on GNP [React. fnc.]										
					GNP: Percentage Deviation					
BEA	−0.04	0.04	0.12	0.22	0.40	0.31	0.25	0.40	−0.07	0.15
DRI	−0.05	−0.06	−0.06	−0.05	0.06	0.14	0.11	0.14	−0.09	0.02
FAIR	−0.12	−0.22	−0.31	−0.38	−0.51	−0.52	−0.62	−0.12	−0.66	−0.54
IND	0.00	0.00	−0.05	−0.06	0.06	0.11	0.04	0.11	−0.06	0.02
LM&A	0.03	0.07	0.12	0.17	0.27	0.20	0.09	0.27	0.02	0.12
MICH	−0.06	−0.04	−0.02	0.00	0.22	0.21	0.10	0.24	−0.44	−0.03
WEFA	0.07	0.04	0.02	0.03	0.14	0.17	0.46	0.46	0.02	0.14
FRB[a]	−0.09	−0.12	−0.08	0.12	1.16	1.87	1.91	2.20	−0.12	1.33
Average	−0.03	−0.02	−0.03	−0.01	0.09	0.09	0.06	0.21	−0.18	−0.02
Standard deviation	0.06	0.09	0.13	0.18	0.27	0.26	0.31	0.18	0.24	0.22
[3BC] The Effects of the Decrease in Wage on GNP Deflator [React. fnc.]										
					PGNP: Percentage Deviation					
BEA	−0.17	−0.34	−0.17	−0.49	−0.47	−0.58	−0.64	−0.17	−0.74	−0.48
DRI	−0.15	−0.26	−0.37	−0.47	−0.69	−0.85	−1.59	−0.15	−1.59	−1.09
FAIR	−0.28	−0.34	−0.40	−0.44	−0.56	−0.57	−0.57	−0.28	−0.58	−0.51
IND	0.00	0.00	−0.05	−0.10	−0.28	−0.39	−0.57	0.00	−0.58	−0.40
LM&A	−0.17	−0.34	−0.17	−0.33	−0.31	−0.44	−0.64	−0.17	−0.65	−0.47
MICH	−0.05	−0.11	−0.13	−0.30	−0.29	−0.41	−0.56	−0.05	−0.56	−0.36
WEFA	−0.45	−0.77	−0.83	−1.05	−1.21	−1.45	−2.10	−0.45	−2.10	−1.48
FRB[a]	−0.16	−0.24	−0.32	−0.39	−0.40	0.19	10.70	10.70	−0.46	3.20
Average	−0.18	−0.31	−0.30	−0.45	−0.54	−0.67	−0.95	−0.18	−0.97	−0.69
Standard deviation	0.14	0.22	0.25	0.27	0.31	0.35	0.58	0.14	0.57	0.40

[a]FRB is not included in the average and the standard deviation.

Table A2.10.

[1A] The Effects of the Increase in Defense on Consumptions [M₁ at base]

Consumption: Percentage Deviation

	1975.1	1975.2	1975.3	1975.4	1976.4	1977.4	1984.4	High	Low	Average
BEA	0.42	0.65	0.97	1.22	1.06	0.85	-1.24	1.22	-1.24	0.28
DRI	0.38	0.70	0.88	1.01	1.18	0.87	1.70	1.70	0.01	0.78
FAIR	0.05	0.11	0.16	0.19	0.23	0.23	0.95	0.95	0.05	0.45
FRB	0.38	0.68	0.94	1.19	1.16	0.31	0.91	1.29	-3.31	-0.80
IND	0.05	0.11	0.14	0.17	0.14	-0.05	-0.89	0.18	-0.89	-0.39
LM&A	0.10	0.19	0.23	0.21	0.20	-0.06	-1.05	0.27	-1.28	-0.61
MICH	0.12	0.20	0.27	0.32	0.53	0.64	1.37	1.37	0.12	0.83
WEFA	0.18	0.37	0.54	0.66	0.67	0.45	1.83	1.83	0.02	0.54
Taylor	0.66	0.99	0.83	0.53	0.28	0.10	-0.13	0.99	-0.13	0.06
Average	0.26	0.44	0.55	0.61	0.60	0.37	0.38	1.09	-0.74	0.13
Standard deviation	0.20	0.30	0.34	0.41	0.41	0.34	1.15	0.54	1.06	0.57

[1A] The Effects of the Increase in Defense on Investment [M₁ at base]

Investment: Percentage Deviation

	1975.1	1975.2	1975.3	1975.4	1976.4	1977.4	1984.4	High	Low	Average
BEA	1.74	3.12	4.55	5.87	6.01	1.11	-7.61	6.97	-7.61	-0.76
DRI	0.00	1.08	1.93	2.80	3.46	0.33	-0.80	3.98	-4.05	-0.65
FAIR	0.56	1.48	2.11	2.73	3.09	1.99	1.57	3.18	0.56	1.63
FRB	1.57	4.29	6.42	7.84	7.93	2.04	-1.04	8.87	-10.84	-1.66
IND	0.16	0.31	0.42	0.49	0.51	0.07	-0.12	0.56	-0.23	-0.02
LM&A	2.00	3.50	4.30	4.47	4.30	1.96	-4.30	4.88	-5.68	-1.92
MICH	-0.01	0.84	1.84	2.36	2.82	2.19	1.37	2.93	-0.01	1.68
WEFA	0.72	1.53	2.42	3.24	4.12	1.31	-7.01	4.47	-7.43	-3.05
Taylor	0.01	1.84	3.15	3.17	1.98	1.05	-0.78	3.17	-0.88	0.31
Average	0.75	2.00	3.02	3.66	3.80	1.34	-2.08	4.33	-4.02	-0.49
Standard deviation	0.77	1.26	1.70	2.02	2.05	0.73	3.22	2.28	3.87	1.50

Table A2.11.

	1975.1	1975.2	1975.3	1975.4	1976.4	1977.4	1984.4	High	Low	Average
[1B] The Effects of the Increase in Defense on Consumption [r at base]										
					Consumption: Percentage Deviation					
BEA	0.42	0.66	1.00	1.28	1.24	1.19	−1.38	1.28	−1.38	0.57
DRI	0.00	1.08	2.00	2.98	4.97	4.04	5.09	7.28	0.00	4.54
FAIR	0.06	0.14	0.21	0.27	0.42	0.53	1.62	1.62	0.06	0.85
IND	0.14	0.32	0.45	0.59	0.98	1.22	2.44	2.44	0.14	1.50
LM&A	0.17	0.40	0.56	0.67	1.22	0.98	0.10	1.22	0.10	0.74
MICH	0.12	0.20	0.27	0.33	0.55	0.67	1.49	1.49	0.12	0.90
WEFA	0.18	0.37	0.54	0.66	0.85	0.90	3.46	3.46	0.18	1.45
FRB[a]	0.44	0.86	1.33	1.86	3.79	5.98		8.32	0.44	4.81
Average[a]	0.36	0.78	1.06	1.25	1.58	1.35	1.58	2.77	−0.12	1.41
Standard deviation	0.55	0.90	1.04	1.11	1.40	1.05	1.96	1.90	0.49	1.23
[1B] The Effects of the Increase in Defense on Investment [r at base]										
					Investment: Percentage Deviation					
BEA	1.74	3.15	4.63	6.02	6.72	2.32	−9.11	7.37	−9.11	−0.18
DRI	0.00	1.08	1.97	2.91	4.27	2.53	0.62	4.48	0.00	2.43
FAIR	0.56	1.51	2.15	2.80	3.36	2.41	1.88	3.42	0.56	1.94
IND	0.17	0.35	0.49	0.60	0.77	0.38	−0.24	0.77	−0.33	0.15
LM&A	2.17	4.14	5.59	6.42	9.23	8.26	3.76	9.23	2.17	5.97
MICH	−0.01	0.85	1.87	2.41	3.03	2.50	2.32	3.11	−0.01	2.30
WEFA	0.72	1.53	2.42	3.24	4.87	4.33	−0.12	4.87	−0.50	1.82
FRB[a]	1.64	4.64	7.39	9.74	17.06	21.33		26.49	1.64	17.52
Average	0.91	2.47	3.89	4.86	5.90	4.11	−0.19	6.08	−0.98	2.40
Standard deviation	0.84	2.13	3.43	4.06	4.16	3.13	3.65	4.28	3.18	1.96

[a]Average and standard deviation include some simulations not shown separately.

Table A2.12.

	1975.1	1975.2	1975.3	1975.4	1976.4	1977.4	1984.4	High	Low	Average
[1C] The Effects of the Increase in Defense on Consumption [React. fnc.]										
					Consumption: Percentage Deviation					
BEA	0.41	0.63	0.90	1.08	0.41	−0.24	−0.07	1.08	−0.47	−0.08
DRI	1.23	1.66	1.92	2.15	2.20	1.71	1.98	2.90	1.23	2.15
FAIR	0.02	0.04	0.03	0.02	−0.04	−0.07	0.68	0.68	−0.07	0.17
FRB	0.41	0.55	0.75	1.01	1.08	−0.03	0.06	1.29	−1.56	0.37
IND	0.08	0.17	0.26	0.35	0.16	−0.31	0.08	0.36	−0.54	−0.09
LM&A	0.17	0.18	0.02	−0.26	−0.80	−0.78	−0.48	0.18	−0.93	−0.67
MICH	0.12	0.20	0.27	0.33	0.52	0.63	1.34	1.34	0.12	0.81
WEFA	0.17	0.34	0.48	0.56	0.60	0.57	2.84	2.84	0.17	1.10
Average	0.33	0.47	0.58	0.65	0.52	0.18	0.80	1.33	−0.26	0.47
Standard deviation	0.37	0.49	0.59	0.71	0.82	0.72	1.08	0.97	0.78	0.82
[1C] The Effects of the Increase in Defense on Investment [React. fnc.]										
					Investment: Percentage Deviation					
BEA	1.72	3.06	4.39	5.50	3.48	−3.23	−4.04	5.96	−4.43	−0.91
DRI	−0.05	0.01	0.08	0.18	0.63	1.13	7.89	7.89	−0.05	3.16
FAIR	0.56	1.44	2.04	2.55	2.62	1.52	1.55	2.86	0.56	1.46
FRB	1.61	4.19	5.88	7.03	8.03	1.27	−0.28	8.58	−6.57	2.06
IND	0.16	0.32	0.44	0.53	0.56	0.00	−0.13	0.62	−0.30	0.07
LM&A	2.17	3.53	3.69	2.91	−0.57	−2.38	−3.34	3.69	−5.96	−3.00
MICH	−0.01	0.84	1.84	2.35	2.75	2.08	1.08	2.89	−0.01	1.50
WEFA	0.66	1.34	2.09	2.73	3.23	1.65	−1.92	3.43	−2.18	0.13
Average	0.85	1.84	2.56	2.97	2.59	0.26	0.10	4.49	−2.37	0.56
Standard deviation	0.81	1.45	1.85	2.16	2.47	1.86	3.48	2.56	2.71	1.80

Table A2.13. J-Curve Simulation Results

	1984.1	1985.1	1986.1	1987.1
J1. Depreciation of the U.S.\$ by 10% with Pass-Through as Specified in the Model				
Real Imports of Goods and Services (% deviation from baseline)				
Michigan	−8.58	−9.32	−7.71	−5.88
Indiana	−0.52	−0.84	−1.01	−1.26
DRI	−2.64	−3.58	−3.28	−3.32
WEFA	−1.50	−2.72	−3.28	−3.45
SINAI	−4.01	−3.40	−3.61	−4.73
FRB	−3.20	−4.98	−5.88	−6.04
Average	−3.41	−4.14	−4.13	−4.11
Nominal Imports of Goods and Services (% deviation from baseline)				
Michigan	−0.05	−0.61	0.90	2.06
Indiana	2.97	2.69	3.26	3.81
DRI	3.33	3.24	3.83	4.05
WEFA	1.92	2.73	2.35	2.86
SINAI	1.24	2.15	1.93	0.77
FRB	1.01	1.52	1.23	1.49
Average	1.74	1.95	2.25	2.51
Real Exports of Goods and Services (% deviation from baseline)				
Michigan	3.55	5.69	6.96	7.72
Indiana	4.68	6.39	6.42	5.22
DRI	3.26	3.24	3.02	3.29
WEFA	2.55	4.41	4.40	4.47
SINAI	3.89	2.30	1.84	1.48
FRB	2.39	3.11	2.75	2.19
Average	3.39	4.19	4.23	4.06
Nominal Exports of Goods and Services (% deviation from baseline)				
Michigan	3.64	6.15	8.25	10.03
Indiana	4.98	7.02	7.86	7.52
DRI	5.12	6.09	6.41	7.59
WEFA	3.58	5.80	5.93	7.19
SINAI	6.68	6.89	8.09	9.28
FRB	5.03	6.94	7.34	7.47
Average	4.84	6.48	7.31	8.18
J2. Depreciation of the U.S.\$ by 10% with Pass-Through as Specified in the Model				
Real Balance of Trade (deviation from baseline, bl. 82 \$)				
Michigan	49.88	63.02	63.98	62.02
Indiana	19.15	27.38	28.69	26.59
DRI	23.15	27.99	27.37	29.58
WEFA	15.73	28.58	32.67	36.14
SINAI	29.97	22.86	24.74	33.09
FRB	22.48	33.93	39.29	40.91
Average	26.73	33.96	36.12	38.06

	1984.1	1985.1	1986.1	1987.1
Nominal Balance of Trade (deviation from baseline, bl. curr. $)				
Michigan	13.82	25.76	26.58	29.34
Indiana	6.13	15.06	14.20	10.00
DRI	5.17	9.20	6.12	10.11
WEFA	4.74	10.34	12.02	11.49
SINAI	19.72	15.43	21.44	30.66
FRB	14.58	19.62	21.67	22.10
Average	10.69	15.90	17.01	18.95
Real GNP (% deviation from baseline)				
Michigan	1.71	3.08	3.16	2.93
Indiana	0.56	0.75	0.59	0.19
DRI	0.82	1.59	1.38	1.04
WEFA	0.41	0.72	0.60	0.55
SINAI	1.29	0.59	−0.28	−1.14
FRB	0.56	0.66	0.31	0.08
Average	0.89	1.23	0.96	0.61
GNP Deflator (% deviation from baseline)				
Michigan	−0.44	0.12	0.12	0.82
Indiana	0.08	0.43	1.01	1.71
DRI	−0.10	0.36	0.75	1.32
WEFA	−0.08	0.10	0.45	0.78
SINAI	0.30	1.44	2.68	3.72
FRB	0.94	0.91	1.77	3.45
Average	0.12	0.56	1.13	1.97
Import Prices (% deviation from baseline)				
Michigan	9.33	9.60	9.33	8.44
Indiana	3.51	3.56	4.31	5.13
DRI	6.14	7.07	7.35	7.63
WEFA	3.47	5.60	5.81	6.53
SINAI	5.46	5.75	5.75	5.77
FRB	5.64	7.18	7.60	8.04
Average	5.59	6.46	6.69	6.92

Table A2.14. J-Curve Simulation Results

	1984.1	1985.1	1986.1	1987.1
J2. Increase in Foreign Economic Activity with Exogenous Exchange Rate at Baseline Level				
Real Exports of Goods and Services (% deviation from baseline)				
Michigan (assumed)	1.00	1.00	1.00	1.00
Indiana	0.74	0.98	1.10	1.11
BEA	0.52	0.54	0.51	0.50
DRI	1.13	1.21	1.25	1.27
WEFA	1.81	1.78	1.84	1.88
SINAI	0.25	0.26	0.26	0.27
FRB	0.86	0.68	0.75	0.76
Average	0.90	0.92	0.96	0.97

Table A2.14. (*Continued*)

	1984.1	1985.1	1986.1	1987.1
Nominal Exports of Goods and Services (% deviation from baseline)				
Michigan	1.01	1.05	1.10	1.13
Indiana	0.75	1.03	1.23	1.34
BEA	0.51	0.54	0.57	0.59
DRI	1.21	1.40	1.52	1.66
WEFA	1.70	1.34	1.23	1.99
SINAI	0.25	0.28	0.29	0.31
FRB	0.97	0.89	1.09	1.22
Average	0.91	0.93	1.00	1.18
Real Balance of Trade (deviation from baseline, bl. 82 $)				
Michigan	2.41	1.90	2.10	1.96
Indiana	2.68	3.59	3.96	4.11
BEA	1.13	1.16	1.33	1.68
DRI	2.94	2.92	3.35	3.72
WEFA	5.05	4.29	4.28	3.80
SINAI	0.77	0.61	0.60	0.84
FRB	1.66	2.16	3.68	4.90
Average	2.38	2.38	2.76	3.00
Nominal Balance of Trade (deviation from baseline, bl. curr. $)				
Michigan	2.58	2.23	2.56	2.67
Indiana	2.79	3.87	4.52	5.01
BEA	1.16	1.24	1.51	1.94
DRI	3.13	3.26	3.66	4.09
WEFA	5.56	5.65	6.06	5.74
SINAI	0.79	0.68	0.69	0.87
FRB	1.71	1.90	3.12	4.13
Average	2.53	2.69	3.16	3.49
Real GNP (% deviation from baseline)				
Michigan	0.18	0.13	0.09	0.10
Indiana	0.10	0.12	0.11	0.08
BEA	0.11	0.10	0.03	−0.03
DRI	0.24	0.22	0.17	0.15
WEFA	0.31	0.25	0.21	0.28
SINAI	0.04	0.04	0.04	−0.01
FRB	0.21	0.11	0.01	−0.06
Average	0.17	0.14	0.09	0.07

J3. Lower U.S. Economic Growth (1% lower than baseline)

Real Imports of Goods and Services (% deviation from baseline)				
Michigan	−1.30	−3.24	−4.51	−5.92
Indiana	−0.21	−0.72	−1.49	−2.61
WEFA	−2.59	−6.19	−10.30	−14.52
Average	−1.37	−3.87	−6.42	−7.08
Nominal Imports of Goods and Services (% deviation from baseline)				
Michigan	−1.43	−3.85	−6.07	−8.52
Indiana	−0.21	−0.73	−1.52	−2.73
WEFA	−2.29	−7.06	−11.66	−16.72
Average	−1.54	−3.87	−6.42	−9.32

	1984.1	1985.1	1986.1	1987.1
Real Balance of Trade (deviation from baseline, bl. 82 $)				
Michigan	5.63	14.59	22.31	31.57
Indiana	0.88	3.55	8.72	16.64
WEFA	10.56	26.53	48.50	73.04
Average	5.69	14.89	26.51	40.42
Nominal Balance of Trade (deviation from baseline, bl. curr. $)				
Michigan	5.94	15.82	26.40	39.19
Indiana	0.86	2.20	3.80	5.61
WEFA	10.62	24.33	43.72	69.51
Average	5.81	14.12	24.64	38.10

COMMENTS ON FEDERAL RESERVE BOARD MODEL RESULTS CONTAINED IN THE APPENDIX TO THE KLEIN–ADAMS PAPER
Albert Ando

The set of multipliers reported by Professors Klein and Adams includes a few calculations prepared using the quarterly econometric model maintained at the Board of Governors of the Federal Reserve System. A part of these calculations appear to be quite extreme, and this note briefly describes some of the reasons for the results.

The somewhat unusual pattern of multipliers for the FRB model is due partly to the inherent structure of the model and partly to the use of a trial version of the model that contained some alternative formulations for several equations. Implications of choosing one alternative over another were not fully analyzed at the time.

When the nominal rate of interest is exogenous and the system is subjected to a positive demand shock, as was done in Table A2.2, the response of the FRB model can be explosive in the long run. When aggregate demand is pushed up, the rate of inflation accelerates, and, given the policy of letting the nominal interest rate not respond, the money supply will expand to accommodate both the higher level of output and accelerating inflation. In this model, the actual rate of inflation feeds into the expected rate of inflation with a fairly long distributed lag. Since the real rate of interest is defined as the nominal rate of interest minus the expected rate of inflation, under these circumstances the real rate of interest must gradually fall. Since, in this model, most components of private aggregate demand are significantly decreasing functions of the real interest rate, aggregate demand will be further stimulated as the real rate falls.

This is clearly a destabilizing mechanism, although it is rather slow to develop its full impact as it is represented in the FRB model. It can, of course, be counterbalanced by other mechanisms, such as automatic stabilizers on the fiscal side and imports under some conditions. We believe, nevertheless, that a mechanism such as this is not an artificial feature of the FRB model, but is a reflection of an important aspect of the real economy. It should be noted that a critical part of this destabilizing mechanism is the monetary policy of letting the nominal rate of interest be fixed exogenously, and, hence, the instability can be avoided by replacing this policy by a more appropriate policy rule that would not create the perverse response of the real interest rate to demand shocks. In the real economy, realistic monetary policies in fact manage to limit the perverse reaction of the real rate at most to a relatively short period of time, especially since the process is fairly slow to develop. For this reason, we do not observe economies of most countries exhibiting severe instabilities associated with this mechanism.

This brings us to the question of why, in computations reported to Klein and Adams, the apparently unstable response of the system is so fast and violent. The most important cause of this dramatic instability is a changed nature of one critical equation, namely, the equation for expenditure on residential construction, reinforced by changes in a few additional equations.

Investment in residential construction went through very large fluctuations in the late 1970s and early 1980s, more or less synchronously with aggregate income and output. Because of this, any equation or a system of equations that is capable of tracking closely the time pattern of housing investment during the period tends to involve parameter values implying a very large response of housing expenditure to changes in income. Furthermore, in most specificiations of equations for housing investment that we have tried, parameter values seem quite unstable, depending on minor changes in the sampling period or details of specifications, making the implied short-run elasticity of housing investment with respect to income also quite unstable, ranging from a little over 1 to as much as 7. Quite clearly, either our specification of the equation is seriously defective, or the behavior of housing investment has been seriously unstable over time, or both. We are inclined to think that both problems are involved. At any rate, this equation has been under investigation for some time, and at the time when computations for Klein and Adams were prepared, several alternative equations were on file for comparison and analysis. It so happens that the one used for the computations in question was the one for which the short-run elasticity with respect to income was the largest, close to 7, making the dynamic response of this model to any demand shock unreasonably large. The multiplier pattern for the FRB model reported in Table A2.2 was a result of this choice of the housing investment equation, aggravating the basic instability described in the earlier paragraph.

To assess the contribution of the housing investment equation, we have rerun the experiment with the housing investment taken as exogenous. The result is given in Table 2.5. In column (1), we duplicate the result reported in Klein–Adams Table A2.2. In column (2), we report the same experiment except that the housing investment is taken as exogenous. In column (1), the GNP multiplier reaches 7.9 in the twelfth quarter, and soon thereafter, the solution of the system becomes impossible. In column (2), the multiplier is still rather large, but it moves up much more slowly, and between the twelfth and fortieth quarters, it fluctuates between 3.5 and 5.5. The pattern of column (2) is almost reasonable for the fiscal multiplier under the monetary policy of keeping the nominal rate of interest fixed exogenously, although we feel that it still expands a little too fast compared to similar calculations that we have done in the past. We believe that this is a result of the experimental nature of two or three additional equations in the model at the time. Similar comments apply to some additional tables in Klein–Adams, for example, Table A2.11.

Table 2.5. Difference in Multipliers Due to the Housing Expenditure Equation[a]

	(1)	(2)
1	1.3	1.1
2	1.9	1.5
3	2.5	1.8
4	3.0	2.2
8	5.3	3.3
12	7.9	3.8
40	—	5.4

[a]Column (1) is a result of the same experiment as the one reported for the FRB model for Table A2.2 of Klein and Adams. Although the FRB model has changed slightly from the one used to generate results for the Appendix of Klein and Adams, the changes are slight enough so that the pattern of the multiplier (changes in GNP in constant dollars divided by GNP in the base run, that is, historical values) is virtually unchanged between two sets of results. Column (2) is the same computation except that housing investment is exogenized.

When the nominal rate of interest is used as the instrument, and the rate is given a step shock that is sustained, the response of the FRB model is rather similar to the case in which some other expenditure is shocked with the nominal rate held constant. This is because the initial movement of the nominal rate will shock some components of aggregate demand up, and, thereafter, the same destabilizing mechanism under the policy of keeping the nominal interest rate constant described earlier becomes dominant.

When a demand shock is applied to the model with M_1 held exogenous, the situation is of course different. In such an experiment, the FRB model can respond to the shock in a more or less stable pattern under some circumstances, since the nominal rate of interest responds negatively to changes in output and in prices. The real rate of interest, however, is not guaranteed to respond countercyclically, since its movement depends on movements of both the nominal rate and the rate of inflation.

M_1 in recent years has three main components: currency, demand deposits, and the so called "other checkable deposits." When M_1 is taken as exogenous, to solve the model, we must decide on which of these three equations is to be solved for the rate of interest, leaving the other two as they are. Traditionally, it is the demand equation for demand deposits that is solved for the rate of interest.

In the current version of the FRB model, however, the demand function of demand deposits is formulated as an "error correction" mechanism with the quantity of demand deposits as the dependent variable, and when it is solved for the interest rate, the interest rate exhibits cyclical response to changes in other variables. Furthermore, the equation for other checkable deposits is a function of the difference between the rate solved from the equation for demand deposits and the rate for other checkable deposits that was taken as exogenous here, making the response of other checkable deposits too large. In this setup, the solution process of the whole system with M_1 exogenous may encounter difficulties of convergence. It becomes much easier if other checkable deposits is taken as exogenous, but cyclical response of the rate of interest generated by solving the equation for demand deposits remains. If these equations reflect the characteristics of demands for demand deposits and for other checkable deposits in the real world, the problems described here argue for the desirability of having a well-designed reaction function as a part of monetary policy instruments.

One final point on multiplier calculations with M_1 exogenous should be made. When the target is defined in nominal quantities such as M_1 and the whole system is shocked upward, the structure of the model is such that the inflation rate will become higher and remain higher while the unemployment rate remains below its natural rate as a result of the shock. Even assuming the prevailing conditions to be such that the system exhibits a stable response pattern, when unemployment returns to the neighborhood of the natural rate, the level of prices will be higher than it would have been as a result of the higher inflation rate, while the level of M_1 has not been adjusted. Hence, the level of M_1 is too low relative to the price level at full employment, creating a condition under which the real rate of interest will be too high for full employment equilibrium. Thus, the system must overshoot beyond the neighborhood of the natural rate, and the multiplier must exhibit a cyclical pattern. This feature is not unique to the choice of M_1. A policy of keeping any nominal quantity exogenously fixed will have similar features. Although the pattern of the multiplier would be cyclical, it may or may not be stable depending on other conditions.

ACKNOWLEDGMENTS

Observations contained in this note are originally due to Ignazio Visco; my review of results submitted to Professors Klein and Adams confirms Visco's observations. We are greatly indebted to Dr. Visco for his careful analysis of the difficulties in results reported to Professors Klein and Adams earlier by one of our associates.

BUREAU OF ECONOMIC ANALYSIS (BEA) MODEL

The BEA quarterly model is a "mainstream" macro model in that it is an augmented Keynesian system. Its chief distinctive features are (1) the determination of real personal consumption expenditures by a hybrid "top-down/bottom-up" approach that uses both an aggregate consumption equation and separate equations for consumption components (components are influenced by, but not constrained to sum to, single-equation determined total PCE); (2) endogenous setting of monetary policy through a Federal Reserve "reaction function"; and (3) inclusion of several ancillary subblocks that provide much Federal fiscal information in addition to NIPA receipts and expenditures, viz. unified budget receipts and outlays, the size, maturity composition, and effective interest rates on the short-term and long-term Federal debt (thus permitting structural determination of Federal net interest), the "cyclically adjusted" Federal deficit and debt, and Social Security and Medicare trust fund balances.

There is less endogeneity in some sectors of the model than in comparable sectors of other models, for example, in state and local government expenditures and in the international sector. In "alternative scenario" forecasts, BEA makes judgmental adjustments to such not directly affected exogenous variables when it is felt to be warranted.

DATA RESOURCES, INC. (DRI)/McGRAW-HILL MODEL

The DRI Model blends insights from many theoretical schools—Keynesian, neoclassical, monetarist, supply-side, and rational expectations—in its interpretation of short-run, private sector behavior. One particularly distinguishing extension beyond other macroeconometric models is the careful integration of this behavior with a long-term growth model following the work of James Tobin and Robert Solow. Another is the expanded representation of international and government policy responses to domestic economic phenomena. These two features are believed to improve significantly the model's accuracy and utility in its two primary applications, policy evaluation and short- to long-run forecasting. Finally, the model is relatively large (1215 variables) to provide sectoral specificity required for commercial and regional planning.

The "Neoclassical Synthesis"

In specific goods markets, spending, production, and price levels are jointly determined. Typically, the level of inflation-adjusted spending is driven by income, relative prices, wealth, expectations of growth and inflation, and financial conditions. Supply potential is endogenously modeled as a Cobb–Douglas composite of labor hours, capital stocks, and energy usage; total factor productivity is determined by the embodied state of technology as modeled by the age of the stock and the accumulated, depreciated stock of research and development expenditures. (This novel feature was fully implemented in 1977, long before the "supply side" revolution, and it explains the otherwise curious decline in labor productivity growth seen since 1970.) Prices and wages adjust fully to one another and to gaps between sectoral demands and capacity, producing an "accelerationist" view of the "Phillips Curve."

Finance, Monetarism, and Rational Expectations

The Federal Reserve sets the supply of banking reserves and fractional reserve requirements. Deposit demands, on a highly disaggregated basis, are driven by appropriate transactions, own-rate, and competing yields on securities and physical assets. The monetarist emphasis on portfolio choice is respected, but significant interest elasticities and the endogeneity of the physical capital stock temper the naive monetarist link between inflation and money growth. Interest rates are modeled as a term structure, pivoting off the federal funds rate. Yield spreads are driven by appropriately lagged adaptive inflation expectations, plus endogenous models of expected structural government deficits and monetary policy regimes.

International and Fiscal Policy Reactions

Since 1984, the exchange rate has been fully endogenized; the inflation-adjusted value of the dollar is a sensitive function of the spread between United States and foreign real bond yields and the current account deficit. Foreign bond rates and inflation, in turn, shift (relative to preset baseline values) in response to domestic developments, based on econometrically estimated reaction functions; the same is true of the foreign activity levels that appear in the export equations. This substantially improves the estimated impacts of monetary and fiscal policy in situations such as the early 1980s. Fiscal policy is itself partially endogenous. All state–local parameters are endogenous functions of national income, interest rates, and prior state–local surpluses. Many federal tax rates are endogenous, and spending can be user specified to be fixed in either nominal or real terms; government purchase prices are endogenous.

RAY FAIR (FAIR) MODEL

This model consists of 128 equations—30 stochastic and 98 identities. There are slightly over 100 exogenous variables and many lagged endogenous variables. The stochastic equations are estimated by two-stage least squares, with account taken when necessary of autoregressive error terms. The data base for the model begins in the first quarter of 1952. The model was constructed in 1974–1976. The most complete description of it is in Ray C. Fair, *Specification, Estimation, and Analysis of Macroeconometric Models,* Harvard University Press, 1984.

Three goals in the development of the model were to (1) base the estimated equations on microeconomic theory, (2) account for all flows of funds among the sectors and all balance sheet constraints, and (3) account explicitly for possible disequilibrium effects. The model is divided into five sectors: household, firm, financial, government, and foreign.

There are nine stochastic equations for the household sector: three consumption, one housing investment, four labor supply, and one demand for money. The theory behind the household equations is that households maximize a multiperiod utility function, possibly subject to a disequilibrium constraint regarding the amount that they can work at the current set of wage rates. The firm sector determines production given sales (inventory investment), nonresidential fixed investment, employment demand, the price level, the wage rate, and its demand for money, among other things. The financial sector includes, among other equations, two term structure equations and an equation explaining stock prices. There is a demand for imports equation, which is put in the foreign sector. The government sector has an interest payments equation and an equation determining unemployment benefits. Monetary policy is endogenous in the model. An interest rate reaction function is estimated, where the Fed is estimated to "lean against the wind" regarding its interest rate policy.

FEDERAL RESERVE BOARD (FRB) MODEL

In the long run, when markets clear and expectations are fulfilled, the FRB model behaves like a neoclassical growth model in which the real growth rate of the economy is determined exogenously by population and technology growth, the level of per capita output depends on the capital-output ratio, which is affected by fiscal policy, the rate of inflation depends on the rate of growth of money, and money is neutral in the sense that permanent changes in the level of money cause a proportionate change in the price level leaving all real magnitudes unchanged. However, short-run properties are Keynesian because neither labor nor goods markets are continuously in equilibrium, reflecting the presence of adjustment costs and the assumption that expectations are formed autoregressively. Changes in the supply of money have important real effects in the short run through interest rates, which directly influence investment decisions and indirectly affect consumption (through the market value of wealth) and net exports (through the exchange rate).

The IS block of the model consists of equations for real spending on consumption (three components), fixed investment in residential structures, nonresidential structures (three components), and equipment, inventory investment (four components), state and local government purchases (three components), exports (three components), and imports (three components); federal purchases are exogenous. The core of the supply block consists of a labor demand equation that is an inverted production function, a Phillips curve relationship for wage inflation that permits no long-run output-inflation trade-off, and a markup equation for an aggregate price. Equations for money demand, deposit own rates, the term-structure of interest rates, and an arbitrage relationship between the yields on bonds and equity comprise the financial block. The exchange rate is determined with a portfolio balance model.

INDIANA UNIVERSITY CENTER FOR ECONOMETRIC RESEARCH (IND) MODEL

The Indiana University model of the U.S. economy contains 100 equations, 151 identities, and 56 exogenous variables. The model is Keynesian in that output is affected by aggregate demand, and prices are a variable markup over unit labor costs. Wage rates are determined in an inflation augmented Phillips curve and expectations are adaptive. Twenty endogenous components of real GNP are modeled including 11 components of consumption expenditures, 2 inventory components, 3 components of fixed nonresidential investment, residential investment, exports, imports, and state and local government purchases. Federal government defense and nondefense purchases are exogenous.

Government and rest-of-world output are modeled separately and subtracted from real GNP to yield real private domestic output. Factor demand equations for real private domestic employment and manhours depend on output and the capital stock and are derived from a production function.

The wage bill is derived from the wage rate and hours equations, and other income components are modeled separately. Profits are obtained as a residual as in the economy. The model maintains consistency among wage rates, hours, employment, productivity, unit labor costs, the wage bill, and prices for the private domestic economy.

The basic monetary policy aggregate is nonborrowed reserves. M_1 and M_2 are endogenously determined and the treasury bill rate is obtained from an inverted M_2 money demand equation. The bond rate is related to the treasury bill rate through a term structure equation.

The model is used to generate 12-quarter forecasts regularly and to test empirical macroeconomic hypotheses.

WASHINGTON UNIVERSITY MACRO MODEL (WUMM) (LM&A)

WUMM is a quarterly econometric system of over 350 equations and 135 exogenous variables. The model explains entries from all major tables of the National Income and Product Accounts, and provides much additional detail on labor and financial markets.

WUMM has an income/expenditure structure in which short-term fluctuations in real output are caused primarily by changes in aggregate demand. However, a distinguishing characteristic of WUMM is that the equilibrium properties of all key behavioral equations are explicitly derived from the neoclassical paradigm, imparting to the model both monetarist and supply-side characteristics in the long run. This emphasis on theory endows the model with an internally consistent structure that renders WUMM well suited not only for short-run forecasting but also for long-term policy analysis.

WUMM incorporates eight key theoretical elements: a life-cycle model of consumption, a transactions model of money demand, an expectations model of the term structure of interest rates, a long-run neoclassical model of fixed investment, a long-run neoclassical model of labor demand, a long-run neoclassical model of pricing, a vertical long-run Phillips curve, and a long-run neoclassical distribution of income. Particular attention is also given to the role of demographics in determining household decisions regarding saving, household formation, and labor force participation. Short-run dynamic properties of the model are either determined empirically or constrained by the assumption that factor proportions are variable ex ante but fixed ex post.

The menu of exogenous variables offers users considerable flexibility in specifying monetary and fiscal policies: there are 18 components of government outlays and 34 tax parameters. Reserves, the money stock, or short-term interest rates can be chosen as the instrument of monetary policy; alternatively, interest rates may be determined by a reaction function. Other important exogenous factors include food and energy prices, a complete age/sex decomposition of the population, and the rate of technical advance.

MICHIGAN QUARTERLY ECONOMETRIC MODEL (MQEM)

The MQEM is maintained by the Research Seminar in Quantitative Economics at the University of Michigan. The current (January 1989) version of the model contains 86 stochastic equations, 89 identities, and 68 exogenous variables (excluding dummy variables). The model is designed primarily for short-term forecasting and policy analysis but is also used as a vehicle for research on econometric methods. The short-term nature of the model derives from the fact that output is determined primarily by aggregrate demand. Supply-side considerations enter the model through the impact of labor and capital utilization rates on wages and prices and hence on interest rates and aggregate demand.

The major blocks of equations in MQEM determine wages and prices including the exchange rate (25 equations), productivity and employment (3 equations), expenditure on consumption (9 equations), investment, exports, and imports (14 equations), the distribution of income (19 equations), interest rates and monetary aggregates (12 equations), and the composition of output (4 equations). The most important exogenous variables in the model are nominal government expenditures, foreign prices, domestic agricultural prices, and the monetary base. Most of the equations in the current version of MQEM have been estimated over the period 1954.1–1985.4 using least squares with serial correlation corrections where appropriate. A more detailed discussion of the properties of MQEM is given in Chapters 4 (Green et al.) and 6 (Fair and Alexander) of this volume and in Belton, Hymans, and Lown, "The Dynamics of the Michigan Quarterly Econometric Model of the U.S. Economy," Research Seminar in Quantitative Economics, The University of Michigan, Ann Arbor, December 1981. A complete listing of the equations of the model can be obtained by writing to the Research Seminar in Quantitative Economics, Department of Economics, The University of Michigan, Ann Arbor, Michigan, 48109.

FEDERAL RESERVE BANK OF St. LOUIS (St.L.) MODEL

The St. Louis Model is a small monetarist model of the U.S. economy purporting to explain the movements of certain key economic aggregates—nominal and real GNP, the GNP deflator, the unemployment rate, and the corporate Aaa bond rate. The model's focus is on the role of monetary aggregates, in particular, M_1, in the determination of these economic variables. There are eight equations of which four are estimated; the remaining equations are identities or definitions of intermediate variables.

The exogenous variables of the model are the M_1 money stock, cyclically adjusted federal expenditures, potential output (and the "full-employment unemployment rate"), exports of goods and services, the relative price of energy, and price-control and velocity-shift dummies. The equations are estimated by ordinary least squares with lag structures estimated by the polynomial lag technique. Autocorrelation adjustments are made where necessary.

The properties of the model are that monetary actions (changes in the growth rate of money) have a large short-run effect on nominal and real GNP and unemployment; over the long run, however, the effect on nominal GNP is almost entirely reflected in the price level, with very little effect on output and unemployment. Fiscal actions have small short-run effects that disappear quite quickly. Supply-side effects are not strong unless, for example, energy prices move dramatically.

TAYLOR MULTICOUNTRY MODEL

The model is built to explain macroeconomic fluctuations in the G-7 countries: the United States, Canada, France, Germany, Italy, Japan, and the United Kingdom. It is designed for policy evaluation through stochastic simulation, rather than for forecasting. It is a nonlinear quarterly model fit to observations from 1971 through 1986 with the exact starting and ending quarters depending on the number of leads and lags in each equation. There are a total of 98 stochastic equations and several additional accounting identities. (In the simulations in this volume, the full multicountry model was used, but only the results for the United States are reported.)

The rational expectations assumption is a highlight of the model. Although this assumption may not be appropriate in periods immediately following a policy reform (when market participants are learning about the policy), it is appropriate for estimating the longer term effects of a new policy. For the deterministic simulations reported in this volume, the fiscal and monetary policy shocks are assumed to be unanticipated and permanent. Because of the rational expectations assumption, the model is solved using the extended path algorithm of Fair, Ray and John B. Taylor (1983), "Solution and Maximum Likelihood Estimation of Dynamic Nonlinear Rational Expectations Models." *Econometrica*, 51, 1169–1185.

Nominal wages and prices are sticky and evolve according to a staggered contracts equation estimated in each country. Hence, monetary and fiscal policies have an effect on real output, though of a qualitatively different type than in "conventional" models without rational expectations. If the model is not continually shocked, output and employment eventually return to an exogenously growing level of "potential" output.

Financial capital is mobile across countries, and within each country bond markets are efficient. However, time-varying "risk premia" exist in both foreign exchange markets and in domestic bond markets. The nominal interest rate spread between each pair of countries is equal to the expected rate of change in the exchange rate between the same two countries, plus a random serially correlated disturbance.

Aggregate demand determines production in the short run. Aggregate demand is built up from disaggregated spending decisions—consumption, investment, government, and net exports. The important price variables in these demand equations are the real interest rate (rational expectations of future inflation are a factor here) and the relative price of domestic goods to foreign goods (the real exchange rate is a factor here). Consumption is disaggregated into durables, nondurables, and services in the United States. A forward-looking permanent income model is used for consumption. Significant negative real interest rate effects are found in most countries. In the United States investment is disaggregated into equipment, nonresidential structures, residential structures, and inventory investment. The real interest rate has a strong negative impact on investment, including inventory investment. The "accelerator" terms relating investment to changes in demand are also strong.

For additional information see John B. Taylor (1988) "The U.S. Trade Deficit, Savings-Investment Imbalance, and Macroeconomic Policy: 1982–87," *The U.S. Trade Deficit: Causes Consequences and Cures, 12th Annual Economic Policy Conference Proceedings,* Federal Reserve Bank of St. Louis, Boston: Kluwer.

WHARTON ECONOMIC FORECASTING ASSOCIATES (WEFA) MODEL

Mark 9 is a quarterly econometric model of the U.S. economy built and maintained by the WEFA Group. It was estimated in 1988 using postwar data extending through 1987. The model contains about 750 variables of which approximately 280 are stochastic and 130 are exogenous. The remaining variables are definitions. All equations were estimated using ordinary least squares. Mark 9 is designed primarily for short-term (up to 5 years) forecasting of the U.S. economy, and is also intended for use in the development of alternative scenarios and for policy and contingency analysis.

Mark 9 is in the neo-Keynesian tradition, with important supply-side and financial influences. Short-run movements in output are primarily determined by changes in aggregate demand. The components of aggregate demand are modeled from the bottom up using standard approaches that employ various measures of permanent income–output and relative prices. Relative price variables for investment goods incorporate detailed "cost of capital" specifications that include a variety of tax policy levers. In addition to detailed consumption, fixed investment, and inventory sectors, Mark 9 contains fully specified housing, auto, and energy sectors. The model also includes a detailed trade sector in which eight categories (six of goods and two of services) of both exports and imports are modeled individually. Each is related to appropriate income–demand variables as well as to relative prices. The demand and domestic price variables in the import equations are aligned with the corresponding final demand terms.

Industry-specific I/O weights are applied to the components of spending to construct measures of output produced by each of the 1-digit industries. These industry output variables determine labor and capital requirements by industry. The stage-of-processing price sector starts with unit labor costs and other input prices, which determine producer prices. Producer prices are major determinants of the various implicit price deflators, which then finally determine the consumer price indexes. The process is simultaneous, however, since the deflators (along with a measure of labor market tightness) are also determinants of the key wage index via a standard Phillips curve equation.

Mark 9 features important linkages between the financial and real sectors of the economy. Outcomes in the economy affect short-term interest rates through a Fed reaction function formulation. Long-term rates are modeled as functions of short-term rates and inflation expectations. In addition to their impact on interest income flows, interest rates affect the user cost of capital variables, relative prices of consumer durables, and the consumer sentiment index that influence investment and consumption.

Key fiscal policy levers, demographics, oil prices, the exchange value of the dollar, inflation and growth in the rest of the world, and seasonal patterns are exogenous variables.

SINAI-BOSTON MODEL

The Sinai-Boston Model of the U.S. Economy (1987–1988 version) encompasses a considerable amount of detail on real final demands, production and the supply-side of the economy, the financial markets and interaction of the financial system with the real economy, trade, and money flows.

The model is open economy in its orientation and considers extensively the interactions of the financial system and sectoral, balance sheets with the real economy. Trade and international capital flows are integral to the determination of the exchange rate, which has substantial impacts on inflation, interest rates and the economy.

The formation of expectations in financial and real markets distinguishes the model from many others, with model-consistent, "permanent," and extrapolative expectations appearing in different markets. Quick expectations formation characterizes key financial markets, in turn, impacting sooner in real markets through the financial-real interactions of the model.

The Sinai-Boston Model contains over 500 variables, 400 endogenous and 100 exogenous, with some 350 stochastic equations.

The model describes the quantity adjustments of simultaneous real and financial activities, as various sectors of the economy move toward desired equilibrium levels of real and financial assets and liabilities. In this sense, it is disequilibrium in nature.

There is a "goods" market, "money" market, numerous "fixed income" security markets, an "equity" market, and a "currency" market. There is a "labor" market. There is a "depository institutions" sector, comprising commercial banks and thrifts. There is a "rest-of-the-world" sector, where trade and international capital flows are modeled. Flows-of-funds sectors and balance sheets include households, nonfinancial corporations, the federal government, state and local government, commercial banks, thrift institutions, and the rest of the world.

Prices, wages, interest rates, and exchange rates are determined in the process of adjustments to new equilibria as demands, supplies, and costs all interact in a stage-of-processing approach to the determination of inflation.

Interest rates are modeled in a segmented market approach, with some 27 fixed income markets showing demands and supplies for the various assets across the various sectors with interrelated behavior between different markets. Monetary policy, fiscal policy and deficits, the banking system, and inflation are key factors in the behavior of fixed income markets. The equity market reflects the demands and supplies for equities in a fundamental valuation approach.

The supply-side of the model determines potential output from fully employed labor, the fully utilized capital stock of business, research and development, energy inputs, effects of the financial system on production as measured by real money balances (M_2), and a measure of innovation and technological change. Demographics and population determine the labor market input. The capital stock evolves from the pace of business capital formation in the system. Taxes and tax incentives significantly affect the labor and capital inputs that impact on potential output.

Expectations and lagged adjustments play a large role in the behavior and processes that are modeled. Expectations are model consistent in some variables in the fixed income, equity, and currency markets. In many other markets, expectations are "backward-looking" or extrapolative.

None of the currently used phrases or depictions for large-scale macroeconometric models is appropriate for the Sinai-Boston model, such as "Keynesian," "monetarist," "supply-side," "rational expectations," "real business cycle," etc.

CHAPTER 3

Comparing Macroeconomic Model Forecasts under Common Assumptions

STEPHEN K. McNEES

Experts typically have a wide variety of views on the future economic environment. Insofar as their views are based on explicit, systematic methods of assessing economic information, we can say forecasts differ because forecasters use different models. However, even if everyone used the same model, all forecasts would not be identical. First, most models are conditional; the predicted outcome depends on the specific input assumptions a forecaster uses to solve the model. A single model can generate an infinite number of forecasts, depending on what assumptions are made. Second, forecasters have different beliefs about the degree to which the predictive value of all information can be fully captured by a formal model. Some econometricians place their faith solely in their model and regard judgmental adjustments of their models as "unscientific" and more likely than not as counterproductive. Other forecasters, typically those whose models have evolved, or even dissolved, are more open to the possibility that special events that cannot be formally modeled from historical data can still have predictive values. Differences in these attitudes affect the extent to which mechanically generated forecasts are modified.

Most forecasts, in other words, reflect a complex interaction among three elements: (1) a model, (2) the conditioning information or input assumptions used to generate a model forecast, and (3) the model user's attempts to incorporate extramodel information through judgmental adjustments.

Unfortunately, little is known about the relative importance of these elements. This chapter addresses three kinds of questions:

1. What are the relative roles of the model and the modeler in generating a forecast? To what extent do forecasts reflect judgments by the forecaster in the form of input assumptions and judgmental adjustments?
2. Why do ex ante forecasts differ? Clearly, different forecasters use different models. In addition, individual forecasters adopt different assumptions about future macroeconomic policy and economic developments in the rest of the world. Forecasters also have different philosophies about how much to override the mechanically generated model results with their own judgment. Do these differences in assumptions and adjustments increase the dispersion of forecasts, exaggerating differences among models, or do they decrease the dispersion of

forecasts, masking larger differences in what the models would predict on the basis of a common set of assumptions and adjustments?

3. What are the sources of forecast errors? Do modelers' adjustments help or hurt forecast accuracy? When, in particular, have they helped and when have they hurt? Does lack of knowledge about future input variables impair forecast accuracy? Or, as some previous research indicates, can modelers somehow compensate for the deficiencies of their models through judicious choice of forecast assumptions?

The initial stage of the Model Comparison Seminar's project, starting in early 1986, has been the collection of relevant data, a laborious and time-consuming part of the project. The following results are a preliminary report on an ongoing effort. The conclusions, based on the limited experience so far, must be regarded as highly tentative. Any success that has been achieved should be largely credited to the modelers who participated in this exercise.[1]

AN OVERVIEW

This chapter compares model solutions based on different sets of conditioning information. In general, a model can be thought of as a conditional statement about the relationship between inputs (Xs) and outputs (Ys), or $Y = f(X)$.

The most frequently observed model solution, the ex ante published forecast, or ($Y^{p,i}$), is the model solution based on the individual forecaster's expected values of the input variables (EX) and any judgmental adjustments (Ad) he chooses to make.

$$Y^{p,i} = f(EX^i) + Ad^i \tag{1}$$

The mechanically generated forecast, $Y^{m,i}$, is the solution of the model based on the individual modeler's input assumptions and a fixed, predetermined rule for adjustments based on the pattern of recent residuals.

$$Y^{m,i} = f(EX^i) + Rule^i \tag{2}$$

A comparison of the published and mechanical forecasts, (1) and (2), measures the importance for Y forecasts of the nonroutine adjustments made in generating the published forecast.

The conditional model forecast, $Y^{C,i}$, is the model solution based on a common input assumption, $E\bar{X}$, as well as the rule.

$$Y^{C,i} = f(E\bar{X}) + Rule^i \tag{3}$$

Note that the individual modeler has no influence on the conditional model forecast, above and beyond that of constructing the model and the explicit adjustment rule. A rule, once it has been formalized, can properly be regarded as part of the model, as some models already include some form of residual adjustment in their estimation procedures. A comparison of the mechanical forecast and the conditional model forecast, (2) and (3), constitutes a measure of the role of the modeler's individual input assumptions relative to common assumptions. In fact, models employ many different kinds of input assumptions, a matter pursued more fully below.

The ex post forecast, $Y^{ep,i}$, is the model solution based on the actual values of the input assumptions, X, which are, of course, not observed until after the forecast period has ended.

$$Y^{ep,i} = f(X) + Rule^i \qquad (4)$$

A comparison of the conditional model forecast and the ex post model solution, (3) and (4), reveals the importance of the knowledge of the actual values of the input variables relative to the common values that were assumed before the fact. The difference between the ex post model solution and the actual historic outcome will be regarded as the model error, the discrepancy between the actual value of Y and the value that the model indicates conditioned on the actual historic input information.

In summary, comparisons of model solutions based on varying sets of input information provide measures of the relative importance of the various factors that are blended together to generate a model-based forecast: the judgmental adjustments, the modeler's assumptions, and the model per se.

MODEL ADJUSTMENT PROCEDURES

Most forecasters adjust their mechanically generated, "pure model" results to try to account for a multitude of considerations outside of their formal model or its inputs. These factors can range from the mundane—for example, the incorporation of revisions of historical data and of incoming high-frequency data—to the purely subjective—the results look "unreasonable" for no stated reason—to the nefarious—the results are manipulated to induce the forecast user to adopt a certain course of action. Some adjustments are intended to incorporate the effects of special events not formally modeled, such as regulatory changes or the imposition and relaxation of wage and price controls. Because the rationales for these adjustments are seldom documented, different commentators characterize adjustments in different ways.

Conceptually, forecasters could be asked to document their motives for each adjustment and these could be categorized to assess the extent to which the adjustments are "scientific," that is, grounded in theory or evidence. Because the object of this seminar is to compare models rather than various forms of judgment, the participants decided, for the purpose of this exercise, to permit only adjustments that could be written down explicitly in the form of a predetermined rule based on observed residuals. Each modeler was permitted to devise the rule for his own model, or even a different rule for each equation in the model, but it was agreed that the rules, once adopted, would not be changed over time. With no room for individual discretion, once these adjustment rules were formulated, adopting this convention amounts to redefining the model as the model *plus* the appended adjustment rules. Except for published forecasts, all forecasts examined below employ the adjustment rule and no other form of adjustments.

INPUT ASSUMPTIONS

Even if there were only one model, it would be a challenge to understand how that model performed and the inputs used to generate forecasts with that model. In fact, because there are numerous alternative models and one wishes not only to understand each but to contrast and compare them, comparisons must confront the fact that model outcomes (Ys) are conditioned on the assumed values of the input variables (Xs) used to solve the model. This fact poses a dilemma. (1) On the one hand, Ys based on *any* Xs other than their actual values cannot be compared to the actual Ys to assess the model's accuracy.

Counterfactual values of Xs can either increase or decrease discrepancies between the model solution and the actual outcome. To isolate the performance of a model defined as a conditional statement, the model must be solved with the actual Xs. Ex ante forecasts intermingle the quality of the model with the skills of the model user in selecting future values of input assumptions. A clever model user may compensate for a deficient model by judicious choice of inputs. A foolish model user could confound even a perfect model by providing unreliable inputs. Ex ante forecast accuracy therefore does not provide a clear comparison of models as conditional statements. This is the reason why early model comparisons focused on ex post simulations, where none of the error can be attributed to counterfactual Xs. (2) On the other hand, different models are conditioned on different, nonoverlapping, sometimes even logically inconsistent, input information sets. Due to these differences in their "degree of exogeneity," comparisons of ex post simulations can be difficult to interpret. Models that require large amounts of input enjoy an informational advantage from the actual values of these additional variables in an ex post simulation.

The first step in this exercise was to examine the input assumption (or "exogenous variable") set of each participating model. That examination confirmed that models differ greatly in the informational input they require. Even when all models embody the same broad concept, such as "monetary policy" or economic growth outside the United States, typically each model uses a different specific measure of that concept. Complete standardization would therefore require supplementary procedures for reconciling alternative concepts and measures. Without building a supermodel to encompass all individual models, complete standardization across fairly similar models is virtually impossible. When different models adopt logically inconsistent assumptions, standardization becomes literally impossible.

Despite such differences, all these models contain similar *types* of input assumptions.[2] For example, all participating models employ some assumptions about fiscal and monetary policy. The most obvious standardization of input assumptions is to solve each model on a common set of policy assumptions. With regard to fiscal policy, all models were constrained to follow common paths of nominal federal expenditures and were requested to introduce no changes in the tax code beyond those that had already been legislated.

Standardization for monetary policy was more difficult because of the lack of a consensus on the appropriate instrument to represent monetary policy. Rather than attempt to resolve this long-standing controversy, forecasts were generated under two alternative monetary policy assumptions—a given path of M_1 and also a given path of short-term interest rates (the federal funds rate, or, for some models, identical changes in the Treasury bill rate).

All these models are also conditioned on input assumptions about economic developments in the rest of the world (ROW). These models vary greatly in the extent to which their external sectors are developed and disaggregated. A complete model of the world economy might require information on ROW macro policies, and perhaps the world price of oil, providing extensive linkages between these and the U.S. economy. At the other extreme, some models were developed essentially as closed models of the U.S. economy, excluding all these linkages and treating only real exports and import prices as input variables. The appropriate standardization for the world model would require other modelers to develop the additional linkages between foreign economies and the U.S. economy. This could be expected to change the character of these models. To "let the models be models," standardization for the ROW was made on the basis of the "lowest common denominator"—the closed economy model with the least-developed external sectors. Specifically, the closed economy forecasts are all based on the same assumptions about the path of real exports and the import price deflator. Auxiliary assumptions were provided on the world price of oil, ROW real growth, and ROW inflation rates to help the more open economy models conform to the common external assumptions.

This exercise did not attempt to standardize across all input assumptions but only for two different, important types of assumptions: macroeconomic policy and external sector. Extending the notation introduced earlier, the published forecast ($Y^{p,i}$) becomes

$$Y^{p,i} = f(EP^i, EX^i, EO^i) + Ad^i \tag{1A}$$

Here EP^i, EX^i, and EO^i are, respectively, the individual forecaster's policy assumptions, external sector assumptions, and other input assumptions. The mechanical forecast becomes

$$Y^{m,i} = f(EP^i, EX^i, EO^i) + Rule^i \tag{2A}$$

The conditional model forecast now consists of two parts:

The open economy forecast,

$$Y^{o,i} = f(\overline{EP}, EX^i, EO^i) + Rule^i \tag{3A}$$

and the closed economy forecast,

$$Y^{c,i} = f(\overline{EP}, \overline{EX}, EO^i) + Rule^i \tag{3B}$$

A comparison of the mechanical forecast with the open economy forecast, (2A)–(3A), measures the impact of the individual modeler's macro policy assumptions relative to the common assumption. A comparison of the open economy forecast with the closed economy forecast, (3A)–(3B), illustrates the importance of the individual modeler's treatment of the external sector relative to the common assumption. Even the mechanically generated model solution with common policy and common external sector assumptions depends on the modeler's assumptions about other input variables. Like all ex ante forecasts, it does not isolate the role of the model as a conditional statement. The model is isolated only in an ex post simulation:

$$Y^{ep,i} = f(P, X, O) + Rule \qquad (4)$$

when P, X, and O are actual values.

In principle, any values could be used as the common core input assumptions. In fact, some combinations of input variables may be economically or politically infeasible. One way to try to avoid such inconsistencies would be to employ one individual's assumptions as the common ones. This would ensure that the common assumptions were consistent in at least one individual's eyes. In this case, the common input assumptions imposed on the models were a simple average among several forecasters, only some of whom participated in this project. Under this approach, the results measure the impact of an individual modeler's assumptions relative to "the" consensus view prevailing among forecasters generally.

THE PRELIMINARY RESULTS

The array of data collected so far is a rich one, covering 21 variables, each over an eight-quarter horizon for as many as eight models under as many as six sets of input assumptions. Some models participated in the early rounds, but subsequently dropped out for a variety of reasons. Other models joined the project after the first two rounds had been completed. The results presented here cover the five models that participated in the six sets of forecasts conducted in 1987 and early 1988. The results focus on two of the most important variables, the real GNP growth and the inflation rate, over three horizons—the first year, the second year, and the first 2 years.

Recall that the models were simulated under two alternative representations of monetary policy—a common M_1 path and a common short-term interest rate path. The dispersion among the real GNP forecasts was smaller under the common M_1 assumption than under the common interest rate assumption, whereas the dispersion of the inflation rate forecasts was about the same. The rest of this chapter deals only with the common interest rate path representation of monetary policy, because one of the regularly participating models does not contain an M_1 variable.

The results are grouped into three sections—forecast dispersion, forecast decomposition, and error decomposition—that correspond to the three questions posed in the introduction to this chapter.

Forecast Dispersion

The answer to the question "Why do forecasts differ?" depends critically on the variable of interest. For example, although real GNP forecasts differ primarily because the underlying models differ, mechanically generated model predictions of the inflation rate based on common assumptions are somewhat more similar than published inflation rate forecasts (see Table 3.1). This result reflects the differential impacts of individual forecasters' assumptions relative to common "consensus" assumptions and adjustments of their model forecasts.

Table 3.1. Sources of Forecast Dispersion: Ranges, Annual Growth Rates

	(1) First Year	(2) Second Year	(3) Two Years
Real GNP			
Closed[a]	3.4	3.6	2.7
Policy[b]	2.8	3.4	2.5
Mechanical[c]	2.6	2.5	1.8
Published[d]	1.3	2.6	1.4
Inflation rate			
Closed	1.7	2.3	1.8
Policy	2.6	3.0	2.8
Mechanical	2.9	3.3	3.1
Published	2.0	2.4	2.1

[a]Closed: mechanical forecasts with common policy and external sector assumptions.
[b]Policy: mechanical forecasts with common policy assumptions.
[c]Mechanical: mechanical forecasts with individual assumptions.
[d]Published: forecasts with individual assumptions and adjustments.

Forecasters' choices of external assumptions have had a negligible impact on the dispersion of their real growth forecasts but a major impact on the dispersion of their inflation rate forecasts. This reflects both the diversity of opinion about future import prices and the different sensitivities across models to changes in import prices.

In contrast, as shown in column three, the individual forecasters' choices of policy assumptions had a fairly small impact on the dispersion of their inflation rate forecasts over a 2-year horizon, but a major impact on the dispersion of their real GNP forecasts. This result can be interpreted as illustrating the modeler's role as an implicit reaction function or policy rule that tends to push real GNP back toward a satisfactory path. Specifically, if a model exhibits particularly weak (strong) real growth, the modeler is more likely to employ more stimulative (restrictive) macroeconomic policy assumptions in his forecast. It is interesting to note that the implicit policy rules increase the conformity of real GNP growth, but not the inflation rate, at least over a 2-year horizon.

The forecasters' adjustments virtually always work to make the forecasts more similar. Their importance is relatively large for the dispersion of inflation rate forecasts and of real GNP forecasts in the first (column 1), though not the second (column 2), year of the forecast period. This tendency of convergence toward the consensus may reflect a greater reluctance to rely on the model as the model deviates further from the consensus. The consensus view, for example, may be the most likely outcome and the model an indicator of the most likely deviation from the mode. For real GNP, the tendency to adjust the forecast toward the consensus reinforces the unifying impact of individual policy assumptions, so that published forecasts are far more similar than mechanical model forecasts based on common assumptions. For the inflation rate, the unifying adjustments serve to offset the diverging impact of individual external sector assumptions, so that the dispersion of published forecasts is about the same as the dispersion of standardized model forecasts.

Forecast Decomposition

These data also help to measure the relative roles of the model and the modeler in generating a forecast. In Table 3.2 the modeler's role is divided into three parts: columns 1 and 4 show the impact of external sector assumptions, measured as the difference between the forecast based on common policy assumptions and the forecast based on common assumptions for both policy and the external sector; columns 2 and 5 show the impact of policy assumptions, measured as the difference between the forecast based on common policy assumptions and the one based on the modeler's individual policy assumptions; and columns 3 and 6 give the impact of adjustments, measured as the difference between the published and mechanical forecasts. We focus on the mean *absolute* differences rather than the mean differences to avoid equating a forecaster who never makes adjustments (for example, model 3) with a forecaster whose upward adjustments just happen to be as large as his downward adjustments. The results vary by both model and variable. For real GNP over a 2-year horizon, adjustments were most important for models 4 and 5, policy assumptions for models 2 and 3, and external sector assumptions for model 1. For these five models taken as a group, each of these three forms of modeler's judgment is roughly equally important for each of the forecast horizons examined.

For the inflation rate, adjustments have the largest impact on the forecasts of four of the five models. The only exception was model 3, which was never adjusted and where the external sector assumptions were the most important form of judgment embodied in the inflation forecast. Differences in policy assumptions had relatively little impact on the inflation rate forecasts, except for model 2.

Combining the information on forecast dispersion with the information on the impact of assumptions and adjustments suggests a stylized description of the forecasting process: (1) When different models are solved initially with "consensus" values of external sector and policy assumptions, real growth forecasts differ by more than 3 percentage points and inflation rate forecasts by less than 2 percentage points. (2) When the modelers impose their individual assumptions, real growth forecasts converge (reflecting a real-growth-stabilizing implicit policy rule) but inflation rate forecasts diverge further. (3) Judgmental adjustments are imposed to narrow forecast dispersion, offsetting the divisive impact of individual assumptions on the inflation rate and reinforcing the converging impact on real growth forecasts.

The mean absolute deviation of the published real GNP forecasts from the average or "consensus" published forecast is about half as large as the deviation of "pure model" forecasts based on common assumptions. In contrast, the mean absolute deviation of the published inflation forecasts from the consensus forecast is about the same as the deviation of "pure model" forecasts based on common "consensus" assumptions. The net effect of the individual modelers' assumptions and adjustments is to draw their real GNP forecasts together—the forecasts are more similar than the models. The *net* effect is essentially nil for their inflation rate forecasts—the dispersion among published forecasts is similar to the dispersion among models, once the role of the individual modeler has been minimized.

Over this period the models, as a group, based on common consensus assumptions, generated higher forecasts of both real growth and inflation rates than the published

Table 3.2. Importance of Three Forms of Forecasters' Judgment: Mean Absolute Change (Percentage Points)

	Real GNP			Inflation Rate		
	External Sector Assumptions (1)	Policy Assumptions (2)	Adjustments (3)	External Sector Assumptions (4)	Policy Assumptions (5)	Adjustments (6)
			First Year			
Model 1	0.7	0.2	0.4	0.5	0.0	0.9
Model 2	0.3	1.0	1.1	0.4	0.8	1.1
Model 3	0.3	1.1	0.0	0.8	0.1	0.0
Model 4	1.5	1.1	0.7	0.6	0.5	0.8
Model 5	0.4	0.2	0.8	0.0	0.0	0.6
Mean	0.6	0.7	0.6	0.5	0.3	0.7
			Second Year			
Model 1	0.9	0.3	0.6	0.4	0.0	0.9
Model 2	0.1	1.2	0.9	1.0	1.1	1.8
Model 3	0.6	0.3	0.0	0.9	0.2	0.0
Model 4	1.4	0.9	0.8	0.7	0.5	1.5
Model 5	0.8	0.3	0.7	0.1	0.0	0.9
Mean	0.8	0.6	0.6	0.6	0.4	1.0
			Two Years			
Model 1	0.8	0.3	0.4	0.4	0.0	0.9
Model 2	0.2	0.7	0.6	0.7	0.9	1.5
Model 3	0.2	0.7	0.0	0.8	0.1	0.0
Model 4	0.4	0.4	0.6	0.7	0.5	1.2
Model 5	0.5	0.2	0.7	0.1	0.0	0.7
Mean	0.4	0.5	0.5	0.5	0.3	0.9

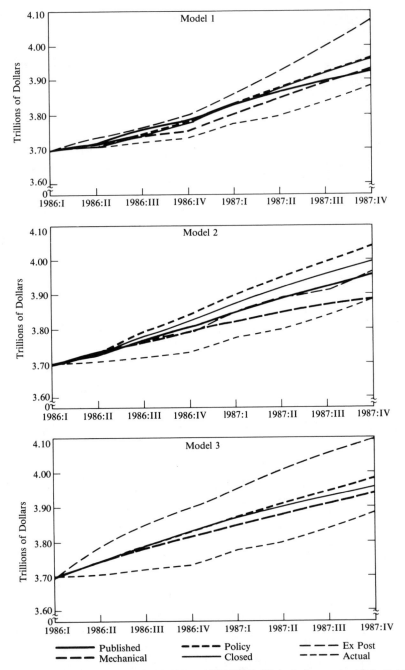

Figure 3.1. Forecasts of real GNP, 1986:I to 1987:IV. Published, forecast with individual assumptions and adjustments. Mechanical, mechanical forecast with individual assumptions. Policy, mechanical forecast with common policy assumptions. Closed, mechanical forecast with common policy and external sector assumptions. Ex Post, simulations using actual values of exogenous variables.

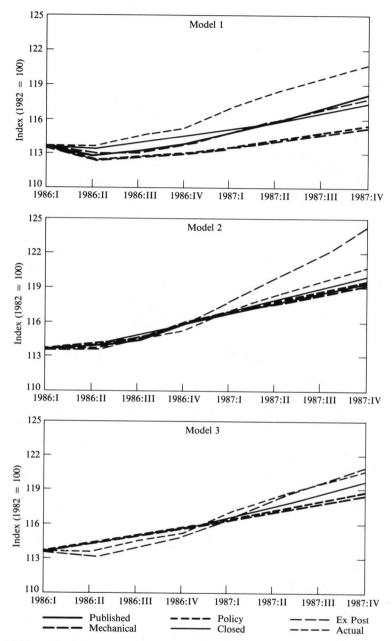

Figure 3.2. Forecasts of the personal consumption deflator, 1986:I to 1987:IV. See Figure 3.1 for definition of terms.

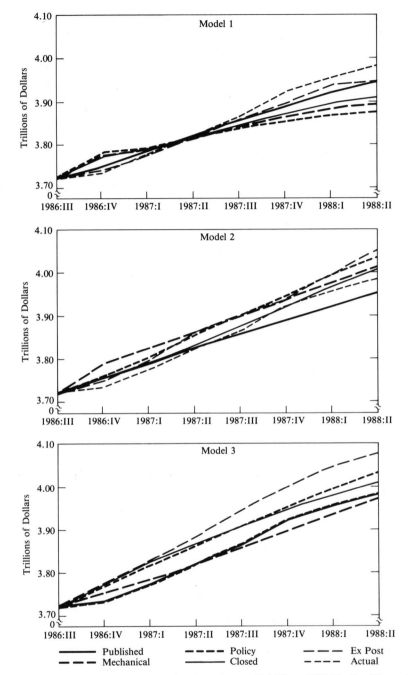

Figure 3.3. Forecasts of real gross national product, 1986:III to 1988:II. See Figure 3.1 for definition of terms.

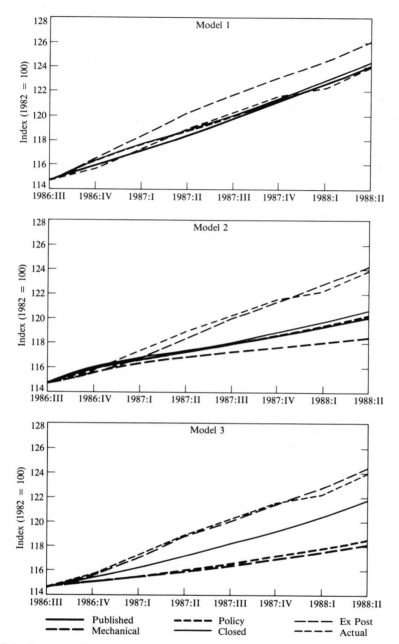

Figure 3.4. Forecasts of personal consumption deflator, 1986:III to 1988:II. See Figure 3.1 for definition of terms.

forecasts. About half of the difference was due to adjustments, and the other half was due to the individual modelers' nonconsensus assumptions.

Error Decomposition

All the preceding information describes the evolution of individual ex ante forecasts and the dispersion of those forecasts. We have seen how the forecasters' judgments affect their forecasts and the disparity among forecasts. This section describes two forecast periods for which the actual outcome is now known. This enables us to examine not only how judgments affect the forecasts but also whether they aid or impair the accuracy of the forecast.

Figure 3.1 shows the quite general tendency to overestimate real GNP from 1986:I to 1987:IV, especially early in the period. For models 1 and 3, the extent of overestimation was greater with the actual values of exogenous variables than with any set chosen ex ante. The forecaster's own ex ante assumptions led to slightly better forecasts than did imposing consensus assumptions. For model 2, the overestimation was worse with the common, ex ante assumptions and less with the forecaster's individual assumptions than with their actual values. For models 1 and 2, the published, adjusted forecasts were less accurate than the mechanically generated forecasts.

Figure 3.2 shows forecasts of the deflator for personal consumption expenditures over the same period. The ex ante forecasts from models 1 and 3 tended to underestimate the price level. The ex ante forecast of model 2 was quite accurate. Using the actual values of the exogenous variables, the model 1 forecast remained too low, the model 2 forecast started to overestimate, and the model 3 forecast became highly accurate. The proprietor of model 2 was able to offset his model's deficiencies to give "the right forecast for the wrong reasons." In contrast, model 3's ex ante error was solely attributable to the modeler's ex ante choice of assumptions; the model as a conditional statement was on track.

Figures 3.3 and 3.4 graph the ex ante forecasts, ex post simulations, and actual data for the period from 1986:III through 1988:II. Figure 3.3 shows that all these forecasts tracked real GNP fairly closely. Although the ex post forecasts of model 1 were somewhat better than its ex ante forecasts, the ex post forecasts of model 3 were somewhat worse. The adjustments to models 1 and 2 improved their forecasts, particularly early in the period.

Figure 3.4 shows the inflation forecasts over the same period. Ex ante, model 1 forecasts were quite accurate; the forecasts of models 2 and 3 were too low. However, with actual values of the exogenous variables, the forecasts of models 2 and 3 were quite accurate and model 1's forecast was slightly too high.

SUMMARY AND CONCLUSIONS

The chapter opened by posing three questions. This conclusion summarizes the limited evidence that has been presented.

1. Although the importance of judgment adjustments varies among individual models, for the models as a group the choices of macroeconomic policy assumptions

and external sector assumptions, relative to consensus assumptions, are as important to real GNP forecasts and nearly as important to inflation forecasts as are modelers' judgmental adjustments.

2. The reason for the dispersion among forecasts depends critically on the variables analyzed. The differences between the modeler's individual policy assumptions and the consensus assumptions tend to narrow differences in real GNP forecasts. Differences between individual and consensus external sector assumptions tend to increase the disparity among inflation forecasts. Model adjustments seem to narrow the dispersion among forecasts of both real GNP and the price level.

3. The role of adjustments. Do judgmental adjustments help or hurt? This evidence shows instances of both "good" judgment and "bad" judgment, depending primarily on which forecast period is examined. The adjustments hurt the real GNP forecasts of models 1 and 2 in the first forecast period, but helped in the second period, especially for model 2 in the short term. Adjustments had little impact on the inflation forecasts. The sole exception is for model 1 in the first round, when adjustments improved the inflation forecast at the same time they hurt the real GNP forecasts. This evidence is not consistent with the widespread belief that mechanically generated forecasts are wildly inaccurate compared to adjusted forecasts. It is consistent, however, with the view that judgmental adjustments can either help or hurt. Other evidence, covering longer periods, does suggest that adjustments do tend to help on average over time, but very little is known about when adjustments are likely to hurt and when they are likely to help.

4. Consensus versus individual ex ante assumptions. Two very different concepts of a model coexist. To some, the main virtue of using a model is that it gives the same answer to a precise question regardless of who poses the question. A model can be viewed as a disembodied system or formula like the laws of the natural sciences, totally independent of who uses it. From this perspective, there is no particular reason to believe that the person who built a model will necessarily be more skilled in formulating ex ante assumptions to generate a model-based forecast. If the model and the forecast assumptions were totally independent, there is no particular reason to think the model builder's individual assumptions would produce a more accurate forecast than any other feasible set of assumptions, such as the consensus assumptions.

Others tend to think of models, at least in a forecasting context, as tools the forecaster can use to enhance his skills. Just as not all craftsmen use the same kind of tools and not all athletes use the same brand of equipment, the performances of the model and the modeler are not independent and the two must be viewed as a team. Under this view, a model builder is in the best position to know the particular characteristics of his model and would, therefore, be especially capable of selecting ex ante assumptions to generate more accurate forecasts. Any externally imposed assumptions, such as the ad hoc consensus assumptions, would be less likely to be compatible with a specific model.

The evidence provides some insight into which of these perspectives is the more fruitful. Fortunately, these data are fairly clear across models and forecast periods. Unfortunately, the results differ depending on which variable is examined. Individual assumptions tend to produce more accurate real GNP forecasts than the common "consensus" assumptions, reflecting perhaps the forecasters' implicit policy reaction function which attaches major importance to stabilizing real GNP. In contrast, the common consensus assumptions tended to produce more accurate inflation forecasts than the modeler's own individual assumptions. This result is more consistent with the traditional view of a model as independent of the model user. The individual's unique knowledge of the model is not particularly helpful for generating accurate inflation forecasts, at least over a 2-year horizon.

5. Model (ex post) accuracy versus forecast accuracy. Forecast errors may either overestimate or underestimate the deficiency of a model viewed as a conditional relationship between input and output variables. The input assumptions chosen ex ante to generate a forecast are bound to be counterfactual. To the extent that the actual assumptions enhance accuracy, the forecast error overstates the deficiency in the conditional model. In practice, much evidence suggests that the counterfactual (ex ante) assumptions work to offset model deficiencies—that ex post model solutions, those based on actual input assumptions, are typically inferior to the ex ante forecast. These results are consistent with the view in Lucas (1976) that conditional models are severely flawed but that the model users can somehow offset these model deficiencies and generate reliable ex ante forecasts.

The limited evidence on this issue presented here is extremely mixed. For model 3, the ex post forecasts of real GNP were distinctly inferior to the ex ante real GNP forecasts, but the inflation forecasts were clearly superior. For model 1, the ex post real GNP forecasts were distinctly inferior in the first forecast but somewhat superior in the second period, when ex post inflation rate simulations were inferior to the ex ante. The results for model 2 are even more ambiguous, except for the inflation rate in the second forecast period where the ex post simulation was more accurate than the ex ante forecasts. This evidence, in other words, does not provide support for either extreme position on the relative accuracy of ex post and ex ante forecasts.

As noted at the outset, these conclusions are based on a very limited number of observations and may well not hold in the future. The experiment is an ongoing one, to try to determine under what circumstances the conclusions hold and when they do not. In addition, future research on this topic should examine more variables and perhaps include more models. Much more experience will be required to understand better the reasons why forecasts differ and to evaluate the reasons for their differences.

ACKNOWLEDGMENTS

The author is grateful to Lawrence Klein and Allen Sinai for helpful comments and to James Clark for able research assistance.

NOTES

1. The five models participating were those of Data Resources, Incorporated of Lexington, MA; Fairmodel, Macro Inc; Center for Economic Model Research, Indiana University, Bloomington, IN; Research Seminar in Quantitative Economics at the University of Michigan; Allen Sinai's model developed at Lehman Brothers, Shearson Lehman Brothers and most recently at The Boston Co. Inc.

2. Using what appears to be a more heterogeneous group of models, Wallis et al. (1986) argue that differences in the degree of exogeneity are of little practical importance for comparisons of models of the United Kingdom's economy. Accordingly, they consistently find that differences in exogenous variable assumptions account for little of the differences among forecasts.

REFERENCES

Evans, Michael K., Yoel Haitovsky, and George I. Treyz. (1972). "An Analysis of Forecasting Properties of U.S. Econometric Models." In *Econometric Models of Cyclical Behavior,* Bert G. Hickman, ed. New York: National Bureau of Economic Research.

Haitovsky, Yoel, and George Treyz. (1972). "Forecasts with Quarterly Macroeconomic Models, Equation Adjustments, and Benchmark Predictions: The U.S. Experience." *Review of Economics and Statistics* 54, 317–325.

Lucas, Robert E., Jr. (1976). "Econometric Policy Evaluation: A Critique." In *The Phillips Curve and Labor Markets* (Carnegie-Rochester Conferences on Public Policy #1), K. Brunner, and A. H. Meltzer, eds., pp. 19–46. New York: American Elsevier.

Wallis, K. F. ed. (1984–87). *Models of the UK Economy: A Review by ESRC Macroeconomic Modelling Bureau,* Vols. 1–4. New York: Oxford University Press.

COMPARISONS OF
MODEL STRUCTURES

CHAPTER 4

The IS–LM Cores of Three Econometric Models

R. JEFFERY GREEN, BERT G. HICKMAN, E. PHILIP HOWREY,
SAUL H. HYMANS, and MICHAEL R. DONIHUE

Large scale macroeconometric models are frequently used to simulate responses to various policy changes and external shocks. Because of the complexity of these models, it is not always easy to predict the outcomes of these simulation experiments, to explain the results in an intuitive way, or to determine why alternative models produce different results. These difficulties have led to the development of expository models and methods that are intended to be useful for pedagogical and comparative purposes.

One such approach to the problem of exposition and model comparison is the construction of a similar but simpler model that preserves the basic structural features of the original system. This approach has been pursued, for example, by Deleau, Malgrange, and Muet (1984), Klein, Doud, and Sojo (1985), and Hickman (1987, 1988). Deleau et al. propose a simple 26-equation model that is "intended to offer a *common structural reference* [sic] for *econometric model* comparisons." Klein et al. have a somewhat more limited objective, namely the construction of an IS–LM nucleus model that they obtain both by direct estimation and by simulation of the Wharton Quarterly Model. Hickman uses numerical results from a set of standardized simulation experiments on energy shocks and policy responses to estimate the slopes or elasticities of the implicit IS, LM, AD, and AS curves of 13 U.S. models in his 1987 paper and performs similar calculations for fiscal and monetary shocks to 12 multinational models in his 1988 paper. The estimated elasticities are then used to characterize similarities and differences among the models.

The purpose of this chapter is to discuss the methodology of IS–LM and AD–AS system reduction and to illustrate its application to three U.S. econometric models: the Hickman–Coen (HC) Annual Growth Model, the Indiana University Econometric Model (EMUS), and the University of Michigan's Quarterly Econometric Model (MQEM). In the first section, Hickman compares the estimation of the short-run IS, LM, and AS loci by partial simulation techniques and full-model comparative-static experiments and illustrates the methodology using the HC Model. In the next section, Green measures the short- and long-run elasticities of the IS, LM, AD, and AS loci of the Indiana Model by partial simulation methods. In the third section, Howrey, Hymans, and Donihue illustrate the use of IS–LM analysis to interpret macroeconometric model simulations in a detailed examination of the responses of the

MQEM model to a fiscal shock over a 10-year horizon. The final section offers some concluding observations on the usefulness of the general approach.

THE CONCEPTUAL FRAMEWORK

In the common textbook formulation, the IS–LM framework taken by itself serves to determine the nominal interest rate (R) and real income (Y) consistent with equilibrium in the markets for goods and money when prices are predetermined. The IS locus is shifted by exogenous changes in tax rates or real government spending and the LM curve by exogenous changes in the nominal money supply. Simultaneous solution of the IS and LM equations yields a reduced-form equation for income as a function of tax rates, government purchases, and real money balances. Once the system is broadened to include an endogenous price (P), the income equation is no longer a reduced form, but rather defines an aggregate demand (AD) locus in P–Y space, summarizing the aggregate demand conditions yielding equilibrium in the goods and money markets at alternative price levels.

The corresponding aggregate supply (AS) curve determines the short-run response of price to production and incorporates the labor-market Phillips curve for wage determination and the markup mechanism for price determination typical of econometric models. The AS schedule depends on lagged prices and is shifted contemporaneously by autonomous changes (innovations) in wage rates, markups, payroll taxes, or import prices.

The first conceptual experiment is for a fiscal shock and is illustrated in Figure 4.1. The initial equilibrium occurs at R_0, P_0, and Y_0. Now assume that the IS curve shifts rightward because of an increase in government purchases, moving from IS_0 to IS_1. An equivalent shift of the aggregate demand curve will carry it from AD_0 to AD_1. Next, suppose that contrary to Figure 4.1, the AS curve were perfectly elastic. The

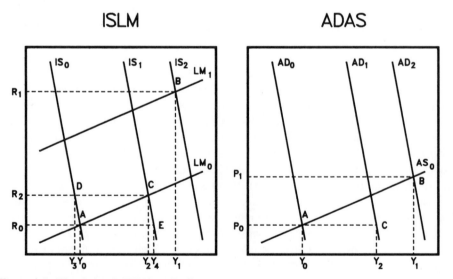

Figure 4.1. Fiscal shock (ISLM, ADAS).

price level would then remain at P_0 and LM_0 would stay fixed. The new equilibrium would be at point C, with interest rate R_2, price P_0, and income Y_2. The slope of the unshifted LM curve could then be calculated from the observations at points A and C on the ISLM diagram. Assuming approximate log linearity, the result would be the estimated elasticity of LM.

One expects, however, an upward sloping AS curve on general theoretical grounds. An increase of output will increase the demand for labor and hence the wage rate, and the resulting rise in unit labor cost will put upward pressure on the price level. The wage pressure may be mitigated by an induced cyclical increase in manhour productivity, but this effect is insufficient in most U.S. models to prevent prices from rising along with wages.

The expansionary fiscal shock will, therefore, increase the price level along the positively sloped AS curve in Figure 4.1, leading to price-induced shifts in the IS and LM curves. The LM curve will necessarily shift leftward as real money balances are reduced by the higher price level. The outcome for the IS curve is ambiguous, however. In most U.S. models, induced productivity increases mitigate the inflationary effects of induced wage increases at least in the short run, so that not only the price level but real wages and disposable income increase under a demand stimulus, augmenting consumption demand at any GNP level and shifting IS to the right. On the other hand, if real balance or wealth terms are included in the aggregate demand equations, as in some U.S. models, a price increase will tend to shift IS leftward. The net outcome for IS therefore depends on specific model characteristics. In Figure 4.1 it has been assumed that the real wage stimulus is dominant and moreover that the price-induced upshift of IS is sufficiently large to outweigh the corresponding upshift of LM, so that Y_1 is greater than Y_2, in accord for the empirical findings for the HC Model (which has no wealth terms) reported below. Correspondingly, it is assumed on the ADAS diagram that the induced rightward shift of AD from higher real wages is sufficient to cause equilibrium income to exceed the level that would occur if wages and prices were invariant under the demand stimulus.[1]

Clearly an elasticity calculated between A and B on the ISLM diagram would be a biased measure of the true LM elasticity. One way to estimate the latter is to simulate the ISLM sector under the fiscal shock but holding prices constant at P_0, to obtain a solution for point C. A comparison of the two simulations will then show the magnitude of the bias when the AD side is not isolated from the equilibrium computation.

Finally, a direct derivation of the original IS schedule and its elasticity may be obtained from points A and D, where the latter point is from a simulation of the IS sector alone, with government purchases at their baseline level and the interest rate at its value from the ISLM fixed-price fiscal-shock simulation. Similarly, a direct estimate of the shifted IS schedule under fixed prices is obtained by solving the IS sector under the fiscal shock but with the interest rate and prices at their baseline values, to yield point E for comparison with C. Comparison of these alternative estimates will show whether the IS elasticity tends to be invariant to shocks that shift the fixed-price IS locus.

A similar conceptual experiment involves a monetary shock and may be used to estimate the IS and LM slopes in a model. Assume a decrease in the money stock to shift the LM curve upward and to the left (Figure 4.2). At fixed prices, the new equilibrium is at point C, permitting calculation of the elasticity of the unshifted IS locus

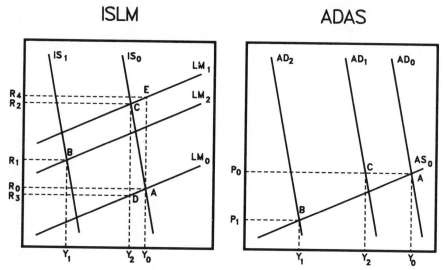

Figure 4.2. Monetary shock (ISLM, ADAS).

in comparison with the baseline equilibrium at A. If AS is positively sloped, however, the price level will decrease and induce a rightward shift of the LM curve to a position between LM_0 and LM_1. The IS curve will also be affected by the price decrease, and in Figure 4.2 it has been assumed that the real wage effect dominates the wealth effect and causes IS to shift down enough so that the final equilibrium at B is at a lower income than if prices were unchanged by the monetary contraction. The extent to which including the AS sector in the money shock simulation biases the estimate of the underlying IS elasticity may again be judged by comparing the two cases.

An estimate of the elasticity of the unshifted LM curve may be obtained from a comparison of points A and D of Figure 4.2, where the latter point is found by solving the LM sector alone, with the money supply at its baseline level and income at its estimated value from the fixed-price ISLM solution under a monetary shock. Similarly, solving the LM sector for point E, with M_1 at its reduced level and prices and income at their baseline values, permits evaluation of the shifted LM locus under fixed prices from points C and E.

With regard to the supply side, note that the two demand-shock scenarios also provide estimates of the short-run elasticity of the AS curve between points A and B in the ADAS diagram of Figures 4.1 and 4.2. Again, however, the estimated supply elasticity will be biased in the complete model simulations if the AS curve itself shifts because of the demand shocks. Interdependences between AD and AS and a method of direct estimation of the elasticity of the unshifted AS schedule will be discussed below.

Finally, the initial postshock equilibrium illustrated in Figures 4.1 and 4.2 is temporary. The positive and negative short-run responses to the fiscal and monetary shocks arise because prices adjust gradually in the model. Equilibrating price changes will build up over time, however, inducing additional shifts in IS–LM locuses and tending to restore the preshock level of real income. This process is not traced beyond the second year in the simulations of the HC Model, but those for the Indiana and MQEM Models cover a longer time span.

BLOCK STRUCTURE OF THE HICKMAN–COEN MODEL

The HC Model is designed for analysis of the medium and long-run growth path of the U.S. economy. First published in 1976, it has subsequently been augmented with a disaggregated model of labor supply, a representative-agent model of personal taxation incorporating the (changing) structure of the tax code, a detailed model of social

Table 4.1. Block Structure of the Hickman–Coen Model

Block	Principal Endogenous Variables
1. CONS (consumption)	1. Expenditures on automobiles; other goods; nondurable goods; services; energy
2. INV (business investment)	2. Gross business fixed investment; stock of fixed business capital; inventory investment; inventory stock
3. HOUS (housing and residential construction)	3. Rent; nonfarm households; stock of nonfarm dwelling units; occupancy ratio; nonfarm housing starts; value per nonfarm housing start; residential construction expenditure
4. GOVT (government purchases of goods and services)	4. State and local government purchases of goods and services
5. FORT (foreign trade)	5. Imports; exports
6. OUT (output)	6. GNP in current and constant prices; gross private nonresidential product in current and constant prices
7. INC (income)	7. Gross corporate profits; dividends; capital consumption allowances; labor income; national income; personal income; disposable personal income
8. TXTR (taxes and transfers)	8. Unemployment compensation; unemployment contributions; contributions to social insurance; federal personal taxes; federal corporate taxes; indirect business taxes; investment tax credit
9. LBIN (labor input)	9. Private man-hours
10. EMLF (employment and labor force)	10. Labor force participation rate; average hours; labor force; employment; unemployment
11. WAGE (money wages)	11. Change in aggregate wage rate
12. PRIC (product prices)	12. Implicit price deflators for GNP; gross private nonresidential product; 12 final demand sectors
13. MONY (money stock and interest rates)	13. Money stock; commercial paper rate; average Moody's corporate bond rate
14. UTIL (resource utilization)	14. Levels and rates of utilization of capacity output; full-employment output; potential output; full-employment labor force; average hours at full employment; man-hours at full employment

security taxation and expenditures, and a model of the natural growth path of potential output. The 1988 version is described in Coen and Hickman (1987).

The equations of the model are organized by blocks as shown in Table 4.1. The first five blocks contain the demand functions for purchases of final goods and services and the sixth incorporates the GNP identities in current and constant prices. Block 7 determines the income side and block 8 contains the tax and transfer equations. Together these eight blocks comprise a disaggregated IS structure. The LM structure is represented by the MONY block (13), with the real demand for M_1 a function of real income and the short-term interest rate. Either the supply of M_1 or the interest rate may be treated as exogenous.

Aggregate supply is modeled in the five remaining blocks. Blocks 9–11 comprise the labor market and 12 is the price determination sector. The final block, UTIL, determines various measures of capacity output and utilization.

For the purpose of describing some basic properties, it is useful to think of a model of this type as a disaggregated AD–AS structure, with AD in turn disaggregated into IS and LM sectors. But how may the core elasticities of the implicit aggregative IS, LM, and AS functions be estimated numerically? Most econometric models are much too detailed to provide convenient algebraic reductions of the underlying structural equations to IS or AS curves, although this may be feasible for the LM equation. It is a practical necessity to obtain the locuses by simulation techniques.

SIMULATION METHODOLOGY

Direct Estimation of Isolated IS and LM Curves

The simplest case is the LM locus. In the HC Model, the demand for real money balances (measured by M_1/P, where P is the implicit GNP deflator) increases with real GNP (Y) and lagged real balances and decreases with the 4–6 month commercial paper rate (RS). The partial elasticity of LM can be estimated by solving the MONY block for the value of RS corresponding to a fixed real money supply and two different levels of Y, by declaring P and Y to be exogenous along with M_1. This is the computational counterpart to estimating points A and D in Figure 4.2. The money block also contains a term-structure equation to determine Moody's corporate average bond rate (RL) as a function of RS and the lagged value of RL, so the LM solution is for a vector of interest rates, with RS the key rate used to define the slope of LM.

With regard to the IS sector the procedure is the same in principle but must allow for the fact that a disaggregated set of final demand functions will include many-valued vectors of prices as well as several concepts of income and interest rates. Holding "P" constant and solving for "Y" at two different levels of "R," as between points A and D in Figure 4.1, now requires specifying predetermined vectors rather than scalars. Moreover, these must be internally consistent vectors, capable of actually solving the complete model and satisfying the LM and AS equations as well. In the example of Figure 4.1, the exogenized interest rate and price vectors used to establish points A and D so satisfy the complete model.

Estimation of IS and LM Locuses from Market Equilibria

This approach relies on the fact that both the IS and LM sectors must be satisfied in an ISLM equilibrium. The elasticity of LM is estimated from a comparison of two market equilibria differing only because of a shift of IS. This procedure allows for estimation both of the elasticity of the unshifted LM curve when prices are held constant, as between A and C in Figure 4.1, or of the LM elasticity incorporating price feedbacks, as between pints A and B. Similarly, the IS elasticities excluding and including price effects may be established in a monetary shock comparison, as in Figure 4.2.

The Simulation Procedures

The methodology exploits two features of the computational design used in the HC model:

1. Any endogenous variable may be declared exogenous, and in addition, the user may declare any subset of the 14 equation blocks to be exogenous, in which case the left-hand variables that are normally endogenously determined in a block, instead retain whatever values are currently present in the internal data matrix of the model.
2. The internal data matrix is not overwritten when the model is solved. Rather, the solution values are written to a separate matrix. However, the solution matrix may itself be read into the data matrix on command.

Together, these two facilities provide the capability for a systematic approach to estimation of the core elasticities of a model. The procedure is as follows, first using the example of a fiscal shock.

Baseline ADAS Solution

This is a standard complete-model solution to establish the initial equilibrium denoted by point A in Figure 4.1. The solution output for R_0, P_0, and Y_0 and such other diagnostic variables as desired, is saved in a permanent file.

Fiscal-Shock ADAS Solution

Real federal purchases of goods and services (GF), an exogenous policy variable, is incremented and the model re-solved. This provides the equilibrium values corresponding to point B in Figure 4.1 (R_1, P_1, and Y_1) for computation of the *mutatis mutandis* LM elasticity between points A and B, after allowance for the price-induced shift of the *ceteris paribus* LM locus.

Fixed-Price ISLM Fiscal-Shock Solution

1. The baseline solution is written to the data matrix, so that each block now contains model-consistent values for the endogenous left-hand variables deter-

mined in that block, corresponding to point A in Figure 4.1. (This step is unnecessary if a perfect tracking solution to replicate the historical data is used as the baseline.) In particular, the vectors represented by R_0, P_0, and Y_0 are now stored in the data matrix.

2. Declare the AS blocks to be exogenous, fixing wage rates, prices, employment, unemployment, hours, and other variables proximately determined in the AS blocks at the values corresponding to point A—the vector equivalent of holding P_0 in Figure 4.1 constant. Note that the same values of these variables also satisfied the ISLM sector in the baseline solution wherever they appeared on the right-hand side of equations in the ISLM blocks.

3. Increment government spending by the same constant-dollar amount as before and solve the ISLM blocks simultaneously for the endogenous values of the ISLM variables, holding prices constant at the baseline level. This provides the solution values for point C in Figure 4.1 (R_2, P_0, and Y_2). Points A and C both satisfy the ISLM sector for fixed prices and provide an estimate of the slope of the *ceteris paribus* LM curve.

Fixed-Price IS Solutions

1. Copy the solution matrix from the previous fixed-price ISLM shock solution to the data matrix, restore government purchases to the baseline level, and solve the IS blocks alone by exogenizing the AS and LM blocks. This provides an estimate of Y_3 at point D, with the interest rate and price vectors fixed exogenously at values corresponding to R_2 and P_0 in Figure 4.1. The *ceteris paribus* elasticity of the original IS locus may then be calculated by comparison with point A.

2. Copy the baseline solution to the internal data matrix to fix P_0 and R_0. Increment GF as before and solve the IS sector alone for Y_4 at point E to obtain the IS_1 locus.

A Monetary Shock

The same general procedures are followed in the case of a monetary shock. The illustration in this paper is for an exogenous decrease in M_1 relative to the baseline solution.

RESULTS FOR THE HICKMAN–COEN MODEL

The simulation results are presented in Table 4.2. The baseline solution (BA) is the same for both sets of simulations and refers to point A in Figures 4.1 and 4.2. The four fiscal-shock simulations, denoted FB, FC, FD, and FE, refer to points B to E in Figure 4.1, whereas the monetary simulations corresponding to Figure 4.2 are similarly labeled in order with an M prefix. The AS simulations will be described later.

The IS and LM elasticities measure the percentage change of income per unit percentage change in the interest rate and the AS elasticities similarly show the percentage income response per unit of percentage price change. The interest responses could be

Table 4.2. Short-Run Elasticities and Multipliers[a]

Simulation Comparison	Year	Percentage Differences			Elasticities			Absolute Differences						Percentage Differences		
		P	Y	R	IS[b]	LM[b]	AS[c]	C	I	G	X	M	Y	W	P	Y/L
FB–BA	1979	0.26	1.45	5.55	—	0.26	5.58	6.7	6.6	10.0	-0.3	1.6	21.3	0.47	0.26	0.68
	1980	0.86	1.25	8.27	—	0.15	1.45	7.4	4.0	10.2	-1.0	2.2	18.4	0.98	0.86	0.14
FC–BA	1979	0.00	1.10	2.61	—	0.42	—	2.6	4.7	10.0	0.0	1.2	16.2	0.00	0.00	0.00
	1980	0.00	1.02	2.43	—	0.42	—	3.6	3.0	10.1	0.0	1.7	15.0	0.00	0.00	0.00
MD–BA	1979	0.00	-0.35	-0.84	—	0.42	—	—	—	—	—	—	—	0.00	0.00	0.00
	1980	0.00	-0.38	-0.92	—	0.42	—	—	—	—	—	—	—	0.00	0.00	0.00
ME–MC	1979	0.00	0.35	0.83	—	0.42	—	—	—	—	—	-	—	0.00	0.00	0.00
	1980	0.00	0.39	0.93	—		—	—	—	—	—	—	—	0.00	0.00	0.00
AS–BA	1979	0.47	2.04	0.00	—	—	4.34	—	—	—	—	—	—	0.59	0.47	0.95
	1980	1.55	2.04	0.00	—	—	1.32	—	—	—	—	—	—	1.63	1.55	0.41
MB–BA	1979	-0.08	-0.46	34.2	-0.01	—	5.43	-1.8	-5.6	0.0	0.1	-0.5	-6.8	-0.12	-0.08	-0.14
	1980	-0.29	-0.48	10.4	-0.05	—	1.66	-2.4	-5.8	0.0	0.3	-0.8	-7.1	-0.43	-0.29	-0.14
MC–BA	1979	0.00	-0.35	35.5	-0.01	—	—	-0.5	-5.0	0.0	0.0	-0.4	-5.1	0.00	0.00	0.00
	1980	0.00	-0.39	12.5	-0.03	—	—	-1.1	-5.4	0.1	0.0	-0.6	-5.7	0.00	0.00	0.00
FD–BA	1979	0.00	-0.04	2.61	-0.01	—	—	—	—	—	—	—	—	0.00	0.00	0.00
	1980	0.00	-0.05	2.43	-0.02	—	—	—	—	—	—	—	—	0.00	0.00	0.00
FE–FC	1979	0.00	0.03	-2.55	-0.01	—	—	—	—	—	—	—	—	0.00	0.00	0.00
	1980	0.00	0.05	-2.37	-0.02	—	—	—	—	—	—	—	—	0.00	0.00	0.00
AS–BA	1979	-0.24	-1.02	0.00	—	—	4.25	—	—	—	—	—	—	-0.35	-0.24	-0.41
	1980	-0.79	-1.02	0.00	—	—	1.29	—	—	—	—	—	—	-0.87	-0.79	-0.27

[a] P, implicit deflator, gross private nonresidential product; Y, real gross national product; R, 4–6 month commercial paper rate; C, real consumption; I, real gross private fixed investment; G, real government purchases of goods and services; X, real exports; M, real imports; W, nominal wage rate; Y/L, man-hour productivity.
[b] Column 2 divided by column 3.
[c] Column 2 divided by column 1.

measured in absolute terms to compute semielasticities for IS and LM, but this has the disadvantage that the measures are not dimensionless. This aspect could be troublesome when comparisons are made for different initial conditions or for dynamic response patterns in a given model, and for comparisons across models not standardized on a given historical tracking solution.

The calculations show that IS is quite steep in the HC Model, whereas LM is considerably flatter. The IS curve is steeper than in models that include the market interest rate in the demand function for business fixed investment. In the HC Model, business fixed investment is assumed to depend on a constant required rate of return instead of a variable nominal or real interest rate, although market rates do directly affect residential construction and automobile sales. Since the IS locus is the frontier for monetary policy, the model predicts a small income response to a monetary shock.

The LM curve is only moderately elastic, owing to the rather small estimated interest elasticity of real money demand in the model (-0.12 in the short run and -0.27 in the long run). The LM curve is sufficiently elastic, however, to permit a substantial income response to a fiscal stimulus.

The fixed-price IS and LM curves are isoelastic over the range of these simulations, showing the same elasticities before and after being shifted by the demand shocks.

Both the fiscal and monetary multipliers for income are larger when the induced changes in wages and prices are taken into account. The induced upshift of LM from a price increase under a positive fiscal shock does exacerbate the rise in the interest rate as predicted, and the interest rate increase under a negative monetary shock is similarly mitigated by the induced downshift of the LM curve. As noted earlier in the theoretical section and documented in the last three columns of Table 4.2, however, the real wage rises under a positive demand shock and falls when the shock is negative, resulting in induced shifts of IS which more than offset the induced shifts in LM and augment the income responses. Conceivable, of course, a wealth effect could dominate the real wage effect in models with wealth terms in the aggregate demand equations.

The AS curve is fairly elastic in this model, moderating the price response to demand shocks. As shown in the last column, induced changes in manhour productivity substantially mitigate the impact of higher wages on prices in the short run. The wage response to unemployment is also small and the feedback of prices to wages is lagged 1 year. Since the position of the AS function depends on lagged wages and prices, it shifts up in the second year of response to a positive demand shock and downward in the second year of a negative shock. The calculated elasticity of AS in the second year therefore refers to a "long-run" AS function corrected for induced shifts from the adjustment dynamics especially in the labor market, and the AS schedule is substantially steeper than in the first year. Recall, however, that the estimates of the AS slopes in either year may be biased by contemporaneous interaction between AD and AS.

The estimated impact elasticities of IS and LM under the fixed-price assumption are virtually the same (apart from rounding) whether obtained from the market equilibria of the ISLM model or by partial simulation of the IS or LM sectors. The same should be true of other models, in the absence of significant interdependences between the IS and LM sectors such as are evidently not present in the HC Model. If the elasticities as estimated by the market-equilibrium approach did differ substantially from the partial-equilibrium results, this would indicate that interdependences were present and should be located and understood.

The impact elasticity for the variable-price IS locus is about the same as for the fixed-price estimate. The lack of bias is doubtless traceable to the small price and real wage declines under the monetary shock. When these changes build up in the second year, the induced downshift of the IS curve increases the estimated *mutatis mutandis* elasticity considerably relative to the *ceteris paribus* estimates for fixed prices.

The bias in the *mutatis mutandis* estimate for LM is fairly large in the first year, however, and is larger still in the second year owing to the steepening slope of the AS curve. Since the LM curve responds to the change in the absolute price level whereas the IS curve is shifted only by the much smaller induced change of real wages, it is not surprising that the price-induced bias is larger in the former case.

The IS and LM elasticities may differ between the first and second years of adjustment even apart from price-induced shifts. For the fixed-price simulations, the dynamic elasticities may differ because of adjustment lags in the demand functions for goods and money. In the HC Model, this is not a factor in the case of LM, because only real balances are lagged in the money demand function. The elasticity of IS is greater in the second year even with fixed prices, however, because of the stock-adjustment processes specified for consumer durables, residential construction, and business fixed investment and the permanent-income formulation of the consumption functions for nondurables and services.

DEMAND SHOCKS AND SHIFTS IN AGGREGATE SUPPLY

The foregoing discussion has abstracted from the possibility that a demand shock may shift the AS schedule, contrary to the situation depicted in Figures 4.1 and 4.2. Several important factors may induce AS shifts from demand shocks, however, as noted in Hickman (1987): (1) If interest rates are included in the price equations, AS will shift on that account when AD is perturbed—and the shifts of AS will be in opposite directions for expansionary fiscal and monetary shocks. (2) If anticipated inflation depends on monetary growth in excess of income growth and is a term in the wage equation, the AS curve will be shifted by fiscal or monetary actions, again in opposite directions according to type of shock. (3) In models with endogenous exchange rates, capital flows induced by interest rate responses to demand shocks will alter import prices in domestic currency and shift AS (Hickman, 1988).

None of these factors is operative in the HC Model, but others are present, as shown by a comparison of the estimated AS elasticities from the demand-shock scenarios with two direct estimates for an unshifted AS curve. The latter were made by simulating the AS blocks in isolation for two different predetermined levels of output, one above the baseline output for comparison with the *mutatis mutandis* estimate from the expansionary fiscal-shock scenario and the other below the baseline output for the corresponding comparison with the contractionary money-shock scenario. As shown in Table 4.2, the new estimates of the *ceteris paribus* AS elasticities are somewhat smaller than those derived from the comparative market equilibria for the two demand shocks. The difference is partly attributable to the fact that a demand shock alters the product composition of consumption in the model and hence alters the weights in the identity for the implicit consumption deflator in the price block. Another weak feedback between endogenous variables in AD and AS is found in the wedge between the private hourly wage including and excluding social security contributions by employers. These small endogenous interactions between demand shocks and the AS curve are insufficient to bias seriously the estimated supply elasticities from the complete model simulations or to alter the basic conclusion that the overall response of price to demand shocks is small in the HC Model.

The purpose of this second section is to describe the results of a series of simulations designed to determine approximate IS and LM and AS and AD curves implied by the Indiana University Econometric Model of the United States (EMUS).

The EMUS model is a medium-size macroeconometric model containing 100 behavioral equations, 150 identities, and 57 exogenous variables. The blocks of equations defining the model are given in Table 4.3. The EMUS model is neo-Keynesian and the components of aggregate demand are determined in the first four blocks. The supply side contains an expected inflation augmented Phillips curve where inflationary expectations are adaptive. Prices are a variable markup over unit labor costs. Monetary aggregates and interest rates are determined in the money block. The first version of the EMUS model was constructed in 1982 and it has been revised and expanded since. It is used by the Center for Econometric Model Research to produce regular quarterly forecasts.

Table 4.3. Block Structure of the Indiana University Model

Block	Principal Endogenous Variables
1. CONS (consumption)	1. Expenditures for four components of durable goods consumption, four components of nondurable consumption, and two components of services consumption
2. INV (business investment)	2. Two components of inventory investment single and multifamily housing starts, residential investment, three components of nonresidential fixed investment
3. FEDG and SLG (government)	3. Federal corporate and individual taxes, social security taxes, Federal transfers, net interest, state and local purchases, taxes, and transfers
4. TRADE (foreign trade)	4. Two components of imports, two components of exports, exchange rate
5. EMP (employment and hours)	5. Labor force, employment, and hours
6. WAGPR (wages and prices)	6. Twenty-one component implicit price deflators, 13 consumer price indexes, private nonfarm wage rate, deflator for private nonfarm output, nominal expenditures
7. MONEY (money and interest rates)	7. Currency, M_2, four interest rates, free reserves
8. INC (incomes)	8. Rental income, proprietors income, interest income, dividend income
9. MISC (miscellaneous)	9. Cost of capital, identities for major aggregates such as GNP

Because theoretically the IS, LM, AS, and AD curves are static and depend on fixed values of other variables, we must estimate the curves for a given period. We have selected 1987.1, the first quarter of 1987, for the IS and LM curves and 1987.3, the third quarter of 1987, for the AS and AD curves.

ESTIMATING THE IS AND LM CURVES

The LM curve is obtained by simulating the monetary sector of the model in isolation. The important equations in the monetary sector are given in Table 4.5 with definitions of the variables in Table 4.4. The standard form of the monetary sector of the Indiana model begins with nonborrowed reserves and average reserve requirement ratios as exogenous monetary policy variables. These exogenous variables plus a behavioral equation for free reserves determine total deposits. There are also behavioral equations for currency and M_2. These equations jointly determine both M_1 and M_2. A behavioral demand for the M_2 equation then determines the 3-month treasury bill rate. Term structure equations are used to determine long rates from short rates.

Table 4.4. Indiana Model Monetary Sector: Definitions of Variables

Variable	Definition
Endogenous	
CURR	Currency
DD	Demand deposits
FR	Free reserves
GNP	Nominal gross national product
GNP82	Real gross national product
M_1	Money supply
M_2	Money supply
PDGNP	GNP deflator
RAAA	Moodys AAA bond rate
RR	Required reserves
RTB3M	91-day treasury bill rate
Exogenous	
NBR	Nonborrowed reserves
OCD	Other checkable deposits
RRR	Average required reserve ratio

Table 4.5. Indiana Model Monetary Sector: Main Equations

Behavioral
$$CURR = f_1 (GNP, RTB3M)$$
$$FR = f_2 [RTB3M, DD(-1), FR(-1), NBR]$$
$$M_2 = f_3 (M_1)$$
$$RTB3M = f_4 (M_2/PDGNP, GNP82)$$
$$RAAA = f_5 [RTB3M, RTB3M(-1), RAAA(-1)]$$
Identities
$$DD = RR/RRR$$
$$RR = NBR - FR$$
$$M_1 = CURR + DD + OCD$$

One way to solve the monetary sector is to make M_1 exogenous. In this case non-borrowed reserves are made endogenous and set at that level necessary to produce the exogenous level of M_1. A second alternative is to allow the 3-month treasury bill rate to be determined by a reaction function similar to that of Fair (1984) rather than the money demand function. For these simulations we have chosen to solve the model with M_1 exogenous since the standard textbook treatment of the LM curve has money constant along any particular LM curve.

Before estimating the IS and LM curves, a tracking solution for the period in which the curves are to be simulated must be obtained. The first step in estimating the LM curve is to exogenize the behavioral equations in all of the sectors in the model except the monetary sector.

With all sectors except the money sector exogenized, one can shock real GNP in a given period and obtain a simulated value for the 3-month bill rate. Together with the tracking solution GNP–bill ordered pair, the simulated values constitute two points on the LM curve. To obtain more points on the curve, one need only specify different values for GNP and solve the monetary sector to obtain corresponding values of the bill rate.

To obtain a sequence of n-period LM curves, one needs to extend the original GNP shock back n-periods. For example, if GNP is shocked by a fixed amount in the current period, then the 1-period LM curve would contain the same magnitude GNP shock in the previous period as well. The 2-period LM curve would shock GNP in each of the past two quarters, and so on for the n-period LM curve. To obtain more points on the long run LM curve the same exercise is performed with different sized GNP shocks.

Figure 4.3 shows the current (1987.1) or 0-period LM curve as well as the four period or long-run curve. Differences in the n-period LM curves became very small for $n>4$. The kink in the curves shows that all curves pass through the tracking solution values for 1987.1 for the bill rate and GNP. The semielasticity, measured as $\Delta \text{RTB3M}/\Delta \ln \text{GNP82}$, of the long run or 4-period LM curve evaluated at the tracking solution value is 41. In other words, a 1% increase in real GNP implies a 41 basis point increase in the bill rate. The corresponding value for the 0 period LM curve is 35. Thus, the LM curve is steeper in the long run than in the short run. To shift the LM curve all that is required is to solve the monetary sector for the LM curve with a different value of M_1.

To estimate the IS curve, the 3-month treasury bill rate must be exogenized. All of the other behavioral equations that were exogenized in the LM curve simulations except the private nonfarm deflator are endogenous in these simulations. This simulation will yield a GNP value corresponding to the now exogenous value of the bill rate. To obtain more points on the IS curve, one need only solve the model with the bill rate exogenized at different values.

The 0-period IS curve is almost vertical. The semielasticity evaluated at the actual 1987.1 value is -376, which implies a decrease of 1% in real GNP is associated with an increase in the bill rate of almost four full percentage points. Figure 4.4 shows the current period, and 3-period IS curves. There was no significant difference between the n-period IS curves beyond three periods. The semielasticity of the long-run or 3-period IS curve evaluated at the actual 1987.1 value is -330. In other words, a 1% decrease in real GNP is associated with a 330 basis point increase in the bill rate. One

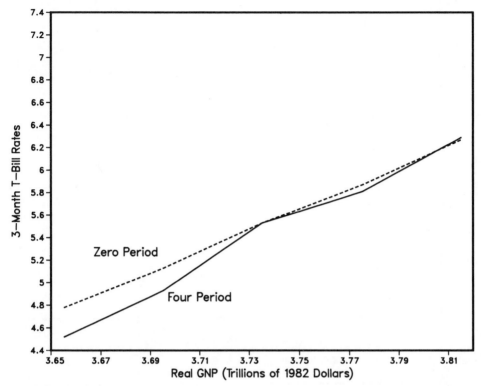

Figure 4.3. 1987.1 LM curves.

reason for the very steep IS curves is that interest income in the model rises with increases in interest rates and offsets a significant portion of the decline in demand coming from higher rates.

The IS curves in Figure 4.4 are based on a fixed price level as in the classic textbook IS–LM analysis. If the price level is allowed to change, an increase in the bill rate will tend to reduce real GNP, which, in turn, will produce a lower price level than in the tracking solution. This lower price level will produce a higher level of real wealth and real income and tend to stimulate consumption and real GNP. The result is a smaller decline in real GNP in the endogenous price level case than in the exogenous price level case and hence a steeper IS curve. However, because the IS and LM curves stabilize after such a short period of time and because the lags between changes in GNP and price changes are significantly longer, there is not much difference in simulating these IS curves with prices endogenous rather than exogenous.

It is important to remember that M_1 is exogenous in the IS curve simulations. We imposed this constraint because in the standard textbook case the IS curve is independent of M_1, and, hence, a change in M_1 will shift the LM curve but leave the IS curve unchanged. The slope of the IS curve measures the net influence of interest rate changes on various components of final demand. The complication here is that in our model consumption expenditures depend on wealth, which, in turn, depends on money. Hence, a change in the money supply changes wealth and consumption expen-

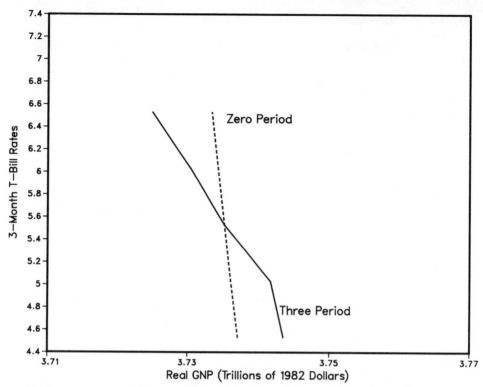

Figure 4.4. 1987.1 IS curves.

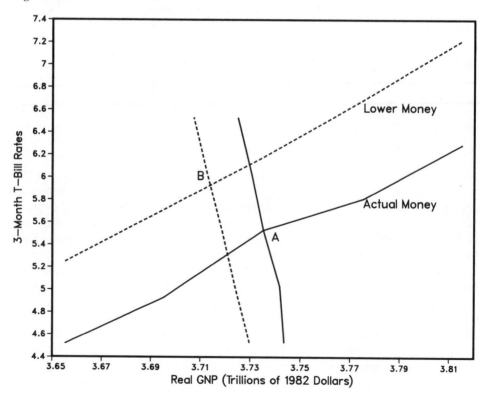

Figure 4.5. Long-run IS–LM curves.

ditures and shifts the IS curve. As a result, it is misleading to predict the change in real GNP and interest rates flowing from a change in money by examining a shifting LM curve against a constant IS curve. In this case both curves shift. The situation is illustrated in Figure 4.5. The semi-elasticities of the long run IS curve with and without wealth effects are -330 and -68. The semielasticity with wealth effects is calculated by comparing points A and B on Figure 4.5.

ESTIMATING THE AS AND AD CURVES

In the Indiana model, prices are determined as a variable markup over unit labor costs. Wages are determined by the degree of slack in labor markets and by inflationary expectations. The main equations in the wage–price block of the model are shown in Table 4.6.

The model assumes adaptive expectations and so the rate of change of current wages depends on lagged values of the inflation rate. As the level of output rises, employment rises and the unemployment rate falls tightening labor markets and putting upward pressure on wages. The upward pressure on wages then is translated into upward pressure on prices with a lag. Thus, an increase in output leads eventually to a rise in prices. Although this is the general reason for an upward sloping aggregate supply curve there is another factor at work in the very short run.

In the Indiana model, employment and hours adjust with a lag to changes in output and thus produce a procyclical movement in productivity. Consequently, a rise in output produces a short-term rise in productivity, which then produces a short-term decline in unit labor costs, which produce downward pressure on prices. This effect disappears as employment adjusts. As we shall see, however, it has implications for the estimated aggregate supply curve in the very short run.

To estimate the aggregate supply curve, we must vary real GNP while holding all variables except those directly determining prices constant. Specifically, we exogenized all blocks in the model except the wage and price block and man-hours and employment. Man-hours and employment had to be made endogenous to allow the degree of slack in labor markets to change and to allow productivity to change since both of these directly affect prices. To obtain the 0-period AS curve, we then varied the level of real GNP (GNP82) in 1987.3 and calculated the resulting price level. These simulations, like those used to estimate the IS–LM curves, are run off the tracking solution

Table 4.6. Main Wage and Price Equations: Indiana Econometric Model of the United States[a]

$$d\,\ell n[\text{WRCPNA}(t)] = f[\,1/\text{NRUT}(t),d\,\ell n\,\text{PDC}(t),\dots,d\,\ell n\,\text{PDC}(t-11)]$$
$$\ell n(\text{PXPD}(t)) = g\{\ell n[\text{XPD82}(t)] - \ell n[\text{POTGNP}(t)],$$
$$d\{\ell n[\text{WRCPNA}(t)] - \ell n[\text{PROD82}(t)]\},$$
$$\dots,$$
$$d\{\ell n[\text{WRCPNA}(t-11)] - \ell n[\text{PROD82}(t-11)]\},$$
$$\text{DON}(t),\text{DOFF}(t)\}$$

[a]WRCPNA, compensation per man-hour private nonfarm sector; NRUT, civilian unemployment rate; PDC, deflator, total consumption; PXPD, deflator, private domestic output; POTGNP, potential GNP; PROD82, output per man-hour private nonfarm sector; DON, DOFF, dummy variables for Nixon price controls; $d\ell n[x] = \log[x(t)] - \log[x(t-1)]$.

so the actual combination of PXPD and GNP82 for 1987.3 is the point on the AS corresponding to a zero shock to GNP82.

Likewise, the n-period AS curve is obtained by changing the level of GNP n periods prior to 1987.3 and maintaining that change in all periods until 1987.3. This allows lagged effects to impact on the price level in 1987.3. After performing these calculations, the elasticities of the price level PXPD with respect to an n-period change in GNP82 were calculated. In Table 4.7, the elasticities are reported in the form $\delta\ln$ GNP82/$\delta\ln$ PXPD to correspond with standard usage. Graphs of the 5-, 11-, and 35-period AS and AD curves are shown in Figures 4.6–4.8.

The first interesting result in Table 4.7 is the negative slope for the 0-period AS curve. As mentioned before, the increase in GNP82 produces a short-run rise in pro-

Table 4.7. Elasticities of n-Period Aggregate Supply and Aggregate Demand Curves: $d\ \ell n$ GNP82/$d\ \ell n$ PXPD

n	AS	AD
0	−18.00	0.00
5	4.72	−0.10
11	1.14	−0.26
23	0.58	−0.38
35	0.43	−0.40
$d\ \ell n[x] = \log[x(t)] - \log[x(t-1)]$		

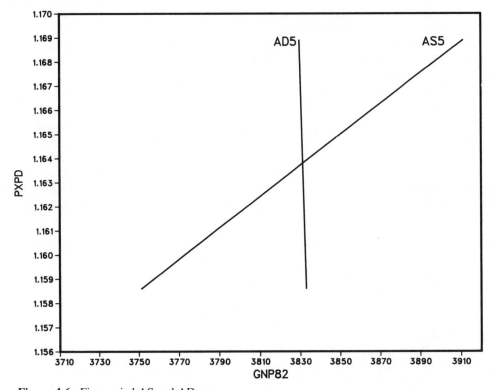

Figure 4.6. Five-period AS and AD curves.

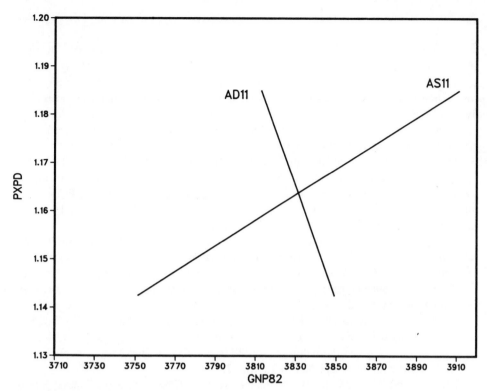

Figure 4.7. Eleven-period AS and AD curves.

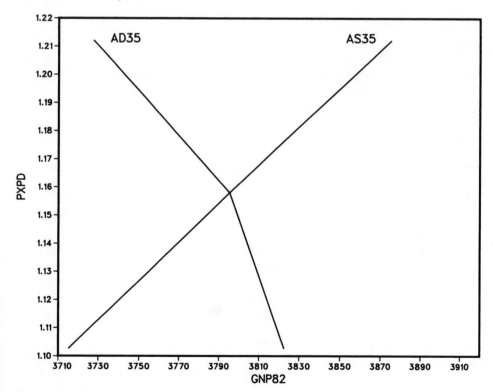

Figure 4.8. Thirty-five period AS and AD curves.

ductivity because hours and employment respond to the increase in output with a lag and the productivity increase lowers unit labor costs and reduces prices. Thus, for the 0-period AS curve, a rise in output leads to a decline in prices. By the 5-period AS curve, hours and employment have responded and the temporary increase in productivity has disappeared. The rise in employment leads to a reduction in the unemployment rate, tightens labor markets, and leads to an increase in prices. The increases in prices then produces a rise in wages with a lag.

The other interesting result with respect to the slope of the AS curve in Table 4.7 is that in the long run the AS curve becomes steeper. A given increase in output, sustained for longer and longer periods, leads to higher and higher prices. In the long run, the AS curve for the Indiana model appears to be approaching a classical vertical aggregate supply curve. However, the convergence is fairly slow.

The aggregate demand curve is estimated by exogenizing only the basic price variable, the deflator for private domestic output (PXPD). By simulating the model with different levels of PXPD, we allow aggregate demand to adjust to the new level of PXPD and trace out the aggregate demand curve. As with the other estimated curves the simulations start with a tracking solution. For the 0-period AD curve the value of PXPD is changed only in 1987.3 and the value of GNP82 calculated for 1987.3. For the n-period AD curve the change in PXPD is maintained for n periods prior to 1987 as well as for 1987.3 and the value of GNP82 is calculated. The elasticities for the n-period AD curve are also reported in Table 4.7.

The 0-period AD curve is approximately vertical. The elasticity of the n-period AD curve gradually increases with increasing n. It appears that the rate of change in the elasticity declines with increasing n and consequently in the long run the elasticity would not be much larger than for $n = 35$. However, in the absence of longer simulations we cannot be sure.

The negative slope of the AD curve comes from two sources. The first source works through interest rates. As the price level rises, nominal income and the demand for money increase, pushing up interest rates. The supply of money increases only slightly in the Indiana model as a result of the increase in interest rates. The increase in interest rates has a depressing effect, with a lag, on the demand for consumer durables and nonresidential and residential investment, and thus has a depressing effect on aggregate demand. However, the elasticities of the components of final demand to a change in interest rates appear small. Since the effects of interest rate changes on the components of final demand occur with a lag, it takes about 2 years for the full effects to be felt.

The second source of the negative slope of the n-period AD curve occurs through wealth effects. The increase in the price level reduces the real value of the money stock which is a component of wealth in the model. Real wealth affects consumer demand and so a reduction in real wealth depresses consumer spending and aggregate demand.

In this third section we derive IS and LM curves for the Michigan Quarterly Econometric Model of the U.S. Economy (MQEM). We then demonstrate how these IS and LM curves can be used to analyze and interpret the comparative static policy responses generated by the model. MQEM is maintained and operated by the Research Seminar in Quantitative Economics at the University of Michigan. The first version of the model was the now-classic Klein–Goldberger model, an annual model containing 20 equations. Today, MQEM contains 172 equations, 84 of which are stochastic, and is used to produce quarterly forecasts on a regular basis throughout the year. The forecasting operation based on MQEM has twice (1984 and 1987) received the national Theodore H. Silbert Award for economic forecasting.

The block structure of MQEM is summarized in Table 4.8. Block 1 (wages and prices) and block 2 (productivity and employment) together comprise the AS portion of the model. The core wage rate (private nonfarm hourly compensation) is modeled as a generalized Phillips curve with price expectations adaptively determined. The corresponding core price level is determined by a variable markup on standard unit labor cost, but depends additionally on crude materials prices and interest rates. Productivity growth depends on output growth in the short run, and on capital accumulation in the long run.

The AD sector of the model is represented in blocks 3–5 and can, as usual, be thought of in terms of IS and LM curves. The IS curve is derived from the blocks that explain expenditures and income flows (blocks 3 and 4, respectively); the LM curve derives from the monetary sector block.

Numerical simulation experiments have traditionally been used to study the properties of dynamic econometric models. For example, a simple fiscal policy experiment might involve a permanent increase in real government expenditure. To determine the impact of the government expenditure increase, the solution of the model corresponding to the higher government expenditure path would be compared with a baseline solution. The baseline solution is frequently the so-called perfect tracking solution in which the exogenous variables are set equal to their historical values and sample-period residuals are added to each of the stochastic equations of the model. The difference between the perturbed and baseline solution is often scaled by dividing by the expenditure increase to obtain a sequence of dynamic expenditure multipliers.

As an illustration of this approach, MQEM was used to generate a perfect tracking solution over the 10-year period ending in the first quarter of 1987 (1987.1). The path of real government defense purchases (GFD82) was then increased by $40 billion (1982 dollars) and the model was solved over the same 10-year period. Two alternative accompanying monetary policy regimes were selected for study. The first, referred to as Policy A, varied the discount rate and the monetary base in such a way as to hold the money supply and unborrowed reserves fixed at their historical values. The alternative policy, Policy B, held unborrowed reserves and the discount rate fixed and allowed the money supply and the monetary base to vary according to the equations of the model. For reasons that will become apparent subsequently, each of these monetary policy regimes was simulated with wage and price levels first held at their historical values and then with wages and prices allowed to vary endogenously as determined by the equations of the model.

The results of these simulation experiments are shown in Figure 4.9 for the 3-month treasury bill rate and real GNP. The interest rate trajectories shown in the top panel indicate that the interest rate is more responsive to the fiscal stimulus under monetary Policy A than under Policy B. In addition the interest rate increases more when wages and prices respond endogenously than when wages and prices are fixed exogenously. As shown in the second panel of Figure 4.9, the fiscal stimulus is more

Table 4.8. Block Structure of MQEM

Block	Principal Endogenous Variables	Block	Principal Endogenous Variables
1. Wages and prices	Compensation per hour	4. Income flows	Private wages and salaries
	Private nonfarm GNP deflator		Profits
	15 GNP component deflators		Interest income
	3 energy price deflators		Dividends
	Index of the exchange value of the dollar		Other labor income
	Automobile price index		Nonfarm proprietor income
			Farm proprietor income
			Government unemployment benefits
			Taxes
			Capital consumption allowances
			Interest on government debt
2. Productivity and employment	Output per hour	5. Monetary sector	M_1 plus total savings deposits
	Employment rate, males 20 and over		M_2 plus short-term treasury securities
	Aggregate unemployment rate		90 day treasury bill rate
			Budget identity
			Four term structure equations
			Monetary base
			Government demand deposits

3. Expenditures, purchases

Unit auto sales
  U.S. cars
  Imported cars
Consumption
  Autos, new
  Autos, net used and parts
  Furniture and household equipment
  Other durables
  Nondurables
  Services
Business fixed investment
  Structures
  Equipment
    Agriculture
    Production
    Autos
    Other
Residential building
  Housing starts
Inventory investment
  New autos
  Nonfarm, nonauto
Imports
  Petroleum
  Nonpetroleum
  Autos
Exports

6. Output composition

Services component of real GNP
Manufacturing index of industrial
  production
Index of available capacity in manufacturing
Gross auto product

3 Month Treasury Bill Rate

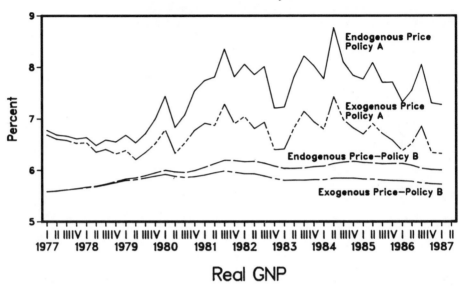

Real GNP

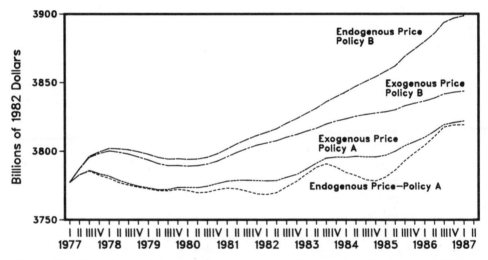

Figure 4.9. Dynamic simulation paths in response to an increase in real government defense spending.

expansionary under Policy B than under Policy A. Under Policy A the endogenous price response simulation is slightly less expansionary than the simulation with no price response. Under Policy B the opposite is true.

The standard textbook IS–LM analysis explains all but the last of these results quite simply. If the LM curve corresponding to Policy A is steeper than the LM curve for Policy B, a given shift in the IS curve with wages and prices fixed would be expected to lead to higher interest rates and lower real income with Policy A than with Policy

B. And this is precisely what is observed in the fixed-price simulation results. Any price increases generated by the expansionary fiscal policy would be expected to shift the LM curve upward, leading to a still higher interest rate and lower output compared to the fixed-price results. This impact on income and the interest rate would be reinforced by any real-balance effects that shift the IS curve downward. The simulation results under Policy A are precisely consistent with this explanation. With Policy B the interest rate behavior is consistent with this standard explanation but the real income response is not.

Such an attempt to use stylized IS–LM arguments to explain the qualitative aspects of the simulation results leads to two questions. First, do the IS and LM curves of MQEM have the standard textbook properties alluded to above? Second, how can the seemingly perverse income effect obtained under Policy B with flexible wages and prices be explained?

DERIVATION OF AN LM CURVE FOR MQEM

The LM curve represents the locus of income and interest rate combinations which equate the demand for money with the supply of money. In order to derive the LM curve implied by MQEM, the monetary sector is separated from the rest of the model. The five equations shown in symbolic form in Table 4.9 constitute the core of the monetary sector of MQEM. They show that the demand for broadly defined money (M) depends on a long-term interest rate (RG5), nominal GNP, and the change in government debt (GDEBTP). The supply of money depends on a short-term interest rate (RTB), the discount rate (RDIS), the monetary base (MBASE), and the change in government debt. The change in unborrowed reserves (FDCUR) depends on the change in the monetary base and the differential between the short-term interest rate and the discount rate. The last two equations determine the differential between long-term (RAAA and RG5) and short-term interest rates, allowing for different inflation (PPNF%) premia in long- and short-term interest rates.

The LM curve can be obtained by solving these core equations for the interest rates corresponding to alternative values of real GNP (GNP82), holding the price level and the level of government debt fixed and using either Policy A or Policy B, as defined above, for setting the monetary policy instruments.

The monetary sector of MQEM contains lagged values of endogenous (monetary-sector) variables to reflect the fact that the adjustment process is not instantaneous.

Table 4.9. The Core of the Monetary Sector of MQEM

Equation	Form[a]
Money demand	$M = f_1(\mathbf{RG5}, \text{GNP}, \Delta\text{GDEBTP})$
Money supply	$M = f_2(\mathbf{RTB}, \text{RDIS}, \text{MBASE}, \Delta\text{GDEBTP})$
Unborrowed reserves	$\mathbf{FDCUR} = f_3[\Delta\text{MBASE}, \Delta(\mathbf{RTB} - \text{RDIS})]$
Term structure	$\mathbf{RG5} = f_4(\mathbf{RTB}, \mathbf{RAAA})$
Term structure	$\mathbf{RAAA} = f_5(\mathbf{RTB}, \text{PPNF\%})$

[a]Endogenous variables are in bold type. GNP, GDEBTP, and PPNF% are endogenous in MQEM but are taken to be exogenous to the monetary sector. RDIS and MBASE are policy instruments.

This leads to a distinction between short-run and long-run equilibria in the money market. Obtaining the short-run LM curve is a straightforward exercise of perturbing real GNP and solving for the values of the interest rates, which equate the demand for money with the supply of money, holding all the exogenous and lagged endogenous variables at their predetermined (historical) values.

There are two alternative approaches to the determination of a long-run LM curve. The first involves solving analytically for the relationship between income and the interest rate implied by the "steady-state" form of the core money sector model in which all lagged endogenous variables are set equal to their current values. This approach ignores the dynamic adjustment process inherent in the model and is, at best, impractical for large nonlinear econometric models. A more tractable procedure for obtaining a long-run LM curve involves dynamic simulation of the model over successively longer time horizons. As the time horizon of the simulation increases, the solution converges to a point on the long-run LM curve, provided the model is stable. In this analysis we have computed LM curves corresponding to the response of the short-term interest rate to a maintained perturbation in the path of real GNP after 0, 2, 4, 8, 16, 32, and 40 quarters. Each simulation ends on the same date and all exogenous variables other than real GNP are held at historical levels. In addition, a perfect tracking solution was used so that the LM curve is centered on the observed values of incomes and interest rate at the end of the simulation period.

The LM curves computed for the first quarter of 1987 are presented in the two panels of Figure 4.10. For both policies, stability is achieved after just 16 quarters as

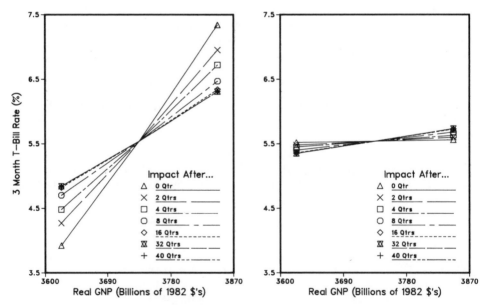

Figure 4.10. Dynamic LM curves. Left: monetary Policy A: unborrowed reserves and money supply held constant. Right: monetary Policy B: unborrowed reserves and discount rate held constant.

Table 4.10. LM Curve Semielasticities $\left(\dfrac{\Delta RTB}{\Delta \ell n\ GNP82}\right)$

Impact After (Quarters)	Monetary Policy	
	A	B
0	57.00	0.57
2	44.72	1.95
4	37.37	3.13
8	29.48	4.78
16	25.33	6.17
32	24.65	6.43
40	24.65	6.43

the LM curves for simulations over 32 and 40 quarters virtually coincide with the 16 quarter LM curve. The most striking feature of this figure is the much flatter LM curve that is obtained under Policy B when unborrowed reserves and the discount rate are held constant and the money supply is allowed to respond to changes in real GNP and the interest rate. Table 4.10 presents semielasticities, measured as the number of basis points change in RTB per percentage point change in GNP82, calculated from the different simulations for the two monetary policies. Under Policy A, with the money supply held constant, in the short run a one percent increase in real GNP is accompanied by a 57 basis point increase in the treasury bill rate. On the other hand, when the money supply is allowed to vary (Policy B) almost no change in the interest rate is required to maintain short-run equilibrium in the money market ($\Delta RTB/\Delta \ln\ GNP82 = 0.57$). Thus, MQEM has a very interest elastic short-run money supply equation, which leads to a very flat short-run LM curve when the money supply is allowed to respond to changes in the interest rate.

As a result of the dynamic adjustment mechanisms inherent in the monetary sector, Figure 4.10 and Table 4.10 show that the LM curve becomes flatter in the long run under a Policy A-type regime. Under Policy B, allowing the money supply to vary leads to an LM curve, which is steeper in the long run than in the short run. Note, however, that the LM curve for Policy A remains steeper in the long run than that for Policy B.

DERIVATION OF AN IS CURVE FOR MQEM

The IS curve is the locus of income and interest rate combinations that equilibrate the market for goods and services. The traditional textbook IS curve is typically obtained with wages and prices taken as given. Thus, almost by definition, an IS curve can be obtained from the equations of MQEM that remain after deleting the wage, price, and money demand and supply equations while retaining the equations for the term structure of interest rates. After these equations are removed from the model, the short-term interest rate is treated as an exogenous variable and wages and prices are set equal to predetermined (historical) values. The solution of this system of equations for the

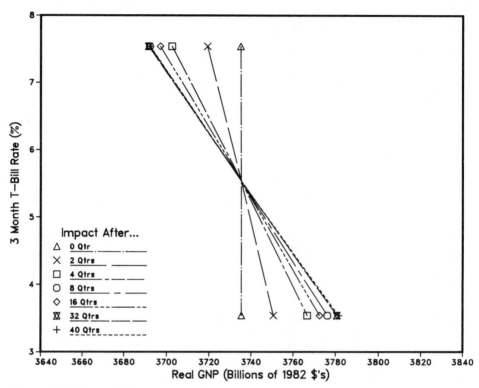

Figure 4.11. Dynamic IS curves.

Table 4.11. IS Curve Semielasticities

Impact After (Quarters)	$\dfrac{\Delta RTB}{\Delta \ell n\ GNP82}$
0	∞
2	475.0
4	232.2
8	177.1
16	197.6
32	167.4
40	167.3

value of real GNP corresponding to alternative values of the short-term interest rate yields the desired IS curve for the model.

As in the case of the LM curves, successive dynamic simulations of 0, 2, 4, 8, 16, 32, and 40 quarters, all ending in 1987.1, were computed to distinguish between short-run and long-run IS curves. The results of these experiments are shown graphically in Figure 4.11 while Table 4.11 presents the semielasticities corresponding to each of the curves. The most striking feature of these plots is that the instantaneous IS curve is vertical. Thus, a change in the interest rate yields no immediate change in real GNP. This is because in MQEM, the initial drop in investment-type expenditures associated with an increase in interest rates happens to be offset by the increase in consumption resulting from the higher personal interest income, which derives from the same increase in interest rates. The fact that the (impact) IS curve is vertical has important implications for the role of monetary policy in MQEM—changes in monetary policy that shift the LM curve will have no immediate effect on real output. As the forecast horizon lengthens, the IS curves become more elastic and the dynamic adjustment process appears to be essentially complete after 32 quarters.

COMPARATIVE STATIC ANALYSIS

An attractive feature of the IS–LM framework is that it can be used to perform qualitative comparative statics analyses in which the economic model is shocked in such a way so as to induce a shift in either the IS or LM curve (or both) and the resulting equilibrium is then determined. This section describes a single experiment in which the time path of real government defense purchases is increased by $40 billion (1982 dollars) to show how the IS and LM curves of MQEM can be used to interpret the results.

In the absence of any feedbacks between the monetary sector and the rest of the model, this experiment simply involves a shift in the IS curve.[2] Therefore we can compute the same set of the IS curves as those presented above but now holding real government spending at a higher level relative to its historical, or baseline, path throughout the simulation period. The results are shown in Figure 4.12. As the simulation horizon is increased so that the shock persists over a longer period of time, the IS curve not only changes slope but shifts outward. The immediate impact of such a shock is to shift the IS curve to the right by $40 billion in real terms as shown by IS'_0. Nonlinearities in the model prevent the shift from being absolutely parallel, but it is nearly so. A simple Keynesian-type multiplier, $\Delta GNP82/\Delta GFD82$, with interest rates held constant, can be computed to evaluate the "steady-state" impact of a shift in the (long-run) IS curve. Holding wages and prices at their historical levels, this multiplier is equal to 2.7 after 40 quarters.

To complete the comparative static analysis, the new equilibrium that results from the shock to government spending must be determined. Four different cases will be considered corresponding to the two alternative monetary policy rules and to two different assumptions about prices and wages. In the first instance we continue to assume that prices and wages are fixed. We then allow prices and wages to vary according to the equations of the model, and show how the price and wage changes shift the IS and LM curves. The results are shown in the four graphs of Figure 4.13.

Figure 4.13a depicts the result of the increase in defense spending with the fixed money supply of monetary Policy A and with the price level given. As a result of the shift in the IS curve from IS_0 to IS'_0, the new instantaneous equilibrium is given by the intersection of the IS'_0 and the LM_0 curves, which corresponds to a level of real GNP equal to $3777 billion and a 3-month treasury bill rate (RTB) of 6.2%. After 40 quarters, the equilibrium values are given by the intersection of the IS'_{40} and LM'_{40} curves, which occurs at the point where real GNP equals $3830 billion and RTB equals 6.2%. The reason LM'_{40} differs from LM_{40} is that LM_{40} was obtained holding the

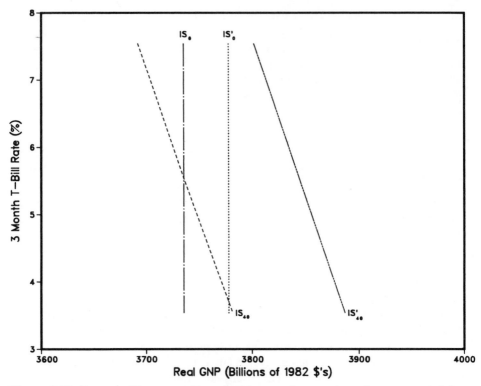

Figure 4.12. Dynamic IS curves with and without an increase in real government defense spending.

government debt constant. As a result of the hypothetical increase in defense spending, the government debt would increase, according to the model, and the LM curve shifts very slightly from LM_{40} to LM'_{40} as a result of this increase in the government debt.

The solid curve in Figure 4.13a traces the actual response of output and the interest rate to the shift in government spending implied by the fixed-price version of the model.[3] The instantaneous response to the increase in government spending results in a level of real GNP equal to $3777 billion and RTB equal to 6.7%. The reason that the interest rate is higher than predicted by the intersection of the IS'_0 and LM_0 curves is that the increase in government spending generates an increase in the federal deficit, which has an immediate impact on the short-term interest rate that is not captured in LM_0 since LM_0 is drawn for a fixed government deficit. After 40 quarters, the solution values are $3822 billion for real GNP and 6.3% for RTB, which are quite close to the intersection of the IS'_{40} and LM'_{40} curves.

Figure 4.13b shows the fixed-price level response to an increase in government spending when monetary Policy B is in effect. The actual simulation path originates and terminates very close to the corresponding intersections of the IS and LM curves. In addition, the transition path is much smoother for Policy B than for Policy A.

The results depicted in Figure 4.13a and b were obtained with prices and wages held constant at their historical values. This counterfactual experiment with the model

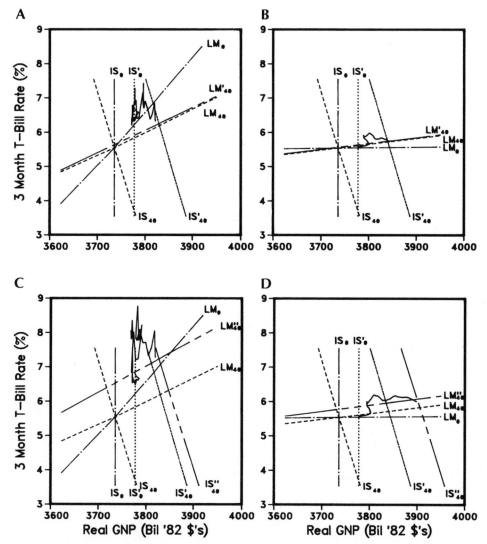

Figure 4.13. IS–LM comparative statics analyses. Exogenous prices: (a) monetary Policy A; (b) monetary Policy B. Endogenous prices: (c) monetary Policy A; (d) monetary Policy B.

is a useful first approximation, but does not capture the complete model response to an increase in government spending. As a result of the exogenous expenditure increase, output and employment increase, thus reducing the unemployment rate and putting upward pressure on wages and prices. The increase in wages and prices shifts the IS and LM curves and this needs to be taken into account as discussed in the theoretical analysis in the first section of this chapter.

To characterize the full-model results, the impact of the wage and price changes on the IS_{40} and LM_{40} curves must be determined. To do this, a 40 quarter simulation of the complete model (with wages and prices endogenous) was performed. The trajectory of this response to the increase in real defense spending is illustrated by the solid curve in Figure 4.13c and d. This simulation produced the higher wage and price paths, which the model predicts would accompany an increase in real government expenditure. IS and LM curves that reflect the higher simulated wage and price paths were then obtained by solving the IS and LM subsystems with the historical wage and price paths replaced by the simulated paths.

The results are shown as IS''_{40} and LM''_{40} in Figure 4.13c and d. The position of the LM''_{40} curve relative to LM_{40} reflects the higher price level as well as the change in government debt that accompanies the expenditure increase, but the price effect dominates and shifts the LM curve in the expected direction. The higher wage and price levels shift the IS curve to the right relative to IS'_{40}—thus adding to the initial expansionary impulse. The reason for this is that wages react more quickly than prices to the increase in expenditure so that the real wage rises. The increase in both the real wage and employment produces an increase in labor income, which translates into an increase in consumption expenditure and an outward shift in the IS curve. This income effect outweighs any real balance effects in the model which would shift the IS curve in the opposite direction. The important point to notice is that once again the terminal values of the 40 quarter simulation of the complete model are quite closely approximated by the intersection of the IS''_{40} and LM''_{40} curves.

A comparison of the results shown in Figure 4.13c and d indicates that the endogenous wage and price movements reduce real GNP under Policy A but increase real GNP under Policy B. With Policy A, the upward shift of the LM curve more than offsets the outward shift of the IS curve so that income falls relative to the IS'_{40}–LM_{40} intersection point.

The quantitative difference in the shifts of the LM curves in the two cases has a fairly simple explanation. The endogenous money supply of Policy B results in a flatter LM curve and also reduces the amount by which the LM curve shifts in response to a given change in the price level.[4] Thus, even though the price level increase is greater with Policy B than with Policy A, the LM curve shifts considerably more with Policy A than with Policy B.

The difference in the amounts by which the IS curves shift in the two cases is primarily a consequence of the relative magnitudes of the wage and price increases. Wages and prices both increase more under Policy B than under Policy A. A larger *real* wage increase under Policy B, however, generates a larger increase in labor income and hence a larger outward shift in the IS curve than under Policy A. This results from the fact that the smaller rise in interest rates under Policy B reduces inflationary pressure so that prices lag further behind wages in the Policy B scenario. An additional, but relatively minor shift in the IS curve occurs under Policy B as a result of an increase in interest income, which is absent when the money supply is held fixed as in Policy A.

SUMMARY

These experiments with the Michigan Quarterly Econometric Model of the U.S. Economy indicate that IS and LM curves can readily be derived from model simulations, and that these curves can be used to examine and explain the comparative static properties of the model. Although the structure of MQEM is too complicated to satisfy the strict decomposability condition of simple textbook models, the simulation results indicate that the feedback between the IS and LM curves through intermediate endogenous variables is sufficiently weak that the IS–LM decomposition is still informative.

The short-run IS curve for MQEM is nearly vertical. This means that, in the very short run, monetary policy has no effect on real output. The long-run IS curve, assuming constant wages and prices, indicates that a 167 basis point decrease in the short-term treasury bill rate generates a 1% increase in real GNP. The slope of the LM curve depends on the monetary policy imposed on the model. Assuming a fixed money supply (Policy A), the short-run LM curve semielasticity is 57 basis points and decreases to 25 basis points in the long run. Assuming instead that the level of unborrowed reserves is held constant (Policy B), the short-run LM curve is nearly horizontal (ΔRTB/Δln GNP82 $= 0.57$) and semielasticity increases to 6.4 in the long run. In short, MQEM is characterized by a relatively steep IS curve and a relatively flat LM curve regardless of whether the monetary authority follows Policy A or B. This indicates that any crowding out of increases in government expenditures that takes place in MQEM is due primarily to price level effects and not interest rate effects. Similarly, the predominant short-run effect of a change in any exogenous variable that shifts the LM curve is a change in the interest rate with little or no change in real income.

When wages and prices are allowed to vary in response to an autonomous expenditure increase, the LM curve shifts in the usual textbook fashion: a higher price level reduces the real stock of money, which increases the intercept of the LM curve. In addition, the fiscal stimulus tightens the labor market and generates higher wage rates before prices begin to respond, so that real wage rates rise. Higher real wages shift the IS curve outward and this accentuates the initial expansionary impact of the increase in autonomous expenditure. In other words, an autonomous expenditure increase has an effect that is analytically similar to a positive real-wage shock.

The interpretation of the IS and LM curves obtained from dynamic simulation as long-run, equilibrium curves hinges on the assumption that MQEM is a stable model of the U.S. economy. One obvious area for further research is to attempt to verify this assumption, possibly by calculating the characteristic roots of an appropriate linear approximation to MQEM.[5] Another important issue involves the question of the statistical precision with which IS and LM curves can be computed for a large econometric model. Thus, further work in this area might focus on the construction of confidence bands about the IS and LM curves, which take account of the uncertainty due to the disturbances and the sampling variability of the coefficients of the model.

CONCLUDING REMARKS

This chapter has demonstrated the methodology for estimating some core relationships of macroeconometric models by simulation techniques. These core relationships are defined as the implicit IS, LM, AD, and AS locuses of a model, and hence represent a reduction of large systems to two diagrams and three endogenous variables. The approach is illuminating because real income, the price level, and the interest rate are major concerns of economic policy and because most operational models are elaborations of the elementary Keynesian ISLM model on the aggregate demand side and incorporate aggregate supply structures derived from a labor-market Phillips curve for wage determination and a markup hypothesis of price setting in imperfectly competitive markets.

On the most general level, the credibility of an empirical model is dependent on a showing that its major features are consistent with mainline theory, and the latter is usually formulated in the ISLM terms for the analysis of stabilization policy and in ADAS terms for the analysis of the macroeconomic effects of supply shocks. One sometimes hears the complaint that econometric models are black boxes and that their structures cannot be comprehended or their properties understood because of their large and intricate nature. It is accordingly appropriate to analyze the basic properties even of elaborate systems in these highly simplified and aggregative terms as a first step in model verification.

It is well known that establishing the elasticity of the IS and LM curves provides basic information about the predicted outcome of fiscal and monetary policies in a given model, with the combination of inelastic LM and elastic IS implying fiscal crowding out and potent monetary policy, whereas elastic LM and inelastic IS lead to potent fiscal and weak monetary effects. Estimation of these locuses therefore provides a useful diagnostic tool for characterizing these policy responses in a given model, and it may direct attention to particular equations or parameters in one or the other sector in need of further examination and testing.

The dominant structural specification in macroeconometric models embodies sticky wage and price adjustments to shocks. Broadly speaking, the models equilibrate more through induced changes in the absolute wage–price level, with associated Keynes and Pigou effects on aggregate demand, than by a neoclassical process of real-wage adjustment. This means that the equilibrating properties and response patterns of a model are strongly influenced by the elasticity of its AS curve in the short and long runs. Deeper investigation of the determinants of the AS elasticity will require analysis of the equations determining factor demands and supplies, productivity behavior, and wage and price setting.

Measurement of the implicit core elasticities can be a useful diagnostic tool for a particular model, but the technique may have a comparative advantage in comparing models, when it may be able to pinpoint key differences in structural specifications or coefficients as causes of observed differences in response patterns and multipliers.

Ideally such comparisons should be based on carefully standardized partial simulations to isolate the *ceteris paribus* elasticities. One could go further in comparing the IS and LM and AD and AS curves across models, by not only comparing the slopes of the overall curves but also by measuring the extent to which each curve shifts in response to a change in selected exogenous variables. For example, the strength of the monetary policy channel operating from interest rates to residential construction to aggregate demand could be estimated by exogenizing residential construction and determining the resulting change in the IS curve. A set of such exercises might provide a useful framework for comparing the properties of several models.

In the absence of such partial simulations, standardized complete-model simulations may be used to provide biased estimates of the slopes of the underlying unshifted locuses. In the case of the HC Model, the results in Table 4.2 indicate that the biases in the *mutatis mutandis* estimates are rather small. Other models may be less decom-

posable, however, leading to larger biases from imposing the ISLM and ADAS paradigm in interpreting the complete-model reduced-form predictions.

One technique to discover the degree of interdependence of the various locuses in
a given model is to undertake a comparison along the lines of Table 4.2. Large discrepancies in the estimates of the elasticity of a given locus by the different approaches
is evidence of substantial interdependences among the locuses. This evidence is itself
important information about the model structure, however. Partial simulations may
measure the *ceteris paribus* elasticities with greater precision, but if the interdependences among the locuses are neglected, misleading inferences may be drawn about
the response patterns of the model as a whole.

NOTES

1. Since the AD locus is a semireduced form of the IS–LM model relating P and Y endogenously, it might be thought that AD should not shift when prices rise under a demand shock.
   This is true insofar as the real wage does not change as the price level varies, for in that case
   all of the change in spending will be attributable to induced changes in the real values of the
   money stock and household wealth along a fixed AD locus. Whenever *relative* prices change,
   however, and whether they do so endogenously or exogenously, the AD schedule will shift.
   Induced shifts of the AD locus owing to induced changes in the real exchange rate provide
   another important example in the open economy case (Hickman, 1988).
2. There are, in fact, two indirect feedbacks in MQEM that were ignored in deriving the IS and
   LM curves presented here. The first exists between the money supply and personal interest
   income and the second captures the effect that the level of the federal government budget
   surplus has on the money supply through changes in the government debt held by the public
   (see Table 4.9).
3. The trajectory of this response was computed by imposing the shock on real government
   defense expenditures throughout the simulation period of 1977.1 through 1987.1 and then
   performing a dynamic simulation using the fixed-price version of MQEM. The resulting
   deviations between historical and predicted values for both real GNP and RTB were then
   added to the actual values beginning in 1987.1 to yield a dynamic path that corresponds to
   the IS and LM curves.
4. Suppose that the money demand and money supply curves are given by

$$m^d = \alpha_0 + \alpha_1 y + \alpha_2 p - \alpha_3 r$$

and

$$m^s = \beta_0 + \beta_1 r$$

so that the LM curve is

$$r = \lambda_0 + \lambda_1 y + \lambda_2 p$$

where

$$\lambda_0 = \frac{\alpha_0 - \beta_0}{\beta_1 + \alpha_3}$$

$$\lambda_1 = \frac{\alpha_1}{\beta_1 + \alpha_3}$$

$$\lambda_2 = \frac{\alpha_2}{\beta_1 + \alpha_3}$$

With an exogenous money supply, as in Policy A, $\beta_1 = 0$. With an endogenous money supply, as in Policy B, $\beta_1 > 0$ and the LM curve is flatter $\left(\dfrac{\alpha_1}{\beta_1 + \alpha_3} < \dfrac{\alpha_1}{\alpha_3} \right)$ and less responsive to price changes $\left(\dfrac{\alpha_2}{\beta_1 + \alpha_3} < \dfrac{\alpha_2}{\alpha_3} \right)$ than is the case with an exogenous money supply.

5. Kuh, Neese, and Hollinger (1985) calculated the characteristic roots of a linear approximation to an earlier (1982) version of MQEM and found 22 roots greater than one. Whether this indicates that the model is unstable is problematic, however, because of the way the model was linearized. To illustrate the potential difficulty, consider the log-linear model

$$\ln y_t = \beta \ln y_{t-1} + x_t$$

The corresponding linear approximation is

$$\frac{1}{y_t} dy_t = \left(\frac{\beta}{y_{t-1}} \right) dy_{t-1} + dx_t$$

$$dy_t = \left(\frac{\beta y_t}{y_{t-1}} \right) dy_{t-1} + y_t \, dx_t$$

The characteristic root of this equation is $\lambda_t = \dfrac{\beta y_t}{y_{t-1}}$. If x_t is a trending variable so that y_t is also a trending variable, λ_t may exceed unity even though β is less than unity. Thus, the linear approximation to a stable log-linear equation may appear to be unstable.

REFERENCES

Coen, Robert M., and Bert G. Hickman. (1987). "Keynesian and Classical Unemployment in Four Countries." *Brookings Papers on Economic Activity* 1, 123–193.

Deleau, Michel, Pierre Malgrange, and Pierre-Alain Muet. (1984). "A Study of Short-Run and Long-Run Properties of Macroeconometric Dynamic Models by Means of an Aggregative Core Model." In *Contemporary Macroeconomic Modelling,* Pierre Malgrange and Pierre-Alain Muet, eds., Chapter 9. Oxford: Basil Blackwell.

EMUS Quarterly Econometric Model Equation Book. (1987). Center for Econometric Research, Indiana University.

Fair, Ray C. (1984). *Specification, Estimation, and Analysis of Macroeconometric Models.* Cambridge: Harvard University Press.

Hickman, Bert G. (1987). "Macroeconomic Impacts of Energy Shocks and Policy Responses: A Structural Comparison of Fourteen Models." In *Macroeconomic Impacts of Energy Shocks,* B. G. Hickman, H. G. Huntington, and J. L. Sweeney, (eds.). Amsterdam: North-Holland.

Hickman, Bert G. (1988). "The U.S. Economy and the International Transmission Mechanism." In *Empirical Macroeconomics for Interdependent Economies,* Ralph C. Bryant, Dale W. Henderson, Gerald Holtham, Peter Hooper, and Steven A. Symansky, eds., pp. 92–130. Washington, D.C.: Brookings Institution.

Hickman, Bert G., and Robert M. Coen. (1976). *An Annual Growth Model of the U.S. Economy.* Contributions to Economic Analysis 100. Amsterdam: North-Holland.

Klein, L. R., A. Doud, and E. Sojo. (1985). "Simplification of Large Scale Macroeconomic Models." *Eastern Economic Journal* xi, 28–40.

Kuh, Edwin, John W. Neese, and Peter Hollinger. (1985). *Structural Sensitivity in Econometric Models.* New York: Wiley.

CHAPTER 5

A Comparative Analysis of the DRI and BEA Models

ROGER E. BRINNER and ALBERT A. HIRSCH

Chapter 2 presented comparative multipliers for 10 models calculated over the decade 1975–1984 using apparently common sets of changes in exogenous inputs. As in previous exercises, the spans of outcomes among the models for such aggregates as real GNP and the GNP implicit price deflator are distressingly large, both in terms of the amplitudes of the multipliers and their time profiles. Although there is some tendency toward clustering, the persistence of such sharp differences is disturbing, particularly insofar as models share a common theoretical basis. Such an outcome tends to breed exaggerated cynicism among economists and noneconomists alike: if the methods of economic science cannot extract common empirical findings in an apparently controlled experiment, then how much science is really involved? The proper answer is that considerable science is employed; indeed, the differences are analogous to the ambiguity of empirical results from natural sciences where the opportunities for experimental controls are limited.

Two main categories of causes underlying the intermodel differences in outcomes can be identified. First, there is the familiar fact that single-equation specifications for the same endogenous variable differ across models, and the associated unpleasant truth that available statistical methodology all too often fails to offer strong tests for selecting among competing behavioral hypotheses. Even subtle variations in the specification of, say, a household automobile demand equation, not to mention variations in the estimation period, can yield substantial differences in response characteristics that may be magnified over long simulation spans. This problem is often exacerbated in economists' time-series regressions by multicollinearity, that is, high correlations among cyclical explanatory phenomena such as income, wealth, inflation, and credit conditions. Such difficulties are, in fact, common to most empirical sciences. For example, medical researchers are apt to be frustrated in cross-section regressions by high correlations among dietary choice, exercise, location, and age—the principal non-pharmaceutical explanatory factors in the analysis of the incidence of particular diseases. Second, some models treated important macroeconomic variables as exogenous for the multiplier experiments; others treated them as fully or partly endogenous. Examples include the dollar exchange rate, the macrovariables of the trading partner economies (production, prices, and interest rates), the rigidity of the Federal budget in real or nominal terms, and state–local government expenditures and tax rates. This source of differences did turn out to be quite important. There is once again a parallel

Table 5.1. Principal Sources of Contrasting Results

	Underlying Model Specifications	
Comparative Responses	DRI	BEA
Differences due Mainly to Differences in Specifications		
1. Larger interest rate responses to fiscal and monetary shocks for DRI	Standard equations used in shocks and forecasting. Normal interest elasticities of money demand. Disposable income, rather than GNP, used in M_2 component equations	Inverted money demand (M_2) equation (optionally used in these simulations with money stock controlled) has high interest elasticity
2. Larger responses of unemployment to given (sustained) shift in real GNP for BEA	"Okun's Law" approach to forecasting unemployment implies significant cyclical productivity variation	Unemployment determined by separate equations for labor force and employment (including establishment-basis to household-basis employment bridge)
3. Greater long-run wage and price response to output for DRI, although muted by cyclical productivity model	Strong price sensitivity to demand pressure; near 100% pass-through of wages to prices and vice versa gives essentially vertical long-run Phillips curve	Larger unemployment response (together with only transitory productivity response—see B3) dominates flatter Phillips curve
4. Larger decline in consumer spending in response to higher prices for BEA	Near neutrality of personal saving rate with respect to inflation. Full indexation available at user discretion	Substantial attitudinal responses and "Pigou effects" with respect to inflation
4. Greater cyclicality in BEA's real GNP multiplier	Accelerator factors not found to be as important as incomes	Strong accelerator responses of both business fixed investment and consumer durables spending

126

Differences due Mainly to Difference in Exogeneity

1. Real net exports fall in response to interest rate rises only for DRI and fall significantly in response to price rises only for BEA	Exchange rate endogenous (responds to domestic/foreign interest rate and inflation differentials); foreign interest rates, incomes, and prices react to U.S. economy according to historically estimated simulation rules	Exchange rate and foreign activity (prices, income, and interest rates) exogenous
2. Real Federal government purchases decline under stimulus for BEA, but not for DRI; real state and local purchases increase for DRI, but not for BEA	Federal spending can be exogenized in real or in nominal terms to fit exercise requirements. State/local purchases and taxes modeled behaviorally	Federal purchases set exogenously in current dollars; thus, higher prices force lower real spending. State/local purchases set exogenously in constant dollars
3. Sustained productivity increase occurs in response to sustained higher output for DRI, but not for BEA	Long-run microeconomic consistency emphasized by DRI. Production function guides labor productivity; net investment tied to utilization rates	Long-run productivity trend, which influences short-run employment and average work week, is exogenous; hence, no capital stock feedback
4. Overall interest elasticity of real demand greater for BEA	Freely estimated coefficients for cost of funds, changes in output and cash flow estimated for all capital spending categories. Vacancy rate feedback estimated for housing	Strong interest sensitivity of residential investment dominates BEA's overall interest rate effects; vacancy rate (affects only multifamily structures) exogenous

to medical science: different cancer therapy studies, for example, may try to isolate the impact of a particular chemical, but the control groups are not comparable; hence therapy effectiveness estimates will vary substantially.

The discussion of intermodel differences presented in Chapter 2 was largely descriptive, not analytical. In Chapter 4, the analysis was carried a step further by relating differences in multipliers for real GNP to differences in Hicksian "IS–LM" reductions of the models' demand relationships. This chapter seeks to deepen the analysis by relating differences in selected multipliers of two models—the DRI/McGraw-Hill (DRI) and the Bureau of Economic Analysis (BEA) models—to underlying structural differences. Because of the large size and the complexity of the models, this cannot be accomplished in anything like an exhaustive sense. Rather we try to identify the major sources of differences by using fairly powerful analytical shortcuts.

The DRI and BEA models can both be characterized as "mainstream" models in that they are augmented Keynesian systems; thus they do not display the most extreme intermodel differences in fiscal and monetary policy multipliers. However, differences are substantial and stimulate investigation of their causes. Although the restriction of this in-depth comparison to two models was a practical necessity, we hope that it has heuristic value by at least indicating where sensitive modeling decisions may occur in other models. Table 5.1 summarizes the major analytical findings, categorized by (1) differences in outcomes that are mainly attributable to differences in model specification and/or critical parameters and (2) differences that are mainly attributable to differences in endogenous versus exogenous treatment.

To some extent, these sources of differences—especially those in the second category—are traceable to somewhat different modeling philosophies of the two modeling groups. In particular, although both groups use the respective models for both forecasting and policy analysis, BEA tends to limit its policy analysis horizon to 2–3 years, and, accordingly, to be somewhat less concerned about fulfilling theoretical long-run properties insofar as this is believed by BEA to conflict with short-term predictability. DRI model managers do not believe there is a trade-off: better long-run properties are believed to enhance forecasting performance in the short run as well. Moreover, the BEA group has traditionally relied on the expert judgment of sector specialists outside the modeling group to project important variables that can plausibly be treated as essentially—or, at least substantially—exogenous, such as the dollar exchange rate, foreign production and prices, and (nominal and real) government expenditures. The DRI group uses such experts for baseline forecasts, but prefers automatic, endogenous adjustment of such elements during the development of alternative scenarios (including these multiplier experiments).[1]

STUDY FORMAT: DISSECTION OF TWO MODELS
WITH A COMMON THEORETICAL FOUNDATION

The analytical approach used to understand the sources of multiplier differences has several aspects: (1) the decomposition of multipliers into partial multipliers obtained through "partial" simulations, that is, repeated simulations of the multiplier experiments with key equations or blocks of equations suppressed and the dependent variables of these equations frozen at baseline or alternative levels; (2) the decomposition of real GNP multipliers into major final demand components or categories (e.g., the aggregates of "interest-sensitive" or "acceleration-sensitive" components); and (3) resort to direct knowledge of each model's structure and specific equations or parameters. The partial simulations serve to isolate the broad categorical sources of differences, whereas disaggregation and investigation of individual equations or parameters pinpoint more specific causes. Closely related investigative tools are (1) the simulation of small subblocks of equations to determine certain gross response characteristics for the aggregated group of equations, and (2) simulations that use selected endogenous responses of one model as predetermined inputs for the other.

We confine the study to the first 5 years (1975–1979) results for two reasons. First, this period is sufficient for each model to reveal a full cyclical response to a fiscal or monetary shock. Second, anomalies that occur in longer term multipliers may reflect the implausible maintenance of the commonly imposed controls within the context of one or both models.

We shall analyze only the differences for the fiscal and monetary shock experiments; the alternative suppression and inclusion of the price–wage blocks (one of the partial simulation mechanisms) reveals most of the information that would be provided by the separate analysis of, say, the oil price shock.[2] Moreover, we shall concentrate on one variant of the fiscal shock from Chapter 2—Simulation IA—and one variant of the monetary shock—Simulation IIA. Simulation IA, it will be recalled, involves a controlled increase in national defense purchases in the face of a fixed money supply. Simulation IIA involves a controlled increase in the money supply.

In the case of the fiscal shock, our investigation of multiplier path differences focuses on four sets of response components: (1) the core real demand or "multiplier–accelerator" mechanism; (2) the price–wage response to the higher level of demand induced by the fiscal stimulus, and the price feedback to demand; (3) the "crowding-out" effect of higher interest rates occasioned by the fiscal stimulus in the face of a fixed money supply; and (4) the response, mainly to higher interest rates, of the exchange rate in the DRI simulation and its system repercussions. A sequence of three partial simulations was used to isolate these four response classes.

In the case of the monetary shock, the analysis is divided into two sections. The first explores the interest rate profiles required to stimulate the hypothesized increase in money demand. The second explores the reactions within both models to a given interest rate shift.

FISCAL SHOCK SIMULATIONS

Overview

In Simulation IA, real (noncompensation) defense purchases are increased over baseline solution levels by 1% of real (baseline) GNP and the money stock is fixed at baseline levels. Because of differences in model structure, there are differences in the way both assumptions were implemented in the two models. First, in the DRI simulations, the increments to Federal purchases were implemented in real terms as prescribed. Because Federal purchases are exogenous in current dollars in the BEA model, in that model current-dollar defense purchases were modified instead: the change was calculated as the prescribed increase in real purchases multiplied by the baseline level of the noncompensation defense purchases implicit price deflator. Thus, as the defense purchases deflator rises in response to the fiscal shock, the realized real increase becomes smaller with the BEA model.

Second, the models were managed differently to keep money demand or supply unchanged during the fiscal experiment. In the DRI simulation, the M_1 money stock was held at baseline levels by searching for the path of nonborrowed bank reserves that would endogenously produce the baseline time path of M_1. This largely involved restricting reserves to raise interest rates and thus offset the higher money transaction demand initially produced by the fiscal stimulus. In the BEA model, M_2 is the exogenous money supply entering directly into the key short-run interest rates equation, the specification of which is that of an inverted standard money demand function. Normalization on M_2 instead of M_1 does not appear to be a significant source of difference, because the companion BEA M_1 equation produced results close to baseline values.

The partial simulations were conducted in sequence as follows: in Simulation IA(1), prices—including the exchange rate index—and wage rates, labor productivity, and short-term interest rates were set exogenously at baseline levels, essentially leaving both models with their (open-economy) multiplier–accelerator cores in operation. Because prices were frozen in Simulation IA(1), the interest rate term structure equations also effectively freeze long-term rates. In Simulation IA(2) prices, wage rates, and productivity were released, leaving the treasury bill rate and the exchange rate at baseline levels. This partial simulation isolates price responses to the demand shocks and highlights the models' reactions to new relative and absolute prices. In Simulation IA(3) (conducted only with the DRI model), only the exchange rate remained frozen. A comparison of this with the full fiscal shock reveals the significance of the DRI open-economy approach to domestic policy evaluation (which involves foreign production, price, and interest rate responses as well as an endogenous exchange rate).[3]

As shown in Figure 5.1, in Simulation IA, the BEA model eventually yields a significantly higher multiplier path for real GNP than the DRI model. For the first 3 years (1975–1977), the paths are quite similar: the timing of peak levels is identical

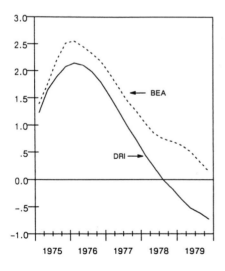

Figure 5.1. Real GNP multipliers: simulations IA–BL, DRI vs BEA (percentage difference).

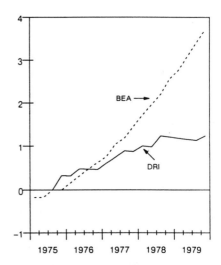

Figure 5.2. Implicit price deflator, GNP: simulation IA–BL, DRI vs BEA (percentage difference).

(1976.1) and the average levels are 1.6 and 2.0, respectively, for the DRI and BEA models. Moreover, both models' multipliers decline rapidly from their peaks, but the spread increases markedly in 1978 and 1979, with DRI's multiplier becoming negative after 1978.2. These declines reflect the combined effects of accelerator feedbacks, higher prices, higher interest rates, and, for the DRI model, higher exchange rates.

The price responses, as measured by the GNP implicit price deflator, are quite similar for the first 2.5 years, then diverge with BEA's deflator rising much more sharply (see Figure 5.2). This divergence largely reflects demand pressures arising from BEA's greater 1978–1979 real GNP multiplier.

Although the GNP multiplier paths are not too dissimilar, they result from sharply contrasting, and largely offsetting comparative displacement effects of higher prices and interest rates, respectively, as revealed by the partial simulations (see Figure 5.3a and b). The multiplier–accelerator cores of the models, as reflected in Simulation IA(1), are quite similar, although BEA's stronger accelerator responses make for somewhat greater cyclicality. Endogenizing the price–wage–productivity sector [Simulation IA(2)] powerfully reduces the GNP multiplier for the BEA model, but hardly at all for the DRI model. Letting the treasury bill rate rise to hit the money stock target [Simulation IA(3) for the DRI model and Simulation IA for the BEA model], in contrast, has a much larger negative impact on the GNP multiplier in the DRI model than in the BEA model. Finally, for the DRI model, this negative impact is reinforced by the rise in the exchange rate, which, in turn, is principally a response to higher interest rates. Higher interest rates, through their depressing effect on final demand, of course, have a negative feedback on prices as well. Similarly, a rise in the dollar's value feeds back negatively to prices.

Underlying BEA's eventually larger price response are the larger and more sustained higher real demands, plus a larger decrease in unemployment relative to the increase in real GNP and a fallback in productivity in contrast to DRI's sustained higher levels. Offsetting these are the DRI model's greater price sensitivity to demand pressure and near 100% pass-through of wages to prices and prices to wages. Several factors underlie BEA's much larger quantity-depressing effect of higher prices, includ-

(a)   **(b)**

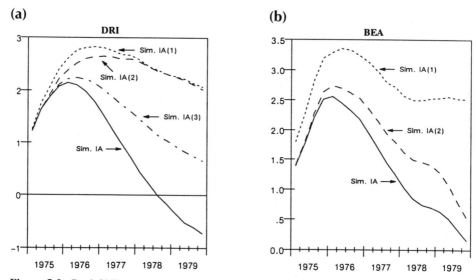

Figure 5.3. Real GNP multipliers: partial fiscal shock simulations. (a) DRI, (b) BEA (percentage difference from baseline).

ing stronger Pigou and consumer confidence effects, the different handling of Federal purchases input, and significantly smaller effects of real net exports.

DRI's much stronger interest rate response stems from a much lower interest elasticity of demand for money, so that for a given increase in the transactions demand (quantity and price components have different impacts) and a fixed money supply, a much larger increase in the interest rate must occur to deter cashholders. Higher interest rates, in turn, not only directly reduce domestic demand for the interest-sensitive components of GNP, but also (in the DRI model) raise the value of the dollar, which further constrains the GNP response through lower net exports; these comparative effects are somewhat mitigated by a lower interest elasticity of demand for the interest-sensitive components for DRI.

We now proceed by first analyzing in considerable detail the final comparative fiscal shock results, and then, in succession, the comparative contributions of the real demand (i.e., multiplier–accelerator) cores, the price–wage effects, and the interest rate effects through progressively more inclusive partial simulations.

Full Simulation (IA)

DRI's real GNP multiplier peaks in the fifth simulation quarter (1976.1) at 2.15 or $60.3 billion (1982 prices), then recedes, reaching zero in the fifteenth quarter (1978.3). BEA's peak multiplier, 2.56 ($71.7 billion), also occurs in 1976.1; the multiplier remains positive throughout the 5-year period, almost reaching zero by 1979.4.

As noted above, the primary cause of the relative weakness of DRI's multiplier is its greater interest rate sensitivity to the fiscal stimulus, given a fixed money target. Figures 5.4 and 5.5 reveal DRI's much larger responses of short-term and long-term rates, respectively. The treasury bill rate rises to 1 percentage point above the baseline solution by 1976.3 in the DRI run and hovers near there through 1979.1, then edges

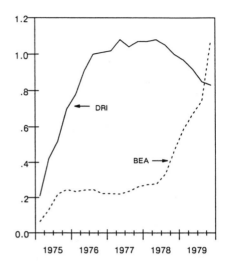

Figure 5.4. Three-month treasury bill rate: simulation IA–BL, DRI vs BEA (percentage points).

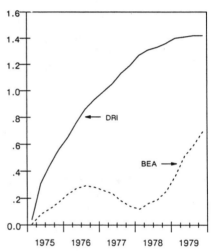

Figure 5.5. AAA corporate bond yield: simulation IA–BL, DRI vs BEA (percentage points).

down. By end of the 5 years, a new equilibrium has been approximately defined: little change in real output (with a substitution of defense spending for other demand), a price level about 1% above the baseline level (implying real money balances about 1% below baseline), and the real, short-term interest rate about 1 percentage point higher.

For BEA, in contrast, the bill rate rises roughly one-fourth as much as for DRI, remains nearly steady in 1978.3, and then rises sharply in response to higher prices.[4] The comparative bond yield responses primarily reflect the differences in the short-term rates. The different interest rate responses can be largely traced to the money demand submodels of the two macro models. Although both submodels implicitly estimate inflation-adjusted money demand as a function of three basic drivers—real transactions, market interest rates, and "own rates" on deposits—the exact specifications are sufficiently different to produce a much steeper "LM curve" in the DRI model. The implied semielasticity of money (M_1 for DRI, M_2 for BEA) with respect to the treasury bill rate over the 1975–1979 period is six times higher for the BEA model than the corresponding weighted-up semielasticity for the DRI model: -9.9 vs -1.7; in its normal operating mode (which uses a Federal Reserve "reaction function" to determine the treasury bill rate), the BEA model incorporates a traditional M_2 demand function with a semielasticity of -4.0.

The interest rate consequences of this difference can be directly calculated as the semielasticities of the treasury bill rate with respect to quantity and price components of the relevant transactions variables in each model's money demand function(s) (Table 5.2). Because both the money measures and the transactions variables differ between the models, the elasticities are not precisely comparable, but they do indicate the order-of-magnitude differences.[5] Both the transactions and price elasticities are much larger for the DRI model than the BEA model; however, the divergence is most pronounced for the price elasticities. A fiscal shock produces much less crowding out with the BEA model than with the DRI model because of its relatively small interest rate response. The vastly different money demand functions naturally also dominate the results in the monetary shock simulations, and a detailed exploration of the specification differences is presented in that section.

We now examine the effects of the fiscal stimulus on the major components of final demand. Table 5.3 shows the breakdown of the real GNP response for each model as annual averages. As noted earlier, during the first 3 years, BEA's GNP multiplier is moderately higher than DRI's. For 1975–1976 the difference primarily reflects smaller responses of fixed nonresidential investment and inventory investment in the DRI model, with smaller reductions in net exports as a partly offsetting factor. Differences in the multipliers for personal consumption expenditures, residential investment, and government purchases are small. Offsetting factors account for the similarity of the consumption responses: higher interest rates in the DRI simulation more strongly repress durable goods purchases; slightly larger increases in real disposable income, a higher marginal propensity to consume, and smaller price increases imply somewhat larger DRI multipliers for consumption of nondurables and services.

The fixed investment components—residential investment and nonresidential fixed investment—are almost consistently weaker (i.e., less positive or more negative) for the DRI model than for the BEA model. This difference primarily reflects DRI's much larger long-term interest rate response. Relative weakness in nonresidential fixed investment in the early simulation quarters also reflects DRI's weaker accelerator response [as we shall see more clearly in the discussion of Simulation IA(1)]. (Toward the end of the simulation period, a secondary response to much lower real net exports

Table 5.2. Semielasticities of 3-Month Treasury Bill Rate with Respect to Real Transactions Variable and Implicit Price Deflator[a]

Model	Transactions Variable	Implicit Price Deflator
DRI	0.44	0.59
BEA	0.15	0.10

[a]The DRI estimates are weighted averages of elasticities derived from the equations for currency and checkable deposits; the shares of these components of M_1 were, respectively, 0.27 and 0.73 in 1977. Because BEA's (M_2) money demand function is fully logarithmic, the semielasticities are estimated on the basis of the average baseline treasury bill rate during the simulation period (6.6%).

Table 5.3. Multipliers for Real GNP, Major GNP Components, and Disposable Income, Simulation IA–BL (Billions of 1982 Dollars)

	1975		1976		1977		1978		1979	
	DRI	BEA	DRI	BEA	DRI	BEA	DRI	BEA	DRI	BEA
Gross national product	46.3	53.2	56.7	67.2	33.1	46.7	3.4	25.6	-17.7	12.9
Personal consumption expenditures	12.8	14.0	20.7	19.7	18.8	17.8	12.1	13.1	4.8	10.5
Durable goods	3.8	7.1	5.6	8.7	4.6	6.6	3.0	3.4	1.7	2.1
Nondurable goods and services	9.0	6.9	15.1	11.1	14.1	11.2	9.1	9.8	3.2	8.3
Nonresidential fixed investment	4.1	10.7	10.8	19.1	5.0	9.3	-5.1	-1.7	-12.4	-4.3
Residential investment	1.1	-0.2	-2.0	-1.1	-6.8	-2.0	-9.8	-0.3	-10.3	1.0
Change in business inventories	3.7	6.3	4.5	11.7	-1.3	4.1	-5.3	-2.2	-5.4	-3.6
Net exports of goods and services	-2.9	-5.4	-7.7	-10.8	-15.8	-11.1	-23.1	-12.0	-28.7	-18.2
Exports	1.5	-0.1	3.0	-0.9	-1.7	-2.6	-8.5	-5.4	-15.3	-9.2
Imports	4.3	5.3	10.7	9.9	14.0	8.4	14.7	6.7	13.4	9.0
Government purchases, goods and services	27.4	27.8	30.4	28.6	33.2	28.4	34.6	28.7	34.2	27.6
Federal	26.9	27.8	28.3	28.6	29.6	28.4	31.1	28.7	31.9	27.6
State and local	0.5	0.0	2.1	0.0	3.6	0.0	3.5	0.0	2.3	0.0
Disposable personal income	19.4	18.2	31.2	27.2	31.2	23.3	23.1	15.1	12.3	9.2

becomes an important additional factor underlying the comparative investment behavior.) DRI's inventory investment multiplier is also consistently lower than BEA's. This is apparently due to DRI's inclusion of "demand surprise" variables: surges in final demand lead to unintended inventory depletion. Such depletion partially offsets desired increases in inventories to match higher levels of sustained spending.

Smaller reductions in DRI's net exports during the first 2 years are due to differences in the responses of exports. Exports are up (from baseline levels) in the DRI simulation, whereas for BEA they are down slightly. This divergence reflects DRI's use of a feedback relation from U.S. production to foreign activity, and hence to the demand for U.S. exports. However, income-induced increases in imports due to the fiscal stimulus dominate the net exports multipliers of both models during this period, with imports being up by similar amounts.

The differences in the reactions of the GNP components become more pronounced after 2 years. In 1977 DRI's residential investment multiplier becomes substantially more negative than BEA's and the net exports response has shifted from less negative to more negative. Partly offsetting these sources of difference is a moderately larger DRI government purchases multiplier. In the final two simulation years (1978–1979), these shifts become highly magnified, particularly that of net exports, and in turn generate greater differences in the consumption, inventory investment, and nonresidential fixed investment multipliers.

The substantial reductions in residential investment in the DRI simulation, in contrast to BEA's slight responses, reflect the impact of DRI's much larger interest rate increases and the inclusion of an endogenous vacancy rate. In 1977–1979, the differences in residential investment multipliers account for about one-third of the differences in the overall GNP multiplier.

The comparative net exports multipliers are sharply reversed in the latter part of the simulation period as export gains turn into losses in the DRI simulation: reductions in exports are considerably larger for DRI than for BEA in the last 2 years, and its import gains are considerably larger. The dominant explanation for this is, as will be elaborated shortly, the behavior of the exchange rate. The index of the dollar's value is up an average 4.3% over baseline levels over the simulation as whole and by a maximum 5.7% in 1978. This lowers the volume of exports and the price level of imports; lower import prices reinforce the positive income effect on the volume of imports. In the BEA simulation, lower real exports are explained by higher export prices, whereas in the DRI run the exports price deflator does not rise above baseline levels at all and eventually falls below them.[6]

Real Federal government purchases of goods and services are somewhat larger for DRI than for BEA (the difference is $4.3 billion in 1979) because, as noted earlier, the exogenous defense inputs were normalized in real terms for the DRI simulation and in nominal terms for the BEA simulation; thus, the resulting higher prices for defense goods reduce real outlays for BEA, but not for DRI. Real estate and local government purchases are exogenous in the BEA model and thus do not respond at all to the fiscal stimulus; for DRI, in contrast, state and local purchases show a small positive response to a rise in "permanent income" (proxied by potential GNP) and increases in past surpluses. In 1979, this source of difference ($2.3 billion) brings the total difference in real government purchases to $6.6 billion.

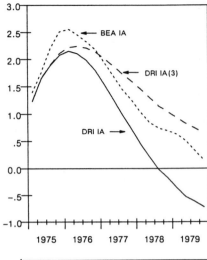

Figure 5.6. Real GNP multipliers with/without exchange fixed [DRI–IA, IA(3); BEA–IA] (percentage difference from baseline).

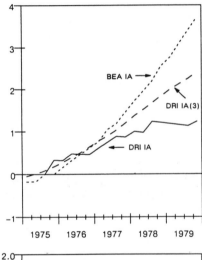

Figure 5.7. Implicit price deflator with/without exchange fixed [DRI–IA, IA(3); BEA–IA] (percentage difference from baseline).

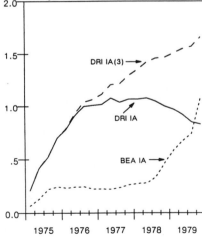

Figure 5.8. Three-month treasury bill rate with/without exchange fixed [DRI–IA, IA(3); BEA–IA] (percentage points, difference from baseline).

Table 5.4. Impact of Higher Exchange Rates in the DRI Fiscal Policy Simulation IA–IA(3)

	1975	1976	1977	1978	1979
Real GNP (1982 dollars)	−0.3	−5.5	−20.3	−35.0	−42.9
Net exports of goods and services	−0.4	−4.4	−11.8	−18.0	−22.7
Exports	−0.3	−3.1	−8.3	−13.3	−18.0
Imports	0.1	1.3	3.5	4.7	4.7
Other GNP	0.0	−1.1	−8.5	−16.9	−20.2
Implicit price deflator, GNP, (percentage difference)	0.0	0.0	−0.2	−0.5	−1.0
3-month treasury bill rate (percentage points)	0.0	−.03	−0.16	−0.37	−0.68

The GNP implicit price deflator in the BEA simulation initially is slightly below the baseline level as the burst in demand raises labor productivity and thus lowers unit labor cost.[7] After 1975, the price deflator rises above the baseline level at a pace greater than DRI's. The more rapid rise clearly reflects BEA's stronger real GNP multiplier, but also, as we shall see more clearly when we analyze Simulation IA(2), a slightly stronger wage response to a given change in demand.

To determine the impact of DRI's endogenous treatment of the exchange rate on real net exports and the overall results, we may compare the results of Simulation IA with those of Simulation IA(3), which differs from Simulation IA only in that the exchange rate is frozen at baseline levels. Figures 5.6–5.8 and Table 5.4 show how the comparative results are altered by this change in the simulation mode. DRI's real GNP multiplier is now actually slightly larger than BEA's beginning in 1977 as a result of much smaller reductions in net exports—indeed, now consistently smaller than BEA's. The large shift in net exports is due to both larger exports multipliers (or a shift from negative to positive multipliers) and smaller imports, but predominantly the former.

Because of the stronger economy, prices and interest rates are higher. Thus, the price response is now closer to BEA's: at the end of the 5-year period, the gap in the increase in the GNP deflator has been halved (from 2.5 to 1.2%). However, the gap in the interest rate response has widened: the treasury bill rate is higher by an average of 25 basis points.

REAL DEMAND SUBMODEL—SIMULATION IA(1)

The comparative multipliers of Simulation IA may be decomposed into the comparative multiplier–accelerator "cores" of the two models (which yield the maximum real GNP responses to the fiscal shock) and the comparative "crowding-out" or "leakage" effects caused by higher prices, interest rates, and exchange rates. By freezing the price–wage–productivity blocks, the 3-month treasury bill rate (and thereby also long-term rates), and the exchange rate, the models are reduced essentially to fully demand-generated (open-economy) systems with passive employment and income responses.[8]

This section examines the comparative results of the fiscal shock applied to these real cores. The remaining sections will examine the effects of freeing, in succession, prices and wages, and then interest rates (under a fixed money supply assumption); we have already examined the effect of freezing the exchange rate for the DRI simulation in the previous subsection.

In Simulation IA(1), as in the full simulation, BEA's real GNP multipliers are generally larger than DRI's. On average, however, the differences are not as great. Over the 5-year period, BEA's GNP multiplier averages 2.75 compared with 2.39 for DRI, a spread of 0.36. This contrasts with an average spread of 0.50 in Simulation IA. Table 5.5 shows the comparative (annual) multiplier effects on real GNP and its major components for this simulation. The most striking contrast to the similar breakdown shown in Table 5.2 (for the full simulation) is the much more similar behavior of the net exports multipliers; we have seen that much of the contrasting responses in the full simulations is due to DRI's exchange rate responses; however, the differences—especially for 1978–1979—are still narrower than when only the exchange rate effects are removed (compare Table 5.4). Similarly, differences in the residential investment multipliers are now relatively small because of the removal of the large interest rate differences. Also, the spreads in government purchases are smaller because price responses have been eliminated as a source of differences in the Federal component.

The time paths of the GNP multipliers for the two models are, however, quite different in character, as can be seen in Figure 5.9. In particular, BEA's path is more cyclical, indicating stronger accelerational behavior. A decomposition of the GNP multipliers into acceleration-sensitive and nonsensitive components highlights these differences, as shown in Figure 5.10a and b and Table 5.5. The acceleration-sensitive components (ASC) are defined as consumer durables purchases, fixed nonresidential investment, and inventory investment.[9]

In the BEA simulation, the ASC display almost a full cycle over the 5-year period with a strong peak in 1976.2 and a trough in 1978.3; DRI's ASC, in contrast, have a weaker single peak in 1976.4. BEA's stronger overall acceleration sensitivity is reflected in each of the ASC's. The stronger cyclicality of BEA's inventory investment

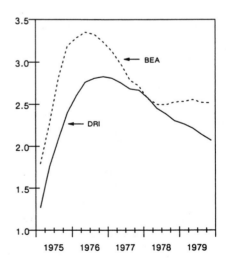

Figure 5.9. Real GNP multiplier: partial simulation IA(1), DRI vs BEA (percentage difference from baseline).

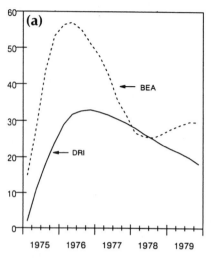 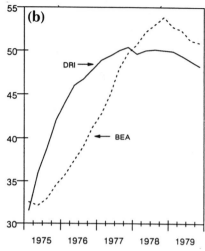

Figure 5.10. (a) Acceleration-sensitive components of real GNP multipliers, partial simulation IA(1), DRI vs BEA. (b) Nonacceleration-sensitive components of real GNP multipliers, partial simulation IA(1), DRI vs BEA. (a, b) In Billions of 1982$.

reflects the greater acceleration sensitivity of the other two components, and the absence of the explicit "demand surprise" factor noted earlier in the DRI model.

BEA's multipliers for consumer durables are not only more cyclical, but are also consistently much larger than DRI's (see Table 5.5): the average increment in the BEA simulation is $15.0 billion (1982 dollars) compared with $8.1 billion for DRI. This difference reflects the "confidence" impact of a substantially larger response of the unemployment rate in the BEA simulation (more on this point below). BEA's larger consumer durables response also produces a larger decline in the personal saving rate.

In the case of the non-acceleration-sensitive components, DRI shows stronger responses for the first 3 years, despite the stronger stimulus provided by BEA's ASC. This results from the following BEA properties: (1) weaker short-run income sensitivity of residential investment, (2) stronger short-run income sensitivity of imports, (3) slightly lower income elasticity of consumption, and (4) exogeneity of real state and local purchases.

As can be seen in Table 5.5 for the longer horizons BEA's residential investment multipliers surpass DRI's and by 1979.4 are opposite in sign. This reflects DRI's inclusion of an (implicit) endogenous vacancy rate in its housing start equations. This rate is equal to the ratio of the gap between the housing stock (endogenous) and the trend level of households to the stock. Thus, the early surge in construction expands the housing stock and reduces the need or incentive for construction later in the simulation.

The drop in unemployment in the BEA simulation is much larger than DRI's—an average of 1.74 percentage points during the 5-year period compared to 0.69 percentage points for DRI, far greater than the relative excess of BEA's real GNP multiplier. The difference stems from different modeling approaches. DRI uses an "Okun's Law"-based determination of the unemployment rate, under which cyclical unemployment falls 0.45 percentage points for each additional percentage point of growth. Extra

Table 5.5. Multipliers for Real GNP, Major GNP Components, and Related Magnitudes Simulation IA(1)–BL (Billions of 1982 Dollars, Except as Noted)

	1975		1976		1977		1978		1979	
	DRI	BEA	DRI	BEA	DRI	BEA	DRI	BEA	DRI	BEA
Gross national product	50.9	68.1	77.8	93.3	80.7	85.8	75.6	78.5	69.4	80.8
Personal consumption expenditures	16.2	24.9	27.8	33.3	31.4	35.8	31.8	37.8	30.6	40.7
Durable goods	5.2	13.5	8.8	15.4	9.4	14.7	9.0	14.7	8.1	16.8
Nondurable goods and services	11.0	11.5	19.0	17.9	22.1	21.1	22.8	23.1	22.5	23.8
Nonresidential fixed investment	4.6	13.4	14.9	24.5	16.6	17.1	14.3	9.7	11.5	10.8
Residential investment	2.2	0.8	2.4	3.0	1.1	4.5	-0.3	4.5	-1.5	3.9
Change in business inventories	4.0	8.2	7.9	15.1	5.1	7.6	2.4	1.7	0.7	1.3
Net exports of goods and services	-3.6	-7.3	-6.1	-11.8	-7.3	-9.7	-8.5	-7.3	-8.3	-8.4
Exports	1.0	0.0	4.6	0.0	5.6	0.0	4.9	0.0	4.2	0.0
Imports	4.6	7.3	10.7	11.8	12.8	9.7	13.4	7.3	12.5	8.5
Government purchases, goods and services	27.6	28.0	30.8	29.3	33.7	30.4	35.9	32.2	36.5	32.4
Federal	26.9	28.0	28.3	29.3	29.6	30.4	31.1	32.2	31.9	32.4
State and local	0.7	-0.0	2.5	-0.0	4.1	0.0	4.7	0.0	4.6	0.0
Acceleration-sensitive components	13.8	35.0	31.6	54.9	31.0	39.4	25.7	26.1	20.3	29.0
Other GNP	37.1	33.1	46.2	38.4	39.7	45.4	49.9	52.4	49.1	51.8
Disposable personal income	24.0	27.6	35.7	37.1	39.3	36.5	40.0	34.2	38.3	35.0
Unemployment rate (percentage)	-0.5	-1.6	-0.9	-1.9	-0.9	-1.9	-0.7	-1.7	-0.5	-1.7

output implicitly or explicitly stimulates four phenomena: greater labor force participation, more hours worked per employee, more output per hour worked, and more employees. Only the last element, the employment gain, serves to reduce the unemployment rate, and this is partially offset by the encouragement (of a stronger economy) for individuals actively to seek jobs and thus be newly counted as part of the labor force: by definition, the change in the unemployment rate is the percentage increase in employees minus the percentage increase in the labor force. These phenomena are all present in the BEA model, but the cyclical responses of labor force participation and weekly hours are more muted; hence the BEA unemployment response tends to be greater for any given output change. [In the BEA model, unemployment is determined residually from labor force and (household-basis) employment. Household-basis employment is determined in two steps: (1) a direct relationship of establishment-basis employment to output and the long-run productivity trend and (2) a "bridge" relationship connecting establishment-basis and household-basis employment.]

An exaggerated divergence in unemployment occurred in Simulation IA(1) due to contrasting implementation of the assumption of productivity equal to the baseline: specifically, changes in average weekly hours take on a greater relative adjustment burden for DRI than for BEA. In the full Simulation (IA), the relative divergence is not nearly so great, but the direction of comparison remains the same. In the peak multiplier quarter (both models) of Simulation IA (1976.1), BEA's real GNP multiplier is 19% larger than DRI's, while the drop in unemployment is 47% larger. The difference is centered in employment, as both models show the same increases in labor force participation.

Endogenizing Prices, Wages, and Productivity—Simulation IA(2)

In Simulation IA(2), the equations of the price–wage blocks and those determining output per hour are released, but the other equations that were suppressed in Simulation IA(1) remain suppressed. Both models show accelerating price responses, as measured by the GNP implicit price deflator, with the BEA model showing stronger acceleration beginning in 1977 (see Figure 5.11). By 1979 (annual average), the GNP deflator is 4.0% above the baseline level in the BEA simulation compared with 2.7% for DRI. This, despite the fact that the price–wage and productivity responses (mainly the former) strongly and increasingly repress the real GNP multipliers in the BEA simulation during 1977–1979, but repress GNP only slightly in the DRI simulation. We shall first focus on the causes of the apparently stronger short-run demand–inflation trade-off in the BEA model, based on the direct comparison of Simulation IA(2) with the baseline solution, and then on the feedbacks of the price–wage responses on demand, comparing Simulations IA(2) and IA(1).

The difference between the two models in the price response to fiscal policy reflects a composite of several factors. First, the unemployment response, which determines the extent of movement along a Phillips curve, is larger in relation to the output response for the BEA model than for the DRI model, as noted previously. The average ratio of the difference in the unemployment rate to the percentage difference in real GNP is about twice as large for BEA as for DRI (-0.6 vs -0.3).

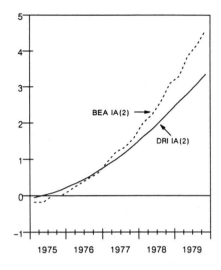

Figure 5.11. Implicit price deflator, GNP: simulation IA(2), DRI vs BEA (percentage difference from baseline).

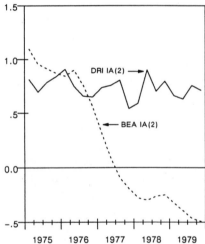

Figure 5.12. Productivity response: simulation IA(2), DRI vs BEA (percentage difference from baseline).

Second, as can be seen in Figure 5.12, the productivity responses are comparable for the first six quarters but diverge sharply thereafter. In the BEA simulation, productivity retreats back toward baseline levels and falls somewhat below baseline levels after mid-1978, as the GNP multiplier reverts toward zero. For DRI, in contrast, the productivity differential remains positive, fluctuating between 0.5 and 1% above baseline levels. This divergent behavior reflects the rather different formulations of the relationships of employment and hours worked to output noted in the previous subsection. Neutralization of BEA's initially positive productivity response contributes, via higher unit labor cost, to a larger inflationary response toward the end of the 5-year period.

DRI links actual labor productivity to potential productivity through cyclical variables. Potential labor productivity is derived from an explicit production function defining potential real GNP as constant-returns-to-scale function of labor hours, fixed capital and energy, plus endogenous total factor productivity tied to the R&D capital stock and the age (technology vintage) of the fixed capital stock. Thus, the significant and sustained labor productivity gains in the DRI simulations are due to both greater fixed business and R&D capital and to a temporary cyclical lift, explaining the previously noted small 0.3% drop in unemployment for each 1.0% gain in output.

In the BEA model, productivity derives definitionally from output, employment, and average weekly hours. The model contains separate (but interrelated) equations for nonfarm private sector employment and average weekly hours. These variables are modeled as functions of long-run productivity, measured as trends through historical peaks, and cyclical output changes. Because the productivity trends are exogenous, there is no feedback of capital stock. Because of the dominance of the cyclical factors in the short run, this "leakage" is not deemed to be a serious deficiency for simulating with horizons up to 3 years.

Third, and offsetting to the first two factors, is an apparently steeper overall (i.e., price and wage) "Phillips curve" for the DRI model. This was established by simulations of each model's price–wage sector response to a standardized demand shock. Standardization was imposed by increasing "demand pressure" variables by common amounts that are roughly consistent with a 1% rise in real GNP: a 0.5 percentage point lower overall unemployment rate and a 2 percentage point higher capacity utilization rate for total manufacturing. Productivity is exogenous and frozen at baseline levels in these simulations.

Table 5.6 shows the comparative results of this experiment—specifically, of the responses of the GNP implicit price deflator and the nonfarm business sector average money wage rate—for 1977.4 (the twelfth quarter) and 1979.4 (the twentieth quarter). The inflation rates of both wages and prices respond more strongly in the DRI model than in the BEA model.

DRI's apparently steeper overall Phillips curve reflects the composite of the comparative effects of four structural elasticities—the sensitivity of wages to unemployment and to prices, and the responsiveness of prices to capacity utilization rates (or other demand pressure measures) and to wages. The semielasticity of the wage rate with respect to the unemployment rate, as a direct calculation from each model's wage rate equation reveals, is virtually the same in both models, about 0.6 after 12 quarters. On the other hand, the sensitivity of wages to prices differs sharply. The long-run elasticity of the wage rate with respect to the consumer price index (CPI) in the BEA

Table 5.6. Comparative Price and Wage Rate Responses to a Sustained 1% Increase in Final Demand

	12 quarters		20 quarters	
	DRI	BEA	DRI	BEA
Implicit price deflator, GNP				
Percentage difference	1.19	0.74	2.78	1.79
Inflation rate[a]	0.67	0.39	0.91	0.65
Compensation per hour, nonfarm business sector				
Percentage difference	1.32	1.01	3.11	2.35
Inflation rate[a]	0.77	0.56	1.03	0.80

[a]Annual rates.

model is 0.68. In the DRI model, the wage rate is a function of both the CPI (short run) and the fixed-weighted GNP price index (long run); a 1 percentage point increase in both indexes yields a wage increase of 0.94% after 12 quarters.

The price–wage and price–demand elasticities are not separately determinable without further simulation. Jointly, they are apparently somewhat larger for DRI, judging from Table 5.6. After 12 quarters, the gross "elasticity" of the GNP deflator with respect to the nonfarm business sector wage rate is 0.90 for the DRI model, compared with 0.73 for BEA; after 20 quarters, the elasticities are 0.89 for DRI and 0.76 for BEA. The fact that the deflators for compensation of general government employees— both Federal and state/local—are endogenous in the DRI model and exogenous in the BEA model contributes to a higher price–wage elasticity for the DRI model.[10] In 1977, general government compensation accounted for 11% of real GNP. Thus, the exogeneity of the deflators for general government in the BEA model is enough of a "leakage" to account for most of the difference in the gross elasticities of the GNP deflator with respect to the nonfarm business sector wage rate.

The apparently nearer-to-full pass-throughs of both prices to wages and wages to prices in the DRI model than in the BEA model makes the former more nearly "accelerationist"; that is, it implies less opportunity for policymakers to trade higher inflation for lower unemployment beyond the very short run. Figure 5.13 shows how these relative trade-offs are effectuated using a stylized simplification of the inflation–demand cores of the models.

We now turn to the comparative feedbacks to real GNP of changing productivity, prices, and wage rates. In addition to the aforementioned tendency of higher productivity to mitigate price increases, it also tends to reduce household income by making profits a greater share of GNP. For the DRI model, as we have seen, higher labor productivity persists throughout Simulation IA(2), whereas for BEA this is transitory. Despite the dropback in BEA's productivity response, BEA's real GNP multiplier falls much more than DRI's between simulations IA(1) and IA(2), and increasingly so in 1977–1979. This clearly shows that higher prices have a strongly negative direct impact on demand in the BEA model.

Because the price increase is eventually larger in the BEA simulation, the quantity reaction should be viewed in relation to the size of the price response. Figure 5.14 shows the elasticity of real GNP with respect to the GNP deflator for each model on the basis of differentials between simulations IA(1) and IA(2). (The chart shows data only from 1976.4 on, after which, for BEA, the productivity factor is no longer significant.) The elasticity is consistently higher for the BEA model than for the DRI model.

What are the causes of this difference? In answering this question, let us first consider the possible reasons why price changes may not be neutral in their macroeconomic impact: (1) they could produce inflation-adjusted asset changes that have "Pigou" effects, although this effect should be small for DRI because nominal asset prices are endogenous; (2) price changes that yield changes in the inflation rate could affect consumer confidence and, therefore, the personal saving rate; (3) they could affect real net exports through changes in the terms of trade; (4) they could affect real government purchases depending on whether such purchases are assumed to be set in nominal or real terms; (5) they might cause shifts in income distribution between economic agents with lower and higher propensities to spend; (6) they might involve changes in relative

The intricate wage-price blocks of both models can be characterized in two equations:

Wage inflation $= \dot{w} = a_0 + a_1\dot{p}_{-1} - a_2(u - u_{FE})$

Price inflation $= \dot{p} = b_1(\dot{w} - \dot{q}) - b_2(u - u_{FE})$

u = unemployment rate (or capacity utilization), with the FE subscript denoting full employment.

$\dot{q}$ = labor productivity growth

Combining the equations to solve for price inflation as a function of productivity growth and unemployment:

$\dot{p} = a_1 b_1\dot{p}_{-1} - (b_1 a_2 + b_2)(u - u_{FE}) + b_1(a_0 - \dot{q})$

In a model, like DRI's, in which wages and prices pass through fully, $a_1 = b_1 = 1$, hence:

$\dot{p} = \dot{p}_{-1} - (a_2 + b_2)(u - u_{FE}) + (a_0 - \dot{q})$

or the change in inflation, the *acceleration* in prices, equals

$\dot{p} - \dot{p}_{-1} = -(a_2 + b_2)(u - u_{FE}) + (a_0 - \dot{q})$

This produces the equation defining what James Tobin has termed "NAIRU," the non-accelerating inflation rate of unemployment, which occurs when $\dot{p} = \dot{p}_{-1}$.

$u = u_{FE} - \dfrac{(a_0 - \dot{q})}{(a_2 + b_2)}$

In the DRI model, prices accelerate by 1/2% per year for each 1% by which unemployment falls below NAIRU. Policymakers cannot force the economy to deviate permanently from this NAIRU. Note that at full employment, if wage inflation exceeds price inflation (on average) by the current productivity growth rate, then $a_0 = \dot{q}$; hence,

$$u_{NAIRU} = u_{FE}$$

In a model, like BEA's, in which a_1 and b_1 are substantially below 1, each unemployment rate corresponds to a unique steady-state inflation rate:

$\dot{p} = [1/(1 - a_1 b_1)][-(b_1 a_2 + b_2)(u - u_{FE}) - b_1(a_0 - \dot{q})]$
$\quad = -c(u - u_{FE}) + d(a_0 - \dot{q})$

where c and d are composites of the earlier subscripted a and b coefficients.

Policymakers can thus choose an "optimal" pair of inflation and unemployment rates.

Figure 5.13. The inflation–demand cores of the DRI and BEA models.

prices with resulting net demand changes due to the failure of the Slutsky condition to hold; and (7) they could change the effective marginal tax rate via shifting tax brackets.

Several of these factors produce the substantial difference between the two models' Simulation IA(1) and IA(2) results. Decomposition of the differences in real GNP multipliers by final demand components between Simulations IA(1) and IA(2) helps to reveal the sources of the differences (see Table 5.7). Differences in the responses

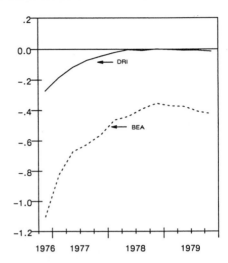

Figure 5.14. Sensitivity of real GNP to price level, DRI vs BEA [percentage difference GNP82/percentage difference PGNP, 1A(2)–1A(1)].

of personal consumption expenditures dominate the differences in the GNP multiplier in 1975–1976. In later years, the differences are more widely spread among GNP components, even as they increase markedly for consumption. Both greater sensitivity of consumption to inflation and the Pigou effect in the BEA model cause this.

The BEA model also displays strongly negative responses in real net exports—mainly lower exports, but also higher imports—than in Simulation IA(1), whereas the DRI model does not. BEA's strong net export response is due to sharp changes in domestic prices without any change in import prices. In the DRI simulation, extra domestic activity and inflation spill over into higher foreign growth and inflation. The magnitudes of these feedbacks are drawn from historical regressions of foreign variables on analogous U.S. concepts. The estimated coefficients are then used in simulation work automatically to translate variations from baseline values in key domestic concepts into appropriately scaled variations in comparable foreign concepts. This DRI "global endogeneity" philosophy is reinforced by the equations for export prices. Export prices, like most U.S. prices, are driven by costs and capacity pressures; they are also sensitive to the exchange rate-adjusted levels of foreign wholesale prices, both influencing foreign price movements and being influenced by them. Such endogeneity makes a critical difference when forecasting or interpreting events such as the U.S. tax cuts and defense buildup during the 1980s.

As was previously explained, real Federal purchases are lower for BEA (but not for DRI) in Simulation IA(2) because, with current-dollar purchases fixed, real purchases are driven down by higher prices. (DRI shows slight reductions in state and local purchases, whereas BEA does not because of its exogenous treatment of state and local purchases.)

Consumer expenditures are depressed more by inflation in the BEA model than in DRI, and inflation is higher in the BEA simulation. But both models do exhibit Pigou-effect characteristics in these fiscal shocks with the nominal money supply fixed. Indicative of these comparative effects is the fact that the personal saving rate is slightly above IA(1) levels in both models' IA(2) simulations, but slightly more so for BEA. To a large extent, however, the differences in consumer spending responses reflect relative feedbacks from disposable income, as can be seen from the decrements in

Table 5.7. Changes in Multipliers for Real GNP, Major GNP Components, and Disposable Income, Simulation IA(2)–IA(1) (Billions of 1982 Dollars)

	1975		1976		1977		1978		1979	
	DRI	BEA	DRI	BEA	DRI	BEA	DRI	BEA	DRI	BEA
Gross national product	-3.3	-13.3	-6.1	-18.5	-3.2	-25.0	-0.4	-32.1	-0.8	-51.6
Personal consumption expenditures	-3.6	-10.5	-5.2	-11.2	-3.8	-12.7	-2.6	-15.3	-2.3	-19.7
Durable goods	-1.4	-6.1	-2.4	-5.4	-2.2	-5.6	-2.1	-7.4	-2.0	-11.0
Nondurable goods and services	-0.8	-4.4	-1.2	-5.8	-0.5	-7.1	0.0	-7.9	0.3	-8.7
Nonresidential fixed investment	-0.3	-2.5	-1.1	-3.9	-1.0	-4.4	-0.3	-6.1	-0.3	-10.1
Residential investment	-0.3	-0.4	-0.4	-1.3	-0.1	-1.4	0.2	2.8	0.5	-1.7
Change in business inventories	0.2	-1.8	-0.8	-2.1	0.3	-1.3	0.9	-1.2	0.7	-2.7
Net exports of goods and services	0.9	2.0	1.9	0.7	1.8	-3.0	1.3	-8.5	0.2	-15.0
Exports	0.0	-0.1	-0.2	-0.9	-0.2	-2.8	0.1	-6.1	-0.1	-11.0
Imports	-0.8	-2.0	-2.1	-1.6	-1.9	0.2	-1.2	2.3	-0.3	4.0
Government purchases, goods and services	-0.1	-0.2	-0.5	-0.7	-0.4	-2.1	0.0	-3.9	0.4	-5.8
Federal	0.0	-0.2	0.0	-0.7	0.0	-2.1	0.0	-3.9	0.0	-5.8
State and local	-0.1	0.0	-0.5	0.0	-0.4	0.0	0.0	0.0	0.4	0.0
Disposable personal income	-5.4	-9.5	-4.5	-9.0	0.0	-11.8	2.7	-15.4	4.5	-24.2
Implicit price deflator, GNP (percentage difference)[a]	0.1	-0.1	0.5	0.4	1.1	1.3	2.0	2.5	3.0	4.0
Implicit price deflator, PCE[a]										
Percentage difference	0.1	0.1	0.5	0.4	0.8	1.2	1.6	2.1	2.4	3.1
Inflation rate	0.2	0.2	0.4	0.5	0.7	0.9	0.7	1.0	1.0	1.1

[a]Differences are measured from baseline levels.

constant-dollar disposable personal income. BEA's somewhat lower marginal propensity to consume is a slightly mitigating factor. Shifts in income distribution, relative prices, and marginal tax rates do not appear to be significant sources of differences in response to price movements in either model.

ENDOGENIZING INTEREST RATES—SIMULATION IA(3)

Endogenizing the 3-month treasury bill rate yields the full fiscal shock simulation for the BEA model and Simulation IA(3) (full simulation less the exchange rate response) for the DRI model. Table 5.8 shows the comparative annualized increments, compared with Simulation IA(2), for the real GNP multipliers, components of the GNP multipliers, and key related variables.

The marked differences in the responses of the treasury bill rate, especially before 1979, have been previously described (they are, by assumption, identical to the responses relative to the baseline solution). There are correspondingly large differences in long-term interest rate responses via term–structure relationships; the latter are, of course, important for the relative responses of the fixed investment components.

Because of the larger interest rate response, the DRI model produces much larger reductions in the GNP multiplier than the BEA model. The intermodel GNP difference grows over the simulation period from $10 billion in 1977 to $27 billion in 1979. Two-thirds of this gap is accounted for by the traditional interest-sensitive components of GNP—consumer durables purchases, nonresidential fixed investment, and residential investment.

However, the reductions of the DRI interest-sensitive outlays are less in relation to the increases in long-term interest rates for DRI than for BEA. This could indicate either different interest rate elasticities or different multiplier–accelerator feedbacks. To understand these full model properties, semielasticities of interest-sensitive expenditures with respect to a sustained 1 percentage point increase in the Treasury bill rate were calculated for important equations and subsectors of the two models; these categories were then aggregated using the 1977 mix of these components as weights. After 12 quarters the relative changes in these expenditures are -3.3 and -5.1%, respectively, for the DRI and BEA models. In other words, the GNP contrasts are moderated because DRI's larger interest rate changes are offset by smaller demand reactions to these changes. (In the following section, we analyze the differential effects of given interest rate changes by an alternative partial simulation approach.)

Comparative responses for the non-interest-sensitive components essentially reflect multiplier–accelerator feedbacks from the primary interest rate-induced responses. Because households are the major net recipients of interest income and this income source rises as a result of higher interest rates—more so for DRI than for BEA (see Table 5.8)—this is another factor tending to compress the differences in GNP responses somewhat. In addition, in the BEA model, but not in the DRI model, the marginal propensity to consume with respect to interest and dividend income is constrained to be substantially lower than with respect to other disposable personal income. Thus, consumer spending is cut more in the BEA model than in the DRI model when interest rates rise for three reasons: (1) a greater income loss due to greater initial declines in

Table 5.8. Changes in Multipliers for Real GNP, Major Components, and Related Magnitudes Simulation IA(3) or IA—Simulation IA(2) (Billions of 1982 Dollars, Except as Noted)

	1975		1976		1977		1978		1979	
	DRI	BEA	DRI	BEA	DRI	BEA	DRI	BEA	DRI	BEA
Gross national product	-0.9	-1.6	-9.5	-7.5	-24.1	-14.1	-36.8	-20.8	-43.3	-16.3
Personal consumption expenditures	0.1	-0.4	-1.9	-2.4	-6.7	-5.3	-11.8	-9.4	-15.6	-10.6
Durable goods	-0.1	-0.3	-1.1	-1.3	-2.8	-2.5	-4.0	-4.0	-4.6	-3.7
Nondurable goods and services	0.1	-0.2	-0.1	-1.1	-1.2	-2.8	-2.5	-5.4	-3.3	-6.8
Nonresidential fixed investment	-0.2	-0.2	-2.4	-1.4	-7.3	-3.4	-12.4	-5.2	-15.1	-5.1
Residential investment	-0.7	-0.6	-4.0	-2.8	-7.4	-5.1	-9.0	-7.6	-9.3	-4.5
Change in business inventories	-0.4	-0.2	-2.1	-1.3	-4.2	-2.1	-5.1	-1.7	-4.2	-2.2
Net exports of goods and services	0.2	-0.1	0.9	0.3	1.6	1.7	2.0	3.7	2.1	5.2
Exports	0.7	0.0	1.7	0.0	1.2	0.2	-0.2	3.7	-1.3	1.8
Imports	0.5	0.1	0.8	-0.3	-0.4	-1.5	-2.2	-3.0	-3.4	-3.4
Government purchases, goods and services	0.0	0.0	0.1	0.0	0.0	0.1	-0.6	0.4	-1.3	1.0
Federal	0.0	0.0	0.0	0.0	0.0	0.1	0.0	0.4	0.0	1.0
State and local	0.0	0.0	0.1	0.0	0.0	0.0	-0.6	0.0	-1.3	0.0
Interest-sensitive components	-1.0	-1.1	-7.6	-5.5	-17.5	-10.9	-25.4	-16.8	-29.0	-13.4
Other GNP	0.0	-0.5	-1.9	-1.9	-6.6	-3.1	-11.4	-4.0	-14.3	-2.9
Disposable personal income	0.8	0.1	0.4	-0.9	-3.9	-1.4	-9.8	-3.7	-14.8	-1.6
Personal interest income	2.1	0.8	8.2	2.1	13.8	3.1	17.7	4.4	21.2	7.9
Interest rates (percentage points)										
3-month treasury bill rates	0.45	0.19	0.94	0.24	1.21	0.24	1.43	0.34	1.58	0.77
Corporate bond yield, AAA	0.33	0.09	0.82	0.27	1.23	0.20	1.75	0.18	2.30	0.54
Implicit price deflator, GNP (percentage)	0.0	0.0	0.0	0.0	-0.1	-0.2	-0.4	-0.4	-0.7	-0.7
Unemployment rate (percentage points)	0.0	0.0	0.1	0.1	0.2	0.2	0.4	0.3	0.5	0.3

interest-sensitive demand, (2) a smaller offsetting gain in interest income, and (3) a smaller propensity to spend out of interest income.

MONETARY SHOCK SIMULATIONS

Simulation 2A is a basic monetary policy exercise: the exogenous monetary drivers of each model are manipulated to provide a temporary increase in money demand growth such that the level of M_1 is permanently raised by 3%.[11] Naturally, a combination of lower interest rates and higher spending is necessary to induce the private sector to hold these additional balances. Initially, lower rates must provide most of the stimulus to money demand. Then, as the lower rates stimulate interest-sensitive investment and consumer durable spending (plus the multiplier feedbacks), transactions demand rises and interest rates must rebound to prevent overshooting of the money target.

This is an accurate qualitative summary of the results in both the BEA and DRI models, but the magnitudes are dramatically different. The fiscal policy discussion has already pointed to the sources: a 6-fold difference between the models in the estimated interest elasticity of money demand, and a collection of smaller differences in the sensitivities of household or business spending to variations in income, inflation, and interest rates.

The large BEA interest elasticity implies that only a very small interest rate decline (0.6 percentage point after 1 year) is required to procure the targeted 3% money demand increase; hence only a small subsequent stimulant to interest-sensitive spending is provided. In contrast, a significant drop in interest rates (2.0 percentage points in the first year) is required in the DRI model, and this initiates a stronger cycle in spending. All of the differences earlier noted—investment responses, consumer reactions, Phillips curves, and exchange rate endogeneity—contribute to the final contrasts. The medium term implications of a monetary impulse (years 3 to 5 of the shock) are an average real GNP gain of 0.6% for BEA versus 3.5% for DRI and an average price level increase of 0.5% for BEA versus 2.5% for DRI. Interest rates remain approximately 0.2–0.3% lower in the BEA results, but swing from a 2.0% drop to a 1.5% gain in DRI. In short, variations in money supply growth are not a major factor in economic performance as portrayed in the BEA simulations, but are a powerful force according to DRI.

Contrasting the Financial Sectors

In the DRI Model, nonborrowed reserves (including extended credit) are the principal exogenous monetary policy instrument. For any legally required reserve ratios, the levels of demand and time deposits determine the level of required reserves; the difference between nonborrowed reserves and required reserves (i.e., "free" reserves) is the primary determinant of the Federal funds rate and all other short-term interest rates.[12] Thus, the money shock experiment required DRI to search for the level of reserves that would cut rates, and subsequently raise spending, sufficiently to boost demand for M_1 by 3%.

The BEA model can be run in two alternative modes, as noted earlier. In its normal operating mode, the financial submodel assumes that the Fed effectively manipulates the treasury bill rate to achieve other policy objectives. Specifically, the bill rate is endogenized by means of an estimated reaction function which assumes the Fed tries to "lean against the wind," and thus interest rate increases occur in response to higher growth and inflation.

In forecasts or simulations in which the money stock is controlled as in the present study, BEA used an inverted M_2 demand equation to project the treasury bill rate: the treasury bill rate was regressed on real M_2, (adjusted) real GNP, and a measure of interest paid on deposits within M_2. M_2 could thus be treated as a purely exogenous variable. Although this appeared to be an innocuous modeling decision, it was highly significant. The estimated interest elasticity of money demand is more than twice as great as the estimate embodied in the conventionally normalized money demand equation used in the BEA's usual operating mode, and six times as great as the equivalent DRI estimate. This specification choice dominates the differences in the money shock simulations because of the dramatically different interest rate changes thereby implied for the two models (Table 5.9 and Figures 5.15–5.18).

Conceptual Differences. The contrasting BEA interest elasticities appear to imply that the estimation of an inverted demand function may bias the critical interest elasticity upward. This is not an unusual outcome when dependent and independent variables are swapped in regression analyses, although the scale of the difference is not

Table 5.9. Money Targets, Required Interest Rate Changes, and Macro Impacts

	1975.4	1976.4	1977.4	1978.4	1979.4
Percent Increase in M_1					
Targeted	2.8	3.0	3.0	3.0	3.0
Achieved					
DRI	2.8	3.0	3.0	3.0	3.0
BEA	2.7	3.1	3.3	3.0	2.9
Difference in Three-Month Treasury Bill Rate (percentage points, Simulation 2A—baseline)					
DRI	−3.2	−1.1	−0.1	0.6	1.4
BEA	−0.6	−0.2	−0.2	−0.2	−0.2
Associated Macroeconomic Impacts (percent difference from baseline)					
DRI					
Real GNP	0.5	2.5	3.8	3.5	2.9
GNP deflator	0.0	0.2	1.3	2.6	4.3
Real consumption	0.1	0.8	1.5	1.4	1.3
Consumption deflator	−0.1	0.2	1.1	2.2	3.5
Real disposable income	−0.3	0.7	1.8	1.9	2.0
M_2	3.1	2.3	3.3	3.8	4.6
BEA					
Real GNP	0.3	0.6	0.6	0.6	0.7
GNP deflator	0.0	0.2	0.3	0.5	1.1
Real consumption	0.1	0.3	0.4	0.5	0.7
Consumption deflator	0.0	0.2	0.1	0.4	0.7
Real disposable income	−0.0	0.0	0.2	0.1	0.1
M_2	4.8	4.8	4.7	4.2	3.9

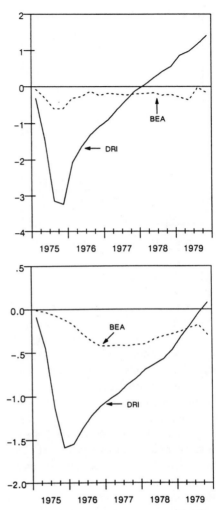

Figure 5.15. Three-month treasury bill rate: simulations 2A–BL, DRI vs BEA (percentage points).

Figure 5.16. AAA corporate bond yields: simulations 2A–BL, DRI vs BEA (percentage points).

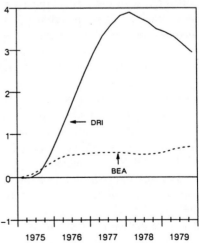

Figure 5.17. GNP multipliers, money shock: simulations 2A–BL, DRI vs BEA (percentage difference).

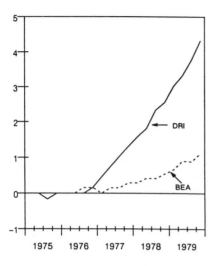

Figure 5.18. Implicit deflator, GNP, money shock: simulations 2A–BL, DRI vs BEA (percentage difference).

typically so large. An alternative explanation is that the sample estimation period was quite different for the two different BEA treatments of M_2.

A second, possibly more important, model specification decision has also influenced the results: transactions demand is driven in the DRI model by consumer spending and household disposable income; transactions are represented by GNP less government spending in the BEA model. Therefore, any shock that causes a significantly different response in household income than in GNP will generate a significantly different transactions demand response in the two models and will thus require a different interest rate profile to match the money demand target—even if the interest elasticities are identical.

Monetary stimulus is likely to produce just such a situation because any cut in interest rates reduces the household share of income significantly (in both models) since consumers are net lenders and businesses are net borrowers. Therefore, if the transactions demand for money is modeled with consumer income or spending rather than total private purchases (as in the BEA model), a higher level of GNP can be consistent with the same expansion of M_1 demand. The simulation results certainly reflect this, as shown in Table 5.9. In the DRI simulation, the consumer spending and income gains are only one-third to one-half the magnitude of the nominal GNP gains; in the BEA simulation, consumer gains are close to those in real GNP, but real income has hardly increased at all. (The implied saving rate shift for BEA is once again due to the strong influence of unemployment, and possibly real wealth, on household spending in the BEA model.)

A third potential source of difference between the money demand models is that BEA has adopted a full logarithmic specification whereas DRI uses semilogarithmic specifications. A final possible source is that the BEA model uses one single equation while the DRI model includes separate equations for eight components of M_2.

Because the goal of this chapter is to deepen the understanding of model contrasts, a thorough test of money demand functions is necessary. It should also be realized that the single equation in the BEA model and the related set of equations in the DRI model dominate the entire "LM" relationships of these macro models. In contrast, the "IS" and aggregate supply relationships are reduced forms of hundreds of equations in both models. Therefore, new empirical testing is truly within the scope of this chapter only for the "LM" relationship.

Empirical Tests. Tables 5.10 and 5.11 summarize the conclusions of tests of coefficient sensitivity to first, the transaction definition (disposable income such as DRI versus GNP excluding government purchases such as BEA); second, the decision to estimate in the standard or inverted form; third, the choice between an aggregated and a disaggregated modeling approach to M_2; and fourth, the specification of a semilogarithmic or full logarithmic relation between money demand and interest rates. Full details of the underlying regressions are reported in the Appendix.

Table 5.10. M_2 Demand Elasticities: Summary of Regression Sensitivity Tests to Alternative Specifications (Estimation Interval 1965.1–1987.4)

Model type[a]	Transaction definition[b]	Direct transactions	Direct t-bill	Direct own rate	Composite t-bill
		Estimated Elasticities[c] of M_2 with Respect to			
Aggregate M_2, standard form	DRI	1.02	−3.14	1.96	−1.69
Same	BEA	1.06	−6.25	5.30	−2.33
Aggregate M_2, inverted form	DRI	1.00	−6.67	6.46	−1.89
Same	BEA	1.10	−4.76	4.38	−1.52
M_2 components estimated separately then aggregated, standard form	DRI	0.95	−5.12	4.86	−2.15
Same	BEA	0.83	−11.80	12.12	−3.79

[a]"Standard form" models have M_2 or its components as the dependent variable; "inverted form" models have the treasury bill rate as the dependent variable. In both, the logarithm of real money demand is related to the level of interest rates and the logarithm of real transactions volume.

[b]The DRI transactions demand driver is real disposable income; the BEA driver is real GNP excluding government purchases.

[c]All are long-run or steady-state parameters derived from the estimated coefficients. The interest rate parameters are semielasticities. The composite treasury bill elasticity equals the reported direct treasury bill coefficient plus the product of the own-rate coefficient and the estimated derivative of the own-rate with respect to the treasury bill rate. This derivative is estimated as 0.74, reflecting a current-quarter impact of 0.14 and lagged impacts of 0.28, 0.23, and 0.09 in subsequent quarters.

Table 5.11. Sensitivity of the Estimated Interest Rate Semielasticity of Money Demand (M_2) to Log versus Semilog Specifications (Estimation interval 1965.1–1987.4)[a]

Equation format	Direct t-bill	Direct own rate	Composite t-bill
Standard Demand Function[b] (M_2 dependent variable)			
Semilog	−3.14	1.96	−1.69
Log	−8.62	7.08	−3.66
Inverted Demand Function (treasury bill rate dependent variable)			
Semilog	−6.67	6.46	−1.89
Log	−6.65	6.23	−2.29

[a]Transaction definition: (BEA) GNP less government purchases.

[b]See footnotes to Table 5.10 for explanation of terms.

The strong conclusion of the new regressions is that a percentage point drop in the treasury bill rate should eventually raise money demand (M_2) by about 2% for any given level of transactions. This is a composite result of a larger direct impact of a treasury bill rate increase, offset by the direct impact of a simultaneous rise in the "own-rates" paid on some deposits within the M_2 aggregate. The own-rates must move with market rates to avoid substantial losses in small time and money-market deposits to certificates of deposits; thus, there is a high correlation between the own-rates and the treasury bill rate. This correlation produces substantial variation in the estimated direct treasury bill semielasticity across alternative specifications, but the own rate semielasticity estimates change in lockstep; as a result, the composite semielasticity estimates cluster around -2.0.

An additional, more tentative conclusion of the regression analysis is that disposable income and consumer spending may be better representatives of transactions demand than adjusted GNP. Equations using the former exhibit substantially greater coefficient stability over the 1965–1987 estimation interval. For example, comparing regressions over the full period with regressions over just 1975–1987, the income version consistently yields transactions elasticities near 1.0 and treasury bill semielasticities near -2.0 in both samples; this is true for aggregate M_2 and for M_2 component regressions. In contrast, regressions using adjusted GNP often break down in the shorter estimation interval.

In regressions explaining demand for individual M_2 components over the entire interval, the two transactions specifications produce very similar results for currency and demand deposits. However, very high treasury bill and own-rate elasticities are estimated for M_2 deposits outside M_1 if adjusted GNP is the transactions proxy: the direct treasury bill semielasticity estimate is -15.1 and that for the own–rate is 14.7. A regression of the own–rate on current and lagged values of the treasury bill rate produces a 0.74 cumulative derivative; thus, the composite elasticity is still -4.2. The corresponding estimates using disposable income are direct treasury bill semielasticity of -6.1, direct own-rate semielasticity of -5.4, and composite semielasticity of -2.1.

There does not appear to be any difference in estimated elasticities that can be attributed to the choice between inverted and standard M_2 demand equations. Surprisingly, there also does not appear to be any difference worth noting between an aggregate M_2 equation and an aggregation of component demand equations.

BEA's inverted M_2 equation has a direct treasury bill semielasticity of -12.7 and an own-rate semielasticity of 11.7. However, the own-rate variation for a full percentage point change in the treasury bill rate is no greater than 0.24; thus, the composite treasury bill elasticity is no lower than -9.9. The semielasticities are not constant because of the full logarithmic equation specification and because BEA used moving weights to estimate the own rate. The weak simulated feedback of the treasury bill rate to the own–rate is thus a major source of the difference in model performance.

In summary, the regression testing and additional simulation tests performed by the authors seem to point to the following conclusion: the large BEA interest elasticity revealed in the shock simulations is caused by the particular estimation interval chosen for the inverted demand function regression; this impact is magnified in the simulations by a quite small estimated translation of movements in treasury bill rates into movements in rates paid on deposits. This produces a BEA composite semielasticity of money demand of -9.9; the DRI model has an implicit semielasticity of -1.7.

Contrasting the Models' Responses to Interest Rates

The remainder of this section on money multipliers uses special simulations of the DRI model to explore differences between the models in their responses to any given set of interest rate changes. In other words, if the money demand functions were the same, what other differences would be important? To gain this knowledge, a sequence of three additional DRI simulations was undertaken. In all three, the treasury bill rate changes of the BEA simulation were exogenously imposed on the DRI model, rather than seeking to match the M_1 change. In addition, one or more of the previously discussed endogenous reactions in the DRI model were "turned off": the exchange rate, the feedback of domestic growth and inflation variations to foreign economies, and the exogeneity of real (rather than nominal) Federal spending.

This set gives a clearer comparative view of the substantial financial-real interactions in the two models. Aside from the foreign trade responses (which have already been discussed), the primary sources of difference are found to be the absence of an accelerator feedback mechanism in the BEA residential construction block and the tendency of the BEA model to produce consumer spending gains well beyond disposable income gains when unemployment drops or real wealth rises.

In the BEA simulation, the money shock requires a 0.6 percentage point lower treasury bill rate after 1 year, followed by a nearly uniform 0.2 percentage point cut relative to the baseline in the next four years (Table 5.12). This stimulates a continually expanding increase in most BEA spending categories throughout the 5 years examined. A rough description is that residential investment responds first, then consumer spending; this ignites extra business fixed investment, which lifts disposable income and hence consumption and housing further. Two factors combine to produce a consumer spending increase eventually 4–5 times greater than the disposable income shift: a jump in wealth and a boost to consumer confidence. The latter is driven by an unemployment rate decline.

Common Exogenous Assumptions. In the first DRI companion simulation, a maximum match of exogenous assumptions was sought. In addition to common bill rates, the change in the long-term bond rate was matched to the BEA outcome, Federal spending was frozen in nominal rather than real terms, and foreign exchange rates, prices, and activity levels were frozen at baseline values. The results are presented in the first of the three DRI lines of Table 5.12.

According to DRI, a shift in nominal interest rates of first 60 and then 20 basis points initiates a shallow cycle in real activity, peaking in the third year. Approximately one-third to one-quarter of the GNP change is found in residential investment, where the stimulus is approximately half as great as the BEA finding during each of the first 3 years. During years 4 and 5, the DRI housing forecast recedes toward the baseline under the pressure of higher vacancies and the gradual disappearance of any significant change in inflation-adjusted interest rates. By year 5, the DRI residential investment change is nil whereas the BEA gain, continuing to expand, has reached $10 billion. Including multiplier–accelerator feedbacks, these contrasts clearly explain most of the $23 billion fifth year BEA GNP gain and the disappearing DRI gains.

Business investment is more sensitive to the direct impact of lower interest rates in the DRI model; thus such spending is $4–5 billion higher in both models in years 3

Table 5.12. Economic Feedbacks from Standardized Interest Rate Shifts[a] (Changes from Baseline, Billions of 1982 Dollars)

	1975.4	1976.4	1977.4	1978.4	1979.4	1975.4	1976.4	1977.4	1978.4	1979.4
Assumed change[a] in treasury bill rate (all simulations)	-0.60	-0.23	-0.20	-0.21	-0.17					
GNP						**GNP Deflator (% points)**				
BEA results	8.5	15.7	17.2	17.5	23.1	0.0	0.2	0.3	0.5	1.1
DRI results										
Maximum match with BEA	1.2	5.4	12.2	9.4	1.7	0.0	0.0	0.1	0.1	0.2
DRI bond rate response	2.7	6.6	6.4	3.4	1.2	0.0	0.0	0.1	0.3	0.4
Full foreign feedbacks	2.6	10.0	14.3	15.1	0.0	0.0	0.1	0.3	0.4	0.4
Residential Investment						**10-Year Treasury Bonds (% points)**				
BEA results	3.6	5.4	6.0	7.5	10.2	-0.11	-0.42	-0.41	-0.28	-0.29
DRI results										
Maximum match with BEA	0.4	2.6	4.2	2.5	1.8	0.0	Same	Same	Same	Same
DRI bond rate response	1.3	2.4	3.0	2.2	0.3	-0.36	-0.19	-0.16	-0.17	-0.10
Full foreign feedbacks	1.3	2.6	1.8	1.2	1.2	-0.36	-0.20	-0.19	-0.21	-0.11
Nonresidential Investment						**Exchange Rate (percent)**				
BEA results	1.0	3.8	4.5	4.7	7.2	0.0	0.0	0.0	0.0	0.0
DRI results										
Maximum match with BEA	0.3	1.7	4.0	4.2	1.8	Same	Same	Same	Same	Same
DRI bond rate response	0.4	2.4	3.0	2.2	1.0	Same	Same	Same	Same	Same
Full foreign feedbacks	0.4	2.8	4.6	4.5	3.8	-0.4	-0.8	-0.9	-1.2	-1.2
Exports						**Imports**				
BEA results	0.0	-0.1	-0.5	-1.3	-2.8	-0.4	1.5	2.3	3.3	6.1
DRI results										
Maximum match with BEA	-1.2	-0.5	-0.5	-0.8	-1.0	-0.9	0.2	1.6	1.6	1.1
DRI bond rate response	-1.2	-0.6	-0.5	-0.8	-0.8	-0.8	0.6	0.8	0.7	0.7
Full foreign feedbacks	-1.0	1.0	2.0	2.8	4.0	-0.8	0.2	0.4	0.0	0.0
Consumer Spending						**Disposable Income**				
BEA results	2.4	5.3	7.6	9.4	13.6	-0.3	0.7	3.6	2.6	2.7
DRI results										
Maximum match with BEA	0.2	1.5	4.3	4.5	3.0	-1.5	1.6	4.4	1.6	1.1
DRI bond rate response	0.6	2.1	3.0	2.5	2.0	-1.1	2.1	2.9	2.3	1.8
Full foreign feedbacks	0.3	2.5	4.5	4.6	5.0	-1.3	2.7	5.1	5.5	6.2

[a] This standardized change was taken directly from BEA Money Shock Simulation (IIA) and imposed on special sequence of DRI simulations. All values are fourth-quarter results for each year indicated rather than annual average values to highlight the short-run cycle in interest rates.

and 4 in spite of the smaller DRI demand expansion. Exports are slightly weaker in both models because only export prices are assumed to have changed. Imports rise by approximately 30–40% of the consumer spending shifts; thus trade does provide a moderate buffer to the monetary stimulus under these assumptions.

The inflation response is proportionately greater in the BEA model, as would be expected from the prior discussion of productivity and unemployment submodels. By the last year, the BEA inflation rate is over one-half percentage point higher than in the baseline; thus, real short-term and long-term interest rates are about three-quarter percentage point lower.

Alternative Yield Curve Effects. Bond rates react more promptly to changing conditions in the DRI model. If the assumption of common nominal long-term rates is relaxed, then the medium-term DRI investment stimulus is significantly muted. These results are displayed on the second of the three DRI lines in Table 5.12.

With the DRI term-structure equation turned on again, the 60 basis point bill rate decline in the first year produces a 36 point cut in bond rates according to DRI (versus 11 points in BEA); the second year convergence to within 23 basis points for treasury bills brings a parallel convergence to within 19 points for bonds for DRI. A very long-lagged reaction within BEA holds the bond rate cut at over 40 basis points in both years 2 and 3, even as inflation is gradually rising.

Impact of Foreign Feedback. In spite of these substantial differences, which on balance produce smaller DRI impacts, a gross equality of the GNP money multipliers of the full models is produced by the offsetting DRI foreign sector feedback. This is revealed by the final simulation in this sequence, summarized in the last DRI lines of Table 5.12.

The drop in U.S. rates and rise in U.S. prices would, according to the DRI equation, produce a 1.2 percentage point decline in the nominal value of the U.S. dollar versus currencies of the major industrial nations; the real exchange value would be about 0.5% lower within 1 year and almost 1% lower thereafter. This would coincidentally nullify the tendency to import more consumer goods and services, and it would bolster export prospects. As a result, DRI estimates that lower interest rates would improve the real trade deficit by almost $2 billion (0.5%) by year 3 and $4 billion by year 5. With exchange rates fixed in the BEA model, the real trade deficit is worse at the end of year five by almost $9 billion.

CONCLUSION

In this study, an analytical microscope has been focused on the results for two models with respect to the fiscal and monetary multiplier experiments; in contrast, Chapter 2 reported macroscopically for 10 models with respect to a broader set of experiments. Like the startling findings in molecular biology obtained with electron microscopy, there were surprises in this (probably unprecedented) effort to determine how and why two models' response mechanisms differ.

Behind the basically similar pattern of the GNP multiplier with respect to the fiscal shock—a fairly quick rise to a peak, followed by a more protracted neutralization—

we found a panoply of largely offsetting contrasts by disaggregation and partial simulation. Thus, although most of the other eight models included in the model comparison study report a broadly similar pattern (as shown in Chapter 2), we strongly suspect that this commonality similarly masks larger, but offsetting differences among the other models. Responses to the monetary shock, in contrast, are markedly different between BEA and DRI, directly reflecting the great differences that the respective money demand functions impart to the "LM curves."

As expected, significant intermodel differences reflect differences in specification and critical parameter estimates. However, to a much greater degree than we expected, they also reflect differences in exogenous versus endogenous treatment of certain variables. Although this might be a cause for concern, two other points should be noted in this regard. First, as often as not, the impacts are offsetting and thus can reduce reported aggregate differences. Second, the design of the comparative model experiment probably exaggerates the differences due to exogenous–endogenous treatment that would emerge in actual practice, inasmuch as model managers interact with their models in carrying out "what if" alternative simulations. For instance, when one model group uses an equation to determine the exchange rate, the other will take into account U.S. and foreign developments and, in a simulation mode, will make warranted judgmental adjustments to the rate. As another example, if inflation were markedly higher in an alternative simulation, nominal Federal purchases would be adjusted by BEA economists so as not to impose the full burden on real purchases. Of course, such model–modeler interactions are too arbitrary to be incorporated in an objective model comparison experiment in the absence of an historically estimated simulation "rule-of-thumb."

In any case, this study confirms what has already been widely perceived: empirical economic science remains a long distance from being an ideal science. Yet our approach is unquestionably scientific. This is not to say that we cannot do better or can never achieve more of a consensus on at least some aspects of model specification. Undoubtedly, in pursuing the enormous and continuous task of large-scale macromodel building, we are not consistently careful about accepting equations that might have been rejected with more careful screening on the basis of single-equation criteria or system validation tests. This study, in particular, has uncovered surprising consequences of some seemingly innocuous modeling decisions; an intermodel comparison, such as this one, has been highly useful in revealing the sensitivity of these decisions. That is in itself a profitable lesson for the future.

NOTES

1. The potential cost of exogenizing arguably endogenous variables is, of course, that leakages of significant feedbacks can occur, thus tending to bias multipliers. Possible remedies, without sacrificing expert judgment for forecasting purposes, are (1) to make judgmental allowances for responses of the "exogenous" variables to policy shifts, and (2) to augment the model with optionally usable equations under a simulation mode, that is, DRI's approach. BEA is now selectively moving toward the second option.

2. Intermodel differences for the effects of an oil shock were extensively analyzed in an earlier study by Bert Hickman: "Macroeconomic Impacts of Energy Shocks and Policy Responses:

A Structural Comparison of 14 Models." In *Macroeconomic Impacts of Energy Shocks,* B. G. Hickman, H. G. Huntington, and J. L. Sweeney, eds., pp. 125–198. Amsterdam: North-Holland, 1987.

3. For the BEA model, Simulation IA(2) is identical to Simulation IB in Chapter 2, although this simulation was treated there as implying an accommodating monetary policy; for DRI, this simulation differs from IB because the exchange rate is frozen. The exogeneity of exchange rates in BEA simulations also means IA is already tantamount to IA(3).

4. The acceleration in the bill rate response in the final year reflects the nature of the inverted money demand function in the BEA model: the rate varies positively (and fairly strongly) both with the lagged price level (a variant of the GNP deflator) and the rate of change in the level; thus a constantly higher inflation rate tends eventually toward a growing interest-rate differential.

5. DRI uses M_1 as the money stock measure, and personal consumption expenditures (for currency) or disposable income (for demand deposits) as the transactions variable. BEA uses M_2 and an aggregate output measure as its transactions variable. The precise formulation of the transactions variable in the BEA model is GDP $-$ GPF $+$ 0.32*GPFXC, where GDP is real gross domestic product, GPF is total Federal Government purchases, and GPFXC is Federal purchases except employee compensation. This formulation focuses on domestic activity and recognizes the exclusion of U.S. Government deposits from M_2, but acknowledges private-sector transactions that are entailed in Federal purchases from the private sector.

6. The rise in the exchange rate in the DRI simulation is sufficient to offset domestic cost pressures on export prices: exchange rates affect export prices both through their impact on prices of imported materials used in producing exported goods and through competitive effects on wage rates.

7. The productivity concept that enters price determination in the BEA model is a weighted combination of "trend" productivity (with the trend drawn through peak levels of historical productivity) and the highest previous level of actual productivity; thus unit labor cost by no means varies proportionally with actual productivity. In the DRI model the productivity measure is an 8-quarter distributed lag of actual values to reflect the common business approach to estimating "standard" unit labor costs as wages relative to average achievable output per hour.

8. Because the BEA model contains behavioral equations for employment and average weekly hours rather than productivity per se, baseline productivity levels were approximated by iterative solution trials.

9. In the DRI model, residential construction outlays might also be regarded as acceleration sensitive because current construction depends partly on the size of the housing stock relative to the number of households; for purposes of this study, however, acceleration-sensitive components are those driven by the change in output or sales.

10. The state–local deflator is implicitly endogenous in the DRI model because the overall purchases (goods and services) deflator is used as a single aggregate price measure.

11. This money acceleration is phased in such that the annualized growth rate of M_1 is greater by 0.6, 2.4, 4.5, and 3.7%, respectively, during the five quarters ending with 1976.1. Although this specific time profile is arbitrary, some phasing was necessary to prevent implausible short-term reductions in interest rates in some of the models. This phased introduction should be kept in mind when evaluating the timing of multipliers, since a peak GNP impact in, say, 1978.1 would actually indicate a mean lag of about 9 rather than 12 quarters (1978.1 vs. 1975.1).

12. The Federal funds rate dominates the determination of other short-term rates such as the commercial paper rate and the 3-month treasury bill rate. The latter is also influenced by the extent of treasury borrowing and state–local income tax rates. The rates for longer

maturity treasury securities are built up from the bill rate, with each yield depending on that of the next lower maturity asset, a distributed lag on inflation, and an endogenous index of the volatility (over the past four years) of bill rates. The volatility index is driven by lagged full-employment government deficits, oil price shocks, and Fed policy shifts. Private long-term yields—corporate bonds and mortgage rates—are keyed to the 10-year treasury bond yield and selected flow-of-funds variables.

APPENDIX

This appendix provides the regression results supporting the money demand discussion in the text. All equations are estimated with ordinary least squares without autocorrelation correction due to time constraints.

Glossary

The transaction definitions are

DRI   Consumer purchases for currency and disposable personal income for all other components of M_1 and M_2. All transaction and money measures are divided by the personal consumption deflator

BEA   Real GNP minus real Federal purchases.

The "own"   Demand deposits: $0.67 \times 5 + 0.33 \times$ (average CD rate, interest rates   current and two lagged quarters)
M_2 and M_2 deposits outside M_1: $w_1 \times 5.5 + (1 - w_1) \times$ (average CD rate, current and two lagged quarters) where w = savings deposits relative to the total of small time deposits and money market deposit accounts at thrifts and commercial banks.

Table A5.1. Estimation Tests: Currency Demand

Interval	Transaction definition	Transactions	Treasury bill	Time	$\bar{R}^2$	SE
1965.1–1987.4	DRI	0.47	−0.83	0.14	0.980	0.017
		(0.07)	(0.08)	(0.05)		
	BEA	0.56	−0.81	0.07	0.970	0.020
		(0.11)	(0.09)	(0.08)		
1975.1–1987.4	DRI	1.00	−0.70	−0.11	0.982	0.012
		(0.09)	(0.06)	(0.06)		
	BEA	1.07	−0.69	−0.16	0.984	0.011
		(0.09)	(0.06)	(0.06)		

Coefficients (Standard errors)

Table A5.2. Estimation Tests: Demand Deposit

Interval	Transaction definition	Time frame	Coefficients (Standard errors)				$\bar{R}^2$	SE
			Transactions	Treasury bill	Own rate	Lagged deposits		
1965.1–1987.4	DRI	Short run	0.080 (0.02)	-.384 (0.06)	0.562 (0.18)	0.875 (0.024)	0.986	0.010
		Long run	0.64	-3.07	4.49			
	BEA	Short run	0.063 (0.02)	-0.339 (0.07)	0.658 (0.19)	0.903 (0.026)	0.985	0.011
		Long run	0.65	-3.49	6.78			
1975.1–1987.4	DRI	Short run	0.277 (0.05)	-0.597 (0.09)	-0.601 (0.31)	0.812 (0.03)	0.990	0.011
		Long run	1.47	-3.18	3.20			
	BEA	Short run	0.242 (0.06)	-0.560 (0.11)	-0.150 (0.32)	0.824 (0.04)	0.987	0.012
		Long run	1.37	-3.16	0.85			

Table A5.3. Estimation Tests: M_2 Deposits Outside M_1

Interval	Transaction definition	Time frame	Coefficients (Standard errors)				$\bar{R}^2$	SE
			Transactions	Treasury bill	Own rate	Lagged deposits		
1965.1–1987.4	DRI	Short run	0.108	−0.609	0.543	0.900	0.998	0.009
			(0.06)	(0.10)	(0.15)	(0.05)		
		Long run	1.08	−6.09	5.43			
	BEA	Short run	0.035	−0.590	0.575	0.961	0.998	0.010
			(0.06)	(0.11)	(0.14)	(0.05)		
		Long run	0.90	15.13	14.74			
1975.1–1987.4	DRI	Short run	0.066	−0.535	0.531	0.912	0.994	0.010
			(0.10)	(0.12)	(0.16)	(0.08)		
		Long run	0.75	−6.08	6.03			
	BEA	Short run	−1.36	−0.306	0.391	1.07	0.995	0.009
			(0.08)	(0.14)	(0.15)	(0.06)		
		Long run	nm	nm	nm			

The letters nm = not meaningful. The long run coefficient is infinite if the lagged deposit coefficient is greater than 1.0.

Table A5.4. Estimation Tests: Aggregate M_2 Standard Money Demand Equation Specification

Interval	Transaction definition	Time frame	Coefficients (Standard errors)				$\bar{R}^2$	SE
			Transactions	Treasury bill	Own rate	Lagged deposits		
1965.1–1987.4	DRI	Short run	0.190	−0.584	0.365	0.814	0.998	0.008
			(0.04)	(0.07)	(0.12)	(0.04)		
		Long run	1.02	−3.14	1.96			
	BEA	Short run	0.105	−0.620	0.524	0.901	0.998	0.008
			(0.05)	(0.09)	(0.11)	(0.04)		
		Long run	1.06	−6.25	5.30			
1975.1–1987.4	DRI	Short run	0.268	−0.529	0.249	0.744	0.995	0.008
			(0.10)	(0.10)	(0.16)	(0.08)		
		Long run	1.04	−2.07	0.97			
	BEA	Short run	−0.094	−0.334	0.421	1.07	0.995	0.008
			(0.09)	(0.13)	(0.13)	(0.07)		
		Long run	nm	nm	nm			

The letters nm = not meaningful. The long run coefficient is infinite if the lagged deposit coefficient is greater than 1.0.

Table A5.5. Estimation Test: Aggregate M_2, Inverted Form (Interval: 1965.1–1987.4)

Transaction definition	Coefficients (Standard errors)				$\bar{R}^2$	SE
	M_2	Lagged M_2	Transactions	M_2 Own rate		
DRI	−0.718 (0.09)	0.568 (0.09)	0.151 (0.05)	0.969 (0.09)	0.906	0.834
	−0.150					
BEA	−0.569 (0.08)	0.359 (0.10)	0.230 (0.04)	0.919 (0.07)	0.922	0.762
	−0.210					

Transaction definition	Implied Long-Run Money-Demand Semielasticities		
	Transactions	T-bill	Own rate
DRI	1.00	−6.67	6.46
BEA	1.10	−4.76	4.38

Table A5.6. Estimation Tests: Aggregate M_2 Logarithm versus Semilogarithmic Specification (Interval: 1965.1–1987.4)

Functional form	Time frame	Transactions	Treasury bill	Own rate	Lagged deposits	$\bar{R}^2$	SE
			Coefficients (Standard errors)				
Standard equation	Specification						
Log	Short run	0.088	−0.046	0.038	0.924	0.998	0.008
		(0.04)	(0.006)	(0.008)	(0.039)		
	Long run	1.16	−0.605	0.500	—		
Semilog	Short run	0.105	−0.620	0.524	0.901	0.998	0.008
		(0.05)	(0.09)	(0.11)	(0.04)		
	Long run	1.06	−6.25	5.30	—		
Inverted equation	Specification						
Log	Short run	0.294	−0.119	0.112	0.745	0.915	0.104
	Long run	1.15	−0.467	0.440	—	0.995	0.008
Semilog	Short run	0.403	−0.0176	0.016	0.631	0.922	0.762
	Long run	1.092	0.048	0.043	—	0.995	0.008

CHAPTER 6

A Comparison of the Michigan and Fair Models

RAY C. FAIR and LEWIS S. ALEXANDER

This chapter compares the predictive accuracy of the Michigan and Fair models using the method developed in Fair (1980). These models are compared to each other and to an eighth-order autoregressive model. The method accounts for the four main sources of uncertainty of a forecast: uncertainty due to (1) the error terms, (2) the coefficient estimates, (3) the exogenous variables, and (4) the possible misspecification of the model. Because it accounts for these four sources, it can be used to make comparisons across models. In other words, it puts each model on an equal footing for purposes of comparison. The method has been used to compare the Fair model to autoregressive models, vector autoregressive models, Sargent's classical macroeconomic model, and a small linear model, but this is the first time it has been used to compare two relatively large structural models.

Ideally, model builders should not be the ones comparing their models to others. Although one may try to be objective, there is always the suspicion that one has stacked the cards in favor of her or his model. This chapter is not intended to be the final word on the relative merits of the Michigan and Fair models. Its primary aim is to demonstrate the application of the comparison method to large models.

As will be seen, the application of the method to the Michigan model reveals two potential shortcomings of the method. First, the results for the Michigan model are highly sensitive to plausible alternative assumptions about exogenous variable uncertainty. This makes comparison difficult because there is no obvious criterion for choosing between the competing assumptions. Second, the Michigan model relies fairly heavily on the use of dummy variables, and the part of the method that accounts for exogenous-variable uncertainty cannot handle dummy variables. It must be assumed that the dummy variables are known with certainty. The method may thus bias the results in favor of models that are heavily tied to dummy variables. It is uncertain how large this bias might be.

THE COMPARISON METHOD

The method was first proposed in Fair (1980), and the latest discussion of it is in Chapter 8 in Fair (1984). The following is a brief outline of the method.

Assume that the model has m stochastic equations, p unrestricted coefficients to estimate, and T observations for the estimation. The model can be nonlinear, simultaneous, and dynamic. Let S denote the covariance matrix of the error terms, and let V denote the covariance matrix of the coefficient estimates. S is $m \times m$ and V is $p \times p$. An estimate of S, say $\hat{S}$, is $(1/T)UU'$, where U is an $m \times T$ matrix of estimated errors. The estimate of V, say $\hat{V}$, depends on the estimation technique used. Let $\hat{\alpha}$ denote a p-component vector of the coefficient estimates, and let u_t denote an m-component vector of the error terms for period t.

Uncertainty from the error terms and coefficient estimates can be estimated in a straightforward way by means of stochastic simulation. Given assumptions about the distributions of the error terms and coefficient estimates, one can draw values of both error terms and coefficients. For each set of values the model can be solved for the period of interest. Given, say, J trials, the estimated forecast mean and estimated variance of the forecast error for each endogenous variable for each period can be computed. Let $\bar{y}_{itk}$ denote the estimated mean of the k-period-ahead forecast of variable i, where t is the first period of the forecast, and let $\tilde{\sigma}^2_{itk}$ denote the estimated variance of the forecast error. $\bar{y}_{itk}$ is simply the average of the J predicted values from the J trials, and $\tilde{\sigma}^2_{itk}$ is the sum of squared deviations of the predicted values from the estimated mean divided by J.

It is usually assumed that the distributions of the error terms and coefficient estimates are normal, although the stochastic-simulation procedure does not require the normality assumption. The normality assumption has been used for the results in this chapter. Let u_t^* be a particular draw of the error terms for period t, and let α^* be a particular draw of the coefficients. The distribution of u_t^* is assumed to be $N(0,\hat{S})$, and the distribution of α^* is assumed to be $N(\hat{\alpha},\hat{V})$.

There are two polar assumptions that can be made about the uncertainty of the exogenous variables. One is that there is no uncertainty. The other is that the exogenous-variable forecasts are in some way as uncertain as the endogenous-variable forecasts. Under this second assumption one could, for example, estimate an autoregressive equation for each exogenous variable and add these equations to the model. This expanded model, which would have no exogenous variables, could then be used for the stochastic-simulation estimates of the variances. The assumption used in this chapter is in between the two polar assumptions. An eighth-order autoregressive equation was estimated for each exogenous variable (with a constant term and time trend included in the equation), and the estimated standard error from this regression was used as the estimate of the degree of uncertainty attached to forecasting the exogenous variable for each period. This procedure ignores the uncertainty of the coefficient estimates in the autoregressive equations, which is one of the reasons it is not as extreme as the second polar assumption. The procedure also assumes that the exogenous-variable errors are uncorrelated with each other and with the structural errors.

This assumption is implemented as follows. Let $\hat{s}_i$ denote the estimated standard error from the autoregressive equation for exogenous variable i. Let v_{it} be a normally distributed random variable with mean zero and variance $\hat{s}_i^2 : v_{it} \sim N(0, \hat{s}_i^2)$ for all t. Let $\hat{x}_{it}$ be the "base" value of exogenous variable i for period t. The base values can be either actual values if the period in question is within the period for which data exist or guessed values otherwise. If the values are guessed, they need *not* be the predictions from the autoregressive equations. The autoregressive equations are used merely to get the values for $\hat{s}_i$.

Let x_{it}^* be the value of variable i for period t used for a particular trial. Given the above setup, one can assume that the v_{it} errors pertain to forecasting either the level of the variable or the change in the variable. If the level assumption is used, the value of x_{it}^* for a given trial is $\hat{x}_{it} + v_{it}$, where v_{it} is drawn from the above distribution. If the change assumption is used, the values are as follows. Let the beginning period be 1 and assume that the overall prediction period is of length K. The values of x_{it}^* ($t = 1, \ldots, K$) for a given trial are

$$x_{i1}^* = \hat{x}_{i1} + v_{i1}$$

$$x_{i2}^* = \hat{x}_{i2} + v_{i1} + v_{i2} \tag{1}$$

$$\vdots$$

$$x_{iK}^* = \hat{x}_{iK} + v_{i1} + v_{i2} + \ldots + v_{iK}$$

where each v_{it} ($t = 1, \ldots, K$) is drawn from the $N(0, \hat{s}_i^2)$ distribution. Because of the assumption that the errors pertain to changes, the error term v_{i1} is carried along from period 1 on. Similarly, v_{i2} is carried along from period 2 on, and so on. Given the way that many exogenous variables are forecast, by extrapolating past trends or taking variables to be unchanged from their last observed values, it may be that any error in forecasting the level of a variable in, say, the first period will persist throughout the prediction period. If this is true, the change assumption is likely to result in a better approximation of exogenous-variable uncertainty.

The stochastic-simulation estimate of the forecast-error variance that is based on draws of the error terms, coefficients, *and* exogenous-variable errors will be denoted $\bar{\bar{\sigma}}_{itk}^2$. It differs from $\bar{\sigma}_{itk}^2$ in that it takes into account exogenous-variable uncertainty.

Estimating the uncertainty from the possible misspecification of the model is the most difficult and costly part of the method. It requires successive reestimation and stochastic simulation of the model. It is based on a comparison of estimated variances computed by means of stochastic simulation with estimated variances computed from outside-sample (i.e., outside the estimation period) forecast errors. Assuming no stochastic-simulation error, the expected value of the difference between the two estimated variances for a given variable and period is zero for a correctly specified model. The expected value is not in general zero for a misspecified model, and this fact is used to try to account for misspecification.

Without going into details, the basic procedure is to estimate the model over a number of different estimation periods and for each set of estimates to compute the difference between the two estimated variances for each variable and lead time of the forecast. The average of these differences for each variable and lead time provides an estimate of the expected value. Let $\bar{d}_{ik}$ denote this average for variable i and lead time k. The stochastic simulations for this work are with respect to draws of error terms and coefficients only, not also draws of exogenous-variable errors. Given $\bar{d}_{ik}$, the final step is to add it to $\bar{\sigma}_{itk}^2$. This sum, which will be denoted $\hat{\sigma}_{itk}^2$, is the final estimated variance; it takes into account all four sources of uncertainty. Another way of looking at $\bar{d}_{ik}$ is that it is the part of the forecast-error variance not accounted for by the stochastic-simulation estimate. Some of the specifics of the above procedure will become apparent in the discussion of the computations under Calculations of the Results.

SOME FEATURES OF THE MODELS

Table 6.1 provides an outline of the models. The Michigan model has 61 stochastic equations and 50 identities. The Fair model has 30 stochastic equations and 98 identities. The following is a brief discussion of some of the differences between the two models.

Even though the Michigan model has more stochastic equations than does the Fair model, it has to some extent more reduced-form like equations. For example, the level of corporate profits is determined by a stochastic equation in the Michigan model, whereas it is determined by an identity (revenue minus costs) in the Fair model. The identity in the Michigan model that would normally determine corporate profits instead determines the statistical discrepancy, which is endogenous. (The statistical discrepancy is exogenous in the Fair model.) Treating the statistical discrepancy as endogenous is a way of allowing a reduced-form like equation for corporate profits to be estimated and used in the model.

The Michigan model is also more reduced form in its determination of the unemployment rate. In the Fair model there are three stochastic equations explaining the labor force (equations for prime age men, prime age women, and all others), a stochastic equation explaining the number of people holding two jobs, and a stochastic equation explaining the demand for jobs by the firm sector. The unemployment rate is determined by an identity. It is equal to one minus the ratio of total employment to the total labor force. Total employment is equal to the total number of jobs minus the number of people holding two jobs. In the Michigan model the unemployment rate is determined by a stochastic equation. It is a function of a dummy variable (DFPR in Table 6.2), a time trend, and one minus the employment rate of adult men. The em-

Table 6.1. The Models

Michigan
   61 stochastic equations
   50 identities
   96 exogenous variables, of which 39 are dummy variables
   Basic estimation period in Belton, Hymans, and Lown (1981): 1954.1–1979.4
   Estimation technique: ordinary least squares, sometimes accounting for first-order serial correlation
      of the error terms
Fair
   30 stochastic equations
   98 identities
   106 exogenous variables, of which 11 are dummy variables
   Basic estimation period in Fair (1984): 1954.1–1982.3
   Estimation technique: two stage least squares, sometimes accounting for first-order serial
      correlation of the errors terms
Autoregressive
   One eighth-order autoregressive equation (with a constant term and time trend included) per
      relevant variable
   No exogenous variables other than the time trend
   Basic estimation period: same as for the Michigan model
   Estimation technique: ordinary least squares

Table 6.2. Dummy Variables in the Michigan and Fair Models

Name	Description	Equation	t-Statistic[d]
Michigan			
DAPACTM	Dummy variable to reflect Canadian auto pact	C16	2.08
DASTRIKE	Dummy variable for auto strikes	C1, C11	6.46, 2.62
DASTRIKE$_{-1}$		C1	−4.23
DAUTO	Dummy variable to reflect 1975 auto rebates and reaction to higher auto prices in 1974; equals 0.90 in 1974.2 and 1974.3, 0.95 in 1975.1 and 1975.2, equals 1.0 otherwise	C1	−5.04[a]
DEX65	Dummy variable for the change in Federal excise tax law, equal to 1 from 1954.1–1964.1, 0 otherwise	D8	3.30[a]
DFPR[b]	Dummy variable to reflect shift in relation between RUM and RUG values (RUM = unemployment rate, males 20 and over; RUG = global unemployment rate)	B3	2.21[a] −5.14[a]
DFROFF	Dummy variable for removal of price controls; equals 0.25 in 1974.2–1975.1, 0 otherwise	A2	4.71
DFRZ1		A1	3.02
DFRZ2	Dummy variables to reflect price freeze and Phase II effects on prices and compensation	A2	−1.83[a]
DFRZ3		A2	−1.83[a]
	DFRZ1 equals −1.0 in 1971.3 equals 0 otherwise DFRZ2 equals 0.5 in 1971.3, 1.0 in 1971.4 DFRZ3 equals 1.0 in 1972.2–1972.4		
DGPAY	Dummy variable to reflect government pay increases	All	4.10[a]
DJGPM	Dummy variable to reflect increased consumer awareness of gas mileage in the cost of running a new car, equal to 0 from 1954.1–1974.4, 1 otherwise	C1	−5.04[a]
		C3	3.56[a]
DM72DOCK	Dummy variable for dock strikes	C16	6.63
DM72DOCK$_{-1}$		C16	−1.77
DM72SS	Dummy variable to reflect steel strike in import equation; equal to 0.5 in 1959.2, 1.0 in 1959.3, 0 otherwise	C16	1.73
DM72SS$_{-1}$		C16	−0.61
DPGAS	Dummy variable for availability of PGAS series, equal to 1 from 1954.1 to 1957.1, 0 otherwise (PGAS = price index for gasoline, motor oil, coolant, and other products)	A6	−1.97
DPROP13	Dummy variable for the effect of Proposition 13 on state and local indirect business taxes; equals 1 in 1978.3; 0 otherwise	D9	−13.36
DRAM	Dummy variable for the effect on MRAM of changes in the structure of reserve requirements on demand and time deposits (part of dependent variable of equation E4) (MRAM = reserve adjustment magnitude)		N.A.[c]

Variable	Description	Equation	Coefficient
DSEAS1	Dummy variable equal to 1 in the first quarter, −1 in the fourth quarter, 0 otherwise	E2–E8, E10	Many coefficients
DSEAS2	Dummy variable equal to 1 in the second quarter, −1 in the fourth quarter, 0 otherwise	E2–E8, E10	Many coefficients
DSEAS3	Dummy variable equal to 1 in the third quarter, −1 in the fourth quarter, 0 otherwise	E2–E8, E10	Many coefficients
DSPRD	Dummy variable for anomaly in spread between RCP and RTB; equals 1 in 1974.2 and 1974.3, 0 otherwise (RCP = 4–6 month commercial paper rate; RTB = 90-day treasury bill rate)	E10	10.87
DTEX[b]	Dummy variable to reflect direct price effects of changes in excise tax laws in 1965	A3 A5	1.51^a 1.30^a
DTIB[b]	Dummy variable to reflect changes in indirect business taxes	D8	16.01
DTP[b]	Dummy variable to reflect changes in personal taxes	An identity	N.A.
DTPR[b]	Dummy variable for personal tax rate	An identity	N.A.
DTSI	Dummy variable that assumes values equal to the revenue effect of changes in social insurance tax law	A1 D1	5.33^a −3.18
DUBEXT	Dummy variable for the extension of unemployment benefits beyond 26 weeks	D5	3.77
DUM74	Dummy variable in IPD072 equation; equals 0 in 1954.1–1973.4, 1 otherwise (IPD072 = producers' durable equipment investment except in agriculture and production)	C11	2.90^a
DUM75	Dummy variable in GDEBTP equation; equals 0 in 1954.1–1974.4, 1 otherwise (GDEBTP = gross public debt of the U.S. treasury held by private investors)	E5	5.09
DVDOWN	Dummy variable to reflect effects of winddown of Vietnam War on employment; equals 1 in 1970.1–1972.2, 0 otherwise	B2	−1.52
DVNUP	Dummy variable to reflect effects of Vietnam War build-up on employment; equals 1 in 1965.3–1966.4, 0 otherwise	B2	−0.68
D5467	Dummy variable for change in trend growth of productivity; equals 1 in 1954.1–1967.4, 0 otherwise	A2 B1	10.99^a 3.82
D5864	Dummy variable in JCAP equation; equals 1 in 1958.1–1964.4, 0 otherwise (JCAP = index of available capacity in manufacturing)	F3	−6.72
D66	Dummy variable in M1BPLUS equation; equals 0 in 1954.1–1965.4, 1 otherwise (M1PLUS = M1B plus total savings at all depository institutions)	E11	−2.97
D674	Dummy variable for state income tax law changes; equals 0 in 1954.1–1967.3, 1 otherwise	D14	2.13
D6873	Dummy variable for change in trend growth of productivity; equals 1 in 1968.1–1973.4, 0 otherwise	A2 B1	2.50^a 3.22

Table 6.2. (*Continued*)

Name	Description	Equation	t-Statistic[a]
D7074	Dummy variable in JCAP equation; equals 1 in 1970.1–1974.2, 0 otherwise (JCAP = index of available capacity in manufacturing)	F3	−6.31
D711	Dummy variable for state personal income tax law changes; equals 0 in 1954.1–1970.4, 1 otherwise	D14	0.91
D763	Dummy variable in IRC72 equation; equals 1 in 1976.3, 0 otherwise	C13	−2.93
D79	Dummy variable for change in trend growth of productivity; equals 0 in 1954.1–1978.4, 1 otherwise	B1	−0.31
Fair			
D593	1 in 1959.3; 0 otherwise	11, 13	1.86, 2.70
D594	1 in 1959.4; 0 otherwise	11, 13	0.64, 0.50
D601	1 in 1960.1; 0 otherwise	11	1.89
D651	1 in 1965.1; 0 otherwise	27	2.18
D652	1 in 1965.2; 0 otherwise	27	1.17
D691	1 in 1969.1; 0 otherwise	27	3.65
D692	1 in 1969.2; 0 otherwise	27	5.42
D714	1 in 1971.4; 0 otherwise	27	2.64
D721	1 in 1972.1; 0 otherwise	27	4.10
DD793	1 from 1979.3 on; 0 otherwise	30	4.20[e]
DD811	1 from 1981.1 on; 0 otherwise	21	6.29

[a]t-statistics are for explanatory variables that are functions of the relevant dummy variable and other variables.

[b]Autoregressive equation estimated from this variable for the estimation of exogenous-variable uncertainty under Calculations of the Results.

[c]N.A., not applicable.

[d]The t-statistics for the Michigan model are as computed for the results in this chapter. They may differ slightly from the values in Belton, Hymans, and Lown (1981).

ployment rate of adult men is determined by a stochastic equation. It is a function, among other things, of real GNP.

The Michigan model has more disaggregation with respect to the expenditure variables. The differences pertain to consumer durable expenditures and nonresidential fixed investment. In the Michigan model durable expenditures are disaggregated into four components: new autos, motor vehicles and parts less new autos, furniture and household equipment, and all other. There is one stochastic equation for each of these components. In the Fair model there is one stochastic equation explaining total durable expenditures. Nonresidential fixed investment is disaggregated into four components in the Michigan model: structures, producers' durable equipment in production, producers' durable equipment in agriculture, and producers' durable equipment except in agriculture and production. There is one stochastic equation for each of these components. In the Fair model there is one stochastic equation explaining total nonresidential fixed investment. There is also a separate equation in the Michigan model explaining the number of new car sales, which is used as an explanatory variable in the automobile expenditure equation. Considerable work has gone into the Michigan model in explaining automobile expenditures.

As noted in the introductory section, there is a fairly heavy use of dummy variables in the Michigan model. Also, many of the dummy variables appear to be subjective. The dummy variables in the Michigan model are listed in Table 6.2. This table also includes the number of the equation that each variable appears in and the associated t-statistic of its coefficient estimate. The description of the variables is taken from Belton, Hymans, and Lown (1981). Two of the more subjective variables are DJGPM, which is a dummy variable to reflect increased consumer awareness of gas mileage in the cost of running a new car, and DAUTO, which is a dummy variable to reflect auto rebates and reaction to higher auto prices. Of the 345 estimated coefficients in the Michigan model, 43 are coefficients of nonseasonal dummy variables or variables that are a function of nonseasonal dummy variables.

Dummy variables play a less important role in the Fair model. The dummy variables in the Fair model are also listed in Table 6.2. There are 11 dummy variables, 6 of which account for the effects of dock strikes in the import equation (equation 27). The other 5 dummy variables appear in 4 other stochastic equations. Of the 169 estimated coefficients in the Fair model, 13 are coefficients of dummy variables or variables that are a function of dummy variables.

The fairly heavy use of dummy variables in the Michigan model poses a problem for the comparison method. With a few exceptions, it is not sensible to estimate autoregressive equations for the dummy variables, and so they have to be taken as fixed for purposes of the stochastic-simulation draws of the exogenous-variable errors.[1] The method may thus underestimate the uncertainty from the exogenous variables for the Michigan model.

Even where autoregressive equations are estimated for dummy variables, it is not clear that the use of these equations is appropriate. Consider, for example, dummy variable DFPR, which plays an important role in the stochastic equation explaining the unemployment rate. It begins to take on positive values in 1965.1. It is 0 before 1965.1; it is 1 in 1965.1 and increases by 1 each quarter until 1970.4; it is flat until 1976.1; it increases by 1 from 1976.1 to 1979.4; and it is flat thereafter. The autoregressive equation for this variable was estimated only over the nonzero observations. The estimated standard error was 0.173. This estimated error is quite low, and so it means that very little uncertainty is assumed for the variable. It is almost like taking the variable to be fixed.

The DFPR variable links the employment rate of adult men to the overall unemployment rate. The former is easier to explain than the latter because the labor force of adult men fluctuates less than does the labor force of other groups. Thus, the Michigan model links a relatively easy-to-explain variable to a relatively hard-to-explain variable by the use of a time trend and the DFPR dummy variable. If the comparison method has underestimated the uncertainty of the DFPR variable, then the uncertainty of the unemployment rate forecasts will be underestimated.

Another example of the dummy variable problem concerns the key price equation in the Michigan model, Eq. (A2), which determines PPNF, the private nonfarm deflator. There are two dummy variables in the equation that pertain to the price freeze, and there is a productivity trend variable that is a function of three other dummy variables. One of the latter three variables takes on a value of 1 between 1954.1 and 1967.4 and 0 otherwise; one takes on a value of 1 between 1968.1 and 1973.4 and 0 otherwise; and one takes on a value of 1 between 1979.1 and 1979.4 and 0 otherwise. The specification of this equation may mean that a fairly large part of the fluctuations in the price deflator is explained by the dummy variables, and if this is true, the method will underestimate the uncertainty from the price equation.

The Michigan model has also used what seem to be questionable explanatory variables in some of the equations. For example, the discount rate is used as an explanatory variable in the bill rate equation. It is by far the most significant variable in the equation. On a quarterly basis the two variables are highly correlated, but this is because the discount rate generally follows the bill rate with a lag of a few weeks. The discount rate is not generally the policy instrument used by the Fed to influence short-term rates.[2] It is simply a passive instrument. Another example of this type is the use of the minimum wage in the wage rate equation. It seems more likely that the aggregate wage rate affects the minimum wage rate rather than vice versa. Both the discount rate and the minimum wage are exogenous in the model.

CALCULATIONS OF THE RESULTS

Many steps were involved in obtaining the final results, and it is easiest to discuss the computation of the results in the order in which they were done. The results for the Michigan model will be discussed first.

Duplication of the Basic Estimates

Data for the Michigan model were taken from the TROLL version of the model that was current at the beginning of 1983.[3] The specification of this version of the model is in Belton, Hymans, and Lown (1981) (BHL). The first step was to duplicate the basic sets of estimates, which we were able to do. For none of the 61 equations were the differences between our estimates and the BHL estimates large enough to call into question our duplication of the results.

Initial Stochastic Simulation Results

Given the basic coefficient estimates, the V and S covariance matrices were estimated. The number of unconstrained coefficients in the model is 345, and so V is 345×345. V was estimated as a block diagonal matrix, with the blocks being the estimated covariance matrices of the coefficient estimates of the individual equations.[4] The estimation of S required more thought (S is 61×61 since there are 61 stochastic equations). The problem was that estimation periods differ across equations. With three exceptions the periods ended in 1979.4, but they generally began with different quarters. The beginning quarters for the longest and shortest estimation periods were 1954.1 and 1963.2, respectively. There are two plausible ways to estimate S. One is to estimate the full S over the period that all the equations have in common, which is 1963.2–1979.4. The other is to take S to be a diagonal matrix and to estimate each diagonal element using the same estimation period that is used to estimate the corresponding equation. In this case the diagonal elements of S would be based on different estimation periods.

To see how sensitive the results are to alternative estimates of S, three stochastic

Table 6.3. Initial Stochastic Simulation Results for the Michigan Model[a–d]

| | Estimated Standard Errors of Forecasts | | | | | | | |
| | 1978 | | | | 1979 | | | |
	1	2	3	4	1	2	3	4
Real GNP								
Full S—small	0.39	0.55	0.72	0.84	0.94	1.04	1.17	1.21
Diagonal S—small	0.43	0.56	0.74	0.87	1.01	1.12	1.23	1.30
Diagonal S—large	0.39	0.62	0.76	0.89	0.98	1.08	1.13	1.21
Private nonfarm deflator								
Full S—small	0.30	0.43	0.57	0.65	0.78	0.90	0.96	1.07
Diagonal S—small	0.29	0.41	0.53	0.65	0.75	0.85	0.96	1.03
Diagonal S—large	0.27	0.40	0.51	0.59	0.70	0.79	0.90	0.99
Unemployment rate								
Full S—small	0.19	0.30	0.38	0.44	0.51	0.55	0.61	0.67
Diagonal S—small	0.22	0.30	0.38	0.45	0.50	0.57	0.66	0.72
Diagonal S—large	0.23	0.35	0.44	0.54	0.58	0.65	0.72	0.76
Bill rate								
Full S—small	0.38	0.46	0.60	0.72	0.71	0.69	0.77	0.96
Diagonal S—small	0.34	0.46	0.62	0.73	0.69	0.63	0.72	0.94
Diagonal S—large	0.41	0.48	0.58	0.70	0.69	0.71	0.80	0.91
Money supply								
Full S—small	0.73	1.16	1.49	1.79	2.07	2.32	2.54	2.66
Diagonal S—small	0.75	1.32	1.78	2.12	2.47	2.77	2.98	3.20
Diagonal S—large	0.76	1.28	1.74	1.99	2.29	2.57	2.77	2.89

[a]Stochastic simulation is with respect to error terms only.

[b]250 trials for each set of results.

[c]Full S—small = full S estimated for 1963.2–1979.4 period. Diagonal S—small = S taken to be diagonal. Estimation period for diagonal elements is 1963.2–1979.4. Diagonal S—large = S taken to be diagonal. Estimation period for each diagonal element is the same as the period used to estimate the corresponding equation.

[d]All errors are in percentage points. Errors for real GNP, the GNP deflator, and the money supply are percentages of the forecast means.

simulations were performed. These results are presented in Table 6.3 for selected variables. The first simulation used the full S estimated for the common period; the second used the diagonal S estimated for the common period; and the third used the diagonal S estimated using the different estimation periods. The period of the simulation is 1978.1–1979.4. The number of trials for each stochastic simulation was 250. These simulations were with respect to draws from the error terms only, since this is all that is of interest with respect to the S matrix. As can be seen, the results are not very sensitive to the alternative S matrices. For the rest of the results in this chapter S has been estimated as a diagonal matrix with the estimation period for each diagonal element being the same as the period used to estimate the corresponding equation.

Although the estimation periods for the Michigan equations ended in 1979.4, the data base contained data through 1982.1. Some of the observations for 1982.1 did not seem sensible, but the data through 1981.4 seemed good. The Michigan model was reestimated through 1981.4. Specifically, new coefficient estimates were obtained along with new estimates of V and S. To see how sensitive the stochastic-simulation results are to the different estimation periods, two stochastic simulations were performed using the two sets of estimates. The simulation period for both simulations was 1978.1–1979.4; both simulations were based on 250 trials and both simulations were based on draws of error terms and coefficients. The results for selected variables are presented in Table 6.4. These results are also fairly close, which means that it does not make much difference which set is taken to be the basic set of estimates of the model. We decided to stay with the first set of estimates (i.e., the estimates through

Table 6.4. More Initial Stochastic Simulation Results for the Michigan Model[a–e]

| | Estimated Standard Errors of Forecasts | | | | | | | |
| | 1978 | | | | 1979 | | | |
	1	2	3	4	1	2	3	4
Real GNP								
Basic	0.46	0.61	0.78	0.91	0.99	1.11	1.23	1.39
Extended	0.55	0.68	0.82	0.95	1.11	1.27	1.43	1.58
Private nonfarm								
Basic	0.28	0.40	0.53	0.66	0.74	0.88	1.01	1.17
Extended	0.32	0.46	0.56	0.67	0.79	0.92	1.04	1.20
Unemployment rate								
Basic	0.25	0.36	0.45	0.54	0.61	0.66	0.74	0.84
Extended	0.24	0.35	0.43	0.49	0.58	0.65	0.72	0.81
Bill rate								
Basic	0.41	0.57	0.73	0.96	1.03	1.06	1.26	1.49
Extended	0.49	0.61	0.75	1.08	1.11	1.03	1.21	1.51
Money supply								
Basic	0.88	1.51	2.10	2.67	3.18	3.42	3.87	4.58
Extended	0.94	1.65	2.15	2.63	3.11	3.53	3.89	4.32

[a]Stochastic simulation is with respect to error terms and coefficient estimates.

[b]250 trials for each set of results.

[c]S matrix is taken to be diagonal.

[d]Basic = estimation periods end in 1979.4. Extended = estimation periods end in 1981.4.

[e]All errors are in percentage points. Errors for real GNP, the GNP deflator, and the money supply are percentages of the forecast means.

1979.4), since this is the set presented in Belton, Hymans, and Lown (1981). We did, however, use the data through 1981.4 for the successive reestimation and stochastic simulation of the model that is discussed below.

Uncertainty with Respect to the Error Terms and Coefficient Estimates

Table 6.5 contains the main results of this chapter. The values in the a rows are stochastic-simulation estimates of the forecast standard errors based on draws of the error terms only. The values in the b rows are based on draws of both error terms and coefficients. The results are based on 250 trials for each of the two stochastic simulations.[5] The coefficient estimates and the estimates of S and V that were used for these simulations are based on the estimation periods that ended in 1979.4. The simulation period is 1978.1–1979.4. In terms of the notation previously given, the b-row values are values of $\tilde{\sigma}_{itk}$.[6]

Treatment of Exogenous-Variable Uncertainty

Eighth-order autoregressive equations were estimated for 48 exogenous variables in the model. The variables and estimation periods are listed in Table A.1 in the Appendix. Of the 39 dummy variables listed in Table 6.2, 5 had equations estimated for them. These are indicated by footnote b in Table 6.2. Two stochastic simulations were performed with respect to exogenous-variable uncertainty. The first was based on the assumption that the errors for the exogenous variables pertain to changes in the variables, and the second was based on the assumption that the errors pertain to the levels of the variables. These two assumptions are discussed under The Comparison Method. Both simulations were based on draws for the error terms, coefficients, and exogenous-variable errors, and both were based on 250 trials.[7] The results are presented in the c-rows in Table 6.5. The results in the left half of the table are for the change assumption, and the results in the right half are for the level assumption. In terms of the previously given notation, the c-row values are values of $\tilde{\tilde{\sigma}}_{itk}$.

Uncertainty from the Possible Misspecification of the Model

For the misspecification results the Michigan model was estimated and stochastically simulated 27 times. For the first set, the estimation periods ended in 1974.4 and the simulation period began two quarters later in 1975.2. For the second set, the estimation periods ended in 1975.1 and the simulation period began in 1975.3. For the final set, the estimation periods ended in 1981.2 and the simulation period began in 1981.4. The beginning quarters for the estimation periods remained unchanged from those for the basic period. The length of the first 20 simulation periods was eight quarters. Since the data ended in 1981.4, the length of the twenty-first simulation period, which began in 1980.2, was only seven quarters. Similarly, the length of the twenty-second period was six, and so on through the length of the twenty-seventh period, which was only one quarter. For each of the 27 sets of estimates, new estimates of V and S were obtained. Each of the 27 stochastic simulations was based on 50 trials.[8]

Table 6.5. Estimated Standard Errors of Forecasts for 1978.1–1979.4 for the Three Models[a-d]

	Change Assumption for Exogenous-Variable Uncertainty								Level Assumption for Exogenous-Variable Uncertainty							
	1978				1979				1978				1979			
	1	2	3	4	1	2	3	4	1	2	3	4	1	2	3	4
Real GNP																
Michigan																
a	0.39	0.62	0.76	0.89	0.98	1.08	1.13	1.21								
b	0.46	0.61	0.78	0.91	0.99	1.11	1.23	1.39								
c	0.51	0.86	1.17	1.61	2.13	2.73	3.34	3.94	0.48	0.74	0.92	1.14	1.30	1.51	1.72	1.84
d	0.83	1.24	1.60	1.86	2.24	2.87	3.91	5.01	0.81	1.16	1.43	1.48	1.47	1.75	2.66	3.61
Fair																
a	0.49	0.66	0.81	0.98	1.10	1.14	1.22	1.32								
b	0.51	0.69	0.89	1.03	1.09	1.22	1.30	1.35								
c	0.61	0.83	1.08	1.34	1.54	1.73	1.88	2.01	0.61	0.78	0.94	1.14	1.31	1.41	1.50	1.66
d	0.91	1.29	1.70	2.47	2.42	2.71	3.00	3.39	0.91	1.25	1.61	1.94	2.28	2.52	2.78	3.20
AR8																
a	0.65	1.01	1.27	1.56	1.67	1.72	1.75	1.76								
b	0.72	1.13	1.50	1.78	1.97	2.11	2.26	2.34								
d	1.14	1.73	2.16	2.08	1.96	2.08	2.47	2.74								
Private nonfarm deflator																
Michigan																
a	0.27	0.40	0.51	0.59	0.70	0.79	0.90	0.99								
b	0.28	0.40	0.53	0.66	0.74	0.88	1.01	1.17								
c	0.30	0.46	0.60	0.74	0.87	1.04	1.16	1.31	0.29	0.44	0.55	0.64	0.79	0.92	1.06	1.17
d	0.36	0.46	0.53	0.71	0.82	0.96	1.09	1.25	0.35	0.44	0.47	0.60	0.74	0.83	0.98	1.11
Fair																
a	0.38	0.55	0.68	0.77	0.84	0.91	0.92	0.98								
b	0.41	0.57	0.70	0.84	0.91	0.99	1.09	1.21								
c	0.44	0.59	0.68	0.80	0.93	1.03	1.18	1.26	0.41	0.63	0.74	0.83	0.93	1.01	1.08	1.16
d	0.68	1.14	1.54	2.03	2.45	2.81	3.20	3.51	0.66	1.16	1.57	2.04	2.45	2.81	3.16	3.47

	1	2	3	4	5	6	7	8	9	10	11	12	13	14	15	16
AR8																
a	0.30	0.48	0.70	0.91	1.11	1.27	1.39	1.50								
b	0.34	0.53	0.77	1.05	1.30	1.55	1.78	1.99								
d	0.70	1.18	1.72	2.57	3.24	3.75	3.98	3.74								
Nominal GNP																
Michigan																
a	0.40	0.64	0.79	0.94	1.00	1.15	1.20	1.20								
b	0.46	0.68	0.89	1.01	1.07	1.24	1.40	1.52								
c	0.58	0.93	1.22	1.62	2.15	2.81	3.89	3.82	0.53	0.81	1.01	1.24	1.38	1.65	1.84	1.90
d	1.08	1.56	1.84	1.92	2.40	3.13	4.53	5.08	1.05	1.49	1.71	1.61	1.75	2.15	2.97	3.85
Fair																
a	0.59	0.85	1.07	1.23	1.36	1.47	1.57	1.62								
b	0.61	0.89	1.12	1.34	1.47	1.70	1.97	2.05								
c	0.79	1.04	1.31	1.56	1.82	2.12	2.50	2.54	0.76	1.06	1.24	1.46	1.71	1.93	2.11	2.21
d	1.05	1.39	1.80	2.06	2.34	2.55	2.77	2.80	1.03	1.40	1.75	1.98	2.25	2.39	2.43	2.50
AR8																
a	0.45	0.69	0.82	0.92	0.95	1.02	1.15	1.21								
b	0.50	0.79	1.01	1.18	1.27	1.37	1.49	1.66								
d	1.25	1.87	2.35	2.42	2.58	3.03	3.66	4.10								
Unemployment rate																
Michigan																
a	0.23	0.35	0.44	0.54	0.58	0.65	0.72	0.76								
b	0.25	0.36	0.45	0.54	0.61	0.66	0.74	0.84								
c	0.25	0.41	0.59	0.76	0.94	1.18	1.46	1.75	0.24	0.37	0.49	0.61	0.69	0.78	0.86	0.96
d	0.34	0.56	0.77	0.92	1.00	1.11	1.40	1.87	0.34	0.53	0.70	0.80	0.78	0.66	0.76	1.17
Fair																
a	0.24	0.38	0.48	0.54	0.61	0.65	0.68	0.68								
b	0.26	0.42	0.52	0.61	0.70	0.77	0.78	0.80								
c	0.27	0.43	0.57	0.67	0.73	0.83	0.89	0.92	0.27	0.43	0.52	0.62	0.72	0.79	0.82	0.91
d	0.39	0.62	0.89	1.08	1.18	1.29	1.36	1.46	0.39	0.62	0.86	1.05	1.17	1.27	1.32	1.46
AR8																
a	0.29	0.58	0.81	0.97	1.06	1.11	1.17	1.23								
b	0.29	0.56	0.83	1.04	1.19	1.30	1.37	1.41								
d	0.31	0.37	0.39	0.29	i	i	i	i								

(continued)

Table 6.5. (*Continued*)

	Change Assumption for Exogenous-Variable Uncertainty								Level Assumption for Exogenous-Variable Uncertainty							
	1978				1979				1978				1979			
	1	2	3	4	1	2	3	4	1	2	3	4	1	2	3	4
Bill rate																
Michigan																
a	0.41	0.48	0.58	0.70	0.69	0.71	0.80	0.91								
b	0.41	0.57	0.73	0.96	1.03	1.06	1.26	1.49								
c	0.61	0.79	0.97	1.28	1.40	1.44	1.98	3.57	0.65	0.80	0.95	1.21	1.22	1.32	1.51	2.18
d	0.78	1.05	1.20	1.52	1.68	1.67	1.93	3.39	0.81	1.05	1.19	1.46	1.53	1.56	1.44	4.87
Fair																
a	0.71	1.00	1.07	1.13	1.17	1.21	1.17	1.19								
b	0.73	0.94	1.04	1.03	1.15	1.25	1.31	1.45								
c	0.72	0.96	1.09	1.16	1.17	1.34	1.49	1.60	0.71	0.99	1.08	1.17	1.29	1.28	1.50	1.37
d	1.37	2.13	2.40	2.54	2.67	2.87	3.08	3.29	1.36	2.15	2.40	2.55	2.72	2.85	3.09	3.18
AR8																
a	0.52	0.82	0.92	0.97	1.00	1.08	1.17	1.23								
b	0.54	0.86	1.00	1.13	1.22	1.35	1.39	1.40								
d	1.52	2.51	2.72	3.08	3.39	3.65	3.89	4.09								
Money supply																
Michigan																
a	0.76	1.28	1.74	1.99	2.29	2.57	2.77	2.89								
b	0.83	1.51	2.10	2.67	3.11	3.42	3.87	4.58								
c	0.89	1.52	2.18	2.88	3.39	3.95	4.62	6.09	0.85	1.39	1.90	2.35	2.78	3.31	3.93	5.00
d	1.60	2.14	2.81	3.81	4.56	5.45	6.54	8.15	1.58	2.05	2.59	3.43	4.12	5.01	6.07	7.37
Fair																
a	0.98	1.35	1.49	1.66	1.82	2.00	2.03	1.98								
b	0.95	1.37	1.57	1.77	2.11	2.32	2.38	2.54								
c	1.07	1.53	1.84	2.03	2.49	2.69	3.12	3.45	1.03	1.47	1.75	1.93	2.13	2.24	2.37	2.44
d	1.49	1.90	1.98	2.06	2.22	2.08	2.17	1.56	1.46	1.91	2.08	2.27	2.32	2.32	2.36	1.78

AR8																
a	0.57	1.11	1.55	1.95	2.43	2.91	3.42	3.92								
b	0.57	1.17	1.68	2.33	3.08	3.89	4.83	5.77								
d	2.10	3.50	4.26	5.27	5.91	7.05	8.85	10.39								
Consumer expenditures, services																
Michigan																
a	0.28	0.39	0.47	0.54	0.59	0.65	0.70	0.74	0.31	0.44	0.54	0.60	0.69	0.77	0.85	0.91
b	0.30	0.41	0.52	0.62	0.67	0.74	0.80	0.85	0.49	0.75	0.91	1.14	1.38	1.64	1.96	2.23
c	0.28	0.45	0.59	0.81	1.03	1.21	1.46	1.72								
d	0.47	0.76	0.97	1.27	1.57	1.89	2.29	2.67								
Fair																
a	0.30	0.40	0.53	0.61	0.72	0.81	0.89	1.00	0.29	0.44	0.56	0.71	0.86	0.99	1.11	1.22
b	0.28	0.41	0.55	0.67	0.81	0.93	0.99	1.10	0.36	0.57	0.87	1.21	1.43	1.71	2.00	2.27
c	0.28	0.43	0.60	0.76	0.91	1.06	1.25	1.37								
d	0.35	0.56	0.90	1.24	1.72	1.75	2.08	2.36								
AR8																
a	0.28	0.40	0.49	0.60	0.69	0.72	0.78	0.81								
b	0.30	0.44	0.54	0.64	0.76	0.84	0.95	1.05								
d	0.51	0.81	1.05	1.31	1.61	1.90	2.27	2.56								
Consumer expenditures, nondurables																
Michigan																
a	0.52	0.70	0.85	0.98	1.14	1.18	1.27	1.38	0.67	0.92	1.23	1.49	1.74	1.95	2.22	2.41
b	0.52	0.70	0.88	1.02	1.14	1.25	1.39	1.45	0.96	1.41	1.77	2.08	2.48	2.86	3.34	3.80
c	0.69	1.16	1.66	2.43	3.34	4.29	5.44	6.68								
d	0.98	1.58	2.10	2.83	3.78	4.77	5.99	7.30								
Fair																
a	0.58	0.73	0.82	0.99	0.99	1.07	1.07	1.16	0.68	0.84	0.96	1.18	1.28	1.27	1.36	1.43
b	0.70	0.78	0.96	1.07	1.11	1.17	1.23	1.33	0.82	0.99	1.02	1.31	1.40	1.26	1.18	1.11
c	0.68	0.93	1.08	1.30	1.45	1.60	1.76	1.95								
d	0.82	1.07	1.13	1.42	1.56	1.59	1.62	1.73								
AR8																
a	0.57	0.89	1.07	1.26	1.37	1.43	1.45	1.48								
b	0.61	0.97	1.16	1.33	1.51	1.62	1.71	1.81								
d	0.88	1.35	1.37	1.12	1.28	1.50	1.73	1.88								

(continued)

183

Table 6.5. (*Continued*)

	Change Assumption for Exogenous-Variable Uncertainty								Level Assumption for Exogenous-Variable Uncertainty							
	1978				1979				1978				1979			
	1	2	3	4	1	2	3	4	1	2	3	4	1	2	3	4
Consumer expenditures, durables																
Michigan																
a	1.15	1.53	1.82	2.20	2.36	2.73	2.98	3.18								
b	1.31	1.93	2.32	2.77	3.33	3.85	4.30	4.85								
c	1.43	2.41	3.71	5.23	7.11	9.09	10.97	12.93	1.19	1.88	2.63	3.16	3.84	4.29	4.87	5.49
d	3.57	4.22	5.70	6.35	8.17	10.43	12.78	14.98	3.48	3.94	5.06	4.80	5.57	6.67	8.16	9.35
Fair																
a	2.17	2.44	2.79	3.26	3.72	3.69	4.09	4.25								
b	2.11	2.55	3.16	3.52	3.94	4.15	4.40	4.61								
c	2.10	2.69	3.00	3.78	4.55	5.03	5.48	5.88	2.36	2.67	3.11	3.79	4.34	4.54	4.82	5.10
d	3.09	3.68	4.99	6.55	8.27	9.41	10.71	12.21	3.27	3.66	5.06	6.56	8.15	9.16	10.39	11.86
AR8																
a	1.91	2.60	3.15	3.36	3.60	3.92	4.18	4.19								
b	2.13	2.82	3.39	3.83	3.80	4.45	4.69	5.12								
d	4.32	5.54	6.39	6.64	6.93	7.97	9.09	9.92								
Housing investment																
Michigan																
a	2.09	3.07	3.68	4.69	5.54	6.41	7.16	7.40								
b	2.24	3.22	3.98	4.86	5.93	7.20	8.61	10.37								
c	2.40	3.51	4.62	5.61	7.00	8.87	10.52	12.36	2.29	3.62	4.52	5.65	6.94	8.52	9.85	11.26
d	5.43	8.65	9.71	10.32	12.69	16.12	19.73	22.52	5.38	8.70	9.66	10.34	12.65	15.93	19.39	21.93
Fair																
a	2.71	4.71	6.36	7.25	8.19	8.99	9.93	10.38								
b	2.80	4.83	6.83	8.46	9.58	10.77	11.88	13.35								
c	2.71	4.54	6.08	7.69	9.05	10.40	11.55	12.34	2.82	4.61	6.13	7.21	8.54	9.99	11.49	12.56
d	4.73	7.09	6.89	6.77	8.92	11.23	12.83	14.82	4.79	7.13	6.93	6.22	8.40	10.85	12.78	14.66

		1	2	3	4	5	6	7	8	9	10	11	12	13	14	15	16
AR8	a	2.61	4.22	5.92	7.06	7.66	8.02	8.21	8.23	1.02	1.44	1.84	2.33	2.65	3.05	3.50	4.09
	b	2.78	4.68	6.20	7.42	8.53	8.96	9.34	9.42	2.50	4.23	5.59	5.82	4.91	6.35	13.53	29.27
	d	6.43	11.25	12.24	10.89	9.58	10.35	12.46	12.77								

Nonresidential fixed investment

		1	2	3	4	5	6	7	8
Michigan	a	1.13	1.47	1.71	1.94	2.20	2.51	2.79	3.09
	b	1.08	1.57	1.85	2.16	2.56	2.88	3.22	3.40
	c	1.16	1.60	2.01	2.51	3.06	3.70	4.42	5.46
	d	2.56	4.29	5.65	5.90	5.14	6.69	13.80	29.49
Fair	a	1.72	2.25	2.60	2.92	3.24	3.32	3.49	3.66
	b	1.81	2.56	2.97	3.05	3.48	3.77	4.00	4.09
	c	1.75	2.37	2.89	3.41	3.83	4.21	4.68	5.04
	d	2.65	3.09	3.94	4.46	5.48	6.36	7.18	8.09
AR8	a	1.24	2.13	2.75	3.29	3.80	4.21	4.30	4.46
	b	1.42	2.05	2.78	3.68	4.27	4.92	5.15	5.45
	d	2.26	2.35	3.41	3.35	2.69	2.03	i	i

Inventory investment

		1	2	3	4	5	6	7	8	9	10	11	12	13	14	15	16
Michigan	a	3.86	4.20	4.38	5.18	5.06	4.81	5.17	5.33	4.31	4.70	4.79	5.05	5.02	5.65	5.89	6.12
	b	4.59	4.75	4.53	5.10	4.76	5.11	5.45	5.57	6.08	6.89	7.52	7.84	7.30	6.56	6.85	7.75
	c	4.39	4.91	5.16	5.49	5.75	6.95	7.73	8.39								
	d	6.14	7.04	7.76	8.12	7.82	7.71	8.48	9.65								
Fair	a	4.66	5.22	5.10	5.52	6.12	5.54	5.38	5.77	4.57	5.28	5.68	5.91	5.53	5.44	5.40	6.23
	b	4.50	5.05	5.52	5.60	4.99	5.93	5.90	6.23	6.38	8.07	9.13	9.29	9.49	9.37	9.59	10.49
	c	4.64	5.34	5.68	6.01	5.81	5.95	6.13	6.22								
	d	6.42	8.11	9.13	9.35	9.66	9.67	10.02	10.49								
AR8	a	5.22	5.45	5.81	5.72	5.69	6.41	6.02	6.38								
	b	5.33	6.18	6.45	6.75	6.64	6.67	6.75	7.32								
	d	6.67	7.66	7.92	7.51	7.78	8.12	8.18	8.61								

(continued)

Table 6.5. (*Continued*)

| | Change Assumption for Exogenous-Variable Uncertainty | | | | | | | | Level Assumption for Exogenous-Variable Uncertainty | | | | | | | |
| | 1978 | | | | 1979 | | | | 1978 | | | | 1979 | | | |
	1	2	3	4	1	2	3	4	1	2	3	4	1	2	3	4
Imports																
Michigan																
a	2.47	3.42	3.68	3.80	3.80	3.65	3.64	3.67								
b	2.65	3.49	3.64	3.90	4.42	4.47	4.63	4.78								
c	2.68	3.34	3.67	3.90	4.60	5.21	5.69	6.66	2.73	3.63	3.75	4.10	4.55	4.81	4.82	5.12
d	3.68	4.91	5.66	6.29	7.10	8.12	9.70	11.65	3.72	5.11	5.71	6.41	7.07	7.87	9.22	10.84
Fair																
a	1.90	2.46	2.60	2.67	2.72	2.71	2.61	2.97								
b	2.22	2.44	2.66	2.76	2.81	3.28	3.56	3.70								
c	1.96	2.42	2.66	2.89	3.03	3.37	3.44	3.65	2.11	2.51	2.55	2.85	2.96	3.20	3.41	3.48
d	3.86	5.73	7.54	8.98	10.30	11.14	12.53	13.08	3.93	5.77	7.50	8.97	10.28	11.09	12.52	13.04
AR8																
a	2.63	3.53	3.98	4.64	4.71	4.87	5.14	5.22								
b	2.79	3.61	4.33	4.91	5.43	5.58	5.77	5.96								
d	5.04	7.54	9.69	11.70	13.11	13.71	14.25	15.26								
Wage rate																
Michigan																
a	0.31	0.42	0.59	0.66	0.78	0.87	0.97	1.10								
b	0.35	0.47	0.59	0.72	0.86	1.00	1.15	1.32								
c	0.35	0.46	0.58	0.68	0.80	0.91	1.06	1.20	0.32	0.44	0.57	0.70	0.86	0.99	1.13	1.25
d	0.28	0.42	0.58	0.71	0.77	0.90	1.05	1.26	0.25	0.40	0.57	0.73	0.83	0.98	1.12	1.30
Fair																
a	0.56	0.86	1.00	1.13	1.20	1.30	1.32	1.38								
b	0.59	0.84	1.01	1.15	1.35	1.48	1.70	1.85								
c	0.60	0.82	1.04	1.19	1.39	1.59	1.83	1.98	0.59	0.85	0.99	1.26	1.49	1.67	1.80	1.97
d	0.38	0.46	0.65	0.78	1.04	1.22	1.59	1.90	0.37	0.51	0.57	0.88	1.17	1.32	1.56	1.89
AR8																
a	0.21	0.33	0.43	0.53	0.60	0.63	0.68	0.73								
b	0.26	0.44	0.58	0.73	0.86	0.95	1.04	1.14								

Profits

Michigan																
a	3.80	4.99	5.90	6.54	7.63	8.87	9.87	10.12	3.90	5.41	6.37	7.25	8.83	10.84	12.05	13.14
b	3.97	5.24	6.07	7.04	7.97	10.29	12.02	13.16	5.31	6.31	7.57	6.36	5.45	5.35	12.43	23.21
c	4.26	5.74	7.45	8.87	11.85	15.77	18.83	21.89								
d	5.97	6.59	8.50	8.16	9.60	12.64	19.07	29.08								
Fair																
a	4.98	6.26	7.61	8.75	8.90	10.07	10.91	11.80	6.34	7.57	8.65	9.61	10.97	11.03	12.69	13.93
b	5.02	6.55	8.35	9.26	10.27	11.55	13.46	15.11	7.98	9.08	9.84	10.00	11.40	11.02	12.87	13.58
c	6.86	8.49	10.27	11.61	12.89	15.52	17.62	18.04								
d	8.40	9.86	11.29	11.94	13.26	15.21	17.75	17.77								
AR8																
a	3.22	4.93	6.39	7.10	7.37	7.59	7.93	8.60								
b	3.72	5.51	7.26	8.58	9.74	10.64	11.77	13.41								
d	9.56	16.32	23.29	27.89	30.69	33.82	37.47	40.43								

[a] a = uncertainty due to error terms; b = uncertainty due to error terms and coefficient estimates; c = uncertainty due to error terms, coefficient estimates, and exogenous-variable forecasts; d = uncertainty due to error terms, coefficient estimates, exogenous-variable forecasts, and the possible misspecification of the model; i = the total estimated variance was negative.

[b] 250 trials for each stochastic simulation.

[c] Errors are in percentage points except for inventory investment, where the errors are in billions of 1972 dollars at an annual rate. Errors for all variables except the unemployment rate, the bill rate, and inventory investment are percents of the forecast means.

[d] The exact variables tabled for each model are the following. See Belton, Hymans, and Lown (1981) for the Michigan notation, and see Fair (1984) for the Fair notation. The variables for the autoregressive model are the same as those for the Michigan model.

	Michigan	Fair
Real GNP	GNP72	GNPR
Private nonfarm deflator	PPNF	P
Nominal GNP	GNP	GNP
Unemployment rate	RUG	UR
Bill rate	RTB	RS
Money supply	M1BPLUS	M1
Consumer expenditures, services	CS72	CS
Consumer expenditures, nondurables	CN72	CN
Consumer expenditures, durables	C72−CS72−CN72	CD
Housing investment	IRC72	IH
Nonresidential fixed investment	IBF72	IK
Inventory investment	IINV72	IV
Imports	M72	IM
Wage rate	JCMH	W
Profits	YCP	Π_f

Table 6.6. Root Mean Squared Errors of Outside-Sample Forecasts for 1975.2–1981.4 for the Three Models[a-f]

	Number of Quarters Ahead							
	1	2	3	4	5	6	7	8
Real GNP								
Michigan	0.80	1.11	1.37	1.36	1.34	1.58	2.53	3.62
Fair	0.83	1.24	1.66	2.02	2.38	2.68	2.99	3.40
AR8	1.14	1.75	2.20	2.20	2.23	2.38	2.73	3.03
Private nonfarm deflator								
Michigan	0.36	0.46	0.51	0.68	0.82	0.95	1.11	1.30
Fair	0.69	1.18	1.64	2.17	2.62	3.03	3.47	3.87
AR8	0.72	1.26	1.92	2.93	3.80	4.57	5.09	5.24
Nominal GNP								
Michigan	1.06	1.46	1.66	1.49	1.63	1.97	2.84	3.90
Fair	0.96	1.38	1.86	2.22	2.54	2.79	3.01	3.28
AR8	1.28	1.90	2.38	2.49	2.70	3.18	3.82	4.29
Unemployment rate								
Michigan	0.34	0.54	0.70	0.77	0.77	0.66	0.78	1.24
Fair	0.41	0.66	0.93	1.14	1.27	1.38	1.48	1.62
AR8	0.34	0.54	0.70	0.81	0.88	0.93	1.01	1.07
Bill rate								
Michigan	0.78	1.04	1.15	1.29	1.42	1.45	1.42	1.42
Fair	1.28	2.05	2.30	2.44	2.58	2.74	2.90	3.08
AR8	1.57	2.58	2.75	3.09	3.42	3.65	3.87	4.04
Money supply								
Michigan	1.60	2.20	2.78	3.64	4.37	5.15	6.10	6.95
Fair	1.43	1.86	2.09	2.45	2.63	2.85	3.10	3.02
AR8	2.22	3.66	4.61	5.83	6.76	8.23	10.25	11.85
Consumer expenditures, services								
Michigan	0.46	0.72	0.90	1.11	1.33	1.60	1.92	2.19
Fair	0.40	0.64	0.98	1.31	1.56	1.87	2.21	2.54
AR8	0.50	0.80	1.05	1.33	1.63	1.92	2.29	2.58
Consumer expenditures, nondurables								
Michigan	0.89	1.33	1.61	1.83	2.17	2.51	2.96	3.42
Fair	0.82	1.08	1.21	1.43	1.58	1.59	1.57	1.65
AR8	0.87	1.34	1.40	1.27	1.46	1.64	1.86	2.01
Consumer expenditures, durables								
Michigan	3.58	4.04	5.10	4.89	5.60	6.79	8.31	9.69
Fair	3.32	4.14	5.67	7.04	8.52	9.67	10.97	12.47
AR8	4.53	5.84	6.81	7.22	7.78	8.55	9.74	10.41
Housing investment								
Michigan	5.65	9.05	10.30	11.18	13.48	16.61	20.41	23.62
Fair	5.39	8.57	9.69	10.65	12.41	14.33	15.70	17.12
AR8	6.88	11.91	13.26	12.42	11.35	12.10	14.03	14.43
Nonresidential fixed investment								
Michigan	2.66	4.58	6.09	6.39	5.63	7.28	14.99	32.03
Fair	2.52	3.08	3.99	4.56	5.66	6.64	7.54	8.51
AR8	2.32	2.90	4.23	4.52	4.56	4.61	4.59	4.61
Inventory investment								
Michigan	6.14	6.72	7.41	7.67	7.05	6.25	6.44	7.57
Fair	6.20	7.64	8.44	8.60	9.04	9.24	9.44	9.92
AR8	6.96	7.95	8.51	8.33	8.79	9.07	9.08	8.98

	Number of Quarters Ahead							
	1	2	3	4	5	6	7	8
Imports								
Michigan	3.83	5.05	5.75	6.33	6.86	7.58	8.99	10.63
Fair	3.89	6.02	8.15	9.96	11.76	13.27	15.46	17.28
AR8	5.33	8.06	10.33	12.55	14.10	15.26	16.43	18.42
Wage rate								
Michigan	0.29	0.48	0.67	0.83	0.94	1.11	1.27	1.49
Fair	0.57	0.89	1.24	1.58	1.92	2.24	2.59	3.00
AR8	0.44	0.78	1.10	1.44	1.88	2.27	2.71	3.21
Profits								
Michigan	5.84	7.31	9.08	9.04	8.99	9.36	16.24	27.80
Fair	7.21	8.79	9.98	10.66	11.80	12.73	13.96	14.57
AR8	9.59	16.56	23.86	28.99	32.15	35.15	38.84	41.71

[a]The results are based on 27 sets of coefficient estimates for each model.
[b]Each prediction period began two quarters after the end of the estimation period.
[c]The predicted values used were the mean values from the 27 stochastic simulations to get the $\bar{d}_{ik}$ values for each model.
[d]There are 27 observations for the one-quarter-ahead forecasts, 26 for the two-quarter-ahead forecasts, and so on.
[e]See note c to Table 6.5 for the units of the errors.
[f]See note d to Table 6.5 for the notation for the variables.

These results produced for the one-quarter-ahead forecast for each endogenous variable 27 values of the difference between the estimated forecast-error variance based on outside-sample errors (i.e., the squared forecast errors) and the estimated forecast-error variance based on stochastic simulation. The average of these 27 values was taken for each variable. In terms of the previous notation, this average is $\bar{d}_{i1}$, where the i refers to variable i, and the 1 refers to the one-quarter-ahead forecast. The total variance for the one-quarter-ahead forecast of variable i is $\bar{\sigma}_{it1}^2 + \bar{d}_{i1}$, which in terms of the notation is $\hat{\sigma}_{it1}^2$. For the results in Table 6.5, t is 1978.1, and the d-row value for 1978.1 for each variable is the square root of $\hat{\sigma}_{it1}^2$. The calculations for the two-quarter-ahead forecasts are the same except that there are only 26 values of the difference between the two estimated variances for each variable. Similarly, there are only 25 values for the three-quarter ahead forecast, and so on.

The d-row values in Table 6.5 take into account the four main sources of uncertainty, and they are the values to be compared across models. This will be done in the Discussion. Two sets of d-row values are presented in Table 6.5 for each variable. The first is for the change assumption regarding the exogenous variables, and the second is for the level assumption. The $\bar{d}_{ik}$ values are the same for both sets of results, but the c-row values (i.e., the values of $\bar{\sigma}_{itk}$) are not.

Outside-Sample Root Mean Squared Errors

For the misspecification calculations one has for each variable 27 one-quarter-ahead outside-sample forecast errors, 26 two-quarter-ahead outside-sample forecast errors, and so on. From these individual errors, one can calculate root mean squared errors. The results of doing this are presented in Table 6.6. The RMSEs in Table 6.6 and the d-row values in Table 6.5 differ in two major respects. First, the d-row values take into account exogenous variable uncertainty, which the RMSEs do not. The outside-sample errors that are used for the RMSE results are all based on actual values of the exogenous variables. Second, the d-row values are for a particular quarter—1978.1 for the one-quarter-ahead forecast, 1978.2 for the two-quarter-ahead forecast, and so on. The RMSEs are averages across all the quarters—27 quarters for the one-quarter-ahead forecast, 26 quarters for the two-quarter forecast, and so on. The RMSEs do not take account of the fact that forecast-error variances vary across time. If the variances did not vary across time and if there were no exogenous variable uncertainty, the d-row values and the RMSEs would be the same except for stochastic-simulation error.

Although the d-row values are better than the RMSEs for comparison purposes, the RMSE results in Table 6.6 provide a rough check on the results in Table 6.5. If a particular d-row value differs substantially from the corresponding RMSE, it is of some interest to determine why this is.

Results for the Fair Model

The results for the Fair model in Table 6.5 are taken from the results in Fair (1984). For the results in Fair (1984) the d-row values were based on 51 sets of estimates of the model. For the present results only the relevant 27 sets of these estimates were used. The values in the a- and b-rows in Table 6.5 for the Fair model are exactly those in Table 8-2 in Fair (1984), although in the present case results for more variables are tabled. The values in the c-rows in the right half of Table 6.5 differ slightly from the c-row values in Table 8-2 of Fair (1984) because a different sequence of random draws was used for the present results. The differences are thus due to stochastic-simulation error. The values in the c-rows in the left half of Table 6.5 are new. The change assumption with respect to the exogenous-variable errors was not used for the work in Fair (1984). Remember that the $\bar{d}_{ik}$ values that are used for the Fair model in Table 6.5 are different from those used in Table 8-2 of Fair (1984) because they are based on 27 rather than on 51 sets of estimates.

Results for the Autoregressive Model (AR8)

The Michigan data base was used for the autoregressive model. The estimation periods are the same as those for the Michigan model.[9] The model consists of a set of eighth-order autoregressive equations with a constant term and time trend. The equations are completely separate from each other. The same steps were followed for the autoregressive model as were followed for the Michigan model except that 100 rather than 50 trials were used for each of the 27 sets of stochastic simulations. The results for the autoregressive model are also presented in Tables 6.5 and 6.6. There are no c-row values for this model because there are no exogenous variables except for the time trend.

A Digression about Stochastic-Simulation Error

Some evidence about the size of stochastic-simulation error is available from the present results. First, there are two sets of c-row values in Table 6.5, and the one-quarter-ahead values for each set should be the same for each variable aside from stochastic-simulation error. (The change versus level difference does not affect the one-quarter-ahead results.) Different random draws were used for the two sets. As can be seen in Table 6.5, the simulation errors are fairly small. Some of the larger errors for Michigan are 1.43 vs 1.19 for durable expenditures, 2.40 vs 2.29 for housing investment, and 4.26 vs 3.90 for profits. Some of the larger errors for Fair are 2.10 vs 2.36 for durable expenditures, 1.75 vs 1.95 for nonresidential fixed investment, 1.96 vs 2.11 for imports, and 6.86 vs 6.34 for profits.

Second, the values in the c-rows in the right half of Table 6.5 for the Fair model should be the same as the c-row values in Table 8-2 in Fair (1984) aside from simulation error. Both sets of results are based on 250 trials, but the random-variable draws were different. The comparisons for the eight-quarter-ahead results are 1.60 vs 1.66 for real GNP, 1.13 vs 1.15 for the GNP deflator, 0.82 vs 0.91 for the unemployment rate, 1.40 vs 1.37 for the bill rate, 2.28 vs 2.44 for the money supply, 1.94 vs 1.97 for the wage rate, and 15.00 vs 13.93 for profits.

Although simulation error is certainly not close to zero for the present results, it seems small enough so as not to affect the basic conclusions that are drawn from the results.

A Digression about Computer Work

The Fair–Parke program (1984) was used for all the computations in this chapter. Once a model is set up in the program, all the estimation and stochastic simulation that are needed for the results in Table 6.5 can be done with a few commands. The program provides an easy way to debug the setting up of the model, and once this debugging has been done, few other errors are likely to arise.

The computer work was done on an IBM 4341 at Yale. The computer time needed for the estimation of the Michigan model was trivial because the estimation technique is simply ordinary least squares. With respect to solution times, the time needed to solve the model for one quarter was about 0.9 second, although this time could be considerably lowered. The Fair–Parke program has an option for efficient coding of the subroutines that are needed to set up the model in the program. This option was not used for the Michigan model. It was used for the Fair model, and the solution time for the Fair model was about 0.2 second per quarter. It is likely that the Michigan time could be lowered to about this value with efficient coding. The total time for an eight-quarter stochastic simulation using 250 trials at 0.9 second per quarter is $250 \times 8 \times 0.9 = 1800$ seconds, or about 30 minutes. Each of the a-, b-, and c-row calculations for Table 6.5 thus took about 30 minutes for the Michigan model, since there is little to the calculations other than solving the model over and over. With efficient coding this time could be reduced to about 7 minutes, which is about the time taken for the Fair model calculations.

DISCUSSION OF THE RESULTS

Sensitivity to Exogenous-Variable Assumptions

The Michigan results in Table 6.5 are in general much more sensitive to the two assumptions about exogenous-variable uncertainty than are the Fair results. The Michigan c-row values for the change assumption, which are in the left half of the table, are in many cases much larger than the corresponding values for the level assumption, which are in the right half of the table. This is unfortunate from the point of view of the method because it makes comparisons more difficult. As previously discussed, the change assumption may be a better approximation, and we have concentrated on the change-assumption results in the following discussion. This is the worst case for the Michigan model. Michigan does best for the RMSE results in Table 6.6, which are based on the assumption of no exogenous variable uncertainty. The results in Table 6.5 for the level assumption are in between the RMSE results in Table 6.6 and the results in Table 6.5 for the change assumption.

It should be noted that the sensitivity of the Michigan results to the exogenous-variable assumptions is not due to the fact that the model is heavily tied to dummy variables. All but four of the dummy variables have been taken to be fixed for the calculations. The sensitivity instead indicates that the Michigan model is more heavily tied to nondummy exogenous variables than is the Fair model. This is probably because variables such as the discount rate and the minimum wage rate have been taken to be exogenous.

Michigan versus Fair

The top half of Table 6.7 contains for each variable and quarter the ratio of the Michigan d-row value in Table 6.5 to the corresponding Fair d-row value. (In what follows M denotes the Michigan model and F denotes the Fair model.) The following is a discussion of the results in Table 6.7.

1. In general, the shorter the lead time of the forecast, the better M is relative to F. For real GNP, for example, M is better than F for the first five quarters and worse than F for the remaining three.
2. The best variable for M is the private nonfarm deflator, where M is about three times more accurate than F. M is also more accurate than F for the wage rate, although not by as much as for the price deflator.
3. M is considerably better than F for the bill rate except for the eight-quarter-ahead forecast, where F is slightly better. F is considerably better than M for the money supply (the money supply variable is M_1).
4. With respect to the components of GNP, F is better than M for the three consumption variables, housing investment, and nonresidential fixed investment. M is better than F for inventory investment and imports. F is thus in general better than M with respect to the components of GNP. There is, however, more error cancellation for M than for F with respect to the predictions of real GNP. As noted above, M is actually better than F for the first five quarters for real

GNP. For nominal GNP F is better than M for all but the four-quarter-ahead forecast.

5. For the unemployment rate M is better than F for the first six quarters and worse for the remaining two. The same is true for profits.

Michigan and Fair versus Autoregressive

The bottom half of Table 6.7 presents the M versus autoregressive and F versus autoregressive ratios. (In what follows AR8 denotes the autoregressive model.) The d-row values in Table 6.5 for AR8 are not sensible for the unemployment rate and nonresidential fixed investment. It sometimes turns out in the successive reestimation and stochastic simulation of the model that the stochastic simulation estimates of the variances are on average much larger than the estimates based on outside-sample errors. This results in large negative values of $\bar{d}_{ik}$, and these values when added to the square of the c-row values (or b-row values in the case of AR8) can yield negative values of the total variance, which is not sensible. What this means is that the sample is not large enough to produce sensible results. This problem occurred for the unemployment rate and nonresidential fixed investment for AR8, and so these two variables have been omitted from the bottom half of Table 6.7.

The results in Table 6.7 in general show that M and F are better than AR8. The main exceptions are as follows. M is worse than AR8 for real GNP for the last four quarters, for nominal GNP for the last three quarters, for nondurable consumption for all quarters, and for durable consumption and housing investment for the last four quarters. F is worse than AR8 for real GNP for the last five quarters, for durable consumption for the last four quarters, and for inventory investment for all but the first quarter.

General Remarks

If the current results are taken at face value, they are obviously mixed. M and F are generally better than AR8, but there is no obvious winner between M and F. M is much better than F for the price deflator and the wage rate. M is also much better than F for the bill rate except for the last quarter. F is much better than M for nondurable consumption, housing investment, nonresidential fixed investment, and the money supply. For the other variables the results are closer.

When all is said and done, however, one may not want to take the current results at face value. There are at least three reasons for this. First, the results are sensitive to the assumptions about exogenous-variable uncertainty. M is more sensitive than F to the exogenous-variable assumptions. If the change assumption has overestimated exogenous-variable uncertainty, then the results are biased in favor of F. If, on the other hand, the change assumption has underestimated uncertainty, which may be true for variables like DFPR (see the discussion under Some Features of the Models), then the results are biased in favor of M.

Second, the heavy use of dummy variables in the Michigan model may have biased the results in favor of M. As previously noted, there are a number of dummy variables in the Michigan price equation, and at least part of the good showing by M for the

Table 6.7. Ratios of d-Row Values from Table 6.5

	Michigan/Fair							
	1978				1979			
	1	2	3	4	1	2	3	4
Real GNP	0.91	0.96	0.94	0.75	0.93	1.06	1.30	1.48
Private nonfarm deflator	0.53	0.40	0.34	0.35	0.33	0.34	0.34	0.36
Nominal GNP	1.03	1.12	1.02	0.93	1.03	1.23	1.64	1.81
Unemployment rate	0.87	0.90	0.87	0.85	0.85	0.86	1.03	1.28
Bill rate	0.57	0.49	0.50	0.60	0.63	0.58	0.63	1.03
Money supply	1.07	1.13	1.42	1.85	2.05	2.62	3.01	5.22
Consumer expenditures, services	1.34	1.36	1.08	1.02	0.91	1.08	1.10	1.13
Consumer expenditures, nondurables	1.20	1.48	1.86	1.99	2.42	3.00	3.70	4.22
Consumer expenditures, durables	1.16	1.15	1.14	0.97	0.99	1.11	1.19	1.23
Housing investment	1.15	1.22	1.41	1.52	1.18	1.10	1.54	1.52
Nonresidential fixed investment	0.97	1.39	1.43	1.32	0.94	1.05	1.92	3.65
Inventory investment	0.96	0.87	0.85	0.87	0.81	0.80	0.85	0.92
Imports	0.95	0.86	0.75	0.70	0.69	0.73	0.77	0.89
Wage rate	0.74	0.91	0.89	0.91	0.74	0.74	0.66	0.66
Profits	0.71	0.67	0.75	0.68	0.72	0.83	1.07	1.64

| | Michigan/Autoregressive | | | | | | | | Fair/Autoregressive | | | | | | | |
| | 1978 | | | | 1979 | | | | 1978 | | | | 1979 | | | |
	1	2	3	4	1	2	3	4	1	2	3	4	1	2	3	4
Real GNP	0.73	0.72	0.74	0.89	1.14	1.39	1.58	1.83	0.80	0.75	0.79	1.19	1.23	1.30	1.21	1.24
Private nonfarm deflator	0.51	0.39	0.31	0.28	0.25	0.26	0.27	0.33	0.97	0.97	0.90	0.79	0.76	0.75	0.80	0.94
Nominal GNP	0.86	0.83	0.78	0.79	0.93	1.03	1.24	1.24	0.84	0.74	0.77	0.85	0.91	0.84	0.76	0.68
Bill rate	0.51	0.42	0.44	0.49	0.50	0.46	0.50	0.83	0.90	0.85	0.88	0.82	0.79	0.79	0.79	0.80
Money supply	0.76	0.61	0.66	0.72	0.77	0.77	0.74	0.78	0.71	0.54	0.46	0.39	0.38	0.30	0.25	0.15
Consumer expenditures, services	0.92	0.94	0.92	0.97	0.98	0.99	1.01	1.04	0.69	0.69	0.86	0.95	1.06	0.92	0.92	0.92
Consumer expenditures, nondurables	1.11	1.17	1.53	2.53	2.95	3.18	3.46	3.88	0.93	0.79	0.82	1.27	1.22	1.06	0.94	0.92
Consumer expenditures, durables	0.83	0.76	0.89	0.96	1.18	1.31	1.41	1.51	0.72	0.66	0.78	0.99	1.19	1.18	1.18	1.23
Housing investment	0.84	0.77	0.79	0.95	1.32	1.56	1.58	1.76	0.74	0.63	0.56	0.62	0.93	1.09	1.03	1.16
Inventory investment	0.92	0.92	0.98	1.08	1.01	0.95	1.04	1.12	0.96	1.06	1.15	1.25	1.24	1.19	1.22	1.21
Imports	0.73	0.65	0.58	0.54	0.54	0.59	0.68	0.76	0.77	0.76	0.78	0.77	0.79	0.81	0.88	0.86
Wage rate	0.65	0.56	0.56	0.53	0.44	0.43	0.42	0.43	0.88	0.61	0.63	0.58	0.59	0.58	0.63	0.64
Profits	0.62	0.40	0.36	0.29	0.31	0.37	0.51	0.72	0.88	0.60	0.48	0.43	0.43	0.45	0.47	0.44

price deflator may be due to this. The same problem may also exist for the unemployment rate, whose equation is heavily tied to the use of a dummy variable.

Third, the misspecification estimates are based on only 27 observations, which is a fairly small sample. More observations are clearly needed before any strong conclusions can be drawn.

NOTES

1. This problem pertains, of course, only to the dummy variables that change values over the simulation periods. The first simulation period in the work below began in 1975.2. Some of the dummy variables in Table 6.2 pertain only to the period before this.
2. Note that if our argument here is correct, many of the policy implications of the Michigan model are suspect. If the discount rate is treated as exogenous for purposes of policy experiments, the interest rate responsiveness to the policy change is likely to be underestimated.
3. We are indebted to Edwin Kuh and Steve Schwartz for providing us with a tape of the data. We are also indebted to Joan Crary for answering a number of questions about the model. These individuals are not accountable for the results in this chapter. We assume responsibility for all errors.
4. The 345 coefficients include serial correlation coefficients. These coefficients were treated as structural coefficients, and so the covariance matrix of the coefficient estimates includes them.
5. It sometimes happens that a particular draw fails to result in a solution of the model. In this case the trial is discarded. There were no failures for the a-row simulation. There was one failure for the b-row simulation, and so the number of trials for this simulation was 249 rather than 250.
6. As indicated in note c to Table 6.5, most of the errors are in units of percentage of the forecast mean. See the discussion in Chapter 8 in Fair (1984) for the exact way in which the percentage errors are computed.
7. There were no failures of the model to solve for the c-row calculations.
8. Of the $27 \times 50 = 1350$ trials, 5 failed to result in a solution of the model.
9. Five of the variables for which autoregressive equations were estimated are determined by identities in the Michigan model—real GNP, the GNP deflator, nominal GNP, consumer durable expenditures, and nonresidential fixed investment. The estimation period used for these variables is 1956.1–1979.4.

REFERENCES

Belton, Terrence, Saul H. Hymans, and Cara Lown (1981). "The Dynamics of the Michigan Quarterly Econometric Model of the U.S. Economy." Discussion Paper R-108.81, Department of Economics, University of Michigan, December.

Fair, Ray C. (1980). "Estimating the Expected Predictive Accuracy of Econometric Models." *International Economic Review* 21, 355–378.

Fair, Ray C. (1984). *Specification, Estimation, and Analysis of Macroeconometric Models.* Cambridge: Harvard University Press.

Table A6.1. Exogenous Variables of the Michigan Model for Which Autoregressive Equations Were Estimated[a]

Variable	Estimation Period	Variable	Estimation Period
AUTOSIZE	1956.1–1979.4	PFP	1956.1–1979.4
BTRP	1956.1–1979.4	PGAS	1959.1–1979.4
DFPR	1967.1–1979.4	PIINV	1956.1–1979.4
DTEX	1956.1–1979.4	PM	1956.1–1979.4
DTIB	1956.1–1979.4	PX	1956.1–1979.4
DTP	1956.1–1979.4	RDIS	1956.1–1979.4
DTPR	1956.2–1979.4	RRDEM	1956.1–1979.4
EGOV	1956.1–1979.4	SDR	1972.1–1979.4
GAID	1956.1–1979.4	SLCSF	1956.1–1979.4
GFD	1956.1–1979.4	TCFR	1956.1–1979.4
GFO	1956.1–1979.4	TCO	1956.1–1979.4
GOLD	1956.1–1979.4	TDEPRAG	1956.1–1979.4
GSL	1956.1–1979.4	TDEPRNC	1956.1–1979.4
GTRF	1956.1–1979.4	TDEPRO	1956.1–1979.4
GTROF	1956.1–1979.4	TDEPRQ	1956.1–1979.4
GTRSL	1956.1–1979.4	TITCR	1956.1–1979.4
IVA	1956.1–1979.4	TSIFR	1956.1–1979.4
JGPM	1956.1–1979.4	TSISL	1956.1–1979.4
JICS	1956.1–1979.4	WCEIL	1956.1–1979.4
KCAC	1956.1–1979.4	WUSMIN	1956.1–1979.4
KCCA	1956.1–1979.4	X72	1956.1–1979.4
MBASE	1956.1–1979.4	YGWS	1956.1–1979.4
PAUTO	1956.1–1979.4	YPINT	1956.1–1979.4
PCRUDE	1956.1–1979.4	YPRENT	1956.1–1979.4

[a]See Belton, Hymans, and Lown (1981) for a description of the variables. See Fair (1984 p. 285) for a discussion of the exogenous variables of the Fair model for which autoregressive equations were estimated.

ADDITIONAL APPROACHES TO MODEL COMPARISONS AND FORECASTS

CHAPTER 7

Reappraisal of the Phillips Curve and Direct Effects of Money Supply on Inflation

ALBERT ANDO, FLINT BRAYTON, and ARTHUR KENNICKELL

This chapter attempts to provide some evidence on two closely related issues. The first is the question of how well or how badly a typical nonmonetarist econometric structure can account for the dynamic pattern of wages and prices in the United States from the 1960s to the 1980s. The second is whether an econometric structure such as this can be successful in fully capturing the effects of the quantity of money on movements of the price level. This second issue is in turn closely related to the question of whether a significant increase in the money supply, regardless of other conditions such as the level of the unemployment rate, is inflationary.

In discussions of macroeconomic theory and policy since the mid-1970s, it is often taken for granted that conventional macroeconometric models have failed in some fundamental way to account for the actual development of the U.S. economy and that the prime culprit in this failure is the Phillips curve (Lucas and Sargent, 1978, 1981). For those who have followed the performance of the modified Phillips curve and associated equations through the 1970s and most of the 1980s, the widespread perception of the complete failure of these equations to "explain" movements of prices and wages during this period has been a complete puzzle, since these equations have been more stable and more reliable over time than most other empirical macroeconomic relationships during the period in question, at least in the United States.[1]

In this chapter we first attempt to exhibit the stability of these empirical relationships and their ability to predict movements of prices and wages during the period in question. For this purpose we will utilize the set of equations embedded in the current structure of the MPS econometric model of the United States, and we also refer to its early predecessors (Brayton and Mauskopf, 1985; deMenil and Enzler, 1971). However, most of our results do not depend on the performance of the rest of the MPS model.

We also present evidence that this set of equations can account for most of the effects of money supply movements on the general price level. The most judicious interpretation of the evidence is that there remains a small direct effect of the money supply on the price level not captured by the MPS equations. The pattern of evidence, however, is rather mixed, and we have not been able to come up with any indication suggesting a specific mechanism generating this direct effect of the money supply.

This issue appears to be very important in affecting our understanding of the dynamic characteristics of the whole economy, as discussed briefly at the end of this chapter.

THE TRADITIONAL PRICE–WAGE SUBSYSTEM

A simple graph plotting the rate of inflation (as measured by the rate of change of the GNP deflator) against the rate of unemployment often exhibited in the popular litera- ture must have contributed, more than anything else, to the establishment of the idea that then prevailing econometric models suffered a "failure on a grand scale" in the 1970s. We reproduce a typical graph of this type as Figure 7.1. For the earlier period between 1954 and 1969, the relationship between the rate of inflation and the rate of unemployment is clearly negative and quite close. Thereafter, however, the line con- necting successive years swirls around and, if anything, the rate of inflation and the rate of unemployment appear to be positively related to each other until the early 1980s.

A moment's reflection would suggest that a graph such as this cannot be very informative concerning the question of whether there exists a stable relationship be- tween the rate of inflation and the rate of unemployment. Such a relationship must be conditional on a number of factors, including past patterns of inflation and unemploy- ment, as well as the supply conditions of some raw materials whose prices are deter- mined in worldwide commodities markets. The graph of an unconditional relationship over time such as Figure 7.1 is therefore meaningless. The figure merely suggests that through most of the 1950s and 1960s relevant conditions were rather stable, whereas

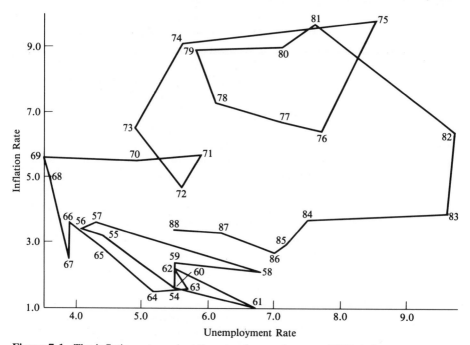

Figure 7.1. The inflation rate against the rate of unemployment (GNP deflator).

in the 1970s and 1980s there were large movements of factors affecting these conditions. Phillips himself (1958) was clearly aware of the conditional nature of the empirical relationship that he observed and referred to several variables that are likely to affect it, including the exchange rate.

The basic specification of a structure determining prices and wages, of which the Phillips curve is a part, was outlined fairly soon after the original work of Phillips, and by the early 1970s it took the form that has remained approximately the same to the present time in the MPS model.[2] The essential features of these equations (in a greatly simplified form for the purposes of exposition) are given in Table A7.1 of the Appendix, together with the derivation of "nonaccelerating-inflation-rate of unemployment" or the natural rate.

(A.1) is the traditional "expectations augmented" Phillips curve. The function $\phi(u)$ must sharply rise to the left as the rate of unemployment, u, goes down significantly below its normal level, say 5 to 6% in recent years. Its form for a very high level of u is less certain since the theory cannot be more specific than that $\phi'(u)$ should remain negative. Other investigators tended to believe that $\phi(u)$ became rather flat as u increased. Our own analysis suggests that when u is above its normal level, $\phi(u)$ is almost linearly declining in u, and its slope does not seem to become less steep. The expected rate of inflation in terms of P^F appearing in Eq. (A.1) is specified in Eq. (A.1a) as an adaptive expectation. This formulation is a part of what is being examined against the data in this chapter. When coefficients of (A.1a) are estimated as a part of Eq. (A.1), their sum is estimated to be very close to unity as soon as data for the first half of 1970s are included in the estimation, implying a "vertical Phillips curve" in the long run. T in (A.1) represents institutional factors affecting the rate of compensation, mainly the employer contribution rates for social security and unemployment insurance.

A number of alternative economic rationales have been proposed for the Phillips curve. The most prominent of these is the formulation of Robert Lucas (1972), in which it is interpreted as a transformation of the supply function of labor. For the purposes of this chapter, we prefer to think of the Phillips curve simply as a description of the standard market adjustment mechanism suggested many years ago by Paul A. Samuelson (1947). That is, the rate of change of the nominal wage rate relative to the expected level of the cost of living is expressed as a function of excess demand in the labor market represented by the unemployment rate:

$$\frac{\Delta\left(\dfrac{W}{P^e}\right)}{\left(\dfrac{W}{P^e}\right)} = \phi(u) \tag{1}$$

$$\frac{\Delta W}{W} = \phi(u) + \left(\frac{\Delta P}{P}\right)^e \tag{1'}$$

There is always the question of why the wage rate does not move quickly enough to equilibrate the labor market continuously. We propose to deal with the specification of detailed behavioral assumptions for workers and employers that are consistent with the above formulation in a separate paper. We record several observations at the aggregate level.

1. The labor market is not an auction market. In many cases, individual workers or a group of workers negotiate with individual employers or a group of employers sequentially. The rate of compensation is usually a part of a fairly complex contract, making it very costly to renegotiate it frequently. Furthermore, both parties usually find it advantageous to be able to rely on the continuous relationship without worrying about renegotiations most of the time. When contracts are renegotiated by individual parties without synchronization and when they tend to last more than one period (quarter of a year), gradual adjustments of the wage rate to excess demand or supply condition in the aggregate can easily be derived as an implication of such an institutional arrangement.

2. The expected rate of inflation appearing in Eq. (A.1a) may be in terms of a number of alternative prices. In particular, it may be in terms of final good prices, or in terms of value added prices.[3] The choice appears to be largely institutional, but, unfortunately, this choice has major impacts on the response of the price–wage sector to supply shocks. Thus, in Japan, the wage rate was informally tied to the final good prices until 1977–1978, but it has become tied to the value added price index after 1978. Because of this, Japan's responses to the first (1974) oil shock and to the second (1979–1980) oil shock were radically different.

3. It is also plausible that the rate of change of the real wage rate responds to changes in labor productivity per hour. Empirically, however, we have never been able to find a role for productivity per man-hour in Eq. (A.1). Since this equation determines the rate of change of the *nominal* wage rate, not the equilibrium real wage rate, this empirical finding is not troubling.

Equation (A.2) is derived as an implication of two basic assumptions concerning the behavior of firms. First, they are assumed to be price takers in factor markets (for labor and capital). Second, all firms in an industry are assumed to have access to the same technology, so that they share the common minimized average cost. They also know the cost of entry into the market by others, so that they know the maximum markup on the minimized average cost they can charge without inducing outsiders to enter their market. The price of output is therefore determined by marking up the value added component of cost and passing through the raw materials cost to final purchasers. Since, at this price, the demand for the output for all firms is well defined, the description of firms' behavior as cost minimization given the output requirement is a meaningful formation.

In this framework, Eq. (A.2) is a slightly modified form of one of the standard efficiency conditions for producers (the price–wage frontier), and its function is to specify the relative price between labor and output that is consistent with the efficient allocation of labor and capital in the production of a given output.

The term $\left(\dfrac{\bar{X}}{E}\right)$ in Eq. (A.2) is the long-run measure of the productivity per man-hour, estimated through the man-hours equation in another part of the MPS model so as to eliminate cyclical fluctuations of productivity per man-hour. Hence, (A.2) can also be interpreted as the expression for the long-term equilibrium share of labor in the value of output, net of raw materials cost. This share should in principle be a function of the gross cost of capital unless the production function is Cobb–Douglas. Empirically, we have never been able to find the gross cost of capital to be significant in this equation. μ is the markup factor that in theory depends in the long run most critically on the entry cost for new firms, but in the empirical representation of (A.2) this cost is assumed to be constant over time. Cyclical variation in the markup factor depends most significantly on the rate of capacity utilization as an indicator of the relative effectiveness of competition among existing firms. Short-run fluctuation of the markup also depends on other factors: for example, when prices of raw materials suddenly and unexpectedly rise (fall), the value added index for output relative to labor cost can fall (rise) temporarily if firms tend to use the actual purchase cost of goods in inventory rather than replacement cost as the basis for setting output prices. Dollar prices of competing imports are also expected to have effects on the domestic value-added prices. These other factors affecting the markup are summarized by the presence of the additional term Z in Eq. (A.2).

Equation (A.3) is a shorthand representation of two sets of equations. The first is a set of allocation equations with the standard adding-up constraints that, given the value of P^v from Eq. (A.2), determine the values of component prices of which P^v is the fixed weight aggregate. Second, there is a set of definitional identities that constructs a group of familiar indices, such as the GNP deflator and the price index of final goods used in Eq. (A.1) in terms of the components of P^v, raw materials prices, and the compensation rate. For purposes of the exposition in this chapter, however, we believe that the representation of all these detailed equations and identities by (A.3) is quite adequate.

Pursuing the purpose of this chapter involves an examination of the stability of the price–wage sector of the MPS model (whose structure is summarized by Eqs. (A.1)–(A.3)) over a fairly long period of time during which the policies of monetary and fiscal authorities changed significantly. For this analysis it is not appropriate to take the *level* of raw materials prices to be exogenous. On the other hand, we wish to focus our attention primarily on the explanation of the movement of the compensation rate and the value added price index and not to get heavily involved in the explanation of the raw materials prices and the exchange rate. We have therefore taken prices of raw materials relative to our basic value added index, P^v, not their absolute level, as exogenous to our analysis. More specifically:

1. The ratio of prices of oil, coal, and natural gas to P^v (not their absolute levels) has been taken as exogenous.
2. The ratio of the price index for agricultural commodities to P^v (not its absolute level) has been taken as exogenous.
3. The real exchange rate for the dollar against the currencies of our main trading partners has been taken as exogenous. Export price indices of our trading partners in terms of their own currencies are sometimes taken as exogenous, and sometimes explained by crude reduced form equations including in their explanatory variables the output price index of the United States.
4. The definition of raw materials for the purposes of analysis in this paper includes agricultural goods, fuel, and imported goods. Other raw materials such

as copper, aluminum, etc., in so far as they are domestically produced, are included as a part of the definition of P^v.

Finally, Table A.7.2 of the Appendix reports the actual empirical estimates of the two basic equations, (A.1) and (A.2), in the currently operating model. The specification and the numerical values of estimated parameters for Eq. (A.2) have been relatively stable since the MPS model was first put together in the late 1960s.[4] Equation (A.1), on the other hand, has gone through one important change. The sum of coefficients a^i in Eq. (A.1a) was considerably less than unity in the late 1960s and early 1970s, but it became unity in the mid-1970s (Pierce and Enzler, 1974). We will have a good deal more to say on this point in the next section.

EMPIRICAL RESULTS: THE PERFORMANCE OF THE PRICE–WAGE EQUATIONS IN THE 1965–1987 PERIOD

Figure 7.2a and b compares the actual historical values of the rate of change of the GNP deflator and total compensation per man-hour against the dynamic simulation of these variables starting in the first quarter, 1964, and continuing through the second quarter, 1988. The simulation is performed using the price–wage sector of the MPS model summarized by the three equations shown in Appendix A. Thus, the unemployment rate and the capacity utilization rate are taken as given, as are genuine exogenous variables such as the growth rate of productivity per man-hour and some features of the tax structure, especially the rate of excise taxes and the contribution rates for social security. The compensation rate is the dependent variable of Eq. (A.1), but the GNP deflator is not the dependent variable of (A.2), and its simulated value is generated as a part of the variables determined by the supplementary set of equations and identities represented by Eq. (A.3). We note, however, that the inflation rate appearing on the right-hand side of (A.1) is generated by the rest of the system so that the simulated value of the compensation rate depends on the performance of the whole system.

These graphs represent variables in the form of four-quarter rates of change; that is, although simulations are run on a quarterly basis, for the purposes of presentation in these graphs, we use information from four quarters earlier to form four-quarter rates of change. The motivation for adopting this mode of presentation is that one-quarter rates of change of these variables are quite erratic with some negative serial correlation, and it is difficult to see the basic pattern of correspondence or lack of correspondence between the actual values and simulated values when the quarterly rate of change is used directly to prepare these graphs.

The system of equations that has generated the simulation results reported in Figure 7.2a and b was estimated using data from 1961 to 1987. These results represent, therefore, mostly the performance of the system within the sample, except the last few quarters. Even so, the ability of the system to track actual history is remarkably good. There are two instances during this period when it would not have been surprising if a system such as the one under consideration exhibited some instability. The first instance is the period around 1973–1975 following a series of significant supply shocks: major devaluations of the dollar against European and Japanese currencies, the sharp

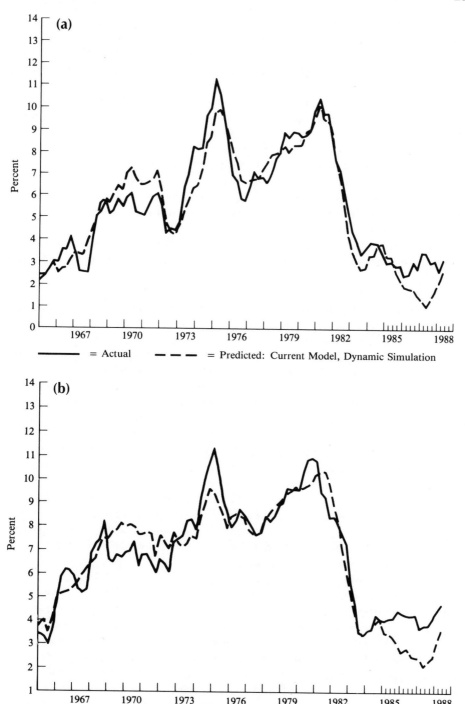

Figure 7.2. (a) GNP implicit deflator (4-quarter rate of change). (b) Compensation per hour (4-quarter rate of change).

rise in commodity prices in 1972, the food price increases of 1973, and the oil shock of 1973–1974. These disturbances clearly were a surprise at the time; not only did they come in rapid succession, but the U.S. economy had not experienced any disturbances of this type and size during the period after the Second World War and prior to 1970. Faced with such a new experience, it would not have been surprising if private agents shifted their behavior in response to it, for example, if they modified the way in which they formed price expectations, especially because in our formulation price expectations are expressed as adaptive. The dynamic simulations show no evidence of such a shift during or immediately after this period.

The second occasion was around 1979 and 1980. The second oil price shock occurred in 1979, while almost simultaneously a new, antiinflationary monetary policy was initiated, resulting in the sufficiently high rate of interest which induced a recession and a decline in the rate of inflation. Here again, it would not have been surprising if the way in which economic agents formed price expectations shifted. The simulation shows no evidence of such a shift, however, and the MPS model with its unchanged adaptive expectations formulation traces the decline of inflation starting in 1981 quite accurately.

When this system is extrapolated to predict the rate of inflation into the 1986–1988 period, it underpredicts the rate of inflation somewhat, about three quarters of one percentage point on average. When individual equations are extrapolated separately to determine which equation is at fault, the underestimation clearly originates with Eq. (A.2), not (A.1) or any part of (A.3). Evidently, when the price of oil fell rather dramatically at the end of 1985, the price of goods did not fall enough to reflect fully the cost reduction. An inspection of detailed data indicates that it is not the retail price of oil as such that remained somewhat higher than expected. Rather, for most goods whose production involved oil or other energy significantly, the markup in their value-added prices seems to have risen somewhat. Moreover, this pattern appears to be repeated in other countries, especially in Japan and in Italy whose data we have studied. This is in clear contrast to the experience of the 1970s, when the rise in the price of energy was almost immediately and completely passed on to the product prices of energy-using industries. Our attempts to build in a simple scheme that permits an asymmetric pass-through of raw material prices in Eq. (A.2) were not very encouraging. Even so, it seems possible that some type of asymmetry in the response pattern to a large change in the price of raw materials is involved, and our simple scheme was not flexible enough to serve as its description.

To check the stability of this system of equations, we have reestimated the entire set of equations using data through the end of 1979, and then extrapolated through the second quarter, 1988. A break at the end of 1979 seemed to be the most logical possibility for a test, because of the widely publicized change in the monetary policy rule initiated in 1979 and the victory of the Reagan team in the presidential election of 1980. Estimated parameters turned out to be almost identical to the ones generated by data running through to 1987, and it is clear that any test of nonhomogeneity would show that the hypothesis of stability is accepted. Perhaps more telling evidence is that the prediction using estimates based on data through 1979 has an almost identical performance in the 1980s as estimates using data through 1987, as a comparison of Figures 7.2a and 7.3a and Figures 7.2b and 7.3b shows. This is an important point because the central point of the so-called Lucas critique of econometric policy evalu-

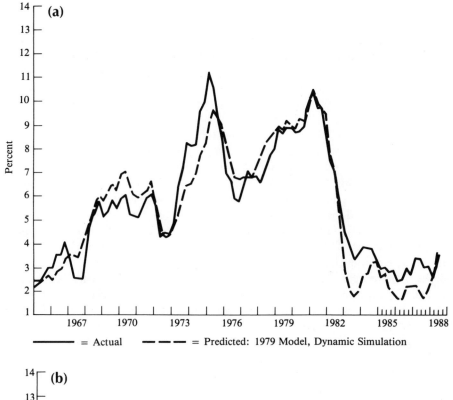

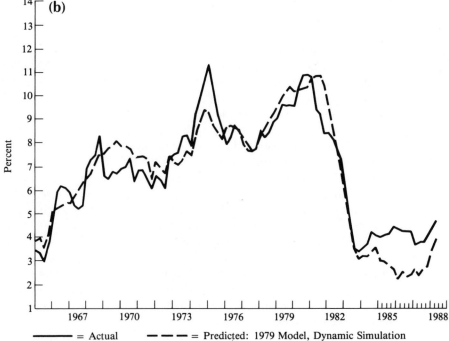

Figure 7.3. (a) GNP implicit deflator (4-quarter rate of change). (b) Compensation per hour (4-quarter rate of change).

ation was that relations such as (A.1) and (A.2) cannot be stable when policy rules change, and hence they cannot be relied on to predict the effects of policy rule changes (Lucas, 1976). As a matter of pure theory, any decision rule of a group of economic agents or a description of market adjustment mechanisms is indeed subject to shifts when policy rules affecting the agents in question change. The critical question is how serious are these shifts, and these results show that the shifts are not visible in equations that have been thought most subject to this problem, even under very large policy rule changes.

As shown in the Appendix, estimates of the wage equation (A.1) were obtained with the constraint that the coefficient a_1 for the expected inflation rate is unity. When data for the period after 1970 are included in the estimation, the free estimate of a_1 turns out to be very close to unity. When we first estimated this set of equations in the late 1960s, however, our estimate of a_1 was considerably smaller than unity, as reported by deMenil and Enzler (1972). In their estimate, the parameter that is equivalent to a_1 is reported at 0.57. Their estimates of other parameters were qualitatively similar to more recent ones.

It would be of some interest, then, to see how well the old deMenil–Enzler estimate would have performed if their set of equations was used to forecast the behavior of prices and wages during the 1970s and beyond. This is a rather difficult task because all of the data have been through several benchmark revisions since the time when deMenil and Enzler estimated their equations. The procedure we have adopted is to utilize only the equation for the compensation rate [equivalent to Eq. (A.1)] estimated by deMenil and Enzler, retaining all other equations in the current model. This decision seems justified because it is Eq. (A.1) that has changed with a significantly different value of a_1, while both the form and the estimated parameter values for other equations are fairly similar between the deMenil and Enzler system and our current system. Also, the shift of the base year and other revisions of the data can more easily be accommodated in Eq. (A.1) because it is formulated in a rate of change form. Since the earlier deMenil–Enzler system was estimated in 1970 using data through 1969, a dynamic simulation of this system can be thought of as a very long-term forecast.

The dynamic simulation of the system in which the current version of (A.1) is replaced by the corresponding equation estimated by deMenil and Enzler is reported in Figure 7.4a and b. We can see that the deMenil–Enzler equation underestimates the rate of inflation throughout the duration of the simulation. This is not surprising because the low value of coefficient a_1 causes an underestimation of the inflation rate, especially when the inflation is caused by a sudden rise in raw materials prices, P^R. However, Figure 7.4a and b shows that the basic time pattern of the historical inflation rate, distinct from the level, is caught reasonably well by the dynamic simulation. This suggests that the deMenil–Enzler equation may do quite well in a static, single period simulation.

Figure 7.5a and b reports the results of a static one-step-ahead simulation of the same system as for Figure 7.4a and b. In this figure, we show quarterly changes at an annual rate rather than the rate of change over four quarters, since in a static simulation short-run movements seemed more significant.

The simulation tracks the inflation rate in terms of the GNP deflator quite well (shown in Figure 7.5a) without serious downward bias. However, this result is somewhat spurious, because the price equation (A.2) has a rather small coefficient for the

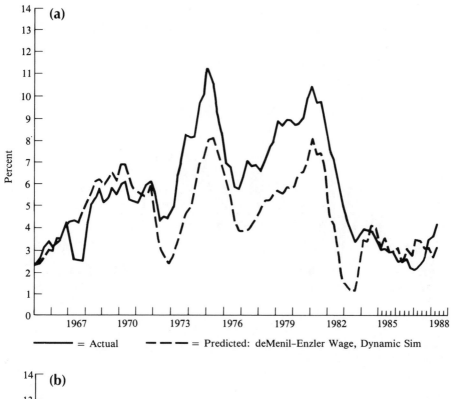

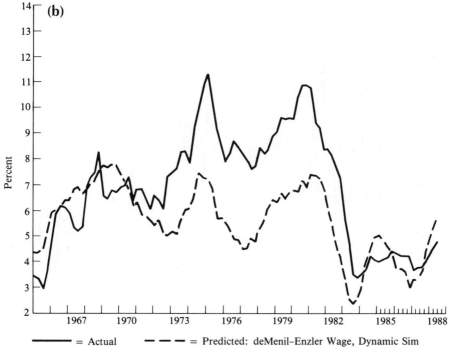

Figure 7.4. (a) GNP implicit deflator (4-quarter rate of change). (b) Compensation per hour (4-quarter rate of change).

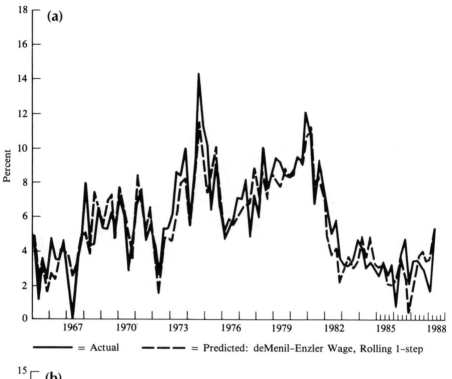

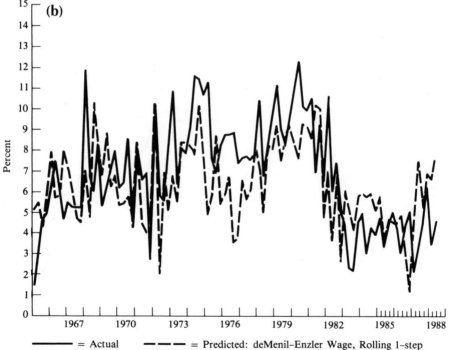

Figure 7.5. (a) GNP implicit deflator (1-quarter change, annual rate). (b) Compensation per hour (1-quarter change, annual rate).

current wage rate, and the result reported in Figure 7.5a depends on the deMenil–Enzler equation quantitatively only very moderately in a static simulation. On the other hand, the simulated value of the inflation rate in terms of the wage rate (shown in Figure 7.5b) reflects directly the behavior of the deMenil–Enzler equation, and it underestimates the rate of change of the wage rate by one to two percentage points on average between 1974 and 1980.

In practice, if an investigator used deMenil–Enzler equations for predicting the behavior of wages and prices during the 1970s conditional on the past values of prices and wages, he would have found that he underestimated the wage rate more than the value-added price. This would have led to some unacceptable features of his overall analysis of the economy as a whole, including, for example, some distortion of the functional distribution of income and an unreasonably low level of real wages and hence an underestimation of the aggregate final demand. Such a situation would have led the analyst to recognize asymmetric biases of predictions for the wage rate and the value-added price, and he would have eventually recognized the source of his difficulties, namely, the size of the coefficient a_1 in Eq. (A.1).

By the mid-1970s, however, it was becoming quite apparent that the coefficient a_1 in Eq. (A.1) must be very close to unity.[5] Once this is recognized, the performance of the system reported in Figures 7.2 and 7.3 rather than that reported in Figures 7.4 and 7.5 becomes relevant. This is a very different situation from that apparently depicted by a naive, unconditional picture such as Figure 7.1.

A TEST OF THE DIRECT EFFECT OF THE MONEY SUPPLY ON INFLATION

Equations (A.1) through (A.3) do not contain the quantity of money or other variables directly related to the money supply. In spite of the apparent absence of the money supply in our price–wage equations, our formulation does not imply that the money has no effect on the price level and inflation when the MPS model is considered as a whole. In our formulation, the direct cause of the movement of prices is excess demand conditions in the labor and goods and services markets, on the one hand, and the relative price of raw materials, on the other, which in turn depends on supply and demand conditions for these raw materials. In the MPS model, some components of final demand for goods and services, especially investment in plant and equipment and in housing, and to some extent consumption, are quite sensitive to variations in the real rate of interest, and because of the formulation of price expectations in the MPS model, the real rate of interest is quite sensitive, particularly in the short run, to movements of the nominal rate of interest. The nominal rate of interest, in turn, is strongly related to the supply of money given the initial levels of price and output. Hence, there is a strong relationship between the supply of money and final demand, and, through final demand, a strong relationship between the movement of prices and the supply of money.

What our formulation does imply is that, given the final demand for goods and excess demand (or supply) conditions in the labor market, there is no further direct effect of the quantity of the money supply on prices. Although this proposition is consistent with a description of the behavior of the more important players in the U.S.

economy and of the country's market structure accepted by many economists, this is a strong empirical hypothesis. The evidence presented in the preceding section establishes the initial plausibility for this hypothesis, but it is by no means conclusive. This section reports a set of tests that is aimed at providing more direct evidence on the hypothesis that effects of the money supply on movements of prices and wages work through the effects of monetary factors on final demand, and that there is no further significant direct effect of the money supply on movements of prices and wages.

Suppose that we generate the predictions of prices and wages by simulating the subsystem consisting of Eqs. (A.1) through (A.3), taking actual values of the rate of unemployment, the capacity utilization rate, and other variables listed previously as given. The output of such a simulation can then be compared with the actual rate of inflation of the corresponding price and wage variables, and the difference between the actual, historical value and the simulated value can be considered as the prediction error. Our test discussed in this section is based on the observation that if our hypothesis is correct, the prediction error described above should not be correlated with the movement of the rate of growth of the supply of money, lagged at least one period.[6] In other words, let us denote the actual, historical value of the inflation rate defined in terms of some price index, say the deflator of GNP, by y, and its corresponding value generated by the simulation described above by ya. Our hypothesis then implies that $y - ya$ should not be correlated with the rate of growth of the money supply, lagged at least one period.

Before carrying out the tests suggested by this observation, however, one technical question must be resolved. Should the simulated value of y, ya, be from a static, one-period simulation, or from a dynamic simulation? Chong and Hendry (1986), and subsequently Pagan (1989), have forcefully advocated that for the purposes of judging the adequacy of a hypothesis in describing data, dynamic simulation results do not contain information that was not already present in residuals generated by the estimation process, which are the same as the static, single-equation simulation errors in most cases. Furthermore, dynamic simulation errors, which accumulate over time, are much harder to characterize and interpret, and, hence, they conclude that we should work with one period ahead forecasting errors, or static simulation errors. Although their argument seems convincing if the system involved is strictly linear, the Chong–Hendry–Pagan argument breaks down if there is any type of nonlinearity present, as shown by Mariano and Brown (1989). The result of Mariano and Brown is rather restricted, but they provide a partial justification for our repeated experience that dynamic simulation over a number of periods seems to provide more stringent tests of the acceptability of many types of specifications, and that the deviation of dynamic simulations from the historical path often points to some specific defects of the specification of the model that were not noticeable from estimation residuals. In what follows, we present results using both dynamic and static simulations. Quite fortunately, conclusions from both results are not materially different.

A preliminary step is to check for bias in the inflation predictions generated by the MPS model. Coefficients from the regression of the form

$$y = \alpha + \beta ya + \varepsilon \tag{2}$$

are reported in Table 7.1. Here ya is generated alternatively by static and dynamic simulations. That α and β in this table are not significantly different from zero and

Table 7.1. Bias Tests for Forecasts from the MPS Model Equations[a]
1. Regression in the form of
$$y = \alpha + \beta ya$$

2. Results

Model Estimate Based on Data for	Sample Period for Bias Test	α	β
	ya is generated by static simulations		
1960.1–1979.4	1965.1–1979.4	0.32 (0.48)	0.96 (0.07)
1960.1–1987.4	1965.1–1979.4	0.12 (0.49)	0.97 (0.07)
1960.1–1987.4	1965.1–1986.4	0.51 (0.31)	0.92 (0.05)
1960.1–1987.4	1980.1–1987.4	0.56 (0.29)	0.91 (0.05)
	ya is generated by dynamic simulations		
1960.1–1979.4	1965.1–1979.4	−0.10 (0.57)	1.00 (0.09)
1960.1–1987.4	1965.1–1979.4	−0.11 (0.55)	1.00 (0.08)
1960.1–1987.4	1965.1–1986.4	0.52 (0.34)	0.93 (0.05)
1960.1–1987.4	1965.1–1987.4	0.72 (0.32)	0.90 (0.05)

[a]y, the actual rate of change of GNP deflator; ya, simulated value corresponding to y. Standard errors are in parentheses.

unity, respectively, except when observations for 1987 are included, is a confirmation of the impression given by Figures 7.2a and 7.3a, that the simulated value is on the whole an unbiased predictor of the actual value.

Returning to the observation that our hypothesis implies the lack of a correlation between $y - ya$ and the lagged value of the rate of change of the money supply, a simple test suggested by this observation is to regress $y - ya$ on a number of lagged values of the rate of growth of the money supply. If our hypothesis is correct, then the coefficients of lagged values of the rate of growth of the money supply jointly should not be different from zero.

Table 7.2 reports results of a regression of the form

$$y - ya = \alpha + \sum_{i=1}^{16} \beta_i \left(\frac{\Delta M}{M} \right)_{t-i} + \varepsilon' \tag{3}$$

$\dfrac{\Delta M}{M}$ is defined in terms of either M_1 or M_2 and the β_i are constrained to lie on a second-degree polynomial. When it is defined in terms of M_1, the result is rather erratic, and the sum of coefficients β_i is not significantly different from zero. On the other hand, when $\dfrac{\Delta M}{M}$ is defined in terms of M_2, the sum of the coefficients β_i is positive and somewhat significant. An earlier version of this paper reported a similar experiment, but on that occasion, only M_1 was used to define $\dfrac{\Delta M}{M}$, and no constraint was imposed on the pattern of β_i. The result was that the sum of the coefficients β_i was not significantly different from zero. The new result reported here suggests that when the rate of growth of the money supply is defined in terms of M_2, and when the latest revision of the data is incorporated into our analysis, there is some evidence that the correlation between $y - ya$ and the rate of growth of the money supply is positive and marginally significant.[7]

Table 7.2. Test of Correlations between the Prediction Errors and the Rate of Growth of Money Supply

1. Test equation

$$y - ya = \alpha + \sum_{i=1}^{16} \beta_i \left(\frac{\Delta M}{M}\right)_{t-i} + \varepsilon$$

where β_i is constrained to be on a second degree polynomial

2. Results[a]

$\frac{\Delta M}{M}$ is Defined in Terms of	Sample Period	α	$\Sigma \beta_i$
M_1	1965.1–1979.4	−0.53 (0.90)	0.06 (0.17)
M_1	1965.1–1987.4	−0.43 (0.44)	0.06 (0.08)
M_2	1965.1–1979.4	−1.57 (1.07)	0.17 (0.12)
M_2	1965.1–1987.4	−1.73 (0.94)	0.20 (0.11)

Note: If the coefficient of *ya* is not restricted to unity, then the results are

$\frac{\Delta M}{M}$ is Defined in Terms of	Sample Period	α	β_y[b]	$\Sigma \beta_i$
M_1	1965.1–1979.4	−0.83 (0.98)	0.90 (0.12)	0.23 (0.26)
M_1	1965.1–1987.4	−0.03 (0.50)	0.93 (0.05)	0.06 (0.08)
M_2	1965.1–1979.4	−1.85 (1.06)	0.84 (0.10)	0.31 (0.14)
M_2	1965.1–1987.4	−1.69 (.90)	0.87 (0.05)	0.28 (0.11)

[a] *y*, the actual rate of change of GNP deflator; *ya*, simulated values corresponding to *y*. Standard errors of estimated coefficients are in parentheses.

[b] Figures under β_y are the estimated coefficients of *ya*.

We wish to review another, parallel set of tests before trying to interpret the results reported in Table 7.2. Let us consider the naive hypothesis that the rate of inflation is completely determined by the rate of growth of money less the expected rate of growth of real output. One such model may be written as

$$\frac{\Delta P}{P} = \gamma + \sum_{i=1}^{N} \beta_i \left(\frac{\Delta M}{M}\right)_{t-i} \tag{4}$$

where $\frac{\Delta M}{M}$ is defined in terms of either M_1 or M_2. γ is meant to represent the long-run, average rate of growth of output with a negative sign. Instead of trying to measure such an average quantity from the historical data, it is estimated as a constant in this equation. Under the assumption that the income velocity of money is stationary, the sum of the coefficients β_i's should be close to unity, and the estimate of γ should be negative and close to the average rate of growth of output.

Estimates of Eq. (4) are reported in Table 7.3. When M_1 is used to construct the rate of growth of the money supply, the results are very erratic and do not make sense, presumably because the role of M_1 and its definition have gone through radical changes in the 1970s and 1980s. The relationship between M_1 and nominal income has been anything but stable during this period. When M_2 is used to construct the rate of growth of the money supply, however, we obtain results that are quite close to our expectation:

Table 7.3. Monetary Models of Inflation

1. Model[a]

$$y_t = \gamma + \sum_{i=1}^{16} \beta_i \left(\frac{\Delta M}{M}\right)_{t-i}$$

2. Estimates

Model	Sample Period	γ	$\Sigma\beta$
M_1	1965.1–1979.4	-3.35	1.74
		$(1.53)^b$	(0.27)
M_1	1965.1–1987.4	6.49	-0.11
		(2.69)	(0.38)
M_2	1965.1–1979.4	-3.43	1.11
		(2.26)	(0.26)
M_2	1965.1–1987.4	-2.68	0.95
		(0.70)	(0.42)

[a]y_t, rate of change of the price index (GNP deflator); $\left(\dfrac{\Delta M}{M}\right)$, rate of growth of money supply. β_i's are constrained to lie on a second degree polynomial.

[b]Standard errors are in parentheses.

the sum of coefficients β_i is not significantly different from unity in the statistical sense, and the estimate of γ is not too far from the rate of growth of real output, although it is a little too large.[8]

Given the results reported in Table 7.3, we can now carry out a simple test of the nonnested hypotheses between this result and our basic hypothesis. The test, suggested by Davidson and MacKinnon (1981) as the "C-test," is based on the restricted regression of the form

$$y = (1-\alpha)ya + \alpha yb + \eta \tag{5}$$

where y is the actual rate of inflation (in terms of the GNP deflator), ya is the predicted value for y generated by our basic model, and yb is the predicted value for y generated by Eq. (4) whose estimated parameter values are reported in Table 7.3. α is the parameter to be estimated, and η is the residual error term. Davidson and MacKinnon (1981) describe why this test is inferior to others they present, but this seems to be the only test that can be implemented without serious difficulty given that the basic model tested here is a multiequation, nonlinear system. In any event, the test provides another indication of whether the introduction of the money supply would improve the predictive ability of the MPS model for the rate of inflation. The results of this test are reported in Table 7.4.

The nonnested test results reported in Table 7.4 are similar to those given in Table 7.2. When the rate of growth of the money supply is defined in terms of M_1, α is mostly insignificant, especially when the data for 1980s are excluded from our test. On the other hand, when the rate of growth of the money supply is defined in terms of M_2, and the data for the 1980s are included in our test, the size of α becomes close to 0.2, and the t-ratio goes above 2.0, in one case more than 3.0.[9]

These results showing a small but significant direct impact of money on prices would seem to indicate that either Eq. (A.1) or (A.2) is misspecified. In particular, the results may be interpreted as pointing to the presence of a positive correlation

Table 7.4. Nonnested Tests

1. Model[a]

$$y = (1 - \alpha)ya + \alpha yb$$

2. Estimates

ya	yb	α	Sample Period for Test
One-step-ahead forecasts			
Model estimated on	M_1 model	$0.13 \ (0.12)$[b]	1965.1–1979.4
1960–1979 data	M_2 model	0.19 (0.10)	1965.1–1979.4
Model estimated on	M_1 model	0.15 (0.07)	1965.1–1986.4
1960–1987 data	M_2 model	0.18 (0.07)	1965.1–1986.4
Model estimated on	M_1 model	0.16 (0.07)	1965.1–1987.4
1960–1987 data	M_2 model	0.20 (0.07)	1965.1–1987.4
Dynamic simulations			
Model estimated on	M_1 model	0.20 (0.13)	1965.1–1979.4
1960–1979 data	M_2 model	0.20 (0.11)	1965.1–1979.4
Model estimated on	M_1 model	0.09 (0.05)	1965.1–1986.4
1960–1987 data	M_2 model	0.15 (0.05)	1965.1–1986.4
Model estimated on	M_1 model	0.11 (0.05)	1965.1–1987.4
1960–1987 data	M_2 model	0.18 (0.05)	1965.1–1987.4

[a]y, inflation rate, GNP implicit deflator; ya, predicted value of y, MPS wage–price model; yb, predicted value of y, alternative model.

[b]Standard errors are in parentheses.

between the rate of growth of the money supply and one or the other of the estimated residuals of Eqs. (A.4) and (A.5). Consequently, we introduced the rate of growth of the money supply in terms of M_2, in the same form as in Eq. (4), into Eqs. (A.4) and (A.5), and reestimated them. Since Eq. (A.5) is formulated in logarithms of level variables, instead of the rate of change of M_2, the level of the expenditure velocity of M_2 was used. Surprisingly, the variable based on M_2 turned out to be totally insignificant in both equations, and its introduction into these equations leaves the coefficients of other variables virtually unchanged.

It is also possible that results reported in Tables 7.2 and 7.4 are due to some complex statistical reasons rather than due to the presence of additional causal channels leading from M_2 to prices. For example, if the true dynamic process is a continuous one, then the variable constructed as the average value over a fixed period of time will have an artificial serial correlation, so that a contemporary causal relation from prices and wages to M_2 may induce nonzero correlation between the current value of P or W and the value of M_2 one period lagged. This possibility, however, seems to be ruled out because the positive contribution of M_2 in the test reported in Table 7.2 remains when the distributed lag of M_2 starts in period $t - 2$.

It is also possible that our results are due to an unusual condition in some specific period. For example, our basic model underestimates the rate of inflation in the 1986–1988 period, though not by a very large margin, and it is conceivable that this is due to some unusual condition in the period 1986–1988. It seems that the rate of growth of M_2 was also somewhat higher than usual during this period. However, as noted earlier, when the rate of change of M_2 is directly introduced into Eqs. (A.4) and (A.5), it is insignificant in both equations.

Our present conclusion, therefore, remains somewhat ambiguous. On the one hand, tests based on the performance of the price–wage subsystem as a whole reported in Tables 7.2 and 7.4 suggest that the MPS model is missing a small but significant direct effect of the rate of growth of M_2 on the rate of inflation.[10] On the other hand, when the individual behavioral equations are tested to see if they should be modified to include the rate of growth of M_2 directly, we find that the data do not support the inclusion of M_2 in either the wage equation or the basic price equation. Equations represented by (A.3) are either definitional identities, or a part of a system of equations with rigid adding-up constraints. Therefore, any misspecification that may be present in (A.3) is more likely to become visible in (A.2), because such misspecification is likely to be transferred into the definition of the value-added price index through identities defining the value-added price index, which serves as the dependent variable of Eq. (A.2). Perhaps the most plausible reason why the rate of growth of M_2 may have a direct effect on the rate of inflation is that the expectation of future inflation appearing in (A.1) is a function not only of the past rates of inflation but also of the past rate of growth of M_2. But if this is the case, the direct introduction of the rate of growth of M_2 into Eq. (A.4) should have produced a significant coefficient.

On the whole, then, it is our tentative conclusion that there remains some small but important misspecification in Eqs. (A.4) and/or (A.5) that is different from the absence of the money supply from these equations, and such misspecification is creating a complex pattern of errors that results in the correlation between the system's error and M_2. The identification of the apparent misspecification must remain an important future task.

SOME FINAL REMARKS

We have presented evidence that supports fairly strongly our contention that the structure describing the price–wage system in the United States summarized by Eqs. (A.1) through (A.3) remained stable from the 1960s to the 1980s. The predictions generated by the currently estimated system, conditional on demand conditions in the domestic markets, especially the labor market, and on the relative prices of raw materials (the ratio of raw materials prices to the private, domestic nonfarm business value-added price index) are unbiased except when very recent data are included, and even then very close to being unbiased. This unbiasedness remains true whether the prediction technique is repeated one-period-ahead forecasts given all past prices, or multi-period-ahead forecasts generated by the dynamic simulation of the system.

Although the system (A.1) through (A.3) does not explicitly contain the money supply or any rate of interest or any other financial variable, the structure of this system does not imply that the development of prices and wages over time is independent of the money supply. The system does imply that any action of the monetary authority, including the rate of growth of the money supply, affects prices and wages only through its effects on the markets for goods and services, and that there is no other "direct" effect of the money supply on the development of prices and wages over time.

We noted that if our hypothesis is true, then the error of prediction of the rate of change of a price generated by our system should be uncorrelated with the rate of growth of the money supply lagged at least one period, and we developed two sets of simple tests based on this observation. Results from these tests indicate that there remain small but nonnegligible effects of M_2 on the movements of prices and wages that are not captured by our system. On the other hand, when M_2 is directly introduced into the two basic equations in our system, (A.4) and (A.5), it does not gain any significance and it does not alter estimates of parameters for other variables in these equations significantly.[11] Our tentative interpretation of these somewhat contradictory results is that there must still be some subtle misspecifications on our basic equations other than the absence of M_2, and that some complex interactions between these remaining misspecifications and the movements of M_2 are causing these mixed signals.

In his contribution to this volume, Ignazio Visco analyzes causes of instability in various econometric models including the MPS model and concludes that the form of the Phillips curve (A.1) is an important source of instability for the MPS model as a whole, especially when the length of the distributed lag in (A.1a) is relatively short. In response to any shock, the model tends to generate moderately unstable cyclical trajectories with a long periodicity if monetary policy is defined as a fixed path for a monetary aggregate. Some type of countercyclical policy rule is needed, therefore, to keep the economy from eventually experiencing serious recessions or inflation. The dynamic properties of the whole system turn out to depend rather critically on specific numerical values of parameters for Eq. (A.1), and, hence, the design of the countercyclical policy rule needed to avoid severe recessions and inflation also depends critically on these numerical estimates of parameters in Eq. (A.1).[12,13] Accurate specification and estimation of the Phillips curve, therefore, remains one of the critical tasks for those of us concerned with dynamic stabilization of the economy.

ACKNOWLEDGMENTS

The material reported here is mostly based on the work undertaken over a number of years at the Board of Governors of the Federal Reserve System. Jared Enzler and Eileen Mauskopf were especially important contributors. Opinions expressed herein, however, are those of the authors and do not necessarily reflect views of the Board of Governors or the staff of the Federal Reserve System.

NOTES

1. See surveys by Gordon (1981, 1982) and Laidler and Parkin (1975). See also Gordon (1988) and Englander and Los (1983).
2. Samuelson and Solow (1960), Tobin (1972a,b), and Friedman (1977).
3. As shown in Table A7.2 of the Appendix, the MPS wage equation uses a final goods price (the personal consumption deflator). We have found that in the United States the substitution for this index by a value added price index causes some deterioration in the ability of this equation to track the historical data.
4. However, fuel prices were not excluded from P^v until the mid-1970s.

5. Pierce and Enzler (1974).

6. Correlation between the current rate of change of money supply and the current inflation rate may be due to the causation going from the former to the latter, or the other way around. Unless the monetary authority controls the supply of money very rigidly without any regard to the demand for it, the short-term movement of the money supply is likely to reflect the demand for money at least partially, and the current demand for money is almost certainly a function of the current price level. Because of this situation, the presence of positive correlation between the prediction errors and the contemporaneous rate of change of the money supply cannot necessarily be interpreted as an indication of a causal relation from the money supply to the inflation rate. Actually, even the rate of change of the money supply lagged one period is suspect because of problems caused by the aggregation of variables over time, but lagging it two periods may bias the result in the opposite direction. As a compromise, we have used a distributed lag on money that starts with the first lag.

7. Equation (3) is the appropriate form to test on whether $y - ya$ and the rate of growth of the money supply are correlated with each other. If our purpose is to determine the optimal combination of ya and the rate of growth of the money supply in the one-period-ahead prediction of the rate of inflation, the coefficient of ya should not be restricted to be unity. The result of removing this restriction is reported in the note in Table 7.2.

8. On the other hand, since M_2 is defined to include a number of additional financial instruments paying the market rate of interest, the demand for M_2 must be based on its role in the portfolios of households and businesses, not on the transactions requirement. Hence, from the theoretical perspective, it is not clear why there should be a stable relationship between M_2 and a measure of nominal income, such as GNP in current dollars.

9. We considered one other monetary model of price determination that is based on the work of Hallman, Porter, and Small (1989). They examine a model in which prices adjust to close the gap between the equilibrium and actual price levels, where the equilibrium price is specified as proportional to M_2 per unit of potential GNP. This model imposes long-run homogeneity between the levels of prices and money. They show that the price gap calculated in logs is arithmetically equal to the sum of the velocity gap (the log of velocity less the log of its mean value) and the output gap (the log of potential output less the log of current output). To focus on the direct importance of monetary variables, it was necessary to simplify the model of Hallman et al. to one in which prices adjust only to the velocity gap. Nonnested tests of the importance of money using the velocity gap model gave uniformly smaller estimates of α than those reported in Table 7.4 for the money models described by Eq. (4).

10. For a parallel result, see the findings of Stockton and Struckmeyer (1989).

11. It is true that by introducing M_2 into Eqs. (A.4) and A.5), even when it is lagged at least one period, its coefficient may be subject to the simultaneous equations bias. On the other hand, lagging M_2 two periods seems to weaken the power of the test too far. We note here, however, that the simultaneous equations bias for the coefficient of M_2 should be in the direction of making it further away from zero due to the causation running from prices and wages to M_2. Hence, we believe that our finding that M_2 is not significant when it is introduced into Eqs. (A.4) and (A.5) remains reliable even when the potential simultaneous equations bias is taken into consideration.

12. We have already dealt with issues of Lucas' critique. We have shown that the Phillips curve has been very stable when conditions in the economy including monetary and fiscal policies have changed quite significantly, so that effects of policy rules on the economy can be cautiously discussed.

13. If the Phillips curve (A.1), which is formulated strictly in terms of rates of change, could be replaced by an equation that is related to an equilibrium level, then the whole model will

become much more stable dynamically, and the dynamic stability of the model will not depend so sharply on estimated numerical values of parameters of the Phillips curve. A formulation of such a level equation for the nominal wage rate, however, has many problems of its own. These points are outlined by Visco in his chapter in this volume, without clear resolution of the basic issues.

REFERENCES

Brayton, F., and E. Mauskopf. (1985). "The Federal Reserve Board MPS Quarterly Econometric Model of the U.S. Economy." *Economic Modelling* 2(3), 170–292.

Chong, Y. Y., and D. F. Hendry. (1986). "Econometric Evaluation of Linear Macroeconomic Models." *Review of Economic Studies* LIII, 671–690.

Davidson, R., and J. G. MacKinnon. (1981). "Several Tests for Model Specification on the Presence of Alternative Hypothesis." *Econometrica* 49, 781–794.

deMenil, George, and J. Enzler. (1972). "Prices and Wages in the FRB-MIT-Penn Econometric Model." In *The Econometrics of Price Determination*, O. Eckstein, ed. Washington DC: Board of Governors of the Federal Reserve System.

Englander, A. S., and C. Los. (1983). *Stability of the Phillips Curve and Its Implications for the 1980's.* A research paper by the Federal Reserve Bank of New York.

Friedman, Milton. (1977). "Nobel Lecture: Inflation and Unemployment." *Journal of Political Economy* 85, 451–472.

Gordon, R. J. (1981). "Output Fluctuations and Gradual Price Adjustment." *Journal of Economic Literature* 9, 493–530.

Gordon, R. J. (1982). "Inflation, Flexible Exchange Rates and the Natural Rate of Unemployment." In *Workers, Jobs, and Inflation,* Martin Baily, ed., pp. 88–157. Washington, D.C.: Brookings Institution.

Gordon, R. J. (1988). "The Role of Wages in the Inflation Process." *AEA Papers and Proceedings* 78, 276–283.

Hallman, J. J., R. D. Porter, and D. H. Small (1989). "M2 per Unit of Potential GNP as an Anchor for the Price Level." Washington DC: Board of Governors of the Federal Reserve System, Staff Study 157.

Laidler, D., and M. Parkin. (1975). "Inflation: A Survey." *The Economic Journal* 85, 741–789.

Lucas, R. (1972). "Expectations and the Neutrality of Money." *Journal of Economic Theory* 4, 103–125.

Lucas, R. (1976). "Econometric Policy Evaluation: A Critique." Carnegie-Rochester Conference on Public Policy (Supplement to *Journal of Monetary Economics*), pp. 7–33.

Lucas, R., and T. Sargent. (1978). "After Keynesian Macroeconomics." In *After the Phillips Curve: Persistence of High Inflation and High Unemployment.* Proceedings of a Conference held in June 1978, Federal Reserve Bank of Boston, Boston, MA.

Lucas, R. (1981). "After Keynesian Macroeconomics." In *Rational Expectations and Econometric Practice,* Robert E. Lucas and Thomas J. Sargent, eds. University of Minnesota Press.

Mariano, R., and B. W. Brown. (1989). "Stochastic Simulation and Validation of Nonlinear Econometric Models." Draft presented at the Stanford Meetings of the NBER Seminar on Model Comparison, February 1989.

Pagan, A. (1989). "On the Role of Simulation in the Statistical Evaluation of Econometric Models." *Journal of Econometrics* 40, 125–139.

Phillips, A. William. (1958). "The Relation between Unemployment and the Rate of Change of Money Wage Rate in the United Kingdom: 1861–1957." *Economica* 25, 283–299.

Pierce, J., and J. Enzler. (1974). "The Effects of External Inflationary Shocks." *Brookings Papers on Economic Activity* 1, 13–61.

Samuelson, Paul A. (1947). *Foundations of Economic Analysis*. Boston: Harvard University Press.

Samuelson, Paul A., and Robert M. Solow. (1960). "Analytical Aspects of Anti-Inflation Policy." *American Economic Review Papers and Proceedings* 50, 177–194.

Stockton, D. J., and C. S. Struckmeyer. (1989). "Tests of the Specification and Predictive Accuracy of Nonnested Models of Inflation." *Review of Economics and Statistics* 71, 275–283.

Tobin, James. (1972a). "Inflation and Unemployment." *American Economic Review* 12, 1–18.

Tobin, James. (1972b). "The Wage-Price Mechanism: Overview of the Conference." In *The Econometrics of Price Determination*, Otto Eckstein, ed. Washington, DC: Board of Governors of the Federal Reserve System.

Table A7.1. Schematic Representation of Basic Equations[a]

$$\frac{\Delta W_t}{W_{t-1}} = \phi(u_t) + a_1\left(\frac{\Delta P^F}{P^F_{-1}}\right)^e_t + a_2 T_t + a_0 \tag{A.1}$$

$$\left(\frac{\Delta P^F}{P^F_{-1}}\right)^e_t = \sum_{i=1}^{Na} a^i \left(\frac{\Delta P^F_{-i}}{P^F_{t-i-1}}\right) \tag{A.1a}$$

$$\ell n\, P^v_t = \sum_{i=0}^{Nb} b^i_1\, \ell n\, W_{t-i} - \ell n\left(\frac{\overline{X}}{E}\right)_t + \ell n\, \mu\left[\left(\frac{X}{X^c}\right)_t, z_t\right] + b_0 \tag{A.2}$$

$$P^F_t = P^v_t\left(\frac{V}{F} + \frac{R}{F}\frac{P^R_t}{P^v_t}\right)(1 + \tau_t) \tag{A.3}$$

[a]Notations:

a's and b's are estimated parameters	
F	Value of final goods sold in the base year
$\mu\left[\left(\frac{X}{X^c}\right)_t\right]$	Markup factor (i.e., the ratio of the output price to the minimized average cost of production); it may be itself a function of the utilization rate, competitiveness of imports relative to their domestic counterparts, and other factors
P^F_t	Price index for final goods for the economy (including indirect business taxes)
$\left(\frac{\Delta P^F}{P^F}\right)^e_t$	Expected rate of change of P^F
P^R	Raw materials price
P^v_t	Value-added price index for nonagricultural, private, domestic, business output (excluding indirect business taxes)
R	The value of raw materials
t	Time
T	Other factors affecting the compensation rate per hour, such as the social insurance contribution rates
u_t	The unemployment rate
V	The value-added recorded in the base year
$\left(\frac{\overline{X}}{E}\right)$	The cyclical average of productivity per man-hour
$\left(\frac{X}{X^c}\right)$	Capacity utilization rate
W_t	The compensation rate per man-hour
Z_t	Other factors affecting markups, such as foreign competition, recent movements of raw materials prices and related handling of raw materials inventory, etc., all in logarithms

Note on the Definition of the "Natural" Rate of Unemployment

Consider a special situation in which

1. The rate of increase $\left(\dfrac{\overline{X}}{E}\right)_t$ is constant and equal to g.

2. Variables μ, Z_t, and $\left[\dfrac{V}{F} + \dfrac{R}{F}\dfrac{P^R}{P^V}\right](1+\tau)$ have been constant for some time and

   expected to remain so in the future, and the variable T_t has been expected to remain zero.
3. The parameter a_1 is assumed to be unity, and $\Sigma a^i = 1.0$ and $\Sigma b_1^i = 1.0$.

4. Given the above three assumptions, $\dfrac{\Delta W}{W_{-1}}$ for periods prior to t has been con-

   stant, and so has $\dfrac{\Delta P^v}{P^v_{-1}}$; $\dfrac{\Delta P^v}{P^v_{-1}} = \dfrac{\Delta W}{W_{-1}} - g$.

Under these assumptions, we can write

$$\frac{\Delta W_t}{W_{t-1}} = \phi(u) + \Sigma f_i\left(\frac{\Delta W_{t-i}}{W_{t-i-1}}\right) - g + a_o$$

where $\Sigma f_i = 1.0$.

In this situation, the rate of unemployment that keeps the inflation rate at its steady past value is given by the solution of

$$\phi(u) - g + a_o = 0$$

This is the operational definition of the non-inflation-accelerating rate of unemployment in the simple case, sometimes called the natural rate of unemployment.

When some of the variables assumed constant in (1) and (2) are not in fact constant, their movements could be incorporated into the definition of the natural rate, but how much of these additional factors should be included in the definition of the natural rate depends on the purposes for which the concept is used.

Table A7.2. Estimated Equations

Estimated Wage Equation[a]

$$\frac{\Delta W}{W} = \underset{[1.15]}{0.82} - \underset{[9.08]}{0.81} \{(U-8)(U>4) - (16/U)(U<4)\}$$

$$+ \sum_{i=1}^{12} a_i \left(\frac{\Delta P^F}{P^F}\right)_{-i} - \underset{[2.26]}{2.34} \Delta LFPART + 1.0\ GTU \qquad (A.4)$$

$$+ \underset{[3.78]}{0.68}\ GTOER + \underset{[1.77]}{0.04}\ GMINW + \sum_{i=0}^{6} b_i\ REPLACE_{-i}$$

$$- \underset{[2.63]}{2.97}\ CONTROL$$

$$(U>4) = \begin{cases} 1 \text{ if } U>4 \\ 0 \text{ if } U\leq4 \end{cases}$$

$$(U<4) = \begin{cases} 0 \text{ if } U>4 \\ 1 \text{ if } U\leq4 \end{cases}$$

Distributed lag coefficients

$$\sum_i a_i = 1.0 \qquad \sum_i b_i = \underset{[1.55]}{7.94}$$

Estimation statistics

$\bar{R}^2 = 0.7672 \qquad DW = 1.90 \qquad SE = 1.28$

Sample period: 1961.3–1987.4

[a]Notation:

$\dfrac{\Delta W}{W}$	Hourly employee compensation, nonfarm business sector, annualized rate of change
U	Civilian unemployment rate
$\dfrac{\Delta P^F}{P^F}$	Implicit deflator for personal consumption, annualized rate of change
LFPART	Female labor force participation rate
GTU	Employer unemployment insurance contributions per hour relative to compensation per hour, annualized rate of change
GTOER	Employer social security contributions per hour relative to compensation per hour, annualized rate of change
GMINW	Minimum wage rate relative to compensation per hour, annualized rate of change
REPLACE	Ratio of unemployment benefits per unemployed worker to wage income net of social insurance contributions per employed worker
CONTROL	Price control dummy (1971.4 = 1; 1972.1 = 0.6; 0 otherwise)
$-i$	An abbreviation for $t-i$

Table A7.2. (*Continued*)

(B.2) Estimated Equation for the Value-Added Price Index[b]

$$\ell n\ P^v = \underset{[13.9]}{0.24} + \sum_{i=0}^{5} a_i\ CAP_{-i} + \sum_{i=0}^{7} b_i\ \ell n\ W_{-i} + 1.0 \times \ell n\ (PROD)$$

$$+ \sum_{i=0}^{4} c_i \left\{ \sum_j w_j^1 \Delta\ \ell n\ (PI1_{j,-i}) \right\} + \sum_{i=0}^{4} d_i \left\{ \sum_j w_j^2 \Delta\ \ell n\ (PI2_{j,-i}) \right\} \qquad (A.5)$$

$$+ \sum_{i=0}^{2} e_i\ \ell n\ (FPC/.01\ PCON \times ER)_{-i} - \underset{[3.53]}{0.10} \sum_j w_j^3\ \ell n\ (PI2_j)$$

Distributed lag coefficients:

$$\Sigma\ a_i = \underset{[5.46]}{-0.0054} \qquad \Sigma\ b_i = 1.0 \qquad \Sigma\ c_i = \underset{[61.5]}{2.63} \qquad \Sigma\ d_i = \underset{[1.89]}{-0.86}$$

$$\Sigma e_i = \underset{[2.55]}{0.04} \qquad \sum w_j^1 = \sum w_j^2 = \sum w_j^3 = 1.0$$

Estimation statistics

$\bar{R}^2 = 0.9999 \qquad DW = 2.10 \qquad SE = 0.0041$

Sample period: 1960.1–1986.4

Autocorrelation coefficient: 0.86

---

[b]Notation:

P^v	Price index for nonfarm business final sales net of crude energy supply and indirect business taxes
CAP	Geometric average of unemployment rate and constructed rate of unused capacity
W	Compensation per employee hour, nonfarm business sector
PROD	Lagged cyclically adjusted productivity, 8-quarter average
PI1	Prices for farm output and nonpetroleum merchandise imports divided by aggregate price level lagged 4 quarters
PI2	Prices for crude energy supply (petroleum, coal and natural gas) and petroleum imports divided by aggregate price level lagged 4 quarters
w_i, w_j	Lagged expenditure shares of prices in PI1 and PI2
FPC	Weighted average foreign consumer price index
PCON	MPS consumption price
ER	Weighted-average exchange rate
$-i$	An abbreviation for $t-i$

CHAPTER 8

New Methods for Using Monthly Data to Improve Forecast Accuracy

E. PHILIP HOWREY

Econometric forecasters continually seek ways to increase forecast accuracy. As new data are released, the residuals of forecasting models are examined for evidence of structural change and equations are modified if necessary. When forecasts are prepared, current economic conditions as reflected in weekly and monthly data releases are factored into the forecast. Several of the participants in the Model Comparison Seminar have recently investigated alternative methods for using monthly data in a systematic way to adjust forecasts produced by quarterly models. These initial studies are reviewed in this chapter and some illustrative results are presented.

We begin with a review of some of the implications of temporal aggregation for the specification and estimation of models and their use in forecasting. This review is intended to provide motivation for the use of high-frequency (monthly) data in forecasting economic aggregates as well as to indicate some of the difficulties that are involved. Ways in which monthly data have been and are currently being used in econometric forecasting are then summarized. The chapter concludes with a presentation of some illustrative results obtained using the Michigan Quarterly Econometric Model of the U.S. Economy.

PREDICTION OF TEMPORAL AGGREGATES

Temporal aggregation has important implications for the specification and estimation of dynamic economic models and their use in forecasting. The usual situation in macroeconometric forecasting is that some of the variables of interest are available more frequently than others. For example, observations on interest rates are available weekly, unemployment rates are published monthly, and estimates of GNP are available on a quarterly basis. The sampling interval at which the data are available may not correspond to either the appropriate time unit of the economic model or the forecast interval of interest.[1]

The purpose of this section is to consider some of the issues involved in the use of mixed-frequency data sets in econometric forecasting. Two simple expository models, both of which have received considerable attention in the literature, are considered here. The first model is a univariate autoregressive model from which forecasts of temporal aggregates are desired. The second model is a bivariate process from which forecasts of temporal aggregates are desired but for which observations on one of the variables are available only as temporal aggregates. The usual approach to the investigation of the effect of temporal aggregation is to formulate a model for what is regarded as the appropriate time unit and then to derive from this model the implications for temporal aggregates. This is the approach that is followed in the illustrative examples considered here.

We consider first the case in which a time series $\{y_t\}$ is generated by an autoregressive process of order one,

$$y_t = \phi y_{t-1} + u_t \tag{1}$$

and the temporal aggregate

$$Y_T = k \sum_{s=0}^{m-1} y_{T-s} \tag{2}$$

is to be forecast. For example, y_t might be the monthly value of some variable and Y_T might be a quarterly average ($m = 3$, $k = 1/m$) or y_t might be a quarterly value and Y_T might be an annual sum ($m = 4$, $k = 1$). It is assumed that observations on the "primary" variable, y_t, are available.

Three approaches to prediction of Y_T will be considered:

1. Forecast y_t using the "micro" model (1) and aggregate the micro forecast to obtain $\hat{Y}_T$,
2. obtain the "macro" model for Y_T implied by the micro model and use the macro model to obtain $\tilde{Y}_t$,
3. combine $\hat{Y}_T$ and $\tilde{Y}_T$ to obtain $\bar{Y}_T$.

Amemiya and Wu (1972) compared the forecast accuracy of procedures (1) and (2) for the autoregressive model of order p and Ahsanullah and Wei (1984) made a similar study of the ARMA(1,1) model. On the basis of their calculations, Amemiya and Wu concluded that method (2) performs "remarkably well" compared to method (1). Ahsanullah and Wei (1984 p. 299) conclude that "an aggregate model performs reasonably well for a well behaved stationary process, particularly if the underlying series are highly negatively correlated. However, an aggregate model leads to a quite substantial loss in efficiency for a non-stationary or close to non-stationary process." In both of these studies the forecast accuracy comparisons are given only for forecast horizons that are a multiple of m and therefore give no indication of the value of observations on y_t that become available during the forecast period. Since the focus of this study is the use of monthly data to improve the accuracy of forecasts from a quarterly model, it will be useful to compare these alternative forecasting procedures for forecast horizons shorter than m.

As a notational matter, let $\hat{y}_{t+s|t}$ denote the forecast of y_{t+s} made at time t so that for the AR(1) process

$$\hat{y}_{t+s|t} = \begin{cases} y_t & s \leq 0 \\ \phi^s y_t & s > 0 \end{cases} \tag{3}$$

The corresponding forecast error is

$$e_{t+s|t} = y_{t+s} - \hat{y}_{t+s|t} \tag{4}$$

$$= \begin{cases} 0 & s \leq 0 \\ \sum_{r=0}^{s-1} \phi^r u_{t+s-r} & s > 0 \end{cases}$$

The forecast of the temporal aggregate Y_T is given by

$$\hat{Y}_{T|t} = k \sum_{j=0}^{m-1} \hat{y}_{T-j|t} \tag{5}$$

so that the forecast error corresponding to the "forecast-and-aggregate" procedure is

$$\hat{E}_{T|t} = Y_T - \hat{Y}_{T|t} \tag{6}$$

$$= k \sum_{j=0}^{m-1} e_{T-j|t}$$

An alternative procedure is to base the forecast on nonoverlapping aggregate observations. The time series model for the aggregate observations implied by the AR(1) model for the primary data is required to implement this approach. The problem of aggregation of AR, MA, and ARMA processes has been treated in some generality by Telser (1967), Amemiya and Wu (1972), Brewer (1973), Stram and Wei (1986), and others. Weiss (1984) provides a useful summary of many of these results. For the AR(1) model, we proceed as follows. The micro process is written as

$$y_t = \phi^m y_{t-m} + v_t \tag{7}$$

where

$$v_t = u_t + \phi u_{t-1} + \cdots + \phi^{m-1} u_{t-m+1} \tag{8}$$

Aggregation of (7) yields

$$Y_T = \phi^m Y_{T-m} + V_T \tag{9}$$

where

$$V_T = k \sum_{j=0}^{m-1} v_{T-j} \tag{10}$$

It follows that the aggregate series $\{Y_T\}$ follows an autoregressive, moving average process

$$Y_T = \Phi Y_{t-m} + W_T - \Theta W_{T-m} \tag{11}$$

where $\Phi = \phi^m$ and Θ and σ_w^2 are obtained by solving[2]

$$(1 + \Theta^2) \sigma_w^2 = \mathrm{Var}(V_T) \tag{12.a}$$

$$-\Theta \sigma_w^2 = \mathrm{Cov}(V_T, V_{T-m}). \tag{12.b}$$

Standard formulas can then be used to obtain the forecast $\bar{Y}_{T/t}$, forecast errors, and corresponding error variances for this aggregate-and-forecast procedure.[3]

A combined forecast, $\tilde{Y}_{T|t}$, can be obtained as follows. The micro and macro forecasts are written as

$$Y_T = \hat{Y}_{T|t} + \hat{E}_{T|t} \tag{13.a}$$

$$Y_T = \check{Y}_{T|t} + \check{E}_{T|t} \tag{13.b}$$

The (minimum variance) combined forecast is then given by[4]

$$\tilde{Y}_{T|t} = \hat{Y}_{T|t} + \lambda(\hat{Y}_{T|t} - \check{Y}_{T|t}) \tag{14}$$

where

$$\lambda = \mathrm{Cov}(\hat{E}_{T|t}, \check{E}_{T|t} - \hat{E}_{T|t})/\mathrm{Var}(\check{E}_{T|t} - \hat{E}_{T|t}) \tag{15}$$

Although some tedious algebra is involved, it is straightforward to show that when the macro process is obtained by aggregating the micro process, $\mathrm{Cov}(\hat{E}_{T|t}, \check{E}_{T|t} - \hat{E}_{T|t}) = 0$ so that in this case $\tilde{Y}_{T|t} = \hat{Y}_{T|t}$.

It is well known that $\hat{y}_{T-j|t}$ is the minimum mean squared error (linear) predictor of y_{T-j} given $y_t, y_{t-1}, \ldots$.[5] Therefore the forecast $\hat{Y}_{T|t}$ obtained by aggregating the micro forecasts $\hat{y}_{t-j|t}$ is the minimum mean squared error predictor of Y_T given $y_t, y_{t-1},$ $\ldots$. It follows that if the micro model is correct, the aggregate-and-forecast procedure will, in general, lead to less precise forecasts. The decrease in precision depends on the value of the parameter ϕ and the forecast horizon. The efficiency of $\check{Y}_{T|t}$ relative to $\hat{Y}_{T|t}$, defined as $\mathrm{Var}(\check{E}_{T|t})/\mathrm{Var}(\hat{E}_{T|t})$, is shown in Table 8.1 for various values of ϕ for the case where $m = 3$ and $k = 1/m$. The entries in the table show the relative efficiency of quarterly forecasts obtained from a correctly specified quarterly model compared to quarterly forecasts obtained by averaging the forecasts from the underlying monthly model.

Consider, for example, the case in which the monthly data follow a random walk ($\phi = 1$). The relative efficiency of the one-quarter (3-month) ahead macro forecast is 0.77. For two, three, and four quarters ahead, the relative efficiency is 0.91, 0.94, and 0.96. As the forecast horizon increases, the relative efficiency of the macro-model forecasts approaches one, but not monotonically. The reason for this is that for the 4-month-ahead forecast, for example, the forecast horizon for the monthly model is indeed 4 months, whereas the forecast horizon for the quarterly model is two quarters or 6 months.

The entries in this table illustrate several important points. For moderate values of the autoregressive parameter ($|\phi| \leq 0.5$), there is little to be gained from the monthly data outside the first quarter of the forecast. Within the first forecast quarter, however, monthly data can provide rather dramatic reductions in the forecast error variance of quarterly averages. For more extreme values of the autoregressive parameter, the use of monthly data can provide substantial improvements in forecast accuracy even outside the first forecast quarter.

Variables frequently enter macroeconometric models as first differences or first

Table 8.1. Relative Efficiency of Quarterly Forecasts for an AR(1) Monthly Model

	Prediction Horizon (months)											
φ	1	2	3	4	5	6	7	8	9	10	11	12
1.0	0.06	0.28	0.77	0.51	0.71	0.91	0.69	0.82	0.94	0.78	0.87	0.96
0.9	0.07	0.31	0.81	0.64	0.81	0.95	0.85	0.92	0.98	0.93	0.96	0.99
0.8	0.08	0.35	0.84	0.76	0.89	0.97	0.94	0.97	0.99	0.98	0.99	1.00
0.7	0.10	0.39	0.87	0.86	0.94	0.99	0.98	0.99	1.00	1.00	1.00	1.00
0.6	0.12	0.44	0.91	0.92	0.98	1.00	1.00	1.00	1.00	1.00	1.00	1.00
0.5	0.15	0.48	0.94	0.97	0.99	1.00	1.00	1.00	1.00	1.00	1.00	1.00
0.4	0.18	0.53	0.96	0.99	1.00	1.00	1.00	1.00	1.00	1.00	1.00	1.00
0.3	0.21	0.57	0.98	1.00	1.00	1.00	1.00	1.00	1.00	1.00	1.00	1.00
0.2	0.25	0.61	0.99	1.00	1.00	1.00	1.00	1.00	1.00	1.00	1.00	1.00
0.1	0.29	0.64	1.00	1.00	1.00	1.00	1.00	1.00	1.00	1.00	1.00	1.00
0.0	0.33	0.67	1.00	1.00	1.00	1.00	1.00	1.00	1.00	1.00	1.00	1.00
−0.1	0.38	0.68	1.00	1.00	1.00	1.00	1.00	1.00	1.00	1.00	1.00	1.00
−0.2	0.42	0.69	0.99	1.00	1.00	1.00	1.00	1.00	1.00	1.00	1.00	1.00
−0.3	0.46	0.69	0.98	1.00	1.00	1.00	1.00	1.00	1.00	1.00	1.00	1.00
−0.4	0.50	0.68	0.96	0.99	1.00	1.00	1.00	1.00	1.00	1.00	1.00	1.00
−0.5	0.52	0.65	0.94	0.98	0.99	1.00	1.00	1.00	1.00	1.00	1.00	1.00
−0.6	0.52	0.60	0.91	0.95	0.98	1.00	1.00	1.00	1.00	1.00	1.00	1.00
−0.7	0.50	0.55	0.86	0.89	0.95	0.99	0.99	0.99	1.00	1.00	1.00	1.00
−0.8	0.46	0.48	0.80	0.79	0.89	0.96	0.95	0.97	0.99	0.99	0.99	1.00
−0.9	0.40	0.40	0.73	0.65	0.79	0.91	0.84	0.91	0.96	0.92	0.95	0.98
−1.0	0.33	0.33	0.67	0.50	0.67	0.83	0.67	0.78	0.89	0.75	0.83	0.92

differences of logarithms. It is therefore of interest to repeat the previous exercise for a model of the form

$$\Delta y_t = \phi \, \Delta y_{t-1} + u_t \tag{16}$$

where $\Delta y_t \equiv y_t - y_{t-1}$ denotes the first difference of the variable y_t. We continue to assume that the aggregate Y_T as defined in (2) is the variable for which a forecast is desired.

It is convenient to rewrite (16) as

$$y_t = \phi_1 y_{t-1} + \phi_2 y_{t-2} + u_t \tag{17}$$

where $\phi_1 = 1 + \phi$ and $\phi_2 = -\phi$. The forecast error of $\hat{y}_{t+s|t}$ is now given by

$$e_{t+s|t} = \begin{cases} 0 & s \leq 0 \\ \sum\limits_{r=0}^{s-1} \psi_r u_{t+s-r} & s > 0 \end{cases} \tag{18}$$

where the coefficients ψ_r are determined according to

$$\psi_s = \begin{cases} \phi_1 & s = 1 \\ \phi_1 \psi_1 + \phi_2 & s = 2 \\ \phi_1 \psi_{s-1} + \phi_2 \psi_{s-2} & s \geq 3 \end{cases} \tag{19}$$

The forecast error variance of $\hat{Y}_{T|t}$ of the forecast-and-aggregate procedure can now be determined by substituting (18) into (6).

Following Amemiya and Wu (1972) a model for nonoverlapping aggregate observations can be obtained by rewriting (17) as

$$(1 - \lambda_1 L)^m (1 - \lambda_2 L)^m y_t = v_t \tag{20}$$

where λ_1 and λ_2 are the zeros of $x^2 - \phi_1 x - \phi_2$ (i.e., $\lambda_1 = 1$ and $\lambda_2 = \phi$) and

$$v_t = (1 + \lambda_1 L + \cdots + \lambda_1^{m-1} L^{m-1})(1 + \lambda_2 L + \cdots + \lambda_2^{m-1} L^{m-1}) u_t \tag{21}$$

After aggregation, we obtain

$$Y_T = \Phi_1 Y_{T-m} + \Phi_2 Y_{T-2m} + V_T \tag{22}$$

where $\Phi_1 = \lambda_1^3 + \lambda_2^3 = 1 + \phi^3$ and $\Phi_2 = \lambda_1^3 \lambda_2^3 = \phi^3$. The appropriate moving average representation for V_T is

$$V_T = W_T - \Theta_1 W_{T-m} - \Theta_2 W_{T-2m} \tag{23}$$

where Θ_1, Θ_2, and σ_w^2 are obtained by solving

$$(1 + \Theta_1^2 + \Phi_2^2)\sigma_w^2 = \text{Var}(V_T) \tag{24.a}$$

$$(-\Theta_1 + \Theta_1 \Theta_2)\sigma_w^2 = \text{Cov}(V_T, V_{T-m}) \tag{24.b}$$

$$-\Theta_2 \sigma_w^2 = \text{Cov}(V_T, V_{T-2m}) \tag{24.c}$$

The usual formulas for the ARMA(2,2) model can then be used to obtain forecasts and forecast error variances for the aggregate-and-forecast procedure.

The relative efficiency of $\bar{Y}_{T|t}$ for the integrated AR(1) model is shown in Table 8.2 for various values of ϕ for the case where $m = 3$ and $k = 1/m$. What this table shows is that monthly data can provide even more dramatic reductions in forecast error variance if the variable to be forecast enters the model as a first difference. Even for moderate values of the autoregressive parameter, sizable reductions in the forecast error variance up to 10 or 11 months ahead can be realized.

Parameter estimation is relatively straightforward for univariate models. Least-squares or maximum likelihood methods can be used to estimate the parameters of either the micro model using the primary data or the macro model using the temporal aggregates. The contribution of the sampling variability of the parameter estimates to the forecast error variance is inversely related to the number of observations used to estimate the parameters. A case could be made for the micro model on these grounds alone.[6] But for a sufficiently large sample, the contribution of sampling variability of the parameter estimates is negligible and the illustrative calculations of Tables 8.1 and 8.2 indicate that the gain in forecast accuracy that results from using the primary data can be substantial, especially if the variable to be forecast enters as a first difference.

Conceptually, it is a relatively simple matter to extend the forecast-and-aggregate and aggregate-and-forecast procedures to higher dimensional linear systems.[7] However, several rather interesting and challenging problems emerge when the values of some of the variables are available only as temporal aggregates. A bivariate system can be used to illustrate some of the problems that now arise and the alternative approaches that are available.

Consider the bivariate AR(1) model

$$y_{1t} = \phi_{11}y_{1t-1} + \phi_{12}y_{2t-1} + u_{1t} \tag{25.a}$$

$$y_{2t} = \phi_{21}y_{1t-1} + \phi_{22}y_{2t-1} + u_{2t} \tag{25.b}$$

which we write in matrix form as

$$y_t = \phi y_{t-1} + u_t \tag{26}$$

We assume that the characteristic roots of $\phi = (\phi_{ij})$ are less than one in absolute value and $u_t = (u_{it})$ is a sequence of serially uncorrelated random variables with mean zero and covariance matrix Σ. We suppose that the vector of temporal aggregates

$$Y_T = k\sum_{j=0}^{m-1} y_{T-j} \tag{27}$$

is to be forecast on the basis of a mixed data set consisting of observations on y_{1t} and nonoverlapping m-period averages of y_{2t}.

The three approaches to forecasting Y_T introduced previously, namely,

1. forecast and aggregate to get $\hat{Y}_T$,
2. aggregate and forecast to get $\tilde{Y}_T$, and
3. combine $\hat{Y}_T$ with the monthly observations on y_{1t}

will now be considered. We suppose initially that the parameter values are known and return to the issue of parameter estimation subsequently.

The minimum mean squared error linear predictor of y_{t+s} given the observations

Table 8.2. Relative Efficiency of Quarterly Forecasts for an Integrated AR(1) Monthly Model

φ	Prediction Horizon (months)											
	1	2	3	4	5	6	7	8	9	10	11	12
1.0	0.01	0.08	0.38	0.15	0.33	0.60	0.32	0.49	0.71	0.43	0.59	0.77
0.9	0.01	0.10	0.41	0.19	0.38	0.65	0.39	0.56	0.77	0.53	0.67	0.83
0.8	0.01	0.11	0.45	0.23	0.44	0.70	0.46	0.63	0.81	0.61	0.73	0.87
0.7	0.02	0.13	0.49	0.28	0.49	0.75	0.52	0.68	0.85	0.66	0.78	0.89
0.6	0.02	0.14	0.53	0.32	0.54	0.79	0.57	0.72	0.87	0.70	0.80	0.91
0.5	0.02	0.16	0.57	0.36	0.58	0.82	0.61	0.75	0.89	0.72	0.82	0.92
0.4	0.03	0.19	0.62	0.40	0.62	0.84	0.63	0.77	0.91	0.74	0.84	0.93
0.3	0.03	0.21	0.66	0.44	0.65	0.87	0.65	0.79	0.92	0.75	0.85	0.94
0.2	0.04	0.23	0.70	0.47	0.67	0.88	0.67	0.80	0.93	0.76	0.86	0.95
0.1	0.05	0.25	0.74	0.49	0.69	0.90	0.68	0.81	0.94	0.77	0.86	0.95
0.0	0.06	0.28	0.77	0.51	0.71	0.91	0.69	0.82	0.94	0.78	0.87	0.96
−0.1	0.06	0.30	0.80	0.53	0.72	0.92	0.70	0.83	0.95	0.78	0.87	0.96
−0.2	0.07	0.31	0.83	0.54	0.73	0.93	0.71	0.83	0.95	0.79	0.88	0.97
−0.3	0.08	0.33	0.86	0.55	0.74	0.93	0.71	0.84	0.96	0.79	0.88	0.97
−0.4	0.10	0.34	0.88	0.56	0.75	0.94	0.72	0.84	0.96	0.79	0.88	0.97
−0.5	0.11	0.35	0.89	0.56	0.76	0.94	0.72	0.84	0.96	0.80	0.89	0.97
−0.6	0.12	0.35	0.89	0.56	0.77	0.94	0.73	0.84	0.97	0.80	0.89	0.97
−0.7	0.12	0.33	0.87	0.56	0.78	0.94	0.73	0.84	0.96	0.80	0.89	0.97
−0.8	0.13	0.31	0.83	0.56	0.79	0.94	0.73	0.83	0.96	0.80	0.89	0.97
−0.9	0.12	0.26	0.74	0.55	0.82	0.93	0.71	0.79	0.93	0.79	0.90	0.97
−1.0	0.10	0.20	0.61	0.54	0.85	0.93	0.64	0.68	0.84	0.79	0.93	0.97

available at time t, $\hat{y}_{t+s|t}$, and the corresponding prediction error covariance matrix can be calculated recursively using the Kalman filter. We first rewrite the model as

$$
\begin{bmatrix} y_{1t} \\ y_{2t} \\ y_{2t-1} \\ \cdot \\ \cdot \\ \cdot \\ y_{2t-m+1} \end{bmatrix} = \begin{bmatrix} \phi_{11} & \phi_{12} & 0 & \cdots & 0 \\ \phi_{21} & \phi_{22} & 0 & \cdots & 0 \\ 0 & 1 & 0 & \cdots & 0 \\ \cdot & \cdot & & & \cdot \\ \cdot & \cdot & & & \cdot \\ \cdot & \cdot & & & \cdot \\ 0 & 0 & \cdots & 1 & 0 \end{bmatrix} \begin{bmatrix} y_{1t-1} \\ y_{2t-1} \\ y_{2t-2} \\ \cdot \\ \cdot \\ \cdot \\ y_{2t-m} \end{bmatrix} + \begin{bmatrix} u_{1t} \\ u_{2t} \\ 0 \\ \cdot \\ \cdot \\ \cdot \\ 0 \end{bmatrix}
$$

(28)

or, more simply, as

$$
y_t = \boldsymbol{\phi} y_{t-1} + u_t \tag{29}
$$

Let x_t denote the information that becomes available at time t so that

$$
x_t = M_t y_t \tag{30}
$$

where

$$
M_t = \begin{cases} \begin{bmatrix} 1 & 0 & \cdots & 0 \end{bmatrix} & [t/m] \neq t/m \\[2ex] \begin{bmatrix} 1 & 0 & \cdots & 0 \\ 0 & k & \cdots & k \end{bmatrix} & [t/m] = t/m \end{cases} \tag{31}
$$

with the convention that $[t/m]$ denotes the integer part of t/m. Thus, y_{1t} is observed every period whereas y_{2t} is observed every m periods. The usual recursive calculations can be performed at time t to obtain $\hat{y}_{t+1|t}$.[8] Given the one-period-ahead forecast, $\hat{y}_{t+s|t}$ can be obtained from

$$
\hat{y}_{t+s|t} = \boldsymbol{\phi} \hat{y}_{t+s-1|t} \tag{32}
$$

for $s > 1$. Finally, the required aggregate forecasts can be obtained by extracting the appropriate elements from $\hat{y}_{t+s|t}$ and inserting them into

$$
\hat{Y}_{T|t} = k \sum_{j=0}^{m-1} \hat{y}_{T-j|t} \tag{33}
$$

It should be noted that this procedure automatically provides forecasts of the unobserved values of y_{2t}.

An alternative procedure is to aggregate first to obtain a model for Y_T and then use the aggregate model to produce the forecast. The mechanics of this approach are quite similar to the univariate case. We first rewrite the model as

$$
y_t = \boldsymbol{\phi}^m y_{t-m} + v_t \tag{34}
$$

where

$$
v_t = u_t + \boldsymbol{\phi} u_{t-1} + \cdots + \boldsymbol{\phi}^{m-1} u_{t-m+1} \tag{35}
$$

and then aggregate to obtain

$$Y_t = \Phi^m Y_{T-m} + V_T \tag{36}$$

where

$$V_T = k \sum_{j=0}^{m-1} v_{T-j} \tag{37}$$

It follows that the process $\{Y_T\}$ of temporal aggregates follows a mixed autoregressive, moving-average process:

$$Y_T = \Phi Y_{T-m} + W_T - \Theta W_{T-m} \tag{38}$$

Forecasts of the vector of aggregates can be generated using the standard formulas for a vector ARMA process.

The forecast-and-aggregate approach has several advantages over the aggregate-and-forecast procedure. As in the univariate case, forecasts from the vector ARMA macro process will generally have larger mean squared errors than forecasts from the underlying micro process. In addition, the micro model provides a unified approach to interpolation of missing values and prediction of temporal aggregates. However, the implementation of the micro-model approach poses serious practical problems in all but the simplest cases.

For small linear systems parameter estimation is relatively straightforward, at least in principle, for both the micro and macro models. Various methods can be used to estimate the parameters of vector ARMA models.[9] The prediction error variance decomposition of the (Gaussian) likelihood function, combined with the recursive calculations of the Kalman filter, can be used to calculate the value of the likelihood function implied by the micro model.[10] However, it does not appear at the current time to be feasible to use full information maximum likelihood to estimate micro-model parameters in systems as large as those that are currently used to produce macroeconomic forecasts.

It should be possible to improve the accuracy of the macro-process forecasts by combining them with the more frequent observations available on y_{1t}. Of course, if we attempt to combine $\hat{Y}_{T|t}$ and $\tilde{Y}_{T|t}$ to obtain a minimum variance (linear) combined forecast, we would get back to $\hat{Y}_{T|t}$. But it may not be possible to implement the forecast-and-aggregate approach with multivariate systems of even moderate size. As a feasible alternative, we could use the univariate ARMA model for y_{1t} implied by (25) to forecast y_{1t}, aggregate the univariate forecasts of y_{1t} to obtain $\check{Y}_{T|t}$ and then combine $\tilde{Y}_{T|t}$ and $\check{Y}_{T|t}$.[11] This would yield a suboptimal forecast in general but would avoid the computational problems of a full-blown forecast-and-aggregate approach.

THE USE OF MONTHLY DATA TO IMPROVE QUARTERLY ECONOMETRIC FORECASTS

The simple examples discussed in the previous section demonstrate that there are certain cases in which monthly data can substantially improve the accuracy of forecasts of quarterly aggregates. As a practical matter, forecasters using quarterly econometric models almost invariably examine currently available monthly data very carefully when making forecasts. Until fairly recently, however, monthly data have been used in a fairly informal way to adjust quarterly forecasts. We turn now to a brief review of the approaches to the systematic use of monthly data in econometric forecasting that are currently being investigated by several participants in the Model Comparison Seminar.

The early work of T. C. Liu (1969, 1974) provides a useful historical perspective on the currently ongoing research in this area. Liu was primarily concerned, at least initially, with the feasibility of constructing a monthly econometric model. The original work was intended to answer three basic questions (1974 p. 329):

> (1) Is it possible to generate all the monthly data necessary to build a monthly econometric model for the United States for making forecasts and policy recommendations? (2) On account of the inertia and continuity of almost all econometric processes and activities, lagged magnitudes of the dependent variable are logically required to be included as explanatory variables for the current magnitude of the same variable in an economic relationship of a short unit period of observation, say, a monthly relationship. High serial correlations in practically all economic variables are plainly observable. Can *other* explanatory variables of theoretical relevance and importance still take on plausible and significant regression coefficients when they are included, together with the lagged magnitudes of the dependent variable itself, in an equation to explain a given variable? (3) Would not the serial correlation in the disturbance term of a monthly relationship be so high that, with lagged magnitudes of the dependent variable included as explanatory variables, consistent and efficient estimates of the regression coefficients in the relationship could not be obtained?

Monthly data were obtained, where necessary, by interpolation from related series that were available on a monthly basis. The method used to estimate the missing monthly data can be summarized as follows. Let $\{x_{jt}; j = 1,2, \cdots, J\}$ denote the basic monthly series to be used to determine the monthly values of y_t and suppose $Y_t = (y_t + y_{t-1} + y_{t-2})/3$ is observed on a quarterly basis. The method Liu used to estimate y_t was first to obtain least-squares estimates of the coefficients in the quarterly regression equation

$$Y_t = \sum_{j=1}^{J} c_j(x_{jt} + x_{jt-1} + x_{jt-2}) + U_t \tag{39}$$

and then form

$$\hat{y}_t = \sum_{j=1}^{J} \hat{c}_j x_{jt} \tag{40}$$

Liu was able to find monthly indicator variables that were highly correlated with the quarterly variables to be interpolated.[12]

A monthly model consisting of 16 stochastic equations and 17 identities was fit to the monthly data. A satisfactory fit was obtained with statistically significant coefficients and plausible values. The forecast accuracy of an expanded version of the original monthly model (51 stochastic equations and 80 identities) was examined subsequently by Liu and Hwa (1974). It was found that for most variables the monthly model forecasts had a smaller root mean squared error than comparable forecasts from

quarterly models, even for forecast horizons of 3–6 months. The within-quarter forecasts of the monthly model were even better. These early results provided evidence
that monthly data could be used in a systematic way to improve the accuracy of econometric model forecasts of quarterly aggregates.

A very elaborate system for real-time processing of monthly data has been devised
by Carol Corrado and her collaborators in the Division of Research and Statistics of
the Federal Reserve Board. Forecasts of quarterly aggregates are obtained by linking
a monthly forecasting model with the MPS quarterly model. The monthly observations
needed to estimate the parameters of the monthly econometric model are obtained from
interpolation procedures similar to those used by Liu. The details of the procedure are
described in Corrado and Haltmaier (1988) and the references cited there.

The estimated standard errors of the forecasts for the rate of growth of real GNP
given by Corrado and Haltmaier (1988) are reproduced in Table 8.3. These results
indicate that for the GNP growth rate the estimated forecast standard error is smaller
for the monthly model than for the quarterly model, even when none of the monthly
data for the first forecast quarter is available. This is consistent with both the tabulations in Tables 8.1 and 8.2 and the results of Liu, which show that monthly data can
be quite useful in making quarterly forecasts. These results also indicate that the pooling of monthly and quarterly FRB forecasts is expected to lead to improvements in the
accuracy of both forecasts. This is an interesting result because, as noted earlier, if the
quarterly model were consistent with the temporally aggregated monthly model, the
minimum variance combined forecast would simply be the aggregated forecasts from
the monthly model. The quarterly and monthly models in this case each has something
useful to contribute to the combined forecast.

Klein and Sojo (1987) have proposed three approaches to the use of monthly data
to construct a "current quarter forecast," which they then use as a basis for adjustment
of the quarterly forecasting model. The adjusted quarterly model is then extrapolated
over a longer forecast horizon. All three approaches involve the estimation of "bridge"
equations, which link quarterly entries in the national income and product accounts
with aggregates of monthly indicator variables. These equations are similar to the
interpolation equations used by Liu and Corrado to construct monthly observations,
but they are used by Klein and Sojo in a different way. Klein and Sojo extrapolate the
monthly indicator variables using univariate time series methods (ARIMA models) and
then substitute the aggregated monthly forecasts into the bridge equations to obtain
short-run projections of the quarterly NIPA entries.

Table 8.3. Estimated Forecast Standard Errors for the Rate of Growth of Real GNP, FRB
Monthly and Quarterly Models

	One Quarter Ahead			Two Quarters Ahead		
Horizon	Monthly Model	Quarterly Model	Pooled Forecast	Monthly Model	Quarterly Model	Pooled Forecast
Beginning of month 1	2.94	4.13	2.50	4.91	6.16	3.82
Beginning of month 2	2.27	4.09	1.94	4.07	5.84	3.44
Beginning of month 3	1.98	4.09	1.70	3.48	5.84	3.00

Source: Corrado and Haltmaier (1988, Table 5).

Bridge equations of the form

$$Y_{it} = \alpha_i + \Sigma_j \beta_{ij} X_{jt} + U_{it} \tag{41}$$

are specified for the major income and expenditure account entries that are not observed monthly. The indicator variables X_{jt} are aggregates of values that are observed monthly, that is,

$$X_{jt} = k(x_{jt} + x_{jt-1} + x_{jt-2}) \tag{42}$$

where the monthly values x_{jt} are available. A short-run forecast of Y_{it} (one or two quarters ahead)) is given by

$$\hat{Y}_{it} = \hat{\alpha}_i + \Sigma_j \hat{\beta}_{ij} \hat{X}_{jt} \tag{43}$$

where $\hat{X}_{jt}$ is obtained by aggregating ARIMA forecasts of x_{jt}. Separate forecasts of income and expenditure are obtained by summing the appropriate $\hat{Y}_{it}$ elements.

A third type of indicator relationship is obtained by regressing nominal GNP, real GNP, and the GNP deflator on the principal components of a number of monthly indicator variables. These equations are used in the same way as the income and expenditure bridge equations. Predicted values of the principal components based on forecasts of the monthly indicator variables from univariate time series models are substituted into the indicator equations to obtain indicative forecasts.

Two additional steps are required to complete the process. First, it is necessary to reconcile the income, expenditure, and indicator forecasts to obtain the current quarter forecast. Once this is done, adjustment constants for the quarterly model that will produce a model forecast that is consistent with the current quarter forecast are determined. The adjusted quarterly model can then be used to produce forecasts over a longer horizon.

The Research Seminar in Quantitative Economics (RSQE) at the University of Michigan has pursued a still different approach to the use of monthly data. The key element of the RSQE approach is the combination of projections of a monthly vector autoregressive model containing a few key macroeconomic variables with the forecasts of the Michigan Quarterly Econometric Model of the U.S. Economy. Two links between the monthly and quarterly forecasts are exploited. First, the forecasts of the two models are adjusted to produce consistent forecasts of the common variables. Second, the correlation between monthly and quarterly forecasts errors is used to update the quarterly forecasts as new monthly observations become available.

These two links between the monthly and quarterly models can be made explicit by writing the quarterly model as

$$F(Y_T, Y_{T-1}, X_T; \Theta) = U_T \tag{44}$$

where Y_T is a vector of G endogenous variables in quarter T, X_T is a vector of K exogenous variables in quarter T, Θ is a vector of parameters, and U_T is a vector of disturbances in quarter T. The evolution of a vector y, of g monthly observations is described by a monthly forecasting model of the form

$$f(y_t, y_{t-1}, x_t; \theta) = u_t \tag{45}$$

where x_t is a vector of k exogenous variables, θ is a vector of parameters, and u_t is a vector of disturbances.

The first link between the monthly and quarterly forecasting models is through a set of aggregation conditions. These aggregation conditions are written as

$$SY_T = (1/3)s(y_{3T} + y_{3T-1} + y_{3T-2}) \tag{46}$$

where S and s are selection matrices that pick out the common variables in the vectors of quarterly and monthly observations.[13] The second way in which the monthly and quarterly variables are related is through the correlation of forecast errors across models (44) and (45). This correlation is captured by supposing that the vector of quarterly and monthly disturbances, defined by

$$U'_T = [U'_T \mid u'_{3T} \mid u'_{3T-1} \mid u'_{3T-2}] \tag{47}$$

is a sequence of independent $N(0,\Sigma)$ random vectors. The nonzero off-diagonal elements in Σ allow for correlation of the quarterly disturbances with the monthly disturbances that occur within the quarter.

At the beginning of quarter $N + 1$, with no monthly data for the quarter yet available, a one-quarter-ahead forecast based on the econometric model alone is obtained by solving[14]

$$F(\hat{Y}_{N+1}, Y_N, X_{N+1}\hat{\Theta}) = 0 \tag{48}$$

for $\hat{Y}_{N+1}$ and forecasts for each of the 3 months of the quarter are obtained by solving the monthly model recursively:

$$f(\hat{y}_{n+1}, y_n, x_{n+1}; \hat{\theta}) = 0 \tag{49.a}$$

$$f(\hat{y}_{n+2}, \hat{y}_{n+1}, x_{n+2}; \hat{\theta}) = 0 \tag{49.b}$$

$$f(\hat{y}_{n+3}, \hat{y}_{n+2}, x_{n+3}; \hat{\theta}) = 0 \tag{49.c}$$

Combining the forecasts from (48) and (49.a)–(49.c) yields a vector of $G + 3g$ predicted values, which is written as

$$\hat{\mathbf{Y}}'_{N+1} = [\hat{Y}'_{N+1} \mid \hat{y}'_{n+3} \mid \hat{y}'_{n+2} \mid \hat{y}'_{n+1}] \tag{50}$$

The procedure for combining the monthly forecasts with the quarterly forecasts requires an estimate of the covariance matrix, Ω, of the vector $\mathbf{V}_{N+1}$ of forecast errors corresponding to this vector of forecasts.[15] This can be obtained by (1) linearization of the monthly and quarterly forecasting models, (2) stochastic simulation as in Fair (1984), or (3) a combination of linearization and stochastic simulation.

In general, the vector of quarterly and monthly predicted values will not satisfy the aggregation condition. The first step in the process of combining the monthly and quarterly forecasts is therefore to adjust them so that the common variables satisfy the aggregation condition. Rewriting the aggregation condition as

$$Q\mathbf{Y}_{N+1} = 0 \tag{51}$$

where

$$Q = [S \mid -s/3 \mid -s/3 \mid -s/3] \tag{52}$$

it follows that

$$QV_{N+1} = Q(Y_{N+1} - \hat{Y}_{N+1}) \tag{53}$$
$$= - Q\hat{Y}_{N+1}$$

On the assumption that V_{N+1} is $N(0, \Omega)$ the standard formulas for the multivariate normal distribution are used to obtain the conditional mean $\hat{V}_{N+1}$ and the conditional covariance matrix, Ψ, of V_{N+1} given $QV_{N+1} = - Q\hat{Y}_{N+1}$:

$$\hat{V}_{N+1} = - \Omega Q'(Q\Omega Q')^{-1}Q\hat{Y}_{N+1} \tag{54}$$

$$\Psi = \Omega - \Omega Q'(Q\Omega Q')^{-1}Q\Omega \tag{55}$$

The combined forecast is then

$$\bar{Y}_{N+1} = \hat{Y}_{N+1} + \hat{V}_{N+1} \tag{56}$$

Monthly updates of the initial combined forecast are obtained by conditioning successively on the observed monthly values as they become available. The observed value for the first month of the quarter, y_{n+1}, provides information about the quarterly variables in two ways. First, the monthly model can be used to calculate the vector u_{n+1} of first-month disturbances, which will in general be correlated with the quarterly disturbance vector U_{N+1} as reflected in the covariance matrix Σ. Thus, the observed u_{n+1} provides information about U_{N+1} and hence about Y_{N+1}. In addition, the aggregation condition must continue to hold for the common variables and now that the first-month values are known, the prediction error variance of the quarterly aggregates of the monthly variables will be smaller than before. Both of these sources of information are incorporated into the revised forecast by calculating the conditional expectation of V_{N+1} given the monthly value u_{n+1} and the aggregation condition $QY_{N+1} = 0$. The forecast made with 2 months of the current quarter known is an obvious extension of the 1-month-known forecast.

SOME ILLUSTRATIVE RESULTS USING THE MICHIGAN MODEL

In this section some preliminary results obtained by the Research Seminar in Quantitative Economics using the Michigan Quarterly Econometric Model of the U.S. economy are summarized. These results are taken from Howrey, Hymans, and Donihue (1987). The monthly model used in this exercise is a simple four-variable vector autoregressive model. The variables are the rate of growth of the manufacturing index of industrial production, the rate of inflation measured by the consumer price index, the 3-month treasury bill rate, and the civilian unemployment rate. The model was estimated using monthly data from the second quarter of 1954 through the fourth quarter of 1985, a total of 380 observations. The Bayesian information criterion (BIC) was used to select a second-order model.[16]

Although not required by the forecasting procedure, each variable in the monthly model also appears in MQEM. The models were linked through the aggregation condition on the four variables and through the covariance matrix of the vector of quarterly and monthly disturbances.[17]

Estimates of ex post quarterly forecast standard errors for 1986.1 are shown in Table 8.4 for a subset of the variables in MQEM. The entries in the column labelled $\sqrt{\Omega}$ are the estimated standard errors of a one-quarter-ahead forecast based on the quarterly model alone.[18] The entries in the $\sqrt{\Psi}$ column are the estimated forecast standard errors of the pooled forecast with no months known. For example, the estimated forecast standard error for the annualized percentage rate of growth of real GNP is 2.72 for MQEM. By linking the MQEM forecast with the four-variable monthly VAR model through the aggregation condition, the estimated forecast standard error is reduced to 2.43. The remaining entries in Table 8.4 give the estimated standard errors for forecasts with one ($\sqrt{\Psi_1}$) and two $\sqrt{\Psi_2}$) months of the forecast quarter known. It is interesting to note that the forecast standard errors given for the combined forecast of the rate of growth of real GNP are very close to the values given in Table 8.3 for the FRB procedure.

The ex post performance of this forecasting procedure for the period 1981.1– 1986.4 is summarized in Table 8.5. One-quarter-ahead ex post forecasts for each of the 24 quarters were obtained from MQEM and then linked with the monthly forecasting model.[19] For each of the variables listed in Table 8.5, the average of the forecast standard errors implied by the model for 1981.1–1986.4 is shown in the AFSE row.[20] This is an estimate of the expected performance of the forecasting procedure. The RMSE row gives the observed root mean squared error of the forecasts. The average forecast standard errors almost invariably understate the standard errors of the actual forecasts and sometimes by a fairly wide margin. However, for virtually all of the variables in Table 8.5, the root mean squared forecast error of the quarterly model is reduced by linking it with the monthly model, even when no monthly observations are available for the current quarter. Monthly data for the first and second months of the quarter almost always help to improve the forecast, as expected.

The practical objective of this research is to develop a forecast procedure that will produce accurate ex ante forecasts. Table 8.6 contains the root mean squared forecast errors for ex ante forecasts for 1986 and 1987 produced by three different procedures. The first procedure, designated as RSQE, refers to actual published forecasts obtained using the quarterly model in conjunction with subjectively determined adjustment constants. These forecasts are based on information available early in the second month

Table 8.4. Estimated Forecast Standard Errors For Ex Post Forecasts of 1986.1, RSQE Monthly and Quarterly Models

Variable	Units	$\sqrt{\Omega}$	$\sqrt{\Psi}$	$\sqrt{\Psi_1}$	$\sqrt{\Psi_2}$
Real GNP	Billions of 1982 $	23.74	21.19	18.12	14.74
Real GNP growth rate	AR	2.72	2.43	2.08	1.69
GNP deflator	1982 = 100	0.34	0.28	0.26	0.25
GNP deflator growth rate	AR	1.21	1.01	0.93	0.90
3-month treasury bill rate	%	0.56	0.50	0.38	0.16
Civilian unemployment rate	%	0.23	0.22	0.14	0.06
Real consumption	Billions of 1982 $	12.26	11.48	10.91	8.07
Real business fixed investment	Billions of 1982 $	7.41	6.64	6.25	5.96
Real inventory investment	Billions of 1982 $	21.66	20.61	19.27	18.79
Real residential construction	Billions of 1982 $	4.86	4.75	4.49	4.22

Table 8.5. Root Mean Squared Forecast Errors, Ex Post Forecasts for 1981.1–1986.4, RSQE Monthly and Quarterly Models

Endogenous Variable	Units	Measure[a]	$\sqrt{\Omega}$	$\sqrt{\Psi}$	$\sqrt{\Psi_1}$	$\sqrt{\Psi_2}$
Real GNP	Billions of 1982 $	AFSE	23.77	20.75	17.91	15.48
		RMSE	28.35	25.98	19.67	19.50
Real GNP growth rate	AR	AFSE	2.93	2.54	2.19	1.90
		RMSE	3.40	3.10	2.42	2.38
GNP deflator	1982 = 100	AFSE	0.31	0.26	0.25	0.23
		RMSE	0.96	0.96	0.96	0.96
GNP deflator growth rate	AR	AFSE	1.25	1.05	1.00	0.95
		RMSE	3.77	3.76	3.79	3.80
3-month treasury bill rate	%	AFSE	0.79	0.60	0.39	0.17
		RMSE	0.96	1.01	0.52	0.20
Civilian unemployment rate	%	AFSE	0.25	0.23	0.14	0.04
		RMSE	0.20	0.20	0.12	0.06
Real consumption	Billions of 1982 $	AFSE	11.92	10.66	10.07	7.60
		RMSE	14.46	11.81	11.15	11.25
Real business fixed investment	Billions of 1982 $	AFSE	7.41	6.45	6.09	5.77
		RMSE	9.30	8.30	8.34	8.76
Real inventory investment	Billions of 1982 $	AFSE	20.99	19.79	18.24	17.45
		RMSE	29.93	29.39	25.63	25.10
Real residential construction	Billions of 1982 $	AFSE	4.86	4.64	4.44	4.16
		RMSE	4.71	4.47	4.09	4.42

[a]AFSE is the average forecast standard error over the 1981–1986 period implied by the model. RMSE is the root mean squared error of the 24 forecasts.

Table 8.6. Root Mean Squared Errors[a] For One-Quarter-Ahead Forecasts Made in 1986 and 1987[b]

Endogenous Variable	Units	RSQE	MQEM[c]	Combined Forecast[c]		
				0 Months Known	1 Month Known	2 Months Known
Real GNP[d]	Billions of 1982 $	24.88	45.87	35.68	24.98	27.09
Real nondurable consumption[d]	Billions of 1982 $	7.67	18.17	11.39	11.31	6.99
Real durable consumption[d]	Billions of 1982 $	14.30	13.74	14.22	14.02	16.44
Real business fixed investment[d]	Billions of 1982 $	15.48	13.62	13.78	12.26	10.99
Real inventory investment[d]	Billions of 1982 $	26.54	27.11	27.17	22.48	22.47
Real net exports[d]	Billions of 1982 $	15.21	12.45	17.96	19.48	19.98
Civilian unemployment rate	%	0.19	0.18	0.18	0.10	0.08
Private nonfarm GNP deflator	% change, AR	2.16	3.30	2.96	3.23	3.36
3-month treasury bill rate	%	0.15	0.91	0.77	0.61	0.18
Corporate Aaa rate	%	0.23	0.80	0.81	0.77	0.69
Exchange value of U.S. dollar	1973 = 100	1.46	3.85	5.73	5.28	5.05
Federal budget deficit[d]	Billions of $	23.83	29.56	31.54	29.27	26.50

[a]Computed for eight forecasts: February, May, August, November 1986 and February, May, August and November 1987.
[b]Note: The results in this table use actual data from the September 20, 1988 NIPA release.
[c]Using no adjustment constants.
[d]RMSE's calculated from differences between predicted and actual changes.

of the quarter. The second procedure, identified in the table as MQEM, refers to fore-casts generated by the Michigan Quarterly Econometric Model of the U.S. economy with no adjustment constants.[21] These forecasts are based entirely on information for the preceding quarter and reflect the collective judgment of RSQE only through the specification of the values of the exogenous variables in the model. The third proce-dure is the combined forecast obtained using the procedure described above. In terms of the information available at the time the forecasts were made, the MQEM and combined forecast with no current-quarter monthly data are comparable and the RSQE forecast is comparable to the combined forecast with monthly data for the first month of the quarter known.

The results for real GNP are shown in the first line of Table 8.6. For a one-quarter-ahead horizon the RSQE forecast has an RMSE of $24.88 billion (1982 dollars). The combined forecast with no months of the current quarter known, with an RMSE of $35.68 billion, represents an improvement over forecasts generated using MQEM alone. With 1 and 2 months of the forecast quarter known the RMSE is further reduced to about $25 billion. The results in Table 8.6 are, in general, consistent with the amount of information on which each forecast is based. This pattern of forecast ac-curacy is not uniform over all the variables in Table 8.6; however, it is the case that the ex ante and the combined forecast with 2 months known are most accurate most often and least accurate least often.

Figure 8.1 illustrates the results obtained from the monthly updating procedure for eight forecasts of the annual rate of growth of real GNP made in 1986 and 1987. One

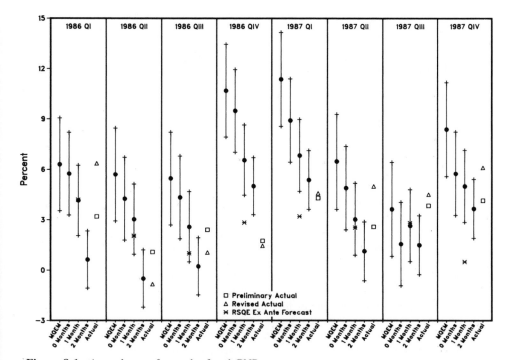

Figure 8.1. Annual rate of growth of real GNP.

standard error forecast intervals have been plotted for (1) the initial one-quarter-ahead forecast using MQEM with no nonzero adjustment constants, (2) the initial combined forecast when no months in the current quarter are known, (3) the combined forecast after data for the first month in the current quarter become available, and (4) the combined forecast with 2 months known. In each of the above cases, the dot at the midpoint of the forecast interval represents the corresponding point forecast. In addition the star shown along with 1-month-known forecast represents the RSQE ex ante forecast made early in the second month of the quarter and thus comparable to the 1-month-known forecast in terms of data available at the time the forecasts were made. Two "actual" values are recorded; the square denotes the rate growth based on the preliminary data released immediately following the quarter and the triangle denotes the growth rate based on the revised NIPA data released in July 1988. As shown in Figure 8.1 the combined forecast with no months known improves on the MQEM forecast in six of the eight quarters. The method is clearly not foolproof, however, since the combined forecasts with observations for 1 and 2 months of the quarter known provide further improvement in only four of the eight quarters. There is also some indication that the estimates of the standard error of the forecast understate the true standard error. However, this sample of eight forecasts is clearly too small to draw any definitive conclusions.

In summary, it has been found that it is feasible to combine monthly and quarterly forecasting models systematically on a real-time basis. The preliminary results indicate that the improvement in forecast accuracy is close to what would be expected on the basis of the theory underlying the method. The results are sufficiently encouraging to warrant continued research on and comparison of alternative methods for using both monthly and quarterly data in a systematic way to generate macroeconomic forecasts.

ACKNOWLEDGMENTS

I would like to thank the members of the Model Comparison Seminar for their helpful comments on an earlier draft of this paper and Michael R. Donihue for his help in providing the results for the Michigan Quarterly Econometric Model.

NOTES

1. The problems posed by aggregation were recognized very early in the econometrics literature. See for example Klein (1950) and Theil (1954).
2. Note that Var (V_T) and Cov(V_T, V_{T-m}) can be expressed in terms of ϕ and Var(u_t), which implies, in turn, that Θ and σ_w^2 can also be expressed in terms of these parameters.
3. See, for example, Box and Jenkins (1976).
4. See, for example, Fuhrer and Haltmaier (1988). For a general discussion of the combination of forecasts the reader is referred to Granger and Newbold (1986) and the references cited there. For a specific applications to econometric forecasting, see Greene, Howrey, and Hymans (1986) and Corrado and Greene (1988).
5. This is an immediate consequence, for example, of Theorem 2.9.1 (p. 75) in Fuller (1976).
6. Lütkepohl (1986) makes a case for using disaggregated data when the process order and parameters must be estimated.

7. Lütkepohl (1987) cites and summarizes much of the work that has been done on temporally aggregated vector ARMA models.
8. See for example Harvey (1981 Chap. 4).
9. See, for example, Tiao and Box (1981) and Hilmer and Tiao (1979).
10. Ansley and Kohn (1983), Harvey and Pierse (1984), and Palm and Nijman (1984) deal with the estimation problem with missing or temporally aggregated data.
11. Nijman and Palm (1986) propose a different approach. They use univariate ARMA models to interpolate the missing values of y_{2t} and then use these interpolated values as proxies for y_{2t} in the micro model.
12. Somewhat more sophisticated procedures for interpolation of missing data are now available. See, for example, Chow and Lin (1971), Fernandez (1981), and Litterman (1983).
13. An obvious modification of this condition is required for such variables as the stock of money, which enters the quarterly model as the end-of-period or third-month value.
14. For an "ex ante" forecast, the exogenous variables, X_{N+1} in the quarterly model and x_{n+1}, x_{n+2}, and x_{n+3} in the monthly model, must also be predicted. For an "ex post" forecast, the values of these exogenous variables are set equal to their realized values.
15. For a nonlinear model this covariance matrix will be state (time) dependent but for simplicity we suppress the time subscript in Ω in what follows.
16. See Lütkepohl (1985) for a comparison of alternative criteria for estimating the order of a vector autoregressive process.
17. The covariance matrix Σ of the quarterly and monthly structural model disturbances was estimated using a maximum likelihood procedure. The covariance matrix Ω of reduced form forecast errors was obtained by using the LIMO option in TROLL to linearize the nonlinear monthly and quarterly forecasting models.
18. The ex post forecasts for MQEM include no nonzero adjustment constants.
19. To reduce computational costs, the same covariance matrix Ω was used for all four quarters of the year. Ideally, this covariance matrix would be calculated at the beginning of each quarter.
20. The AFSE entries in Table 8.5 would be identical to the corresponding entries in Table 8.4 if the covariance matrix of forecast errors, Ω, were time invariant.
21. In a few instances *policy* assumptions for the forecast period were implemented through a constant adjustment rather than an exogenous variable. In such cases an adjustment constant is included to reflect the policy assumption in generating comparable MQEM and combined forecasts.

REFERENCES

Ahsanullah, M., and W. W. S. Wei. (1984). "Effects of Temporal Aggregation on Forecasts in an ARMA(1,1) Process." *Proceedings of the Business and Economic Statistics Section of the American Statistical Association,* 297–302.

Amemiya, T., and R. Y. Wu. (1972). "The Effect of Aggregation on Prediction in the Autoregressive Model." *Journal of the American Statistical Association* 67, 628–632.

Ansley, C. F., and R. Kohn. (1983). "Exact Likelihood of Vector Autoregressive-Moving Average Process with Missing or Aggregated Data." *Biometrika* 70, 275–278.

Box, G. E. P., and G. M. Jenkins. (1976). *Time Series Analysis: Forecasting and Control,* rev. ed. San Francisco: Holden-Day.

Brewer, K. R. W. (1973). "Some Consequences of Temporal Aggregation and Systematic Sampling for ARMA and ARMAX Models." *Journal of Econometrics* 1, 133–154.

Chow, G. C., and A. Lin. (1971). "Best Linear Unbiased Interpolation, Distribution, and Extrapolation of Time Series by Related Series." *Review of Economics and Statistics* 53, 372–375.

Corrado, C., and M. Greene. (1988). "Reducing Uncertainty in Short-Term Projections: Linkage of Monthly and Quarterly Models." *Journal of Forecasting* 7, 77–102.

Corrado, C., and J. Haltmaier. (1988). "The Use of High-Frequency Data in Model-Based Forecasting at the Federal Reserve Board." *Finance and Economics Discussion Series,* 24.

Fair, R. C. (1984). *Specification, Estimation, and Analysis of Macroeconometric Models.* Cambridge: Harvard University Press.

Fernandez, R. B. (1981). "A Methodological Note on the Estimation of Time Series." *Review of Economics and Statistics* 63, 471–476.

Fuhrer, J., and J. Haltmaier. (1988). "Minimum Variance Pooling of Forecasts at Different Levels of Aggregation." *Journal of Forecasting* 7, 63–73.

Fuller, W. (1976). *Introduction to Statistical Time Series.* New York: Wiley.

Granger, C. W. J., and P. Newbold. (1986). *Forecasting Economic Time Series,* 2nd ed. New York: Academic Press.

Greene, M. N., E. P. Howrey, and S. H. Hymans. (1986). "The Use of Outside Information in Econometric Forecasting." In *Model Reliability,* D. A. Belsey and E. Kuh, eds. Cambridge: M.I.T. Press.

Harvey, A. C. (1981). *Time Series Models.* New York: Wiley.

Harvey, A. C., and R. G. Pierse. (1984). "Estimating Missing Observations in Economic Time Series." *Journal of the American Statistical Association* 79, 125–131.

Hilmer, S. C., and G. C. Tiao. (1979). "Likelihood Function of Stationary Multiple Autoregressive Moving Average Models." *Journal of the American Statistical Association* 74, 652–660.

Howrey, E. P., S. H. Hymans, and M. R. Donihue. (1987). "Merging Monthly and Quarterly Forecasts: Experience with MQEM." Paper presented at the session Can Economic Forecasting Be Improved?, AEA Meetings, Chicago, Illinois, December.

Klein, L. R. (1950). *Economic Fluctuations in the United States, 1921–1941.* New York: Wiley.

Klein, L. R., and E. Sojo. (1987). "Combinations of High and Low Frequency Data in Macroeconometric Models." Paper presented at the session Can Economic Forecasting Be Improved? AEA Meetings, Chicago, Illinois, December.

Litterman, R. B. (1983). "A Random Walk, Markov Model for the Interpolation of Time Series." *Journal of Business and Economic Statistics* 1, 169–173.

Liu, T. C. (1969). "A Monthly Recursive Econometric Model of the United States: A Test of Feasibility." *Review of Economics and Statistics* 51, 1–13.

Liu, T. C., and E. C. Hwa. (1974). "A Monthly Model of the U.S. Economy." *International Economic Review* 15, 328–365.

Lütkepohl, H. (1985). "Comparison of Criteria for Estimating the Order of a Vector Autoregressive Process." *Journal of Time Series Analysis* 6, 35–52.

Lütkepohl, H. (1986). "Forecasting Temporally Aggregated Vector ARMA Processes." *Journal of Forecasting* 5, 85–95.

Lütkepohl, H. (1987). *Forecasting Aggregated Vector ARIMA Processes.* New York: Springer-Verlag.

Nijman, T. E., and F. C. Palm. (1986). "The Construction and Use of Approximations for Missing Quarterly Observations: A Model-Based Approach." *Journal of Business and Economic Statistics* 4, 47–58.

Palm, F. C., and Th. E. Nijman. (1984). "Missing Observations in the Dynamic Regression Model." *Econometrica* 52, 1415–1435.

Stram, D. O., and W. W. S. Wei. (1986). "Temporal Aggregation in the ARIMA Process." *Journal of Time Series Analysis,* 7, 279–292.

Telser, L. (1967). "Discrete Samples and Moving Sums in Stationary Stochastic Processes." *Journal of the American Statistical Association* 62, 484–499.

Theil, H. (1954). *Linear Aggregation of Economic Relations.* Amsterdam: North-Holland.

Tiao, G. C., and G. E. P. Box. (1981). "Modelling Multiple Time Series with Applications." *Journal of the American Statistical Association* 76, 802–816.

Weiss, A. A. (1984). "Systematic Sampling and Temporal Aggregation in Time Series Models." *Journal of Econometrics* 26, 271–281.

CHAPTER 9

Stochastic-Simulation Tests of Nonlinear Econometric Models

ROBERTO S. MARIANO and BRYAN W. BROWN

Stochastic simulations of nonlinear dynamic econometric models have been used in various ways in the past. They have been employed to study the dynamic and cyclical properties of estimated simultaneous systems (e.g., Adelman and Adelman, 1959; Hickman, 1972; Klein, 1974 inter alia). They have been used also to obtain prediction bounds for some commercial forecasts, such as WEFA and DRI, and to construct efficient instrumental variable estimators (Kelejian, 1974; Amemiya, 1985). The method of simulated moments (McFadden, 1989) and analogous earlier developments in the statistical literature rely on stochastic simulators instead of numerical integration to solve moment restrictions in estimating polychotomous discrete choice models.

In a series of recent papers, listed in the references, we have devised and analyzed forecasting and testing procedures using stochastic simulations of estimated nonlinear systems. We have found that Monte Carlo and residual-based stochastic simulations provide new statistical techniques for prediction and model validation with desirable statistical properties. These studies, carried out analytically and experimentally through large-sample asymptotics and finite-sample analysis, deal with the following three major uses of stochastic simulations:

1. To center forecasts appropriately and correct for the bias in deterministic simulations due to nonlinearities in the model.
2. To estimate expectations of other functions of endogenous variables, especially the variance and higher order moments. This is done with an eye toward the evaluation of forecast accuracy, the construction of prediction regions and estimation of quantiles, and the estimation of important elasticities in the system.
3. To construct specification tests of significance for the validity of the model as a whole. These tests are designed to possess power against deterioration in the predictive performance of the model. Taking into account the interlinkages among the various endogenous variables, they supplement the usual diagnostics performed separately on each equation in the system.

This chapter focuses on the third item and discusses how stochastic simulations can be exploited to develop appropriate system specification tests for nonlinear systems. The approach we take is through auxiliary regressions of stochastic simulation errors to develop asymptotically valid significance tests of the predictive performance of the model. The tests so devised improve on the common practices that use deterministic simulations, that ignore issues of statistical significance of summary error measures, and that disregard appropriate error covariance structures in diagnostic regressions of model forecast errors.

Because of nonlinearities in the system, stochastic simulations are required to correct the bias in deterministic solutions of the model. In the presence of such bias, tests based on deterministic simulations would have unknown significance level and power. The use of either Monte Carlo or residual-based stochastic simulations allows a large-sample analysis of the tests based on them, starting with the asymptotic behavior of the simulation errors based on these stochastic procedures. Our earlier analysis of stochastic predictors leads to the appropriate error covariance structure in the auxiliary regressions of simulation errors. This addresses complications in the development of the regression tests due to not only heteroscedasticity but also serial correlation in the auxiliary regression disturbances.

The first section discusses Pagan's (1989) critique of the use of simulations in testing nonlinear models for misspecification. The related issue of the informational content of multi-period-ahead predictions (beyond static or one-period simulations) is also analyzed in this section. The stochastic simulations that we use to form our prediction-based tests and their basic asymptotic properties are reviewed in the second section. The last section then develops the auxiliary regressions leading to our prediction-based tests.

The analysis shows that comments made in the context of linear models, that question the utility of model simulations for testing and multiperiod prediction error analysis, do not apply to nonlinear models. The simulation tests developed here provide power against misspecification that affects the forecasting performance of the model. They serve to supplement the usual battery of validation tests and, in fact, provide the main basis for judgment regarding model adequacy if prediction is the main objective of the modeling exercise.

USE OF SIMULATIONS TO VALIDATE NONLINEAR MODELS

Pagan (1989) has actually questioned the marginal utility of specification error tests based on model simulations. Dealing with linear simultaneous equations models, he argues that reduced form errors are linear transformations of structural disturbances and that Wald-type test statistics in terms of quadratic forms in simulation (reduced-form) errors are exactly the same as corresponding quadratic forms in structural residuals. Because of this equivalence and since the analysis based on structural errors is more easily interpreted and suggestive of resolution, he concludes that tests based on reduced form residuals offer no additional value. Using continuity arguments, he also reasons that this conclusion must apply as well to nonlinear models.

Alternative approaches have been suggested in the literature for testing model misspecification concerning the behavior of model disturbances. We consider four categories:

1. Estimation-based tests, such as the tests discussed by Hausman (1978). These tests are designed basically to have power against violations of assumptions that cause the seemingly efficient estimator to be inconsistent.

2. Inference-based tests. These include the White (1982) information matrix test. They have power against misspecification that causes inconsistency in the usual covariance-matrix estimates.
3. Distribution-based tests. These procedures are designed to detect violations of distributional assumptions in the model. A prominent example is the Kolmogorov–Smirnov test.
4. Prediction-based tests. Tests of this type would reject the null if misspecification in the model leads to incorrect first moments for endogenous variables. Tests based on simulation residuals that Pagan (1989) studied for linear models and the Monte Carlo-simulation test, developed in Mariano and Brown (1983b) for the static nonlinear model, fall in this category.

Although Pagan's arguments apply to the linear case, the basis for them disappears when models are nonlinear. Higher order terms due to nonlinearities in the model (with respect to structural disturbances) cause quadratic forms in simulation error to differ from corresponding quadratic forms in calculated structural residuals. Prediction-based tests, in a nonlinear setting, would differ from more standard tests based on the estimated structural model. We argue further, through the following simple example, that prediction-based tests may give results that conflict with the other tests. In cases where conflicts occur, the investigator's decision regarding the validity of the model depends on the objectives of the model. If the main objective is to forecast future values of endogenous variables, prediction-based tests would provide the main guideline. If the model is to be put to multiple uses, then a combination of various types of tests forms a complementary battery of diagnostics for evaluating the model.

For a further illustration of these points, consider the log-linear model

$$\log y_t = \alpha + \beta x_t + \varepsilon_t \qquad t = 1, 2, \ldots, T$$

with "reduced-form" equation

$$y_t = \exp(\alpha + \beta x_t + \varepsilon_t)$$

with the assumption that x_t is exogenous and $\varepsilon_t \sim$ i.i.d. $(0, \sigma^2)$. Under these assumptions, the OLS estimator of α and β would be consistent.

For purposes of predicting y_τ, since

$$y_\tau = \exp(\alpha + \beta x_\tau + \varepsilon_\tau)$$

the predictor with minimum mean square prediction error (MSPE) is

$$Ey_\tau = \exp(\alpha + \beta x_\tau) \, E[\exp(\varepsilon_\tau)]$$

If $\varepsilon_\tau \sim$ i.i.d. $N(0, \sigma^2)$, $E[\exp(\varepsilon_\tau)] = \exp(\sigma^2/2)$; and OLS would give maximum likelihood estimates $(\hat{\alpha}, \hat{\beta}, \hat{\sigma}^2)$. The optimal predictor with lowest asymptotic MSPE (AMSPE) is

$$\hat{y}_\tau^{(c)} = \exp(\hat{\alpha} + \hat{\beta} x_\tau) \exp(\hat{\sigma}^2/2).$$

An alternative predictor based on stochastic simulations is the Monte Carlo predictor

$$\hat{y}_t^{(m)} = \exp(\hat{\alpha} + \hat{\beta}x_\tau) \sum_{s=1}^{S} \exp(\hat{\sigma}\bar{u}_s/S$$

where the $\bar{u}_s$ are independent draws from $N(0, 1)$ for $s = 1, 2, \ldots, S$.

Suppose we are interested in testing distributional assumptions regarding the disturbances ε_t and their consequences on model forecasts. The four types of tests enumerated earlier can be used for this purpose. The ability of these tests to detect misspecification regarding ε_t depends on the "true state of nature"—that is, the extent of departure from null assumptions. The interesting cases can be delineated in terms of violations of the following three properties:

P1. ε_t is normally distributed with mean zero and variance σ^2.
P2. $E(\varepsilon_t^4) = 3\sigma^4$.
P3. $E[\exp(\varepsilon_t)] = \exp(\sigma^2/2)$.

Depending on the user's objectives, a violation of P1 or P2 or P3 need not necessarily vitiate the model away from the use for which it was built. For example, if the model is to be used mainly for prediction purposes, the important requirement is that expected values of endogenous variables, as implied by distributional assumptions on the disturbances, be correctly specified. For the log-linear model under discussion, this will be satisfied as long as P3 holds; ε_t need not be normally distributed—P1 and P2 need not hold.

Three cases concerning the satisfaction of P1, P2, and P3 are summarized in Table 9.1. For each case, we indicate in Table 9.1 whether or not each type of test (E for estimation-based, I for inference-based, etc.) would be consistent—that is, whether the probability of rejecting the null hypothesis of correct misspecification approaches unity as sample size increeaszes.

Under Case 1, the disturbance term does not have the normal distribution assumed under the null. Despite this, however, because of P3, $E(y_t)$ is the same as under the null. For prediction purposes, the model need not be rejected. As indicated on Table 9.1, distribution-based tests would reject the model whereas estimation-based, inference-based, and prediction-based tests would not.

Under Case 2, again, the null hypothesis is violated but $E(y_t)$ remains the same as under the null and the model can still be used for prediction purposes. Prediction-

Table 9.1. Consistency of Specification Tests under Alternative Violations of Null Assumptions[a]

	Property			Consistent test			
Case	P1	P2	P3	E	I	D	P
1	N	Y	Y	N	N	Y	N
2	N	N	Y	N	Y	Y	N
3	N	Y	N	N	N	Y	Y

[a]N, no; Y, yes.

based tests will not reject; neither will estimation-based tests. Inference-based and distribution-based tests, however, will reject the model.

In Case 3, $E(y_t)$ differs from the null. Consequently, prediction-based tests would reject the model. Here, distribution-based tests would also lead to a rejection since the errors are not normally distributed. In contrast, estimation-based and inference-based procedures would not reject the null.

This discussion shows that analysis of structural disturbances would reject the model in Cases 1 and 2 even when predictors based on the model work well. Inference-based tests would lead us to reject the model in Case 2 even though the estimated model would still provide asymptotically unbiased forecasts. Estimation-based tests will tend to accept the model in Case 3 when the model cannot be used for forecasting—appropriate predictors in standard situations are in fact asymptotically biased.

Thus, if predictive accuracy is the primary criterion and the model is nonlinear, the non-prediction-based approaches can be misleading and test results from them should be interpreted with care. In this situation, prediction-based tests should be the main basis for decision regarding the applicability of the model. If, however, the model is to be used for other purposes, such as structural inference, then prediction-based tests alone can be misleading (see Cases 1 and 2); they should be supplemented with other tests.

In the context of linear dynamic models, it has also been claimed that multi-period-ahead simulations carry no incremental information beyond one-period-ahead predictions (Chong and Hendry, 1986; Pagan, 1989). A simple example shows that this claim does not apply to nonlinear dynamic models. Misspecification tests based on one-period simulations measure only the adequacy of one-period-ahead forecasts and can be seriously misleading as far as adequacy of multiperiod forecasts.

Consider the following dynamic model:

$$y_{t1} = \alpha + \beta y_{t-1,1} + \varepsilon_{t1}$$

$$y_{t2} = \lambda + \delta \exp(y_{t-1,1}) + \varepsilon_{t2}$$

where $(\varepsilon_{t1}, \varepsilon_{t2}) \sim$ i.i.d. $N(0, \Sigma)$.

Conditioning on period $t = \tau$, we have

$$E(y_{\tau+1,1}|y_{\tau1}) = \alpha + \beta y_{\tau1}$$

$$E(y_{\tau+1,2}|y_{\tau1}) = \lambda + \delta \exp(y_{\tau1})$$

Thus, the Monte Carlo predictor will be asymptotically unbiased even if the disturbances are nonnormal, since the above expectations do not depend on the properties of the distribution. A prediction-based test would have no power against such a misspecification; it would lead to the correct decision if prediction is important.

For two-periods-ahead prediction,

$$E(y_{\tau+2,1}|y_{\tau1}) = \alpha + \beta(\alpha + \beta y_{\tau1})$$

$$E(y_{\tau+2,2}|y_{\tau1}) = \lambda + \delta \exp(\alpha + \beta y_{\tau1}) \, E[\exp(u_{\tau1})]$$

If $E[\exp(u_{\tau1})] = \exp(\sigma_1^2/2)$, as is assumed by the Monte Carlo predictor based on normality assumptions, then the Monte Carlo predictor will be asymptotically unbiased, and the prediction-based tests will not reject the model. However, if

$E[\exp(u_{\tau 1})] \neq \exp(\sigma_1^2/2)$, then the two-period-ahead Monte Carlo predictor will be biased asymptotically. In this case, although the test based on one-period simulations tends to accept the model, the test based on two-periods-ahead simulations leads to the correct prescription of rejecting the model.

DYNAMIC MODEL AND STOCHASTIC SIMULATORS

To develop our prediction-based tests, we establish the basic concepts in this section. Consider a simultaneous system of n nonlinear stochastic equations

$$f(y_t, y_{t-1}, x_t; \theta) = u_t \tag{1}$$

where f, y_t, and u_t are $n \times 1$. The vectors y_t and x_t of endogenous and exogenous variables, respectively, are observed over the sample period for $t = 1, 2, \ldots, T$. The vector of functions, f, is completely known; θ denotes the vector of unknown parameters; the u_t are unobservable disturbances, assumed to be independently and identically distributed (i.i.d.) with zero mean and identity variance–covariance matrix.

We assume that (1) defines a locally unique inverse

$$y_t = g(u_t, y_{t-1}, x_t; \theta) \tag{2}$$

with finite first two moments

$$\begin{aligned}
Ey_t &= \gamma(x_t, x_{t-1}, \ldots; \theta) = \gamma_t \\
V(y_t) &= E(y_t - \gamma_t)(y_t - \gamma_t)' = \Omega(x_t, x_{t-1}, \ldots; \theta) = \Omega_t
\end{aligned} \tag{3}$$

We will also be considering conditional moments of y_t; for this we introduce the following notation:

$$\begin{aligned}
E(y_t|y_{t-1}) &= \gamma_1(y_{t-1}, x_t; \theta) = \gamma_{t1} \\
V(y_t|y_{t-1}) &= \Omega_1(y_{t-1}, x_t; \theta) = \Omega_{t1} \\
E(y_t|y_{t-\ell}) &= \gamma_\ell(y_{t-\ell}, x_{t-\ell+1}, \ldots, x_t; \theta) = \lambda_{t\ell}, \qquad \ell \geq 2 \\
V(y_t|y_{t-\ell}) &= \Omega_\ell(y_{t-\ell} x_{t-\ell+1}, \ldots, x_t; \theta) = \Omega_{t\ell}, \qquad \ell \geq 2
\end{aligned} \tag{4}$$

Here, all expectations are relative to the model described in (1) and the assumed distribution of u_t.

Given the sample (x_t, y_t): $t = 1, 2, \ldots, T$, from which an estimator $\hat{\theta}$ is calculated, the static one-period, dynamic two-periods-ahead and ℓ-periods-ahead simulations of y_τ given x_τ, for some time point τ are

$$\begin{aligned}
\hat{y}_{\tau 1} &= g(\tilde{u}_1, y_{\tau-1}, x_\tau; \hat{\theta}) \\
\hat{y}_{\tau 2} &= g(\tilde{u}_2, \hat{y}_{\tau-1(1)}, x_\tau; \hat{\theta}) \\
&= g[\tilde{u}_2, g(\tilde{u}_2, g(\tilde{u}_1, y_{\tau-2}, x_{\tau-1}; \hat{\theta}), x_\tau; \hat{\theta})] \\
&= g_2(\tilde{u}_1, \tilde{u}_2, y_{\tau-2}, x_{\tau-1}, x_\tau; \hat{\theta}) \\
\hat{y}_{\tau\ell} &= g_\ell(\tilde{u}_1, \tilde{u}_2, \ldots, \tilde{u}_\ell, y_{\tau-\ell}, x_{t-\ell+1}, \ldots, x_\tau; \hat{\theta})
\end{aligned} \tag{5}$$

The simulations are said to be deterministic if $\bar{u}_1$, $\bar{u}_2$, . . . and $\bar{u}_\ell$ are set to zero, and stochastic if they are random proxies for $u_{\tau-\ell+1}$, $u_{\tau-\ell+2}$, . . . , and u_τ, respectively. In our earlier papers, we have distinguished between two generic stochastic simulations: Monte Carlo, where the proxies are random draws from a prespecified probability distribution such as $N(0, I)$, and residual-based, where the proxies are calculated structural residuals.

Replications of the stochastic simulations for one time point τ generate pseudosamples of y_τ. The pseudosamples of y_τ, ℓ periods ahead, are

Monte Carlo $\{\hat{y}_{m,\tau\ell s}:$ $s = 1, 2, . . . , S\}$

Residual-based $\{\hat{y}_{r,\tau\ell h}:$ $h = 1, 2, . . . , (T-1)^\ell\}$

The elements in the pseudosamples are

$$\hat{y}_{m,\tau\ell s} = g_\ell(\bar{u}_{s_1}, \bar{u}_{s_2}, . . . , \bar{u}_{s\ell}, y_{\tau-\ell}, x_{\tau-\ell+1}, . . . , x_\tau; \hat{\theta}) \qquad (6)$$

$$\hat{y}_{r,\tau\ell h} = g_\ell(\hat{u}_{h_1}, \hat{u}_{h_2}, . . . , \hat{u}_{h\ell}, y_{\tau-\ell}, x_{\tau-\ell+1}, . . . , x_\tau; \hat{\theta})$$

where $(\bar{u}_{s_1}, . . . , \bar{u}_{s\ell})$ are independent draws from the distribution of $(u_{\tau-\ell}, u_{\tau-\ell+1}, . . . , u_\tau)$ while $(\hat{u}_{h_1}, \hat{u}_{h_2}, . . . , \hat{u}_{h\ell})$ is an ℓ-tuple of calculated residuals; that is

$$\hat{u}_{h_i} = f(y_{h_i}, y_{h_i-1}, x_t, \hat{\theta}) \qquad (7)$$

This definition corresponds to a variation of the residual-based procedure that we called complete enumeration in Brown and Mariano (1989a). Each h_i can be any number between 2 and T since $\hat{u}_1$ cannot be calculated. Sampling from the empirical distribution of the calculated residuals modifies the residual-based to what we would call the bootstrap pseudosample.

Stochastic predictors of a future y_τ can be calculated from the simulated pseudosample. As we have done in our previous papers, we use sample means as stochastic predictors. The ℓ-period-ahead Monte Carlo predictor of y_τ, for example, is

$$\hat{y}_{m,\tau\ell} = \sum_{s=1}^{S} g_\ell(u_{s1}, u_{s2}, . . . , u_{s\ell}, y_{\tau-\ell}, . . . , x_\tau; \theta)/S \qquad (8)$$

The large sample properties of these forecasts and the analogous residual-based and bootstrap predictors are studied in Brown and Mariano (1989a) for $\tau = T + \ell$. Under the assumption of correct model specification, it is shown that these stochastic simulation procedures provide asymptotically unbiased predictors and consistent estimators of corresponding conditional means. Their asymptotic mean squared prediction errors AMSPE are derived and used to determine relative prediction efficiencies. These AMSPEs are utilized further in the formulation of the prediction-based tests that we develop in the next section.

STOCHASTIC SIMULATION ERROR REGRESSION TESTS

Utilizing the asymptotic properties of stochastic predictors, we now proceed to construct significance tests for validating the model through sample period simulations of the estimated system. The reduced-form errors

$$v_t = y_t - \gamma_{t\ell} \tag{9}$$

would have mean zero under the null hypothesis, H_0, of correct model specification. However, it would have generally a nonzero mean if the model is misspecified. We can represent this parametrically as

$$E(v_t|y_{t-\ell}) = D_\ell w_{t\ell} \tag{10}$$
$$v_t = D_\ell w_{t\ell} + \eta_{t\ell}$$

where $w_{t\ell}$ is a $q \times 1$ vector of observations on a selected set of nonlinear functions of $y_{t-\ell}, x_{t-\ell+1}, \ldots, x_t$, and possibly other variables, D_ℓ is $n \times q$, and $\eta_{t\ell}$, defined implicitly by the second equation in (10), has mean zero and variance–covariance matrix equal to $\Omega_{t\ell}$. Here, the term $D_\ell w_{t\ell}$ represents the conditional mean of v_t under either null or alternative hypothesis. Thus, $\eta_{t\ell}$ has mean zero under both hypotheses. Under H_0, $D_\ell = 0$, while under H_1, with $w_{t\ell}$ chosen properly, D_ℓ would be different from zero. Consequently, a specification error test on the model can be formulated in terms of testing the null hypothesis that $D_\ell = 0$ in (10).

Since v_t is unobservable, we utilize stochastic simulation errors as proxies for it. Consider the Monte Carlo forecast errors based on ℓ-period-ahead simulations:

$$\hat{v}_{t\ell} = y_t - \hat{y}_{m,t\ell} \tag{11}$$
$$\hat{y}_{m,t\ell} = \sum_{s=1}^{S} \hat{y}_{m,t\ell s}/S$$

Here, for each time t, a Monte Carlo ℓ-period-ahead pseudo sample on y_t is generated with sample mean equal to $\hat{y}_{m,t\ell}$. Combining (10) and (11), we get

$$\hat{v}_{t\ell} = D_\ell w_{t\ell} + \hat{\eta}_{t\ell} \tag{12}$$
$$\hat{\eta}_{t\ell} = \eta_{t\ell} + (\hat{y}_{m,t\ell} - \gamma_{t\ell})$$

Stacking these regression equations for all t, we obtain

$$\hat{v} = W\delta + \hat{\eta} \tag{13}$$

Technically, all the four symbols in (13) should be subscripted by ℓ (for ℓ-ahead prediction) and m (for Monte Carlo simulation). The two indices have been suppressed to streamline the notation.

The asymptotic covariance matrix for $\hat{\eta}$ under H_0 follows from the large-sample analysis in Brown and Mariano (1989a). Tests of correct model specification [H_0: $\delta = 0$ in (13)] can then be constructed from alternative estimators of δ in (13) using the different stochastic simulators introduced earlier.

For example, if we denote the asymptotic covariance matrix of $\hat{\eta}$ by Σ, ordinary least-squares estimation of (13) results in the following test statistic:

$$\hat{\delta}'[(W'W)^{-1} (W'\hat{\Sigma}W) (W'W)^{-1}]^{-}\hat{\delta} \tag{14}$$

where $\hat{\delta}$ is the OLS estimator of δ in (13) and T times the matrix in brackets is the limiting covariance matrix of $\sqrt{T}\,\hat{\delta}$ under H_0. There are cases when this matrix is not of full rank; in such cases, as indicated above, the generalized inverse is used in constructing the quadratic form. Under H_0, (14) is asymptotically a central chi-squared variable with degrees of freedom equal to the rank of the asymptotic covariance matrix of $\hat{\delta}$.

Note that Σ must also be estimated in the numerical calculation of (14). In general, Σ contains the basic reduced-form error covariance matrix (Ω), the matrix (Γ) of partial derivatives of conditional means of endogenous variables with respect to unknown parameters, and the asymptotic covariance matrix (Ψ) of parameter estimates. Ω and Γ can be estimated from the stochastically generated pseudosample. Stochastic simulations can also be employed to estimate Ψ if numerical calculations from analytical formulas are not feasible. Mariano and Brown (1983a,b), Brown and Mariano (1984, 1989a,b), and Brown (1988) provide additional details.

Test statistics such as (14) for static nonlinear models are discussed further using Monte Carlo simulations in Mariano and Brown (1983b) and using the bootstrap predictor in Mariano and Tabunda (1987). Tests of this type, using OLS estimates of δ, can also be developed for one-period and multiperiod stochastic simulations in dynamic models; see Brown (1988) and Brown and Mariano (1989b). Tests based on generalized least-squares estimates of δ can also be developed but technical complications, especially in residual-based and bootstrap simulations, remain to be resolved. Brown (1988) contains a preliminary discussion of this and the important issues of local power behavior of the tests and practical guidelines for the choice of explanatory variables in the auxiliary regressions.

ACKNOWLEDGMENT

Partial support from NSF Grants SES-8520969 and SES-8604219 is gratefully acknowledged.

REFERENCES

Adelman, F., and I. Adelman. (1959). "The Dynamic Properties of the Klein-Goldberger Model." *Econometrica* 27, 596–625.

Amemiya, T. (1985). *Advanced Econometrics*. Cambridge: Harvard University Press.

Brown, B. W. (1988). "Prediction-Based Tests for Misspecification in Nonlinear Dynamic Models." Rice University Discussion Paper.

Brown, B. W., and R. S. Mariano. (1984). "Residual-Based Procedures for Prediction and Estimation in a Nonlinear Simultaneous System." *Econometrica* 52, 321–343.

Brown, B. W., and R. S. Mariano. (1989a). "Predictors in Dynamic Nonlinear Models: Large-Sample Behavior." *Econometric Theory* 5, 430–452.

Brown, B. W., and R. S. Mariano. (1989b). "Measures of Deterministic Prediction Bias in Nonlinear Models." *International Economic Review* 30, 667–684.

Chong, Y., and D. Hendry. (1986). "Econometric Evaluation of Linear Macro-Economic Models." *Review of Economic Studies* 53, 671–690.

Fair, R., and R. Shiller. (1988). "The Informational Content of Ex-Ante Forecasts." Mimeo.

Hausman, J. (1978). "Specification Tests in Econometrics." *Econometrica* 46, 1251–1272.

Hickman, B. (ed.). (1972). *Econometric Models of Cyclical Behavior.* New York: Columbia University Press.

Kelejian, H. (1974). "Efficient Instrumental Variable Estimation of Large Scale Nonlinear Econometric Models." Discussion Paper.

Klein, L. R. (1974). *A Textbook of Econometrics,* 2nd ed. Englewood Cliffs, NJ: Prentice-Hall.

McFadden, D. (1989). "Method of Simulated Moments for Estimation of Discrete Response Models Without Numerical Integration." *Econometrica* 57, 995–1026.

Mariano, R. S., and B. W. Brown. (1983a). "Asymptotic Behavior of Predictors in a Nonlinear Simultaneous System." *International Economic Review* 24, 523–536.

Mariano, R. S., and B. W. Brown. (1983b). "Prediction-Based Tests for Misspecification in Nonlinear Simultaneous Systems." In *Studies in Econometrics, Time-Series, and Multivariate Statistics,* S. Karlin, T. Amemiya, and L. Goodman, eds. New York: Academic Press.

Mariano, R. S., and B. W. Brown. (1986). "Interval and Quantile Prediction in Nonlinear Simultaneous Systems." University of Pennsylvania Discussion Paper.

Mariano, R. S., and B. W. Brown. (1988). "Predictors in Dynamic Nonlinear Models: Finite-Sample Behavior." University of Pennsylvania Discussion Paper.

Mariano, R. S., and A. Tabunda. (1987). "A Test for Misspecification in Nonlinear Simultaneous Systems Using the Bootstrap Predictor." University of Philippines Discussion Paper.

Pagan, A. (1989). "On the Role of Simulation in the Statistical Evaluation of Econometric Models." *Journal of Econometrics* 40, 125–140.

Phillips, P. C. B. (1979). "The Sampling Distribution of Forecasts from a First-Order Autoregression." *Journal of Econometrics* 9, 241–261.

White, H. (1982). "Maximum Likelihood Estimation of Misspecified Models." *Econometrica* 50, 1–25.

CHAPTER 10

Comparisons of Macroeconometric Models of Developing Economies

F. GERARD ADAMS and JOAQUIN VIAL

Comparisons of the performance of econometric models serve a number of purposes:

- To learn about the reliability of the individual models for policy analysis and forecasting and, by comparing a number of different models, to draw conclusions about their relative strengths, weaknesses, and potential areas for improvement.
- To learn about the structure of the economies that these models represent, so to speak, to use them as a "window on the real world."
- To improve individual models as a result of setting standards of performance and as a result of interaction between model builders and operators.

These goals motivate our comparisons of econometric models of less developed countries (LDCs) as they have previous model comparison projects dealing with the United States and other industrial countries.

But, comparing the performance of econometric models of developing economies poses some rather special challenges. The objectives of developing economies, focused toward growth and economic and social transformation, suggest that the performance of LDC models should be considered from perspectives different than those applied to models of developed economies. The tight constraints under which the LDCs operate—shortages of capital and foreign exchange—as well as their structural duality point in a similar direction. Model performance comparisons for LDCs should go beyond the traditional concerns with short- and medium-term forecasting and stabilization. The LDC economies are less stable and more sensitive to external shocks, and there is often a special concern with long-run and sectoral issues. This is one of the reasons why planning models in the 1960s, and "Computable General Equilibrium" (CGE) models now, are being used widely with reference to these countries. Macroeconometric models have to be able to give answers to development related problems, such as the relationship between growth, trade, and the evolution of foreign debt, and the effects of policies on the sectoral composition of output, income distribution, employment. This means that the models should also be compared on these grounds and, perhaps, other types of models such as growth models and CGE models should be included in the comparisons.

The history of econometric modeling in LDCs is sparse, and examples of continuous use of LDC models over many years for forecasting or policy analysis are limited to two or three cases such as CIEMEX-WEFA for Mexico, Metroeconomica in Venezuela, and, perhaps, one or two other proprietary models.

A number of LDC models are currently maintained and operated by international agencies or private consulting firms, especially after the debt crisis showed the need for a close monitoring of these economies, but this is done with little direct input from the local economies. During the last few years, we have witnessed a significant increase in the number of models built and maintained in local centers in LDCs. Project LINK and local offices of the UN (ESCAP and ILPES from ECLA) have played a very important role in this process, giving technical support and providing forums for the discussion of the model themselves, as well as their results in terms of forecasting and policy simulation.

The short history of econometric modeling in LDCs and the relatively novel application of these tools for policy and development planning severely limit the range of comparison exercises that can be made, particularly when trying to assess their reliability for forecasting purposes. On the other hand, a model comparison project provides a unique opportunity to influence the development of models, to improve their specification at an early stage, before they become too large and complex, and subsequently difficult and expensive to analyze and change.

In most LDCs, only one or two macro models are being maintained and operated actively.[1] Consequently, comparisons have to be made across countries. This is an important source of challenges. A project of this type will have to deal with widely diverse economies, and a special effort needs to be made to disentangle results due to differences between the countries from those that are caused by differences in the models. This is particularly difficult for LDCs since there is much diversity between LDCs and there is less agreement on how to model them, than in the case of developed countries.[2]

A FIRST ROUND OF COMPARISONS

The most important goal of the round of LDC model performance comparisons presented in Taiwan in May of 1987 was to get a first idea of the general characteristics of these models and a preliminary diagnostic of their principal strengths and weaknesses.

Simulation Specifications

A request to produce a standard set of simulations was sent to a dozen model groups in different countries. The simulations were defined carefully restricting as much as possible the freedom of individual model builders, so as to attain maximum comparability of results. Yet, even so, since model structures and procedures differ, it is not certain that all the simulations are fully comparable.

First, model managers were asked to perform a simulation for 7 years, to use as a baseline. The 7-year period 1985–1991 was suggested, but groups that would have difficulties simulating that particular period were allowed to use other years.

Alternative "disturbed" simulations were the following:

1. *A sustained increase in real government consumption equivalent to 1% of GDP in the base year,* which is maintained through the whole simulation period, and which is financed by additional foreign loans. This is a standard fiscal policy multiplier. To isolate the pure effect of fiscal policy, special care was taken to

define a neutral way to finance the expansion in government spending. In the case of countries with a fixed exchange rate or currencies pegged to the dollar or other major currency, this exercise leaves open the question of the definition of monetary policy and the treatment of the new foreign loans. To control for this problem, two variants were requested:

- Simulation (1A) with Sterilization: The Central Bank acts to sterilize the increase in the monetary base, so that M_1 remains the same as in the baseline solution.
- Simulation (1B) with Monetary Expansion: There is no sterilization and the monetary impact is the same as if the government had financed the increase in spending resorting to monetary expansion.

2. *A sustained increase in real government investment equivalent to 1% of GDP in the base year.* The purpose of this exercise is to see if these models capture the potential effect on capital formation and relative increase in capacity of investment as contrasted to government consumption. We anticipated that Exercise 2 would yield more growth than Exercise 1 in the long run. Two variants depending on the response of monetary authorities were designed: Simulation 2A implies full sterilization and Simulation 2B full monetization of the additional spending.

3. *A sustained devaluation of the domestic currency by 10% as compared to the baseline.* Devaluation is a standard component of IMF-oriented adjustment programs and there have been important discussions about its effects on LDCs.[3] To give a touch of realism to the exercise, and also to check the consistency of the results of the simulations with some standard results from international monetary theory, two variants were implemented:

- Simulation 3A with Baseline Money Supply: It is assumed that the exogenous components of money supply are kept at the same values as in the baseline solution.

- Simulation 3B with Accommodative Monetary Policy: It is assumed that economic authorities follow accommodative monetary policies, so that M_1 also increases by 10% with respect to the baseline.

4. *A 10% increase in money supply (M_1), maintained over all the simulation period.*

5. *A 1 point rise in international interest rates (LIBOR, for instance) above the baseline values.* This exercise serves to assess the impact of a foreign interest rate shock. It is particularly important since many of these countries have large foreign debts.

We sent preformatted diskettes with LOTUS 1-2-3 files to all the groups that agreed to participate, and a meeting was held in Taiwan in May 1987, to discuss the results of these simulations. In total, we received simulations from 13 groups covering 12 countries. However, not all could be used for this comparison, due to communication problems, or simply because the models were in too much of a preliminary stage of development to publish results. The results that we report here cover Brazil, Chile, Hong Kong, India, Korea, Mexico, Philippines, Taiwan, Thailand, and Venezuela.

For India and Thailand, we have two different models. In these cases one model is operated by ESCAP and the other by a local group.[4]

Expected Performance of the Models

There are many ways to conduct the analysis of the results of the simulations. We choose to present a cross section of the results across models and exercises. We focus here on the short run.

To evaluate the performance of the models, it would be helpful to have a standard for comparison. The ideal instrument would be a "prototype model" estimated for a "prototype country."[5] However, that model does not exist and there are good reasons to think that instead of one prototype we should have to consider several to deal with the wide differences in economic structure and degree of development of LDCs.[6] As an alternative we consider our anticipations of the type of responses that these models should have: In the short run:

- A positive association between *increases in government consumption or investment* and economic activity (GDP) and prices (PDGDP). As a consequence, the balance on current account should deteriorate.
- A similar type of response to *changes in money supply,* even though the magnitude of the impact could be different. (This also means that Simulations 1B and 2B should present a stronger effect on the three variables considered than Simulations 1A and 2A.)
- *Devaluation* should have an impact on prices and also improve the balance on current account when measured in dollars. However, we cannot anticipate if it is going to have a positive or negative impact on GDP in the short run, since contradictory forces interact. (We also expect that Simulation 3B will show a stronger impact on prices, a weaker effect on the current account balance, and produce a more favorable evolution of GDP than Simulation 3A.)
- The *rise in LIBOR* or other international interest rates should reduce GDP, worsen the current account, and, subsequently, reduce prices (although exchange rate impacts may work in the opposite direction). All the countries included are net debtors. Obviously, if any of them were a net creditor, the effects should have the opposite sign.

In the long run, the emphasis of model simulation should be somewhat different. We expect the *long-run multiplier* effects to satisfy the following properties:

- The impact on GDP of an increase in government investment should be stronger and more persistent than a similar increase in government consumption. It should put less pressure on prices due to the increase in productive capacity.
- Monetary variables such as the exchange rate and money supply should not, in most instances, have permanent effects on real variables such as GDP.
- With a continued disturbance all the variables should converge toward a fixed deviation from the baseline, meaning that the models tend toward stable solutions.

Simulation Results

Average results across all models for three variables, Gross Domestic Product (GDP), the GDP deflator (PDGDP), and the Current Account Balance in dollars (TBPCA),

are presented in Table 10.1. The simulations for each individual model are shown in
Appendix Tables A10.1–A10.8. In all cases the results are expressed as percentage
deviations from the values in the baseline solution, with the exception of TBPCA for
which the deviations from the baseline are expressed as a percentage of the level of
imports in the baseline.

The range of the individual model results is wide, but averages of the simulation
results across the different models show reasonable systematic patterns. We evaluate
such average results here.

The average results can be characterized as follows:

Fiscal Policy: Exercises 1 and 2

- Government consumption stimulus produces, on average, multipliers (Sim 1A)
  only a little above unity with sterilization, but considerably more reasonable results ranging from 1.6 to 1.9 in the short run and declining thereafter with monetary expansion (Sim 1B). The average multipliers show only little change over
  time, rising slightly with sterilization and dropping slightly over time with accommodation.
- Price effects are very small with monetary sterilization (Sim 1A), but are quite
  substantial from 2% at the beginning to 4% at the end of the simulation period
  if government spending is financed through credit creation (Sim 1B), demonstrating the strong weight of monetary variables in the price equations, compared
  to almost no effect of capacity constraints in many of the models.
- Trade balance impacts in U.S. dollars (measured as percentage of imports) are
  uniformly negative amounting to 3–4% on average with sterilization and 5% with
  monetary expansion.

Devaluation: Exercise 3

- Devaluation improves the trade balance on average by 3% of imports in the short
  run rising to 7% over a longer period. The balance of payments impact is only a
  little smaller on average if devaluation is combined with increase in money supply (Sim 3B).
- With monetary sterilization the impact of a 10% devaluation is to increase the
  price level by 2–3%. On the other hand, as we have observed earlier, the impact
  of monetary expansion greatly increases the price effect.
- The impact of devaluation on real GNP is positive, somewhat below 1% with
  sterilization and somewhat above 1% with monetary expansion.

Monetary Expansion: Exercise 4

- Monetary expansion (Sim 4) has substantial impact on inflation. A 10% increase
  in the money supply increases prices from 2% initially to 4% later in the simulation period.
- Probably as a consequence of the important price effect, the impact on real GNP
  is moderate, approximately 0.5% early in the simulation and gradually declining
  to 0.26% later.

Increased World Interest Rate: Exercise 5

- The impact of a 1% rise in LIBOR is small except as one would anticipate with respect to the balance on current account, where impacts ranging from -2 to -4% of imports occur.
- There is a small negative impact on real output, ranging from -0.1 to -0.3%, which must reflect trade and interest rate effects rather than financial or debt service constraints.
- The price level is only minimally affected.

Summarizing the findings of this section, on average, in the short run the models exhibit adequate responses to the different shocks with respect to GDP and Current Account Balance. The impact on prices appears on average to be tightly linked to the monetary sector, so that price response in the absence of monetary expansion appears to be relatively weak. There is no basis for determining whether this is a characteristic of the underlying economies as well as of the models.

With respect to long-term effects, the results are somewhat further from expectations, even for the average of all the models. Government investment does not give results that are clearly better than government consumption, for example. In fact, government investment produces a lower impact than consumption in the long run. This is evidence that supply considerations and/or the linkage between investment and production capacity are underrepresented in most of the models. Where monetary policy has the power to affect GDP in the short run, that effect persists and even increases in the long run. On the other hand, most simulations appear to have settled down to what are approximately equilibrium values after 4 or 5 years of simulation.

As we have noted, the diversity between the results of the models is quite striking. We can see in Appendix Table A.10-1 that the first year impacts on GDP of an increase in government consumption, keeping M_1 constant range from almost 3% of GDP in Brazil and Mexico to approximately 0 in India, the Philippines, and Thailand (Ramangkura). Similarly, if we look at the impact on the current account, we see a sharp deterioration in the Indian model (ESCAP) and Mexico (more than 10% of imports), and very small responses in Hong Kong, India (Madhur), Korea, the Philippines, and Thailand (Ramangkura). Similar patterns can be noted further out in the simulation period, and in other simulations as well. The diversity of responses is even higher if we examine the impact of monetary policy, and, in this case, there are some models that show unexpected effects as seen from the point of view of standard economic theory. For example in Table 10.1, even though for a majority of countries an increase in money supply stimulates output, puts pressure on prices, and worsens the current account, some of the models show little response or even an opposite result.

Since these simulations include a number of countries, it is likely that some of the differences can be explained in terms of different economic structures or differing endogenous policy responses. We expect some of the economies to be less sensitive to policy stimulus than others because they have relatively large primary sectors for example, and we expect some to be more sensitive to devaluation because the economies are open or relatively dependent on trade. On the other hand, the differences between the models are so large that it is likely that they are attributable in many cases to the specifics of model coefficients and structure.

Table 10.1. Average Simulation Effects[a]

	1	2	3	4	5	6	7
Effect on GDP of							
Fiscal Policy							
1a Increase in GC, with sterilization	1.07	1.05	1.02	1.08	1.12	1.25	1.24
1b Increase in GC, no sterilization	1.88	1.59	1.46	1.47	1.47		
2a Increase in GINV, with sterilization	0.87	0.88	0.83	0.87	0.90	1.01	
2b Increase in GINV, no sterilization	1.59	1.34	1.17	1.13	1.10	0.99	
Devaluation							
10% devaluation	0.87	0.61	0.53	0.51	0.65	0.73	
10% devaluation and increase in M_1	1.39	0.99	0.89	0.86	1.01	1.04	0.97
Monetary							
10% increase in M_1	0.60	0.44	0.34	0.33	0.32	0.26	
1% increase in LIBOR	−0.07	−0.29	−0.33	−0.31	−0.35	−0.34	
Effect on PGDP of							
Fiscal Policy							
1a Increase in GC, with sterilization	−0.02	0.07	−0.11	−0.20	−0.01	0.09	0.26
1b Increase in GC, no sterilization	2.19	3.16	3.42	3.69	3.81	4.29	
2a Increase in GINV, with sterilization	−1.18	−0.39	−0.55	−0.62	−0.47	−0.47	
2b Increase in GINV, no sterilization	2.24	3.07	3.42	3.71	3.90	4.85	

Devaluation							
10% devaluation	2.11	2.19	2.50	2.71	3.40	2.88	
10% devaluation and increase in M$_1$	4.30	5.62	6.10	6.34	7.31	6.84	6.91
Monetary							
10% increase in M$_1$	1.93	3.29	3.72	3.71	3.92	3.25	
1% increase in LIBOR	−0.02	−0.07	−0.06	−0.09	−0.10		
Effect on TBPCA of							
Fiscal Policy							
1a Increase in GC, with sterilization	−2.90	−3.58	−3.15	−3.48	−3.22	−3.45	−4.40
1b Increase in GC, no sterilization	−5.04	−5.88	−4.82	−4.93	−4.32	−3.38	
2a Increase in GINV, with sterilization	−2.95	−3.48	−2.91	−3.17	−2.85	−3.08	
2b Increase in GINV, no sterilization	−5.02	−5.40	−3.87	−3.70	−2.95	−1.92	
Devaluation							
10% devaluation	3.45	7.38	5.17	5.52	4.62	6.64	
10% devaluation and increase in M$_1$	2.37	6.08	4.14	4.78	4.02	6.57	7.56
Monetary							
10% increase in M$_1$	−0.70	−1.37	−1.05	−1.16	−1.13	−1.40	
1% increase in LIBOR	−3.42	−4.12	−2.89	−2.39	−2.43	−2.60	

ᵃPercentage deviation from baseline. The effects on the Current Account are computed as percentage of the level of imports in the baseline solution.

FINAL COMMENTS

The simulation results presented in this chapter represent a first round of LDC model comparison studies. Although they illustrate the advanced state of econometric modeling in many developing economies, they tend to suggest many of the models operate more effectively for short-run simulation of policy and exchange rate shocks than for the analysis of long-term growth policy issues. Most of the models suffer from excessive "Keynesianism" in the sense that they are too much oriented toward the short run and appear in some cases to have overlooked the role of long-run supply considerations.[7]

On average the results are "reasonable," though the standard of comparison of the performance of models of developed economies is not really appropriate. Individually, the models vary greatly in the results and in some cases the simulations suggest that there are some problems. On the other hand, the diversity of the economies should account for some diversity in the models and in their simulation results. Clearly, considerably more detailed analysis is required to disentangle the effects of different underlying countries, the effect of differences in model structure, and, finally, the differences attributable to the estimated coefficients.

The model comparison effort is ongoing with a number of enthusiastic supporters. A second model comparison conference was held in Seoul, Korea in November 1988. This meeting, from which the results are so far only preliminary, was aimed at measuring the influence of the external sector, trade, and trade policy on economic development. This was a large scale effort. Simulations were submitted for 30 models, covering 16 developing countries. Each participant was asked to run one base simulation and 13 alternative simulations over a period of 7 years providing data for 28 variables. Although not all participants were able to submit all simulations, a very large data bank of simulations has been created that will make possible statistical analysis of the resulting information.

The model comparison work poses substantial theoretical and empirical challenges. More complex techniques of structural analysis are required to disentangle the forces that determined the results of simulation in complex dynamic simultaneous models. Methods must be developed to make meaningful empirical comparisons between models in general, between models based on different time periods, and between models based on different countries such as those compared in this chapter.

Despite the considerable challenges involved, the process of comparing model performance appears to be useful in evaluating the models and, in many cases, in persuading their operators to go back to the "drawing board" to improve them.

ACKNOWLEDGMENT

We gratefully acknowledge the support of National Central University of Taiwan and of the Korean Development Institute for this project.

NOTES

1. Though we have obtained simulations for six models of Korea!
2. Just to give an example, when analyzing the likely impact of a money supply increase, there

are not only the hypotheses that are familiar in the discussion of standard macroeconomic theory, but also some structuralist hypotheses that come to very different conclusions. See Taylor (1983) for a review of structuralist views on macroeconomic policies and models. An attempt to reach a valid synthesis of approaches for Latin American-type economies is made in Cortazar (1986).
3. See Krugman and Taylor (1978) for a discussion of the likely effects of a devaluation in LDCs. Arellano (1986) presents a review of the subject from the perspective of Latin American countries.
4. The model groups participating are listed in Appendix Table A.10-1.
5. For work done along these lines see Adams and Klein (1987), who present simulations comparable to those studied here.
6. A review of different classes of econometric models for LDCs that could form the basis for several "prototypes" can be found in Nam (1987).
7. See Klein (1965) for example.

REFERENCES

Adams, F. G., and Lawrence Klein. (1987). "Performance of Quarterly Econometric Models of the United States: A New Round of Model Comparisons." becomes Chapter 2, this volume.

Arellano, J. P. (1986). "La Literatura Economica y Los Costos De Equilibrar La Balanza De Pagos En America Latina." In *Politicas Macroeconomicas: Una Perspectiva Latinoamericana,* R. Cortazar, ed. CIEPLAN.

Behrman, J., and J. Hanson (eds.). (1979). *Short Term Macroeconomic Policy in Latin America.* NBER.

Beltran del Rio, A. (1979). "Econometric Forecasting for Mexico: An Analysis of Errors in Prediction." In *Short Term Macroeconomic Policy in Latin America,* J. Behrman, and J. Hanson, eds. NBER.

Cortazar, R. (1986). *Politicas Macroeconomicas: Una Perspectiva Latinoamericana.* CIEPLAN.

Hickman, B. (1971). *Econometric Models of Cyclical Behavior,* 2 vols. New York: Columbia Univ. Press.

Klein, L. R. (1965). "What Kind of Macroeconometric Model for Developing Countries?," *Indian Economic Journal* XIII, 313–324.

Klein, L. R., and E. Burmeister. (1976). *Econometric Model Performance.* Univ. of Pennsylvania Press.

Kroch, E. (1987). "Forecasting Performance in LDC Models: Principles of Evaluation Applied to the Mexican Case." Mimeo, Univ. of Pennsylvania.

Krugman, P., and L. Taylor. (1978). "Contractionary Effects of Devaluation." *Journal of International Economics* 8, 445–456.

Nam, S. (1987). "Evaluation of Alternative Models for Developing Economies." Mimeo, World Bank.

Pauly, P. (1987). "Principles of Model Comparisons." Mimeo, Univ. of Pennsylvania.

Taylor, L. (1983). *Structuralist Macroeconomics.* New York: Basic Books.

Vial, J. (1986). "Applied Macroeconometric Models in Latin America." Working Paper, Universidad de Santiago, Chile.

Table A10.1. Increase in GC (1% GDP), with Sterilization[a]

Variable	Country	Group	Year						
			First	Second	Third	Fourth	Fifth	Sixth	Seventh
GDP	Brazil	Reis	3.05	1.61	1.56	1.57	1.55	1.54	*b
	Chile	Vial	1.09	1.24	0.96	0.74	0.65	0.55	0.42
	Hong Kong	Chou	1.14	0.87	0.64	0.51	0.44	0.41	0.38
	India	ESCAP	0.19	0.19	0.19	0.20	0.21	0.24	0.26
	India	Mahdur	0.00	0.24	0.36	0.41	0.44	*	*
	Korea	Han	0.65	0.68	0.62	0.89	1.01	1.42	1.83
	Mexico	CIEMEX	2.88	2.79	2.46	3.02	3.65	4.26	4.27
	Philippines	Mariano	0.04	0.11	0.20	0.25	0.30	0.35	0.39
	Taiwan	Yang	0.84	0.96	0.90	0.93	0.85	0.84	1.13
	Thailand	ESCAP	1.15	1.79	2.05	2.05	1.91	1.67	1.38
	Thailand	Ramangkura	0.00	0.13	0.12	0.12	0.12	0.12	0.11
	Venezuela	Palma	1.83	2.00	2.14	2.24	2.28	2.30	2.27
	Average		1.07	1.05	1.02	1.08	1.12	1.25	1.24
PDGDP	Brazil	Reis	*	*	*	*	*	*	*
	Chile	Vial	-0.19	-0.19	-0.06	0.12	0.33	0.55	0.78
	Hong Kong	Chou	0.20	0.19	0.19	0.19	0.18	0.17	0.16
	India	ESCAP	-0.03	-0.11	-0.16	-0.19	-0.20	-0.24	-0.26
	India	Mahdur	-0.01	-0.23	-0.36	-0.25	-0.33	*	*

	Country	Author							
	Korea	Han	−0.31	0.00	−0.22	−1.18	−0.97	−0.59	−0.75
	Mexico	CIEMEX	0.00	0.00	−1.58	−1.86	−0.10	0.05	1.82
	Philippines	Mariano	0.00	0.01	0.01	0.00	0.00	−0.01	−0.04
	Taiwan	Yang	0.02	−0.04	−0.04	−0.02	−0.01	0.00	−0.01
	Thailand	ESCAP	0.10	0.19	0.15	0.11	0.10	0.05	0.02
	Thailand	Ramangkura	0.00	0.91	0.86	0.90	0.95	0.91	0.89
	Venezuela	Palma	−0.01	−0.02	−0.03	−0.03	−0.04	−0.03	−0.03
	Average		−0.02	0.07	−0.11	−0.20	−0.01	0.09	0.26
TBPCA	Brazil	Reis	−3.14	−3.57	−4.33	−4.34	−4.38	−4.45	*
	Chile	Vial	−2.16	−3.10	−3.04	−2.75	−2.50	−2.38	−2.18
	Hong Kong	Chou	−0.47	−0.22	−0.28	−0.30	−0.31	−0.34	−0.35
	India	ESCAP	−13.06	−6.02	−7.17	−8.08	−8.88	−9.92	−10.70
	India	Mahdur	−0.00	−0.15	−0.37	−0.54	−0.66	*	*
	Korea	Han	−0.81	−0.70	−0.51	−0.48	−0.48	−0.60	−0.79
	Mexico	CIEMEX	−10.01	−7.18	−4.46	−5.47	−2.08	−1.51	−10.59
	Philippines	Mariano	−0.87	−1.74	−2.38	−2.85	−3.22	−3.60	−3.94
	Taiwan	Yang	−1.03	−0.92	−1.23	−0.78	−0.91	−0.74	−1.04
	Thailand	ESCAP	−1.08	−2.76	−3.59	−3.86	−3.71	−3.01	−2.30
	Thailand	Ramangkura	0.00	−1.47	−1.39	−1.40	−1.42	−1.37	−1.34
	Venezuela	Palma	−2.19	−15.09	−9.00	−10.93	−10.04	−9.98	−10.74
	Average		−2.90	−3.58	−3.15	−3.48	−3.22	−3.45	−4.40

[a]Country comparisons (percentage deviations from baseline solutions). The effects on the Current Account are computed as percentage of the level of imports in the baseline solution.

[b]* indicates that the simulation was not reported.

Table A10.2. Increase in GC (1% GDP), no Sterilization[a]

Variable	Country	Group	Year					
			First	Second	Third	Fourth	Fifth	Sixth
GDP	Brazil	Reis	4.52	2.74	2.71	2.88	2.97	3.03
	Chile	Vial	6.51	3.69	1.30	0.61	0.25	−0.22
	Hong Kong	Chou	1.14	0.87	0.64	0.51	0.44	0.41
	India	ESCAP	0.12	−0.09	−0.18	−0.20	−0.19	−0.18
	India	Mahdur	0.00	0.27	0.41	0.48	0.54	*
	Korea	Han	0.89	1.41	1.87	2.10	2.22	2.28
	Mexico	CIEMEX	3.07	3.03	3.03	3.14	3.02	3.19
	Philippines	Mariano	0.36	0.59	0.76	0.92	1.07	1.18
	Taiwan	Yang	0.83	0.83	0.84	0.84	0.93	0.93
	Thailand	ESCAP	1.15	1.79	2.05	2.05	1.91	1.67
	Thailand	Ramangkura	*b	*	*	*	*	*
	Venezuela	Palma	2.06	2.38	2.63	2.87	2.99	3.14
	Average		1.88	1.59	1.46	1.47	1.47	
PDGDP	Brazil	Reis	0.00	0.00	0.00	0.00	0.00	0.00
	Chile	Vial	13.65	19.22	20.27	21.56	23.56	26.14
	Hong Kong	Chou	0.20	0.19	0.19	0.19	0.18	0.17
	India	ESCAP	5.96	8.27	8.62	8.27	7.93	8.01
	India	Mahdur	−0.01	0.66	1.85	2.31	2.25	*
	Korea	Han	−0.31	0.00	−0.22	−0.27	−0.97	−0.59
	Mexico	CIEMEX	−0.31	0.51	0.79	2.17	2.40	6.54

	Philippines	Mariano	2.23	2.13	2.17	2.28	2.35	2.33
	Taiwan	Yang	0.38	0.43	0.43	0.42	0.41	0.41
	Thailand	ESCAP	0.10	0.19	0.15	0.11	0.10	0.05
	Thailand	Ramangkura	*	*	*	*	*	*
	Venezuela	Palma	−0.01	−0.03	−0.07	−0.11	−0.14	−0.18
	Average		2.19	3.16	3.42	3.69	3.81	4.29
TBPCA	Brazil	Reis	−5.96	−6.22	−7.56	−7.97	−8.35	−8.72
	Chile	Vial	−17.83	−16.28	−10.67	−7.34	−5.89	−4.94
	Hong Kong	Chou	−0.47	−0.22	−0.28	−0.30	−0.31	−0.34
	India	ESCAP	−13.06	−6.02	−7.17	−8.08	−8.88	−9.92
	India	Mahdur	0.00	−0.07	−0.10	−0.15	−0.24	*
	Korea	Han	−0.89	−1.13	−1.30	−1.24	−1.36	−1.38
	Mexico	CIEMEX	−10.77	−8.27	−6.11	−5.56	0.42	14.50
	Philippines	Mariano	−1.59	−2.37	−3.01	−3.55	−4.01	−4.42
	Taiwan	Yang	−0.97	−0.85	−0.79	−0.68	−0.89	−0.79
	Thailand	ESCAP	−1.08	−2.76	−3.59	−3.86	−3.71	−3.01
	Thailand	Ramangkura	*	*	*	*	*	*
	Venezuela	Palma	−2.86	−20.54	−12.40	−15.52	−14.35	−14.77
	Average		−5.04	−5.88	−4.82	−4.93	−4.32	−3.38

[a]Country comparisons (percentage deviations from baseline solutions). The effects on the Current Account are computed as percentage of the level of imports in the baseline solution.
[b]* indicates that the simulation was not reported.

Table A10.3. Increase in GINV (1% GDP), with Sterilization[a]

Variable	Country	Group	Year					
			First	Second	Third	Fourth	Fifth	Sixth
GDP	Brazil	Reis	*[b]	*	*	*	*	*
	Chile	Vial	1.21	0.85	0.27	−0.07	−0.20	−0.31
	Hong Kong	Chou	1.16	0.89	0.66	0.54	0.47	0.44
	India	ESCAP	0.19	0.18	0.17	0.17	0.18	0.19
	India	Mahdur	−0.00	0.24	0.42	0.51	0.55	*
	Korea	Han	0.67	0.60	0.27	0.32	0.20	0.46
	Mexico	CIEMEX	2.88	2.79	2.46	3.02	3.65	4.26
	Philippines	Mariano	0.78	1.09	1.55	1.86	2.08	2.27
	Taiwan	Yang	0.84	0.96	0.90	0.93	0.81	0.80
	Thailand	ESCAP	0.79	0.98	0.94	0.77	0.54	0.33
	Thailand	Ramangkura	0.00	0.03	0.33	0.32	0.32	0.32
	Venezuela	Palma	1.06	1.12	1.20	1.24	1.30	1.29
	Average		0.87	0.88	0.83	0.87	0.90	1.01
PDGDP	Brazil	Reis	*	*	*	*	*	*
	Chile	Vial	−0.15	−0.00	0.28	0.58	0.90	1.20
	Hong Kong	Chou	−0.08	−0.07	−0.06	−0.06	−0.06	−0.06
	India	ESCAP	−13.06	−5.04	−6.07	−6.91	−7.17	−7.73
	India	Mahdur	−0.01	−0.23	−0.36	−0.51	−0.57	*

Korea	Han	0.00	0.00	−0.22	0.09	0.16	0.29
Mexico	CIEMEX	0.00	0.00	−1.58	−1.86	−0.10	0.05
Philippines	Mariano	0.00	−0.01	−0.04	−0.10	−0.15	−0.20
Taiwan	Yang	0.02	−0.04	−0.04	−0.02	−0.01	0.00
Thailand	ESCAP	0.25	0.24	0.22	0.21	0.21	0.18
Thailand	Ramangkura	0.00	0.85	1.79	1.68	1.57	1.58
Venezuela	Palma	0.01	0.02	0.02	0.03	0.03	0.03
	Average	−1.18	−0.39	−0.55	−0.62	−0.47	−0.47
TBPCA							
Brazil	Reis	*	*	*	*	*	*
Chile	Vial	−2.42	−2.33	−1.46	−0.75	−0.38	−0.14
Hong Kong	Chou	−0.47	−0.22	−0.27	−0.30	−0.31	−0.34
India	ESCAP	−13.06	−6.02	−7.17	−8.08	−8.88	−9.92
India	Mahdur	−0.00	−0.15	−0.41	−0.64	−0.80	*
Korea	Han	−0.30	−0.32	−0.19	−0.20	−0.24	−0.49
Mexico	CIEMEX	−10.01	−7.18	−4.46	−5.47	−2.08	−1.51
Philippines	Mariano	−1.51	−2.35	−3.33	−4.09	−4.70	−5.32
Taiwan	Yang	−1.02	−0.92	−1.23	−0.78	−0.87	−0.71
Thailand	ESCAP	−0.97	−1.63	−1.51	−1.08	−0.50	0.08
Thailand	Ramangkura	0.00	−1.30	−3.00	−2.78	−2.60	−2.55
Venezuela	Palma	−2.65	−15.90	−8.99	−10.68	−10.01	−9.90
	Average	−2.95	−3.48	−2.91	−3.17	−2.85	−3.08

a Country comparisons (percentage deviations from baseline solutions). The effects on the Current Account are computed as percentage of the level of imports in the baseline solution.
b * indicates that the simulation was not reported.

Table A10.4. Increase in GINV (1% GDP), no Sterilization[a]

Variable	Country	Group	Year					
			First	Second	Third	Fourth	Fifth	Sixth
GDP	Brazil	Reis	*[b]	*	*	*	*	*
	Chile	Vial	6.63	3.28	0.62	−0.18	−0.58	−0.11
	Hong Kong	Chou	1.16	0.89	0.66	0.54	0.47	0.44
	India	ESCAP	0.12	−0.10	−0.18	−0.19	−0.17	−0.15
	India	Mahdur	0.00	0.27	0.48	0.58	0.65	*
	Korea	Han	0.92	1.36	1.60	1.62	1.52	1.38
	Mexico	CIEMEX	3.07	3.03	3.03	3.14	3.02	3.19
	Philippines	Mariano	1.12	1.52	2.16	2.56	2.91	3.20
	Taiwan	Yang	0.83	0.84	0.84	0.84	0.91	0.89
	Thailand	ESCAP	0.79	0.98	0.94	0.77	0.54	0.33
	Thailand	Ramangkura	*	*	*	*	*	*
	Venezuela	Palma	1.22	1.37	1.53	1.63	1.74	1.78
	Average		1.59	1.34	1.17	1.13	1.10	0.99
PDGDP	Brazil	Reis	*	*	*	*	*	*
	Chile	Vial	13.69	19.39	20.63	22.07	24.18	26.87
	Hong Kong	Chou	−0.08	−0.07	−0.06	−0.06	−0.06	−0.06
	India	ESCAP	5.96	7.82	7.71	7.10	6.45	6.19
	India	Mahdur	−0.01	0.66	1.85	2.31	2.25	*

		1	2	3	4	5	6
Korea	Han	0.00	-0.13	0.11	0.27	0.49	0.81
Mexico	CIEMEX	-0.31	0.51	0.79	2.17	2.40	6.54
Philippines	Mariano	2.46	1.85	2.44	2.59	2.72	2.73
Taiwan	Yang	0.38	0.43	0.48	0.42	0.41	0.41
Thailand	ESCAP	0.25	0.24	0.22	0.21	0.21	0.18
Thailand	Ramangkura	*	*	*	*	*	*
Venezuela	Palma	0.01	0.02	0.01	-0.00	-0.02	-0.04
	Average	2.24	3.07	3.42	3.71	3.90	4.85
TBPCA							
Brazil	Reis	*	*	*	*	*	*
Chile	Vial	-18.09	-15.44	-9.03	-5.31	-3.75	-2.68
Hong Kong	Chou	-0.47	-0.22	-0.27	-0.30	-0.31	-0.34
India	ESCAP	-13.06	-5.04	-6.07	-6.91	-7.17	-7.73
India	Mahdur	-0.01	0.66	1.85	2.31	2.25	*
Korea	Han	-0.44	-0.81	-1.07	-1.08	-1.24	-1.31
Mexico	CIEMEX	-10.77	-8.27	-6.11	-5.56	0.42	14.50
Philippines	Mariano	-2.27	-2.92	-4.06	-4.85	-5.57	-6.26
Taiwan	Yang	-0.96	-0.83	-1.16	-0.68	-0.88	-0.76
Thailand	ESCAP	-0.97	-1.63	-1.51	-1.08	-0.50	0.08
Thailand	Ramangkura	*	*	*	*	*	*
Venezuela	Palma	-3.13	-19.53	-11.27	-13.55	-12.74	-12.74
	Average	-5.02	-5.40	-3.87	-3.70	-2.95	-1.92

[a]Country comparisons (percentage deviations from baseline solutions). The effects on the Current Account are computed as percentage of the level of imports in the baseline solution.

[b]* indicates that the simulation was not reported.

Table A10.5. 10% Devaluation[a]

Variable	Country	Group	Year					
			First	Second	Third	Fourth	Fifth	Sixth
GDP	Brazil	Reis	2.75	1.36	1.36	1.36	1.36	1.36
	Chile	Vial	0.78	−0.13	−0.55	−0.37	−0.16	−0.01
	Hong Kong	Chou	2.83	2.42	2.09	1.85	1.69	1.62
	India	ESCAP	0.00	0.00	0.00	0.00	0.00	0.00
	India	Mahdur	*[b]	*	*	*	*	*
	Korea	Han	0.05	0.58	0.86	1.21	1.19	1.63
	Mexico	CIEMEX	−0.83	−0.42	−0.16	−0.22	1.08	1.60
	Philippines	Mariano	−0.38	−0.74	−0.93	−1.07	−1.14	−1.22
	Taiwan	Yang	3.12	2.77	2.14	1.75	1.76	1.55
	Thailand	ESCAP	0.54	1.29	1.83	2.40	2.96	3.52
	Thailand	Ramangkura	0.00	−0.33	−0.23	−0.20	−0.18	−0.21
	Venezuela	Palma	0.70	−0.07	−0.62	−1.08	−1.36	−1.83
	Average		0.87	0.61	0.53	0.51	0.65	0.73
PDGDP	Brazil	Reis	*	*	*	*	*	*
	Chile	Vial	5.09	5.92	5.53	5.11	4.73	4.37
	Hong Kong	Chou	0.00	0.00	0.00	0.00	0.00	0.00
	India	ESCAP	0.00	0.00	0.00	0.00	0.00	0.00
	India	Mahdur	*	*	*	*	*	*

Korea	Han	1.25	0.00	0.87	0.63	0.65	0.88
Mexico	CIEMEX	3.66	5.08	6.10	7.44	13.45	8.14
Philippines	Mariano	7.38	6.57	6.69	6.60	6.68	6.83
Taiwan	Yang	0.04	-0.04	-0.04	-0.02	-0.01	0.00
Thailand	ESCAP	3.02	4.51	4.90	5.15	5.38	5.24
Thailand	Ramangkura	0.00	-1.64	-1.54	-1.24	-1.14	-1.58
Venezuela	Palma	0.67	1.53	2.49	3.41	4.21	4.90
	Average	2.11	2.19	2.50	2.71	3.40	2.88
TBPCA							
Brazil	Reis	-0.67	-0.69	-0.12	0.30	0.70	1.01
Chile	Vial	-1.48	2.11	2.37	2.34	1.90	1.48
Hong Kong	Chou	-6.06	2.00	-1.91	2.77	-2.31	3.46
India	ESCAP	0.00	0.00	0.00	0.00	0.00	0.00
India	Mahdur	*	*	*	*	*	*
Korea	Han	4.30	6.51	6.49	6.02	6.27	6.12
Mexico	CIEMEX	22.38	17.96	13.28	12.54	11.07	27.84
Philippines	Mariano	0.69	0.84	0.89	0.95	0.99	1.01
Taiwan	Yang	5.34	3.99	2.54	1.93	1.69	1.43
Thailand	ESCAP	4.66	6.39	5.14	4.68	4.05	3.67
Thailand	Ramangkura	0.00	8.19	6.93	5.88	5.28	5.45
Venezuela	Palma	8.77	33.91	21.26	23.30	21.20	21.54
	Average	3.45	7.38	5.17	5.52	4.62	6.64

[a]Country comparisons (percentage deviations from baseline solutions). The effects on the Current Account are computed as percentage of the level of imports in the baseline solution.
[b]* indicates that the simulation was not reported.

Table A10.6. 10% Devaluation and 10% Increase in $M_I{}^a$

Variable	Country	Group	Year						
			First	Second	Third	Fourth	Fifth	Sixth	Seventh
GDP	Brazil	Reis	3.37	1.07	1.31	1.37	1.49	1.61	*[b]
	Chile	Vial	3.46	1.41	−0.21	−0.42	−0.37	−0.45	−0.70
	Hong Kong	Chou	2.83	2.42	2.09	1.85	1.69	1.62	1.50
	India	ESCAP	−0.11	−0.43	−0.57	−0.60	−0.59	−0.59	−0.60
	India	Mahdur	*	*	*	*	*	*	*
	Korea	Han	0.32	1.51	2.78	3.49	3.72	3.67	3.69
	Mexico	CIEMEX	−0.33	0.15	0.30	−0.01	0.93	1.37	0.98
	Philippines	Mariano	−0.05	−0.24	−0.29	−0.34	−0.36	−0.38	−0.41
	Taiwan	Yang	3.12	2.64	2.06	1.74	1.70	1.57	1.78
	Thailand	ESCAP	0.54	1.29	1.83	2.40	2.96	3.52	4.13
	Thailand	Ramangkura	*	*	*	*	*	*	*
	Venezuela	Palma	0.78	0.06	−0.44	−0.85	−1.08	−1.50	−1.68
	Average		1.39	0.99	0.89	0.86	1.01	1.04	0.97
PDGDP	Brazil	Reis	*	*	*	*	*	*	*
	Chile	Vial	11.86	15.61	15.75	15.81	16.16	16.75	17.57
	Hong Kong	Chou	0.00	0.00	0.00	0.00	0.00	0.00	0.00
	India	ESCAP	10.07	13.82	14.29	13.53	12.55	11.74	11.20
	India	Mahdur	*	*	*	*	*	*	*

	Korea	Han	−0.31	0.00	0.87	0.63	1.46	1.62	2.65
	Mexico	CIEMEX	3.35	5.84	7.09	9.15	16.62	11.93	10.61
	Philippines	Mariano	9.67	8.85	9.13	9.04	9.05	9.09	9.13
	Taiwan	Yang	0.39	0.44	0.40	0.42	0.41	0.41	0.37
	Thailand	ESCAP	3.02	4.51	4.90	5.15	5.38	5.24	5.26
	Thailand	Ramangkura	*	*	*	*	*	*	*
	Venezuela	Palma	0.66	1.51	2.45	3.36	4.13	4.81	5.40
	Average		4.30	5.62	6.10	6.34	7.31	6.84	6.91
TBPCA	Brazil	Reis	−1.85	−0.29	0.02	0.30	0.39	0.37	*
	Chile	Vial	−9.15	−4.89	−1.87	−0.23	0.11	0.31	0.70
	Hong Kong	Chou	−6.06	2.00	−1.91	2.77	−2.31	3.46	−2.96
	India	ESCAP	0.00	0.00	0.00	0.00	0.00	0.00	0.00
	India	Mahdur	*	*	*	*	*	*	*
	Korea	Han	4.15	6.02	5.33	4.63	4.60	4.52	4.22
	Mexico	CIEMEX	18.12	15.04	11.80	11.91	11.90	32.02	38.13
	Philippines	Mariano	−0.05	0.15	0.12	0.15	0.18	0.18	0.19
	Taiwan	Yang	5.28	4.29	2.64	1.88	1.72	1.43	1.25
	Thailand	ESCAP	4.66	6.39	5.14	4.68	4.05	3.67	3.78
	Thailand	Ramangkura	*	*	*	*	*	*	*
	Venezuela	Palma	8.55	32.11	20.08	21.72	19.56	19.74	22.75
	Average		2.37	6.08	4.14	4.78	4.02	6.57	7.56

[a]Country comparisons (percentage deviations from baseline solutions). The effects on the Current Account are computed as percentage of the level of imports in the baseline solution.
[b]* indicates that the simulation was not reported.

Table A10.7. 10% Increase in M_1 [a]

Variable	Country	Group	Year					
			First	Second	Third	Fourth	Fifth	Sixth
GDP	Brazil	Reis	2.84	1.45	1.45	1.45	1.45	1.45
	Chile	Vial	2.92	1.52	0.26	−0.14	−0.28	−0.51
	Hong Kong	Chou	0.00	0.00	0.00	0.00	0.00	0.00
	India	ESCAP	−0.11	−0.43	−0.57	−0.60	−0.59	−0.59
	India	Mahdur	0.00	0.23	0.17	0.39	0.32	*[b]
	Korea	Han	0.38	0.96	0.94	0.80	0.66	0.48
	Mexico	CIEMEX	−0.13	−0.04	−0.05	−0.05	0.01	0.15
	Philippines	Mariano	0.35	0.52	0.67	0.76	0.82	0.87
	Taiwan	Yang	0.01	0.01	0.01	0.01	0.01	−0.17
	Thailand	ESCAP	0.00	0.00	0.00	0.00	0.00	0.00
	Thailand	Ramangkura	*	*	*	*	*	*
	Venezuela	Palma	0.37	0.63	0.84	0.99	1.10	1.21
	Average		0.60	0.44	0.34	0.33	0.32	0.26
PDGDP	Brazil	Reis	*	*	*	*	*	*
	Chile	Vial	6.93	9.71	10.21	10.67	11.39	12.32
	Hong Kong	Chou	0.00	0.00	0.00	0.00	0.00	0.00
	India	ESCAP	10.07	13.82	14.29	13.53	12.55	11.74
	India	Mahdur	−0.01	6.27	9.58	9.24	10.01	*

Korea	Han	−0.31	0.00	−0.22	−0.27	0.65	0.15
Mexico	CIEMEX	0.00	0.51	0.59	1.24	2.11	2.75
Philippines	Mariano	2.29	2.29	2.45	2.45	2.37	2.25
Taiwan	Yang	0.38	0.42	0.43	0.42	0.41	0.41
Thailand	ESCAP	0.00	0.00	0.00	0.00	0.00	0.00
Thailand	Ramangkura	*	*	*	*	*	*
Venezuela	Palma	−0.02	−0.08	−0.15	−0.22	−0.29	−0.35
	Average	1.93	3.29	3.72	3.71	3.92	3.25
TBPCA							
Brazil	Reis	−2.74	−3.21	−3.99	−4.01	−4.08	−4.17
Chile	Vial	−3.59	−2.30	−1.77	−1.56	−1.52	−1.82
Hong Kong	Chou	0.00	0.00	0.00	0.00	0.00	0.00
India	ESCAP	0.00	0.00	0.00	0.00	0.00	0.00
India	Mahdur	0.00	0.59	1.32	1.50	1.56	*
Korea	Han	−0.15	−0.59	−0.65	−0.52	−0.52	−0.52
Mexico	CIEMEX	0.63	0.17	0.27	0.00	−0.07	0.35
Philippines	Mariano	−0.79	−0.71	−0.81	−0.84	−0.86	−0.88
Taiwan	Yang	−0.01	0.05	−0.00	−0.01	−0.01	0.12
Thailand	ESCAP	0.00	0.00	0.00	0.00	0.00	0.00
Thailand	Ramangkura	*	*	*	*	*	*
Venezuela	Palma	−1.04	−9.03	−5.87	−7.35	−6.88	−7.12
	Average	−0.70	−1.37	−1.05	−1.16	−1.13	−1.40

[a] Country comparisons (percentage deviations from baseline solutions). The effects on the Current Account are computed as percentage of the level of imports in the baseline solution.
[b] * indicates that the simulation was not reported.

Table A10.8. Point Increase in LIBOR[a]

Variable	Country	Group	Year					
			First	Second	Third	Fourth	Fifth	Sixth
GDP	Brazil	Reis	1.33	-0.07	-0.12	-0.15	-0.19	-0.23
	Chile	Vial	-0.48	-0.94	-0.60	-0.25	-0.17	0.00
	Hong Kong	Chou	0.00	0.00	0.00	0.00	0.00	0.00
	India	ESCAP	*b	*	*	*	*	*
	India	Mahdur	*	*	*	*	*	*
	Korea	Han	-0.08	-0.35	-0.59	-0.62	-0.64	-0.61
	Mexico	CIEMEX	-0.13	-0.07	-0.12	-0.12	-0.10	-0.08
	Philippines	Mariano	-0.03	-0.06	-0.08	-0.08	-0.07	-0.07
	Taiwan	Yang	-0.00	0.13	0.08	0.10	-0.06	-0.08
	Thailand	ESCAP	0.01	-0.02	-0.06	-0.08	-0.09	-0.08
	Thailand	Ramangkura	*	*	*	*	*	*
	Venezuela	Palma	-1.21	-1.19	-1.50	-1.57	-1.81	-1.91
	Average		-0.07	-0.29	-0.33	-0.31	-0.35	-0.34
PDGDP	Brazil	Reis	*	*	*	*	*	*
	Chile	Vial	-0.01	-0.22	-0.54	-0.89	-1.32	-1.79
	Hong Kong	Chou	0.00	0.00	0.00	0.00	0.00	0.00
	India	ESCAP	*	*	*	*	*	*
	India	Mahdur	*	*	*	*	*	*

	Korea	Han	−0.31	0.00	−0.22	−0.27	−0.16	−0.59
	Mexico	CIEMEX	0.00	0.00	−0.20	0.16	0.10	0.90
	Philippines	Mariano	0.12	0.19	0.35	0.41	0.47	0.48
	Taiwan	Yang	0.04	−0.04	−0.04	−0.02	−0.01	0.00
	Thailand	ESCAP	−0.00	0.00	0.00	0.00	0.01	0.01
	Thailand	Ramangkura	*	*	*	*	*	*
	Venezuela	Palma	0.03	0.08	0.11	0.15	0.17	0.20
	Average		−0.02	0.00	−0.07	−0.06	−0.09	−0.10
TBPCA	Brazil	Reis	−5.02	−5.10	−7.45	−7.80	−8.35	−8.88
	Chile	Vial	−8.24	−7.27	−4.09	−2.35	−1.57	−0.95
	Hong Kong	Chou	0.00	0.00	0.00	0.00	0.00	0.00
	India	ESCAP	*	*	*	*	*	*
	India	Mahdur	*	*	*	*	*	*
	Korea	Han	−8.81	−6.24	−5.24	−4.39	−4.32	−3.96
	Mexico	CIEMEX	−3.55	−2.92	−2.18	−2.55	−5.54	−8.93
	Philippines	Mariano	−1.81	−1.90	−1.64	−1.31	−1.11	−0.99
	Taiwan	Yang	0.09	−0.01	−0.41	−0.09	−0.04	0.04
	Thailand	ESCAP	−0.03	0.08	0.21	0.30	0.32	0.28
	Thailand	Ramangkura	*	*	*	*	*	*
	Venezuela	Palma	−3.42	−13.70	−5.22	−3.35	−1.28	−0.05
	Average		−3.42	−4.12	−2.89	−2.39	−2.43	−2.60

[a]Country comparisons (percentage deviations from baseline solutions). The effects on the Current Account are computed as percentage of the level of imports in the baseline solution.
[b]* indicates that the simulation was not reported.

EXTERNAL REVIEWS

CHAPTER 11

A New Round of U.S. Model Comparisons: A Limited Appraisal

IGNAZIO VISCO

A first round of U.S. econometric model comparisons took place almost 15 years ago, just before the rational expectations attack on traditional macroeconometric models. Commenting on those model comparisons, Carl Christ (1975, p. 54) observed:

> though the models forecast well over horizons of four to six quarters, they disagree so strongly about the effects of important monetary and fiscal policies that they cannot be considered reliable guides to such policy effects, until it can be determined which of them are wrong in this respect and which (if any) are right.

This new round of comparisons seems to suggest that U.S. models still disagree strongly about the effects of these policies. As Adams and Klein (this volume) observe:

> There is a considerable, one might say astonishing, variation in the performance of the models considering that they were estimated over approximately the same time period and are largely, but not wholly, intended for the same purposes.

Some of the differences in the multipliers reported by Adams and Klein may be the result of basic theoretical differences. The FRB St. Louis model, for example, was intentionally built as a "monetarist" model and the Taylor model, even if similar in structure to more traditional models, is estimated and solved under the rational expectations assumption.

The differences may also be the result of the absence of standardization of the conditions under which models are simulated. The decision to "let the models be models" (Adams and Klein, this volume) implies, among other things, that differences in handling particular variables, considering them as endogenous or exogenous in the simulation exercises, may matter greatly. This is especially so for variables related to international transactions, but it also applies, in some instances, to subsectors of the domestic economy (for example, the farm sector) and it may help to explain why the average multipliers reported in this new round of comparisons cannot be properly considered "consensus" multipliers, given their large variation, while an average of different forecasts is often regarded as a "consensus" forecast.[1]

Clearly, an investigation should also be made to see whether any of the differences can be attributed to substantial divergences in the model specifications and parameter estimates. In principle, carefully designed partial simulations could be used to identify *where* the models differ with satisfactory precision. An attempt in this direction, which also reveals the relative importance of the lack of standardization previously mentioned, is that conducted by Brinner and Hirsch (this volume) with respect to the two models for which they are responsible. In general, a prerequisite for conducting such exercises is thorough knowledge of the models involved. Not only is a high degree of reliability and carefulness needed in designing and carrying out model comparisons, but, just as in the case of building a new model, teamwork is also necessary. A systematic and successful comparison of models of the U.K. economy has been conducted at the University of Warwick over the last 5 years under the direction of Professor Kenneth Wallis.[2]

This chapter is a much more modest contribution to the search for differences in model specifications and estimates. Four models will be considered among those that have participated in the new round of comparisons. Starting from the estimated equations, I shall rely as much as I can on these estimates in seeking to obtain particular forms that might allow comparisons among the different models. These are the fairly small FAIR and TAYLOR models and the relatively large models of the Federal Reserve Board (usually known as the MPS model) and of the University of Michigan (often referred to as MQEM).[3]

Rather than concentrating on the theoretical underpinnings of the model equations, the objective here is to derive "partial" reduced forms that can be easily compared and used to shed light on the different response characteristics of these models. In what follows (1) the price–wage sectors are considered and equations are derived that relate final price deflators to the level of demand; (2) the money demand equations of the four models are considered and the basic properties of the implicit LM curves are extracted from them; (3) the question of how differences in full-model multipliers may be related to basic differences in model structures is briefly examined; the role of the "demand side" is also considered; and (4) a few remarks on the results of this chapter and on the more general issue of model comparisons are advanced.

THE PRICE–WAGE SECTOR

The four models considered in this chapter all have one basic wage and one basic price equation. The MPS and MQEM wage equations belong to the family of "expectations augmented" Phillips curves. The specification is in the form of rates of change so that the rate of change of nominal wages is, in essence, a function of current and past rates of inflation and a demand pressure variable, generally expressed as the deviation of an actual from a potential level that is exogenous or very slowly adapting over time. In FAIR, the wage equation is specified in (logarithmic) level form. The nominal wage is a function of current and lagged values of the price level and a time trend. According to the author, this equation "is best thought of as a real wage equation, where the nominal wage rate adjusts to the price level with a lag" (Fair, 1988, p. 2.4). In TAYLOR, the wage equation is also specified in level form. In contrast with the FAIR model, however, the nominal wage rate is a function of past and future expected wage rates and deviations of past and future expected total demand from a deterministic trend. The specification is based on Taylor's well-known staggered contract model (see Taylor, 1980).

The price equations of the four models refer to value-added (or final sales) deflators and are all specified as functions of current and past cost variables and a term that captures the effect of demand pressures. Except for the MQEM equation, which is estimated in first logarithmic differences, the specification is in level form.[4]

MPS

The two main behavioral equations refer to the growth rate of employee compensation per hour in the nonfarm business sector and the nonfarm business deflator excluding energy and net of indirect business taxes. Using the lag operator L and with log approximations, we have[5]

Wage Rate

$$w_t = w_{t-1} + A(L)(p_t^c - p_{t-1}^c) - 0.207u_t^c + \text{other} \tag{2.1}$$

where w = log of employee compensation per hour in the non-farm business sector,

p^c = log of the implicit deflator of consumption,

u^c = civilian unemployment rate (fraction),

and $A(1) = 1$.

Price Level

$$p_t = B(L)w_t + C(L)f(u_t, y_t, y_t^T) + E(L)(p_t^{MN} - p_t^c) + \text{other} \tag{2.2}$$

where p = log of nonfarm business deflator excluding energy and net of indirect business taxes,

u = unemployment rate of total labor force (fraction),

y = log of nonfarm business output, 1982 \$,

y^T = log of production capacity for nonfarm business output,

p^{MN} = log of nonpetroleum merchandise imports deflator,

$f(u, y, y^T) = 0.01[u(y^T - y)]^{-1/2}$,

and $B(1) = 1$, $C(1) = 0.522$, $E(1) = 0.071$.[6]

Using the results reported in Table 3 of Brayton and Mauskopf (1985) for a previous version of the MPS model, we obtain the following relation between u^c and y:

$$u_t^c = -D(L)y_t + \text{other} \tag{2.3}$$

with $D(1) = 0.34$. Furthermore, linearizing around $u = 0.075$ and $y^T - y = 0.22$ (the average values over the simulation period 1975–1984), considering that $u \simeq 0.98u^c$ and using (2.3), we have

$$f(u_t, y_t, y_t^T) \simeq [0.5D(L) + 0.2]y_t + \text{other} \tag{2.4}$$

where y^T is assumed to be exogenous in view of the fact that in the model it is linked to y through an extremely long and slow distributed lag.

Finally, in the model demand deflators are related to value added and import deflators by means of a complex allocation process. Going through this process and considering all the possible endogeneities,[7] one basically ends up with the following approximations:

$$p_t^c \simeq 0.846 p_t^x + 0.115 p_t^M + 0.039 w_t \tag{2.5}$$

$$p_t^M \simeq 0.53 p_t^{MN} + 0.13 p_t^{MS} + \text{other} \tag{2.6}$$

$$p_t^{MN} \simeq M(L) p_t^x + \text{other} \tag{2.7}$$

$$p_t^{MS} \simeq 0.301 p_t^x + \text{other} \tag{2.8}$$

$$p_t^x \simeq 0.93 p_t + \text{other} \tag{2.9}$$

where p_t^x = log of the nonfarm business deflator,

p_t^M = log of the import deflator,

p_t^{MS} = log of the import services deflator,

and $M(1) = 0.320$.

The coefficients of the polynomials $A(L)$, $B(L)$, $C(L)$, $D(L)$, $E(L)$, and $M(L)$ are reported in Table 11.1. From Eqs. (2.5) to (2.9) we obtain

$$p_t^c = [0.791 + 0.057 M(L)] p_t + 0.039 w_t + \text{other} \tag{2.10}$$

Substituting (2.4) and (2.7) in (2.2) we get

$$\begin{aligned} p_t = \; & B(L) w_t + C(L)[0.5D(L) + 0.2] y_t \\ & + 0.93 E(L) M(L) p_t - E(L) p_t^c + \text{other} \end{aligned} \tag{2.11}$$

Table 11.1. MPS: Prices and Wages, Single Equation Lag Structures

Lag	A(L)	B(L)	C(L)	D(L)	E(L)	M(L)
0		0.237	0.116	0.160	0.019	0.034
1	0.215	0.202	0.222	0.080	0.029	0.057
2	0.172	0.168	0.184	0.010	0.022	0.069
3	0.137	0.136		0.010		0.069
4	0.110	0.106		0.010		0.057
5	0.088	0.077		0.010		0.034
6	0.070	0.050		0.010		
7	0.056	0.024		0.010		
8	0.045			0.005		
9	0.036			0.005		
10	0.029			0.005		
11	0.023			0.005		
12	0.018			0.005		
13				0.005		
14				0.005		
15				0.005		

Table 11.2. MPS: Prices and Wages, Final Lag Structures

Lag	$H(L)$	$K(L)$	$H*(L)$	$K*(L)$
0	0.025	0.033	0.017	0.040
1	0.055	0.036	0.048	0.044
2	0.086	0.003	0.081	0.004
3	0.093	-0.033	0.089	-0.042
4	0.093	0.001	0.091	0.001
5	0.088	0.005	0.088	0.006
6	0.080	0.004	0.080	0.005
7	0.069	0.003	0.070	0.004
8	0.056	0.001	0.057	0.002
9	0.045	0.001	0.047	0.001
10	0.036	0.001	0.038	0.001
11	0.029	0.001	0.031	0.001
12	0.020	0.001	0.022	0.001
13	0.014	0.001	0.016	0.001
14	0.009	0.001	0.011	0.001
15	0.006	0.001	0.007	0.001
16	0.003	0.000	0.004	0.001
17	0.002	0.000	0.002	0.000
18	0.001	0.000	0.001	0.000
19	0.000	0.000	0.001	0.000

Using (2.3) and substituting (2.1) in (2.10) and in (2.11) and solving for p^c and p, we then obtain

$$p_t^c = p_{t-1}^c + H(L)(p_{t-1}^c - p_{t-2}^c) + K(L)y_t + \text{other} \tag{2.12}$$

and

$$p_t = p_{t-1} + H*(L)(p_{t-1} - p_{t-2}) + K*(L)y_t + \text{other} \tag{2.13}$$

The coefficients of the polynomials $H(L)$, $K(L)$, $H*(L)$, and $K*(L)$ are reported, for significant lags, in Table 11.2. We have, in particular, that $H(1) = 0.810$, $K(1) = 0.060$, $H*(1) = 0.802$, and $K*(1) = 0.074$. The total effects of a 1% change in output on the rates of change in the two deflators are then equal to $K(1)/[1-H(1)]$ = 0.316 and $K*(1)/[1-H*(1)] = 0.372$.

MQEM

The two basic wage and price equations are as follows:

Wage Rate

$$w_t = w_{t-1} + A(L)(p_t^c - p_{t-1}^c) - 0.043g(u_t, y_t, y_t^T) + \text{other} \tag{2.14}$$

where w = log of compensation per man hour in the private nonfarm sector,

p^c = log of the implicit deflator of personal consumption expenditure,

u = unemployment rate, males over 20 (fraction),

y = log of manufacturing index of industrial production,

y^T = log of index of available capacity in manufacturing,[8]

and $A(1) = 0.74$.

The demand pressure variable in (2.14) can be written as

$$g(u_t, y_t, y_t^T) = (2/3)u_{t-1} + (1/3)(y_{t-1}^T - y_{t-1}) + \text{other} \tag{2.15}$$

Price Level

$$p_t = p_{t-1} + B(L)(w_t - w_{t-1}) + E(L)h(y_t, y_t^T) + \text{other} \tag{2.16}$$

where p = log of private nonfarm GNP implicit deflator,

$h(y, y^T) = 0.01\,(y^T - y)^{-1}$,

and $B(1) = 0.644$, $E(1) = 0.062$.[9]

$h(y, y^T)$ is a highly nonlinear function of used capacity. Linearizing around $y^T - y = 0.22$ (its average value over the simulation period) we have

$$h(y_t, y_t^T) \simeq 0.2y_t + \text{other} \tag{2.17}$$

Output and import prices are allocated to various demand deflators by means of a number of estimated equations specified as geometric adjustment functions in the rates of change. In particular, there are five equations for the consumer expenditure categories from which the aggregate deflator is obtained. The farm output deflator, energy prices, and import prices[10] are basically exogenous. We start then with five dynamic equations in p. The lags are very short; long-run elasticities range between 0.44 and 0.94. In the case of nondurables we have an elasticity of 0.58; in the case of services, even allowing for a wage effect, the long-run elasticity is 0.56. Aggregating on the basis of the 1982 figures, we get

$$p_t^c = p_{t-1}^c + C(L)(p_t - p_{t-1}) + \text{other} \tag{2.18}$$

with $C(1) = 0.518$.[11]

Working through the productivity and employment equations present in the model and linearizing we also have

$$u_t \simeq -D(L)y_t + \text{other} \tag{2.19}$$

with $D(1) = 0.549$.

The coefficients of the polynomials $A(L)$, $B(L)$, $C(L)$, $D(L)$, and $E(L)$ are reported in Table 11.3. Solving the previous equations we finally obtain

$$p_t^c = p_{t-1}^c + H(L)(p_{t-1}^c - p_{t-2}^c) + K(L)y_t + \text{other} \tag{2.20}$$

and

$$p_t = p_{t-1} + H(L)(p_{t-1} - p_{t-2}) + K^*(L)y_t + \text{other} \tag{2.21}$$

The coefficients of the polynomials $H(L)$, $K(L)$, and $M(L)$ are reported, for significant lags, in Table 11.4. We have, in particular, $H(1) = 0.247$, $K(1) = 0.017$, $K^*(1) = 0.032$, $K(1)/[1-H(1)] = 0.022$, $K^*(1)/[1-H(1)] = 0.043$.

Table 11.3. MQEM: Prices and Wages, Single Equation Lag Structures

Lag	A(L)	B(L)	C(L)	D(L)	E(L)
0			0.249	0.250	
1	0.224	0.161	0.116	0.198	
2	0.224	0.161	0.042	0.101	
3	0.070	0.161	0.023		
4	0.056	0.161	0.018		
5	0.045		0.015		0.037
6	0.036		0.011		0.025
7	0.029		0.009		
8	0.023		0.007		
9	0.018		0.006		
10	0.015		0.005		
11			0.004		
12			0.003		
13			0.002		
14			0.002		
15			0.001		
16			0.001		
17			0.001		
18			0.001		

Table 11.4. MQEM: Prices and Wages, Final Lag Structures

Lag	H(L)	K(L)	K*(L)
0			
1	0.009	0.001	0.003
2	0.022	0.001	0.004
3	0.031	0.002	0.005
4	0.037	0.004	0.013
5	0.032	0.003	0.006
6	0.023	0.002	0.000
7	0.018	0.001	
8	0.015	0.001	
9	0.013	0.000	
10	0.011	0.000	
11	0.009	0.000	
12	0.007	0.000	
13	0.005	0.000	
14	0.003	0.000	
15	0.003	0.000	
16	0.002	0.000	
17	0.002	0.000	
18	0.001	0.000	
19	0.001	0.000	
20	0.001	0.000	
21	0.001	0.000	

FAIR

The two wage and price equations refer to the "firm" (nonfinancial corporate business) sector. The price variable is essentially the deflator of total sales (output less change of inventories) net of farm gross output. The wage rate refers to average hourly earnings in the whole private sector.

Wage Rate

$$w_t = A(L)p_t^s + \text{other} \tag{2.22}$$

where w = log of average hourly earnings, excluding overtime, of workers in the firm sector,

p^s = log of the price deflator of total sales of the firm sector,

and $A(1) = 0.45$. $A(L)$ is an infinite polynomial operator. In particular,

$$A(L) = (0.486 - 0.208L - 0.251L^2)/(1 - 0.940L)$$

Price Level

$$p_t = B(L)w_t + C(L)(y_t - y_t^T) + \text{other} \tag{2.23}$$

where p = log of the price deflator of total sales of the nonfarm business sector,

y = log of production in the firm sector, 1982 \$,

y^T = log of potential output in the firm sector,

and $B(1) = 0.416$, $C(1) = 0.421$.[12] $B(L)$ and $C(L)$ are infinite polynomials. In particular,

$$B(L) = 0.0449/(1 - 0.892L), \qquad C(L) = 0.0455/(1 - 0.892L)$$

The coefficients of $A(L)$, $B(L)$, and $C(L)$ are reported, for the first 20 lags, in Table 11.5.

The price deflator of total sales is obtained aggregating the deflators of total sales of the nonfarm, nonfinancial corporate business sector and of farm gross product, which is exogenous. A geometric average approximation gives

$$p_t^s \simeq \alpha p_t + \text{other} \tag{2.24}$$

with α historically equal to about 0.97.

The previous equations can then be solved to obtain

$$p_t^s = H(L)p_{t-1}^s + K(L)y_t + \text{other} \tag{2.25}$$

and

$$p_t = H(L)p_{t-1} + K^*(L)y_t + \text{other} \tag{2.26}$$

The coefficients of polynomials $H(L)$ and $K(L)$ are also reported, for the first 20 lags, in Table 11.5. Observe that $K^*(L) = K(L)/\alpha$. We have, in particular, $H(1) = 0.164$, $K(1) = 0.418$, $K^*(1) = 0.431$, $K(1)/[1 - H(1)] = 0.500$, and $K^*(1)/[1 - H(1)] = 0.515$.

Table 11.5. FAIR: Prices and Wages, Single Equation and Final Lag Structures

Lag	A(L)	B(L)	C(L)	H(L)	K(L)
0	0.486	0.045	0.046	0.030	0.045
1	0.249	0.040	0.041	0.026	0.040
2	−0.017	0.036	0.036	0.023	0.036
3	−0.016	0.032	0.032	0.020	0.032
4	−0.015	0.028	0.029	0.017	0.029
5	−0.014	0.025	0.026	0.014	0.025
6	−0.013	0.023	0.023	0.012	0.023
7	−0.013	0.020	0.020	0.010	0.020
8	−0.012	0.018	0.018	0.009	0.018
9	−0.011	0.016	0.016	0.007	0.016
10	−0.010	0.014	0.015	0.006	0.014
11	−0.010	0.013	0.013	0.005	0.013
12	−0.009	0.011	0.012	0.004	0.011
13	−0.009	0.010	0.010	0.003	0.010
14	−0.008	0.009	0.009	0.003	0.009
15	−0.008	0.008	0.008	0.002	0.008
16	−0.007	0.007	0.007	0.002	0.007
17	−0.007	0.006	0.007	0.001	0.006
18	−0.006	0.006	0.006	0.001	0.006
19	−0.006	0.005	0.005	0.000	0.005

TAYLOR

The wage equation in Taylor's model is based on his staggered contract model with forward looking rational expectations. The price equation looks like a standard mark-up equation. We have the following.

Wage Rate

$$w_t = \sum_{i=-3}^{3} \alpha_i[w_{t+i} + \beta(y_{t+i} - y_{t+i}^{\mathrm{T}})] \qquad (2.27)$$

where w = log of average hourly earnings index, adjusted for overtime and interindustry shifts, nonfarm sector,

y = log of GNP, 1982 \$,

y^{T} = log of interpolated linear trend of y_t,

and $\alpha_0 = 0.262$, $\alpha_1 = \alpha_{-1} = 0.184$, $\alpha_2 = \alpha_{-2} = 0.120$, $\alpha_3 = \alpha_{-3} = 0.065$, $\beta = 0.030$. Observe that $\Sigma \alpha_i = 1$.

Price Level

$$p_t = A(L)w_t + \text{other} \qquad (2.28)$$

where p = log of the GNP deflator, and $A(1) = 0.944$.[13] $A(L)$ is an infinite polynomial; specifically:

$$A(L) = 0.455/(1 - 0.518L)$$

The coefficients of $A(L)$ are reported, for significant lags, in Table 11.6.

It is possible, even if cumbersome, to solve (2.27) and (2.28) to obtain

$$p_t = H(L)p_{t-1} + K(L)\kappa_t + \text{other} \tag{2.29}$$

In particular, κ_t should be interpreted here as a shock to y_t. The parameters of (2.29) depend, however, on the specification of the aggregate demand sector. An example will clarify this and prove useful for future reference.

I shall explicitly consider the demand side of Taylor's model. It contains, in addition to the national income identity, three consumption and three investment equations, one equation for the change in inventories, and two equations for the foreign sector variables. All equations have a Koyck dynamic adjustment specification. The import and export equations are in logarithmic form and are written as functions of (respectively, domestic and foreign) real GNP and relative price ratios. The other equations are all in linear form. Consumption and investment equations are made to depend on a measure of permanent income and a real interest rate; the change in inventories is also a function of the latter and of the change in real GNP. Writing explicit distributed lags and aggregating these seven equations, on the basis of the 1982 NIA figures and making use of log-linear approximations, the following aggregate demand function has been obtained:

$$y_t = B(L)yp_t + C(L)r_t + D(L)p_t + g_t \tag{2.30}$$

where yp = "permanent income" (a geometric distributed lead of y from one to
eight quarters ahead, with decay factor of 0.9),

Table 11.6. TAYLOR: Prices and Aggregate Demand, Lag Structures

Lag	$A(L)$	$B(L)$	$C(L)$	$D(L)$
0	0.455	0.256	−0.199	−0.035
1	0.236	0.176	−0.137	−0.019
2	0.122	0.125	−0.097	−0.011
3	0.063	0.090	−0.070	−0.008
4	0.033	0.066	−0.051	−0.006
5	0.017	0.048	−0.038	−0.004
6	0.009	0.036	−0.028	−0.003
7	0.005	0.026	−0.021	−0.003
8	0.002	0.020	−0.015	−0.002
9	0.001	0.014	−0.011	−0.002
10	0.001	0.011	−0.008	−0.001
11	0.000	0.008	−0.006	−0.001
12	0.000	0.006	−0.005	−0.001
13	0.000	0.004	−0.003	−0.001
14	0.000	0.003	−0.002	−0.001
15	0.000	0.002	−0.002	−0.000
16	0.000	0.002	−0.001	−0.000
17	0.000	0.001	−0.001	−0.000
18	0.000	0.001	−0.001	−0.000
19	0.000	0.001	−0.001	−0.000
20	0.000	0.001	−0.000	−0.000

$r = i - (p_{+4} - p)$ (where i is a nominal long-term interest rate, which is, in turn, a function, via a term-structure forward-looking equation, of the short-term interest rate present in the money demand equation),

$g = $ log of real public expenditure times a constant scale factor,

and $B(1) = 0.898$, $C(1) = -0.698$, $D(1) = -0.099$. The coefficients of the polynomials $B(L)$, $C(L)$, $D(L)$, and $E(L)$ are also reported, for significant lags, in Table 11.6.

Assume now that y_t can be expressed as a static equation and consider its parameters to be represented by the total multipliers of (2.30). Observe also that the coefficient of p_t reflects only the effect of the net imports leakage. With a given nominal interest rate and a constant permanent income, this equation can then be written as

$$y_t = g_t - \gamma p_t + \lambda(p_{t+1} - p_t) + \text{other} \tag{2.31}$$

where $\gamma = 0.099$ and $\lambda = 0.698$. We can then derive a function such as (2.29) by permanently shocking y_t through g_t (we are thus considering a constant fiscal policy shock, κ, with interest rates constant). Observe that if the endogeneity of the interest rate had been allowed for, substituting the money demand function in (2.31) would have led to a higher γ.

Consider now the system formed by (2.31) and, in place of (2.27) and (2.28), the extremely simplified equations:

$$w_t = 0.25(w_{t-1} + \beta y_t) + 0.5(w_t + \beta y_t) + 0.25(w_{t+1} + \beta y_t) \tag{2.32}$$

$$p_t = w_t \tag{2.33}$$

Solving (2.32) and (2.33) we obtain

$$p_t = 0.5(p_{t-1} + p_{t+1}) + 2\beta y_t \tag{2.34}$$

Ignoring the "other" component, we can then solve equations (2.31) and (2.34) to obtain

$$p_t = \theta p_{t-1} + \psi p_{t+1} + \phi g_t \tag{2.35}$$

where $\theta = 0.5[1 + 2\beta(\gamma + \lambda)]^{-1}$,

$\psi = (0.5 + 2\beta\lambda)[1 + 2(\gamma + \lambda)]^{-1}$,

$\phi = 2\beta[1 + 2\beta(\gamma + \lambda)]^{-1}$.

Starting with constant levels of y, p, and w (normalized so as to have $y_t = p_t = w_t = 0$ for $t = 0$), and for a constant permanent shock $\kappa_t = \kappa$ to y_t from $t = 1$ onward, the only stable solution would then be

$$p_t = \rho p_{t-1} + e_t \tag{2.36}$$

where $e_t = 0$ up to $t = 0$, $e_t = \sigma\kappa$ from $t = 1$ onward and

$\sigma = \phi(\mu + \rho)(\mu - 1)^{-1}$

while μ and ρ are the two roots (with $\mu > 1$ and $\rho < 1$) of the characteristic equation $\psi z^2 - z + \theta = 0$.[14]

It is also easy to show that $\sigma = (1-\rho)/\gamma$; furthermore, we can write

$$y_t = \rho y_{t-1} + u_t \tag{2.37}$$

where $u_t = 0$ up to $t = 0$, $u_1 = [1+\sigma(\lambda\rho-\gamma)]\kappa$, and $u_t = 0$, for $t > 1$.

It is then easy to show that, after a shock κ to y_t, p_t rises continuously towards a long-run level of κ/γ, while y_t first rises by u_1 and then gradually returns to its preshock level. For the parameters of γ and λ given above and for $\beta = 0.03$ as in Eq. (2.27), we obtain $\rho = 0.86$, $\sigma = 1.44$, and $u_1 = 1.72$. It should be remembered that in this case, interest rates are assumed to be fixed and the endogenous dynamics of aggregate demand are ignored. Even so, the results are in line with those of Taylor's model simulations reported in Adams and Klein in this volume. In particular, following a fiscal shock of 1% of real GNP, the price level and the wage rate will continuously rise, approaching new stationary levels 10% higher than the original ones; one-half of the total increase will be completed in about 2 years. Real GNP will instead first rise by about 1.7%; it will then gradually return to its starting point.[15]

It is interesting to observe that the higher γ is, the lower the long-run level of p_t: a fiscal shock with nonaccommodating monetary policy will obviously be less inflationary than a shock with fixed interest rates. However, these shocks, even if permanent, will not result in a permanently higher rate of inflation but will lead only to a higher price level (whereas output will always come back to its "natural" rate). Finally, it should be noted that ρ will now be a function of both γ and λ. Through them it will not be invariant with respect to changes in policy.

MONEY DEMAND EQUATIONS

In this section the main demand for money equations of the four models will be examined and compared. Inverting these equations and solving for the relevant nominal interest rates it is possible to evaluate some of the most important characteristics of the LM curves implicit in the models. As it is possible to derive LM curves with either exogenous or endogenous money supply it should be understood that only the former case is considered here. In view of the complexity of the process of money creation and the variety of specifications adopted in the different models one should be aware of the fact that LM curves obtained with endogenous money supply might be quite different from the simple ones examined in this section. Indeed, the specific characteristics of the four models' financial blocks might cause the full-model properties to differ much more than can be assessed by simply comparing their money demand equations. These equations are all standard liquidity preference functions with the demand for a specific money aggregate depending on a transactions variable and a nominal interest rate. Even so, however, differences in the coefficients and in the dynamic properties of the functions make their comparison useful and revealing.

MPS

The basic equation, as coded in the model, can be written as

$$m_t = 0.958m_{t-1} - 0.166m_{t-2} + 0.600(y_t + p_t)$$

$$-0.157(y_{t-1} + p_{t-1}) - 0.234(y_{t-2} + p_{t-2}) \tag{3.1}$$

$$-0.300i_t - 0.056i_{t-1} + 0.178i_{t-2} + \text{other}$$

where m = log of demand deposits,

$\quad y$ = log of personal consumption expenditure, 1982 \$,

$\quad p$ = log of the deflator of personal consumption expenditure,

$\quad i$ = treasury bill rate, effective annual yield (fraction).

This equation results from an error-correction adjustment process. The interest rate enters in log form in the original equation; linearizing for $i = 0.1$, (3.1) is obtained. Solving for m_t, we obtain

$$m_t = A(L)(y_t + p_t) + B(L)i_t + \text{other} \tag{3.2}$$

where $A(L)$ and $B(L)$ are the infinite lag structures

$$A(L) = (0.600 - 0.157L - 0.234L^2)/(1 - 0.958L + 0.166L^2)$$

$$B(L) = (-0.300 - 0.056L + 0.178L^2)/(1 - 0.958L + 0.166L^2)$$

The long-run elasticity of m with respect to y and p is $A(1) = 1.0$ and that with respect to i is $B(1)/10 = -0.086$. The impact elasticities are much smaller, however, as can be seen from (3.1). In particular, in an experiment that keeps m constant, we would end up inverting (3.1) to obtain

$$i_t = 2.000(y_t + p_t) - 0.523(y_{t-1} + p_{t-1}) \tag{3.3}$$

$$- 0.780(y_{t-2} + p_{t-2}) - 0.187i_{t-1} + 0.593i_{t-2} + \text{other}$$

The dynamics of this equation are likely to play a crucial role, combined with that of p_t, in explaining the simulation results under constant m_t. Observe, in particular, that one of the two characteristic roots of the autoregressive part of (3.3) is negative and large (-0.869, while the second root is equal to 0.682). Notice also that the impact slope of the LM curve is equal to 2 and the long-run slope is equal to 1.173.

MQEM

The relevant demand for money equation is specified in terms of M2PLUS (M_2 plus short-term treasury securities). It is a function of nominal GNP and the yield on U.S.

government securities (5-year issues); the latter is a function of the corporate Aaa bond interest rate, which is in turn a function of the short-term rate. We have[16]

$$m_t = 0.884m_{t-1} + 0.133(y_t + p_t) - 0.288i_t^s + \text{other} \tag{3.4}$$

where m_t = log of M2PLUS,

$\quad y_t$ = log of GNP, 1982 \$,

$\quad p_t$ = log of the GNP deflator,

$\quad i_t^s$ = yield on US government securities (fraction).

Rather than solving for i^s as a function of i (the treasury bill rate), I shall make the extreme assumption that $i^s = i + \text{constant}$, so that, substituting i^s in (3.4) and solving the implicit lag function, we obtain

$$m_t = A(L)(y_t + p_t) + B(L)i_t + \text{other} \tag{3.5}$$

which is a standard distributed lag demand for money function in y, p, and i, with infinite lag structures

$$A(L) = 0.133/(1-0.884L), \qquad B(L) = -0.288/(1-0.884L)$$

The long-run elasticity of m with respect to y and p is $A(1) = 1.147$; that with respect to i is $B(1)/10 = -0.248$, almost three times larger than that of the MPS equation. Keeping m constant and solving (3.5) for i, we obtain

$$i_t = 0.462(y_t + p_t) + \text{other} \tag{3.6}$$

This static equation seems to imply that the slope of the LM curve does not change over time.[17] More importantly, this curve appears to be fairly flat, at least much flatter than the MPS one (but steeper than those implicit in the FAIR and TAYLOR money demand functions considered below.)

FAIR

The FAIR model contains two main money demand equations, one for the household sector and one for the firm sector. The former is the equation considered here; that for the firm sector is a very similar equation. The two sectors cover almost 90% of total demand deposits. We have

$$m_t = 0.910m_{t-1} + 0.048y_t + 0.042p_t - 0.446i_t + \text{other} \tag{3.7}$$

where m = log of demand deposits and currency of households,

$\quad i$ = after-tax bill rate (fraction),

$\quad y$ = log of disposable income of households deflated by p,

$\quad p$ = log of the price deflator of consumer expenditure, plus residential investment of households.

All the explanatory variables have the same Koyck lag structure, so that

$$m_t = A(L)y_t + B(L)p_t + C(L)i_t + \text{other} \tag{3.8}$$

where the polynomials are obvious. In particular, we have $A(1) = 0.533$, $B(1) = 0.467$, $C(1) = -4.956$. This is almost six times larger than the semielasticity of the MPS money demand function.

Keeping m constant and inverting (3.8), we obtain

$$i_t = 0.108y_t + 0.094p_t + \text{other} \tag{3.9}$$

This looks very different from the result of the MPS model; as in the MQEM case, inverting the money demand equation with constant money supply does not seem to be a cause of further dynamic problems in the case of the FAIR model.

TAYLOR

The demand for money comes from a real adjustment process, and we have

$$m_t = 0.953m_{t-1} + 0.040y_t + 0.047p_t - 0.224i_t$$
$$+ 0.953(p_t - p_{t-1}) \tag{3.10}$$

where $m = \log$ of M_1,

$y = \log$ of GNP, 1982 $,

$p = \log$ of the GNP deflator,

$i =$ federal funds rate (fraction).

The inflation term is the result of an adjustment process specified in real rather than nominal terms. Writing (3.10) as

$$m_t = A(L)y_t + B(L)p_t + C(L)i_t + D(L)(p_t - p_{t-1}) \tag{3.11}$$

with obvious Koyck polynomials, we have $A(1) = 0.851$, $B(1) = 1.0$, $C(1) = -4.766$, and $D(1) = 20.277$. The income elasticity is comparable to those of the other models, whereas the semielasticity with respect to i is very close to that of the FAIR model. The inflation term has a very large effect and this seems to be crucial when one inverts this function to substitute it in the IS curve. Keeping m constant, we have

$$i_t = 0.179y_t + 0.196p_t + 4.254(p_t - p_{t-1}) + \text{other} \tag{3.12}$$

THE DEMAND SIDE AND THE FULL-MODEL MULTIPLIERS

Table 11.7 reports the full-model multipliers for two of the experiments considered by Adams and Klein, i.e., those of a fiscal shock under accommodating (nominal interest rate held constant) and nonaccommodating (money supply held constant) monetary conditions. The question is whether the differences in the multipliers can be attributed to differences in model structures. We have already examined some of the differences in the price–wage sectors and in money demand. The latter are particularly important

Table 11.7. Effects of an Increase in Public Expenditures on the Real Gross National Product and Its Deflator

	GNP[a]				GNP Deflator[a]			
	MPS	FAIR	MQEM	TAYLOR	MPS	FAIR	MQEM	TAYLOR
r at base[b]								
7501	1.42	1.00	0.88	2.36	−0.07	−0.03	0.04	0.29
7502	2.08	1.29	1.09	4.35	0.03	0.03	0.02	0.89
7503	2.67	1.41	1.25	4.82	0.22	0.08	−0.25	1.79
7504	3.26	1.45	1.32	4.43	0.43	0.15	0.07	2.97
7604	5.55	1.42	1.41	3.46	2.39	0.42	0.33	8.25
7704	7.93	1.34	1.29	1.92	7.53	0.58	0.41	12.22
7804	8.84	1.31	1.26	0.65	19.30	0.69	0.67	14.01
7904	9.93	1.35	1.28	0.01	35.96	0.85	0.80	14.15
8004		1.42	1.36	−0.04		0.99	1.16	13.49
8104		1.54	1.55	−0.09		1.11	1.45	12.58
8204		1.69	1.59	0.04		1.19	1.69	11.63
8304		1.78	1.63	−0.00		1.25	1.92	10.69
8404		1.88	1.63	0.03		1.33	2.13	9.75
High	10.92	1.88	1.63	4.82	40.57	1.33	2.13	14.23
Low	1.42	1.00	0.88	−0.12	−0.07	−0.03	−0.25	0.29
M₁ at base[c]								
7501	1.38	0.99	0.88	1.23	−0.07	−0.03	0.04	0.09
7502	1.91	1.27	1.08	1.90	0.03	0.03	0.03	0.24
7503	2.23	1.37	1.23	1.67	0.18	0.08	−0.23	0.47
7504	2.45	1.39	1.29	1.18	0.34	0.15	0.08	0.74
7604	2.27	1.25	1.32	0.76	1.46	0.37	0.34	2.02
7704	0.87	1.11	1.17	0.45	2.98	0.51	0.42	3.12
7804	−2.13	1.07	1.10	0.20	4.01	0.59	0.67	3.87
7904	−3.68	1.10	1.04	0.05	4.10	0.73	0.78	4.35
8004	−2.88	1.17	1.08	0.09	3.62	0.84	1.11	4.65
8104	−1.70	1.28	1.21	0.04	2.79	0.96	1.35	4.87
8204	−0.04	1.39	1.23	0.11	1.80	1.05	1.53	5.01
8304	1.23	1.47	1.31	0.05	1.25	1.13	1.72	5.10
8404	1.47	1.56	1.31	0.07	1.67	1.25	1.88	5.09
High	2.51	1.56	1.36	1.90	4.10	1.25	1.88	5.39
Low	−3.68	0.99	0.88	0.02	−0.07	−0.03	−0.23	0.09

Source: Adams and Klein (this volume), Appendix, Tables A2.1 and A2.2 and Figure 2.1.

[a]Percentage deviations.

[b]Real defense spending shocked by 1% of historical GNP for each period with r (nominal short-term interest rate) kept to the baseline path.

[c]Real defense spending shocked by 1% of historical GNP for each period with M₁ (or corresponding monetary aggregate) kept to the baseline path.

in the case of nonaccommodating monetary policy. The former can be summarized, ignoring further unnecessary lags, by means of the following general specification:

$$p_t = \alpha p_{t-1} + \beta p_{t+1} + \delta(p_{t-1} - p_{t-2}) + \varepsilon y_t + \text{other} \qquad (4.1)$$

We have seen that in both the MPS and the MQEM models $\alpha = 1$, $\beta = 0$, and $1 > \delta > 0$: in both models the reduced form of the price–wage sector can be written as a stable autoregressive structure in the rate of inflation, for a given level of the demand pressure variable. In the former model, however, δ is actually close to one (except for the slight leakage of exogenous import prices); in the second, it is nearer to zero. Furthermore, in the MPS case ε is much larger than in the MQEM.

In the case of the FAIR model, instead, we end up having $\beta = \delta = 0$ and $1 > \alpha > 0$. Equation (4.1) then defines a stable process for the price level, not just for the rate of inflation. In the case of the Taylor model, as we have previously seen, $\alpha = \beta = 0.5$, $\delta = 0$, and there exists, due to the particular specification of the wage equation, an embedded tendency for the level of production to return to its exogenous trend level.

In essence, the demand side of all the models examined here can be summarized by means of the following simple expression:

$$y_t = g_t - \gamma p_t + \lambda(p_t - p_{t-1}) + \text{other} \tag{4.2}$$

where g_t reflects the possible effects of autonomous demand components (such as various kinds of public expenditure) and I have either substituted for the nominal interest rate from a money demand equation or kept it constant in the "other" component of (4.2). As in (4.1) all variables are in logarithmic form so (4.2) essentially implies a log-linearization of the national income identity. Observe also that the possibility of complex dynamics in aggregate demand has been totally ignored (and the models that are considered here *do* have complex dynamics), including that stemming from stock–flow relations (wealth effects on consumption, stocks of inventories, capital–output ratios). Forward-looking expectations, such as those considered in Taylor's model, are also ignored, and this is the only practical difference between (4.2) and (2.31).[18]

The coefficient of the rate of inflation in (4.2) should be related to the negative effects that real interest rates might have on the demand components. Although the demand blocks are fairly complex in general (with multiplier–accelerator effects coupled with adjustment or putty–clay specifications for the demand of capital goods), a cursory investigation indicates that λ is generally small (almost zero) in the MQEM and FAIR models, quite high in TAYLOR [with foward-looking rational expectations as we have seen in (2.30)], and possibly very high in the MPS model. In the latter, the block of residential investment seems to be particularly sensitive to real interest rates (and therefore to price changes). This produces, under particular conditions, rather dramatic effects in full-model simulations, which I shall consider briefly later in this section.

As already mentioned, the price level coefficient reflects either the relative price effect on imports and exports or, added to this effect, that of possible shifts in the LM curves in the case of nonaccommodating monetary policy.[19] In the former case, and for the United States, the effect seems to be extremely small. As will be shown, this is a possible cause of instability for the models that have a high δ in (4.1) when they are solved with nominal interest rates kept constant at their baseline values. With money supply held constant, instead, γ will rise as the LM curve becomes steeper. As we have previously seen, this curve is steepest in the case of the MPS model and, as will be shown below, this is a potential cause of an oscillatory response of output and prices to a permanent shock in g_t. These cases will be studied along the same lines as for the TAYLOR model.

Assuming that $\beta = 0$, the "other" terms in (4.1) and (4.2) are constant and

$g_0 = y_0 = p_0 = p_{-1} = 0$, while $g_t = \kappa$ for $t > 0$, the reduced form of the system of equations (4.1) and (4.2) can be written as

$$p_t = \rho p_{t-1} + \chi p_{t-2} + e_t \tag{4.3}$$

$$y_t = \rho y_{t-1} + \chi y_{t-2} + u_t \tag{4.4}$$

where

$$e_t = \begin{cases} 0 & \text{for } t \le 0 \\ \sigma\kappa & \text{for } t > 0 \end{cases}$$

$$u_t = \begin{cases} 0 & \text{for } t \le 0 \\ [1+(\lambda-\gamma)\sigma]\kappa & \text{for } t = 1 \\ [1+(\lambda-\gamma)\sigma]\kappa - (\rho+\lambda\sigma)\kappa & \text{for } t = 2 \\ [1+(\lambda-\gamma)\sigma]\kappa - (\rho+\chi+\lambda\sigma)\kappa & \text{for } t > 2 \end{cases}$$

and

$$\rho = (\alpha+\delta-\varepsilon\lambda)/[1-\varepsilon(\lambda-\gamma)]$$

$$\chi = -\delta/[1-\varepsilon(\lambda-\gamma)]$$

$$\sigma = \varepsilon/[1-\varepsilon(\lambda-\gamma)].$$

Consider first the FAIR model, where $\alpha < 1$ and $\delta = 0$. In this case, $0 < \rho < 1$, $\chi = 0$, and $u_t = u_2$ for $t > 2$. It can immediately be seen that, following a fiscal shock that shifts the aggregate demand curve by $\kappa > 0$,[20] p_t will increase monotonically converging to a long-run level $\varepsilon\kappa/(1-\alpha+\varepsilon\gamma)$, much as with the TAYLOR model. Contrary to the latter, however, after the shock y_t will not return to its initial level, but will converge to a long-run value of $(1-\alpha)\kappa/(1-\alpha+\varepsilon\gamma)$. This difference in the response to a fiscal shock is clearly embodied in the results of the two actual model simulations summarized in Table 11.7.

For the MQEM and MPS models, the results are a little more complex. In both models $\alpha = 1$. In the former, however, δ is rather small; in the latter it is short of unity only for the limited weight of exogenous import prices in the consumption deflator. I shall therefore consider the polar cases of $\delta = 0$ and $\delta = 1$ to shed light on the simulation results for the two models.

When $\delta = 0$ it follows that $0 < \rho < 1$ and $\chi = 0$. Thus, also in this case the price level will rise, after the shock κ, this time converging to a long-run level equal to κ/γ. As with the TAYLOR model, however, after an initial increase equal to u_1 the level of output will gradually return to its preshock level. But in the MQEM model δ, even if small, is larger than zero. This is probably the main reason why y_t does not return to zero in the simulations of Table 11.7. Observe, however, that the path of y_t with this model tends to be below that obtained with the FAIR model, the converse being true for the path of p_t. Indexing by "M" the parameters that refer to the case "$\alpha = 1$, $\delta = 0$" and by "F" those referring to the case "$\alpha < 1$, $\delta = 0$," and assuming $\kappa_M = \kappa_F$, the ratio between the two aftershock long-run price levels can be written as

$$R = \gamma^F/\gamma^M + (1-\alpha^F)/(\varepsilon^F\gamma^M) \simeq 1 + (1-\alpha^F)/(\varepsilon^F\gamma^M) \tag{4.5}$$

For γ^F approximately equal to γ^M, we thus have $R > 1$, so that the price level is higher in case "M" than in case "F." Moreover, the larger the value of γ is the smaller the value of R. This may help to explain why, in the simulations of Table 11.7, the GNP deflator tends to rise more for the MQEM than for the FAIR model, and to a higher level in the experiment with constant interest rates (where γ is lower), than in the experiment with constant money supply.

Turning now to the case of $\delta = 1$, it is easy to show that the critical stability condition is $1 + \chi > 0$, which reduces to $\gamma > \lambda$. Furthermore, inspection of the discriminant reveals that the roots of (4.3) and (4.4) will be complex conjugate if $\gamma > \varepsilon\lambda^2/4$ and, since $\varepsilon\lambda^2/4$ is probably an upper bound for λ, also if $\gamma > \lambda$.

As we have seen, the MPS model has a very steep LM curve: for a solution in fixed money supply mode this implies a rather high value for γ. After a fiscal shock κ, p_t and y_t might eventually converge, if the stability condition is satisfied, to long-run values, respectively, equal to κ/γ and 0. These long-run solutions are apparently equal to those of the TAYLOR model, but it is likely that the two models differ for the values of γ and, perhaps more importantly, for the actual change in government expenditure implied by an identical percentage shock κ (as a consequence of different income multipliers). It should, however, be observed that in the present case the stability of the solution is accompanied by the existence of complex roots. The solution paths might therefore be highly oscillatory with possibly wide fluctuations in output and prices. As is clear from Table 11.7, this is exactly what happens when the MPS model is solved with money supply held constant at its baseline values.

In the case of a model solution obtained keeping the nominal rate of interest constant, γ will be quite small. The MPS model seems to possess a high overall elasticity of aggregate demand with respect to real interest rates; it is thus likely to have in this situation $\gamma < \lambda$ and, for γ also smaller than $\varepsilon\lambda^2/4$, the roots of the characteristic equation will be real. p_t and y_t will then diverge monotonically; as can be seen by considering the case of $\gamma = 0$, the instability might concern not only the price level but also the rate of inflation. Equation (4.3) can now in fact be written as

$$p_t - p_{t-1} = \chi(p_{t-1} - p_{t-2}) + e_t \qquad (4.6)$$

and $\chi = 1/(1 - \varepsilon\lambda) > 1$ for $\varepsilon\lambda < 1$. This is exactly what seems to happen in the actual simulations. As a matter of fact, the results of the simulations described by Adams and Klein and reproduced in Table 11.7 indicate that after 21 quarters it becomes impossible actually to compute a solution for the MPS model with interest rates kept constant at their baseline values.

This result nonetheless seems extreme. Even if holding interest rates constant has the implication of strengthening the destabilizing role of the price–wage spiral in a model such as the MPS, other mechanisms should be at work and provide dampening effects capable of avoiding the explosive response that we observe in the simulation. A careful equation by equation review of the model estimates suggests that this response is basically due to a single equation, the one that explains real unsubsidized housing expenditure. In reestimating this equation on an extended sample period and with the new 1982 $ NIA data, the specification and parameter estimates changed quite substantially from the ones reported in Brayton and Mauskopf (1985). Not only is the elasticity with respect to the measure of real interest rates included in the equation very large but the income elasticity is also extremely high. Besides the intrinsic instability

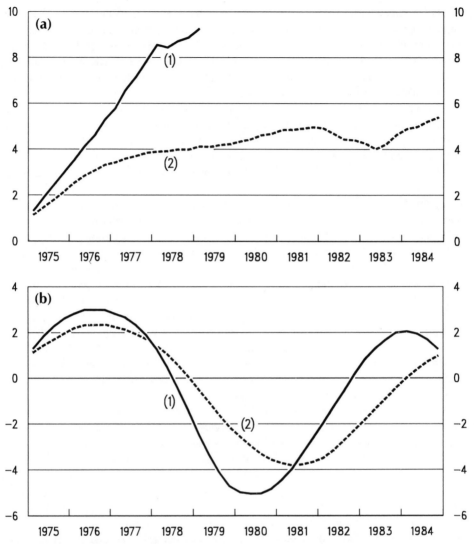

Figure 11.1. MPS model multipliers under different monetary policy regimes.* (a) Constant rate of interest. (b) Constant money supply.

*Percentage deviation of GNP (in 1982 $) from base run (historical values) that results from shocking Federal Government purchases other than labor or construction (in 1982 $) by 1% of historical GNP for each period.
  (1) Full model simulations.
  (2) Simulations with housing expenditures exogenous.

of housing investment behavior in recent years, these results are likely to reflect some serious specification problems that deserve to be further investigated.[21]

Accordingly, the summer 1987 version of the MPS model was therefore simulated, first with the housing expenditure equation fully endogenous and then with this expenditure variable taken to be exogenous. The results for the GNP multiplier are shown in Figure 11.1 (those for the GNP deflator being similar in nature). The full-model simulations (Figure 11.1a) are very close to those reported in Table 11.7.[22] In particular, we observe that with nominal interest rates held constant at their baseline values, in a few years the GNP multiplier (and, correspondingly, the price level) reaches so high a value that it becomes impossible to solve the model.

With residential investment taken as exogenous, instead, the pattern of the multiplier is much more reasonable, even if it rises to values more than twice those of the FAIR and MQEM models (compare the simulation results for these models reproduced in Table 11.7 with those of Figure 11.1a). This is the result of the interaction in the MPS model between the wage–price spiral and the high overall elasticity of aggregate demand with respect to real interest rates: under an extreme policy such as that of keeping nominal interest rates constant, a demand shock first pushes the rate of inflation upward and then reduces the real interest rates. With sufficiently high elasticities, such as those of the MPS model, this will produce further increases in aggregate demand, and then in prices again. The almost unitary root of inflation in the reduced form of the price–wage sector keeps this process going over time.

It is worth noticing that exogenizing housing expenditure, and thus eliminating its extreme and possibly misspecified effects on the simulation, reduces the amplitude of fluctuations in the GNP multiplier when M_1 is held constant at the baseline (Figure 11.1b). It does not, however, eliminate the pronounced oscillatory pattern that results, as we have seen above, from the interaction between a very steep LM curve and the highly autoregressive structure of inflation implicit in the MPS model.

This result makes it clear that multipliers obtained as a result of a fiscal shock in experiments such as those studied in this section are highly dependent not only on the specification and parameter estimates of the single models but above all on the accompanying assumptions on monetary policy. In particular, although these experiments are very useful for a better understanding of the properties and responses of the individual models, the assumptions of fully accommodating and nonaccommodating monetary policy are extreme. Accordingly, on this basis it is not possible to discriminate between the different models to determine, in the words of Christ, "which of them are wrong . . . and which (if any) are right."

To conclude this section, however, I would suggest that perhaps the most important question still concerns the intrinsic stability of the economy. Is it basically stable, as described by Taylor's model, so that following a fiscal shock real output quickly returns toward its preshock value and the price level converges to a new long-run equilibrium? Or does it contain important elements of instability, as the MPS model simulations seem to indicate (apart from the possible specification problems of a few equations) and that we can appreciate from the plots of Figure 11.1, so that one cannot avoid the task of searching for a potentially complex stabilizing reaction function of monetary policy?

SOME FINAL REMARKS

Even if the analysis conducted in the preceding sections is specific to the four models of the U.S. economy considered, it seems possible to conclude this chapter with some observations of a more general nature.

There are many ways of comparing macroeconometric models. In the one adopted in this paper single equations or blocks of equations have been examined and the outcomes of full-model deterministic simulations have been evaluated in view of specific differences in these equations. This showed, in particular, that differences in specifications and parameter estimates of similar behavioral equations were not negligible and accounted for substantial variations in the dynamic response characteristics of the models. It is true that in some instances, as observed in the last paragraph of the previous section, different overall responses to specific shocks may be related to major theoretical disagreements on matters such as the intrinsic capability of the economic system to return smoothly, and independently of policy actions, to equilibrium or "natural" positions of rest. But even models similar in structure and in the basic theoretical underpinnings seem to react very differently under quite similar external conditions.

The results of this chapter indicate that the wide overall variation in the performance of the models owes much to the differences in the four following points:

1. the specification of wage equations;
2. the elasticity of prices with respect to labor costs;
3. the effects of real interest rates on aggregate demand;
4. the slope of the LM curve.

The first two points are related to some extent. On the one hand, there is the question whether wage equations are to be specified in terms of levels or first differences. As we have seen, this has important practical consequences for the dynamic responses to demand shocks (the only kind of shocks considered in this chapter). In a model such as the MPS, for example, the wage–price spiral and the oscillatory behavior of the solution under a policy of constant money supply depend in a critical manner on the augmented Phillips curve specification chosen for the wage equation (and on the homogeneity property of the price equation). On the other hand, this specification does not generate, within the wage–price sector, a long-run relationship between the level of real wages and the rate of unemployment, which would "only reveal the long-run equilibrium level of unemployment when the long-run relationship is combined with the remaining supply-side equations."[23] It determines, instead, a long-run rate of unemployment that depends (for given values of the real exchange rate and of specific labor market variables) only on the long-run growth rate of real wages, which is related, through the price equation, to the change in trend productivity.

This is an important issue: with a wage equation possessing a well-defined long-run solution in terms of the real wage level, a demand shock to the system would be absorbed much more smoothly and with significantly less inflationary effects (as is the case for the FAIR and TAYLOR models). It should also be clear that less than unitary elasticities between value-added deflators and unit labor costs, on the one hand, and between demand and supply deflators, on the other, constitute possibly major leakages that might considerably reduce the inflationary effects of demand shocks (as was apparently the case for the MQEM model, in which direct demand pressure effects on prices and wages are nonetheless quite small).

These two issues are worthy of special investigation, in view of their importance for the full-model simulations discussed by Adams and Klein. In general, the role of long-run constraints and of homogeneities should be given more explicit consideration and, when possible, tests of obvious restrictions should be performed. As Nickell (1988, pp. 217–218) puts it:

> Any model that purports to do more than generate very short-term forecasts should . . . possess a coherent set of supply-side equations. . . . It seems always worth writing down the set of long-run solutions to all the supply-side equations in a model. Inconsistencies will thereby often be revealed.

It has been argued, however, that excessive attention to long-run constraints might be detrimental, since it could end up imposing too much on the data. As put by Fair (1984, pp. 15–16):

> Although it is difficult to argue this in the abstract, my feeling is that long-run constraints may be playing too much of a role . . . It is not obvious, for example, that the assumption of no long-run trade-off between inflation and unemployment warrants so much confidence that it should be imposed on models, given the severe restrictions that it implies.

The examination of the models of the U.S. economy considered in the new comparison exercise discussed in the chapter by Adams and Klein suggests, however, that in many cases this issue has not received enough attention. In my view, the need for further investigation especially regards the homogeneity properties, the dynamics, and the error characteristics of the wage–price sectors of different models, perhaps at a single equation level. This is a different level of model comparison than the one based on full-model simulations. It seems to me that it is equally important, and that it should perhaps be given greater priority. In any case advantage can now be taken of an impressive, sophisticated, and easy to use battery of misspecification tests that have been developed and spread over the last 15 years.[24]

More in-depth analysis of the modeling of IS–LM components also seems to be necessary. In particular, further research on the transmission mechanism of monetary policy is still badly needed. Even similar models differ substantially on the role they assign to interest rate effects (nominal and real) in demand expenditure equations for consumption and investment.[25] And the elasticity between aggregate demand and real interest rates (or the rate of inflation) plays a very important part in the pattern and stability of the full-model simulations previously discussed. Again, it seems to me that it would be desirable to go back to a single equation level, and to compare very basic parameters and dynamic responses.

The same holds true for the interest elasticity of the demand for money. The models considered in this chapter differ greatly in the slopes of their implicit LM curves and this is another factor that plays a significant part in their responses to fiscal policy shocks. It should be observed here that differences in money demand functions have immediate consequences on the kind of monetary policy assumptions that should accompany a fiscal policy experiment to make multiplier analysis of practical interest. But this goes beyond simple exercises in model comparison and opens a Pandora's box containing issues such as the endogeneity of policy instruments, policy reaction functions, and open- versus closed-loop rules for stabilization policy. For these issues to be given concrete treatment, I believe, one cannot do without representations of the working of economic systems such as those provided by the econometric models considered in this chapter. Accordingly, basic research on why and where these models differ should continue and areas of agreement and disagreement should be further clarified.

ACKNOWLEDGMENTS

I wish to thank Albert Ando for many useful discussions on the issues covered in this chapter. Remaining errors are my own and the views expressed are not necessarily those of the Bank of Italy.

NOTES

1. On the effect on ex ante forecasts of differences in assumptions on exogenous variables and judgmental adjustments, see McNees (this volume).
2. This project has resulted in the production of four volumes and several papers. See, inter alia, Wallis et al. (1987) and Fisher et al. (1988).
3. A first broad and clear presentation of Fair's model is contained in Fair (1984); the updated version considered in the present paper can be found in Fair (1988). A first version of Taylor's model is presented in the Appendix to Taylor (1988a); the equations actually used in this chapter are those of Taylor (1988b). The MPS model is described in detail in Brayton and Mauskopf (1985); the reestimated version used for this chapter is unpublished and dates back to Summer 1987. A somewhat older presentation of the Michigan model can be found in Belton, Hymans, and Lown (1981); the list of the equations considered in this chapter is presented in Hymans, Crary, and Howrey (1988).
4. It should be observed that even if some models may be solved with flexible exchange rates, in the calculations that follow exchange rates have been kept constant.
5. Besides variables treated as exogenous in the simulations, the term "other" that appears in some of the equations of this chapter includes variables that, even if endogenous in the full-model simulations, are ignored in the present exercise because their effects are very small and transitory.
6. This equation also contains two very short distributed lags on the deviations of the rates of change of farm and import prices and of crude energy prices from the rate of change of the output deflator. These terms have only transitory and quickly disappearing effects and have been ignored in the calculations.
7. It should be observed that the only prices that are completely exogenous in the MPS model are those of imported and domestically produced energy products.
8. Available capacity is endogenous in the MQEM model and is basically explained by a very long and slow distributed lag on nonresidential structures and producers' equipment. In the present chapter it has therefore been treated as an exogenous variable. In contrast with the MPS model, where production capacity is constructed as a very long distributed lag on actual production with coefficients obtained from the equation of expenditures on produc-

ers' durable equipment, in the MQEM model it is derived from the Federal Reserve Board index of capacity utilization in manufacturing.

9. Even if the price equation refers to the private nonfarm GNP deflator it also contains permanent effects of farm and oil prices (exogenous in the MQEM model), with total elasticities of 0.014 and 0.096. Even considering these effects, the equation falls short, however, of being homogeneous with respect to the cost and price variables included among the regressors.

10. It should be observed that import prices in this model depend on the exchange rate, which is a function, among other things, of the price of exports. This in turn is a function of the nonfarm output deflator. Under the assumption of fixed exchange rates, this linkage has been ignored. It turns out, however, that it does not matter much. Endogenizing the exchange rate would produce only marginally different figures than the ones reported below $[C(1) = 0.584, H(1) = 0.278, K(1) = 0.019, K^*(1) = 0.032]$.

11. Even considering that farm and energy prices, as well as import prices in foreign currencies, are exogenous in the model, the elasticity of the consumption deflator with respect to the nonfarm output deflator seems to be rather small. This result should probably serve as a warning against the unconstrained use of a set of dynamic econometric equations in the linkage between output prices and demand deflators.

12. The dependent variable of the price equation is a value-added deflator (net of the change in inventories). It is permanently influenced, however, by the (exogenous) import deflator with an equilibrium elasticity of 0.42 (so that the sum of the elasticities with respect to the cost and price regressors is 0.84). Potential output is exogenous in the FAIR model.

13. Though specified in terms of the GNP deflator, also the price equation of the TAYLOR model includes a permanent effect of the import deflator. Its equilibrium elasticity and that of the cost of labor variable add up, however, to one.

14. For details on this standard "rational expectations" solution, see Pesaran (1987, pp. 109–110).

15. In the present example, the fiscal shock κ does not embody the standard Keynesian multiplier effect (with constant prices) on aggregate demand. With the exception of imports and inventory investment, the latter depends on the level of permanent income, a variable expressed as a forward-looking function of actual output in the original TAYLOR model and held constant in the derivation of Eq. (2.30). In the derivation of the numerical coefficients of Table 11.6, the transitory effect on aggregate demand of the presence of the change in output in the equation of inventory investment has been ignored. The latter equation also includes a permanent effect of the real interest rate on the change in inventories; this effect has been taken into account in the computations for Table 11.6. Observe also that the simplification of the wage and price equations introduced to exemplify the basic working of the TAYLOR model has the effect of somewhat reducing the response of real GNP to the fiscal shock. Simply replacing Eq. (2.33) with $p_t = 0.5(w_t + w_{t-1})$ has the effect of raising u_1 to a value of 1.91, while keeping ρ practically unchanged.

16. In the original equation i^s enters in log form; (3.4) is then obtained as a linearization around $i^s = 0.1$.

17. It should be observed that (3.6) is obtained keeping M2PLUS constant. However, in the MQEM model the relevant money supply variable is M1PLUS and keeping this aggregate constant in simulation appears to produce LM curves that shift over time, even if the order of magnitude of their slopes does not differ greatly from that of Eq. (3.6). For further details, see Green et al. (this volume, Table 4.10), where the LM curve semielasticity is shown to pass from an impact value of 0.57 to an equilibrium value (reached in 4 years) of 0.25.

18. With the obvious exception of the TAYLOR model, where Eq. (2.31) has been written

keeping the level of permanent income constant, while Eq. (4.2) should be interpreted as a static aggregate demand function solved for the actual level of output. In the latter case, g_t should be interpreted as inclusive of the standard income multiplier effect with constant prices.

19. The parameter γ should also subsume the dampening effect of fiscal automatic stabilizers such as progressive income taxation.

20. As noticed, this fiscal shock is already inclusive of the (static) multiplier effect with prices held constant.

21. See, for further comments on this issue, the note by Albert Ando added to the chapter by Adams and Klein in this volume.

22. To solve the model holding money supply constant, a renormalization routine has been used, endogenizing the treasury bill rate and keeping the sum of currency and demand deposits constant at their baseline (that is, historical) values. A third, small component of M_1 ("other checkable deposits") has, however, been fully exogenized to avoid intractable destabilizing effects on interest rates originating from the pattern of coefficients of the equation explaining that variable.

23. Nickell (1988, p. 216). Nickell's article also contains a thorough analysis of the supply side of macroeconometric models and the treatment of nonneutralities with respect to the rate of inflation.

24. For a recent, clear, and extremely useful monograph on misspecification tests in econometrics, see Godfrey (1988).

25. Not to mention differences in net worth effects and stock–flow interactions in consumption functions and in stock adjustment specifications for (putty–putty versus putty–clay) demand functions of capital goods.

REFERENCES

Belton, T., S. H. Hymans, and C. Lown. (1981). "The Dynamics of the Michigan Quarterly Econometric Model of the U.S. Economy." Discussion paper R-108-81, The University of Michigan, December.

Brayton, F., and E. Mauskopf. (1985). "The Federal Reserve Board MPS Quarterly Econometric Model of the US Economy." *Economic Modelling*, July, 170–292.

Christ, C. F. (1975). "Judging the Performance of Econometric Models of the U.S. Economy." *International Economic Review* 16, February, 54–74.

Fair, R. C. (1984). *Specification, Estimation, and Analysis of Macroeconometric Models*. Cambridge: Harvard University Press.

Fair, R. C. (1988). *Macroeconomics in Practice: Exercises with FAIRMODEL*. MACRO Inc., Southborough, MA.

Fisher, P. G., S. K. Tarma, D. S. Turner, K. F. Wallis, and J. D. Whitley. (1988). "Comparative Properties of Models of the UK Economy." *National Institute Economic Review* August, 69–87.

Godfrey, L. G. (1988). *Misspecification Tests in Econometrics: The Lagrange Multiplier Principle and other Approaches*. Cambridge: Cambridge University Press.

Hymans, S. H., J. P. Crary, and E. P. Howrey. (1988). "The Michigan Quarterly Econometric Model of the U.S. Economy." Discussion paper, Research Seminar in Quantitative Economics, University of Michigan, January.

Nickell, S. (1988). "The Supply Side and Macroeconomic Modelling." In *Empirical Macroeconomics for Interdependent Economies*, R. C. Bryant et al., eds., pp. 202–221. Washington, DC: The Brookings Institution.

Pesaran, M. H. (1987). *The Limits to Rational Expectations*. Oxford: Basil Blackwell.

Taylor, J. B. (1980). "Aggregate Dynamics and Staggered Contracts." *Journal of Political Economy,* 88, February, 1–23.

Taylor, J. B. (1988a). "The Treatment of Expectations in Large Multicountry Econometric Models." In *Empirical Macroeconomics for Interdependent Economies,* R. C. Bryant et al., eds., pp. 161–182. Washington, DC: The Brookings Institution.

Taylor, J. B. (1988b). "An Econometric Evaluation of International Monetary Policy Rules: Fixed versus Flexible Exchange Rates." Mimeo.

Wallis, K. F. (ed.), P. G. Fisher, J. A. Longbottom, D. S. Turner, and J. D. Whitley. (1987). *Models of the UK Economy: A Fourth Review by the ESRC Macroeconomic Modelling Bureau*. Oxford: Oxford University Press.

CHAPTER 12

Model Comparisons and Appraisals[1]

ROBERT J. SHILLER

The Seminar on Model Comparisons has produced some striking findings. The differences in the properties of the major macroeconometric models are much bigger than one might have expected given their emphasized theoretical foundations, or given the similarity of the published forecasts. Adams and Klein conclude that there is "considerable, one might even say astonishing" variation in the behavior of models "largely intended for the same purposes." Brinner and Hirsch refer to these sharp differences as "disturbing, particularly insofar as models share a common theoretical basis." McNees shows that the models themselves agree much less on forecasts than do the forecasters: the forecasts of the exogenous policy variables and the ad hoc adjustments serve to make the different models' forecasts much more similar than they would be if the models alone accounted for the differences in forecasts.

Adams and Klein study 10 models, of which 7 are "neoclassical Keynesian synthesis" models, one is a "micro based" model, one is a "monetarist" model, and one is a "rational expectations" model. They ran simulations to discern multipliers associated with each of various spending shocks, monetary shocks, and supply shocks. These multipliers showed striking differences across models, even among the neoclassical Keynesian synthesis models. For example, the effects on GNP of an increase in defense expenditures with a constant interest rate monetary policy showed a multiplier at a lag of 1 year of 1.31 with the Michigan model, 1.57 with the Indiana model, 2.21 with the DRI model, 2.63 with the BEA model, and 3.26 with the Federal Reserve Board Model. At a 2-year lag from the initial shock, the multipliers among the neoclassical Keynesian models ranged from 1.29 to 7.93. Needless to say, these are big differences. The multiplier is a central theoretical concept to Keynesian models. One would think that now, 50 years after Keynes, we ought to have some agreement, at least among Keynesian econometric model builders, as to what the magnitudes are.

What is the source of these striking differences across models? The conclusion of Adams and Klein is that the differences across models "do not appear to represent so much intended differences in structure as differences in sensitivity" in terms of estimated coefficients in the IS, LM, and AS curves. Brinner and Hirsch present a pessimistic account of the possibility of ever finding out which model is correct: "even subtle variations in the specification of, say, a household demand equation, not to mention variations in the estimation period, can yield substantial differences in response characteristics—differences that may be magnified over long simulation spans."[2] Indeed, our basic theoretical foundations offer only limited guidance about which variables to include and which to omit, or when to end a sample or which episodes to dummy out of a sample.

One might tend to infer from the Brinner–Hirsch paper that with very large models we cannot expect to estimate multipliers accurately just because of the large number of parameters that must go into the multiplier, any one of which might be thrown off by misspecification or other error in one equation. Their account of the source of differences between the BEA (230 behavioral equations) and DRI (450 behavioral equations) models helps us to appreciate the complexity of these models, and the chance that something could go wrong. I am reminded of the space shuttle Challenger, in which a vastly complex craft was destroyed by a minor flaw in an apparently in-consequential part called an O-ring. But then again, the Space Shuttle *is* up again and flying. The large models' dealing with so much complexity may be regarded as their strength, in that they are able to bring so much data to bear on forecasting. Some of the efforts associated with the Seminar to describe the basic structure of the model and to track down the basic causes for differences may be interpreted as steps that will iron out the differences.

If the major macroeconometric models are so different, then why aren't forecasts made from these models more different? The McNees paper confirms that indeed the models themselves would make forecasts that are much more different from each other than are the published forecasts. His paper was written with the cooperation of five macroeconometric modelers who gave him ex ante forecasts under standardized as-sumptions about government policy and the rest of the world and without the ad hoc adjustments that are commonplace. He finds that model forecasters manage to reduce the differences among each other in their forecasts through their judgmental inputs both in policy variables and in the ad hoc factors.[3]

I do not think that it is prima facie evidence of cheating that the forecasts come out closer to each other than the models would indicate. The different model builders may from time to time share certain extramodel information. Consider an extreme case: the imposition of The Phase-I wage and price controls by President Nixon in 1971. The pure models certainly were forecasting many different inflation rates, but the forecasters would be well advised to adjust their short-run forecasts of inflation to a common forecast of zero. They would probably do this with an ad hoc adjustment to some equations, and use the model still to forecast other variables. Using a model this way provides more details of the forecast, while enforcing adding-up constraints and other observed relations in the series. In this example, it is more likely that the different forecasts of inflation should be made to conform by the ad hoc adjustments rather than the policy variables.

Even if modelers do not themselves see any information beyond what is in their own models, they may be following an informal practice of pooling forecasts of dif-ferent models. Alternatively, some of the adjustments made by forecasters may be corrections for known deficiencies in their models, deficiencies that could in principle be remedied by improved estimation procedures but that have not yet been remedied.

A more cynical view of the tendency of forecasts of the different models to con-verge more than the models themselves would dictate is that forecasters are trying to run with the pack. It may be more dangerous to one's career or business to make an outlier forecast that might be wrong than is warranted by the potential benefit to being the one right forecast. To find out the merits of this view, it would be helpful to know if the tendency of the different forecasts to converge is indeed an appropriate one from the standpoint of optimal combining of forecasts. Plainly, however, we do not yet have enough data to make such a comparison. In his decomposition of forecast errors, McNees really has only one observation of the decomposition of forecast errors out 2 years. We will have to wait a long time before we have enough observations to make such an evaluation.

AN INTERPRETATION

The authors of some of these papers deserve to be commended for their candor and commitment toward describing possible shortcomings of their models as a group. They seem to be their own harshest critics, not what one would expect from people who have committed so much to the development of these models.

But I have not seen here any direct criticism of individual models. One interpretation for the results here may be just that not all of the models compared are good ones. The fact that there may be a few "duds" in the pool of models is no reason to question the basic approach that may be carried out appropriately by only a few model builders. Perhaps future work in the Seminar might put more emphasis on testing models and assessing their differences in structure.

One lesson that might be learned from these papers, beyond that there should be more papers like them to learn about differences across models, is that the combining of different models for forecasting, as suggested by Granger and Newbold and others, is something that should be taken more seriously. In this connection, I find the discussion by Howrey of the combining of monthly and quarterly models intriguing. Carol Corrado and others have begun to work on the practical matter of combining forecasts from models of different frequencies. Their efforts might seriously improve the ability to forecast. One might also describe this as bringing in much more degrees of freedom to estimation by allowing more frequent sampling.

But perhaps any thought of combining models should wait until we understand better what the various models mean. What are the WEFA model or the DRI model after all? What unifying principle justifies their separate existence? They are complex systems of equations, difficult to describe in simple terms and changing all the time. The people who are doing the reestimation and forecasting are also changing all the time. Even if we were to learn that one model has forecasted better than another historically, how will we know this will continue to be the case? Perhaps the staff of economists at the loser model have benefited from the experience, and have since repaired the model. Or, perhaps, reestimation of the model with the longer sample will have automatically repaired the deficit, as parameter estimates respond in effect to the forecast errors of the older model.

It is striking to me that in many cases the differences between models studied here appear not to be summarizable in terms of differences in basic principles. Rather than clearly formulated differences in theory or approach, we see differences in a lot of details. Now it is true that the Taylor model, being a rational expectations model, does have a distinctly different theoretical foundation, grounded as it is in rational expectations. The Fair model is based on a setup of individual maximization of objective functions that sets it apart from the Keynesian models. And the St. Louis model is certainly fundamentally different in its assumptions. But most of the other models seem to share a general Keynesian theoretical formulation, and for all we know differ in a lot of small choices made by the modelers. Perhaps that is to be expected; serious forecasters must confront many everyday problems that are not "interesting" and for which no elegant solution is available.

It should be stressed that the sources of the problems identified here are probably unrelated to the "Lucas critique" of macroeconometric models. If that critique were important, it would tend to show up in failures to forecast well after major changes in policy rules. But evaluation of forecasting potential is not the main issue in the papers I have discussed. It is true that if the theoretical foundations of the models are wrong, then this might conceivably account for a lot of differences across models. Modelers might assume that alternative formulations are "similar" from the standpoint of their theory, while the alternative formulations are actually very different from the standpoint of another theory. But I do not see that the rational expectations alternatives are particularly likely to suggest a reason for the differences among models.

One wonders what is the significance of the rather striking differences that the one rational expectations model (the Taylor model) shows from the others in terms of the multipliers that Adams and Klein document. Before trying to guess their significance, it should first be asked how the Taylor model was able to participate in such a simulation comparison. As a rational expectations model, it is not supposed to be used to evaluate multipliers, rather, to evaluate the effects of policy rules in rational expectations equilibrium. Taylor made some assumptions about the process that generated the policy shocks—that they were unforeseen noise. Then, in that case, the multipliers would not be applicable to a consistent countercyclical policy.[4] Rational expectations models just do not have a single set of multipliers as do the conventional macroeconometric models.

This shows that even the approach to comparing models—comparing their multiplier responses—is a model-specific approach. That is why, I suspect, no attention is paid here to the strikingly different approach to macroeconometric modeling that is used by the "real business cycle" modelers, as exemplified by the work of Kydland and Prescott. As rational expectations modelers, they would find it difficult to participate in the model comparison.

NOTES

1. This paper was prepared for the session "Evaluating Structural Econometric Models," American Economic Association, December 28, 1988, New York.
2. Although Brinner and Hirsch single out the BEA and DRI models for study in response to the Adams and Klein paper, these were among the pairs of models that showed the least differences in terms of multipliers.
3. Haitovsky and Treyz had done an analysis somewhat like McNees for two models, the WEFA and OBE models. They found that for both models the actual forecasts were dramatically more accurate than were the forecasts from the models themselves without judgmental adjustment. Judging from the small amount of data on forecast evaluation in their paper and in the McNees paper, the raw models seem to be behaving substantially more similarly now than 15 years ago.
4. See Taylor (1988) for a discussion of these issues.

REFERENCES

Adams, F. Gerard, and Lawrence R. Klein. (1988). "Performance of Quarterly Econometric Models of the United States: A New Round of Model Comparisons." Reproduced, University of Pennsylvania. [Chapter 2, this volume.]

Brinner, Roger E., and Albert A. Hirsch. (1988). "A Comparative Analysis of the DRI and BEA Models." Reproduced. [Chapter 5, this volume.]

Granger, C. W. J., and Paul Newbold. (1986). *Forecasting Economic Time Series,* 2nd ed. New York: Academic Press.

Haitovsky, Yoel, and George Treyz. (1972). "Forecasts with Quarterly Macroeconometric Models, Equation Adjustments, and Benchmark Predictions: The U.S. Experience." *Review of Economics and Statistics* 54, 317–325.

Howrey, E. Philip. (1988). "New Methods for Using Monthly Data to Improve Forecast Accuracy." Reproduced. [Chapter 8, this volume.]

Keynes, John Maynard. (1936). *The General Theory of Employment, Interest, and Money.* London: Macmillan.

Klein, Lawrence R. (1988). "Past, Present and Possible Future of Macroeconometric Models and Their Uses." University of Pennsylvania. [Chapter 1, this volume.]

Kydland, Finn E., and Edward C. Prescott. (1982). "Time to Build and Aggregate Fluctuations." *Econometrica* 50(6), 1345–1370.

McNees, Stephen K. (1988). "Comparing Macroeconometric Model Forecasts under Common Assumptions." Reproduced, Federal Reserve Bank of Boston. [Chapter 3, this volume.]

Taylor, John B. (1988). "The Treatment of Expectations in Large Multicountry Models." In *Empirical Macroeconomics for Interdependent Economies,* R. C. Bryant et al., eds. Washington, DC: Brookings Institution.

Index

DATE DUE